GOVERNOR ANDREW GREGG CURTIN
(Pennsylvania Historical and Museum Commission. Division of Archives and Manuscripts, Harrisburg)

The Training of an Army

Camp Curtin
and the
North's Civil War

By

William J. Miller

WHITE MANE PUBLISHING COMPANY, INC.

This White Mane Publishing Company, Inc. publication
was printed by
Beidel Printing House, Inc.
63 West Burd Street
Shippensburg, PA 17257

In respect to the scholarship contained herein, the acid-free paper used in this book meets the guidelines for permanence and durability of the Committee on Production Guidelines for Book Longevity of the Council on Library Resources.

For a complete list of available publications
please write
White Mane Publishing Company, Inc.
P.O. Box 152
Shippensburg, PA 17257

Library of Congress Cataloging-in-Publication Data

Miller, William J., 1959-
　　The training of an Army: Camp Curtin and the North's Civil War /
by William J. Miller.
　　　　p.　　cm.
　　Includes bibliographical references.
　　ISBN 0-942597-15-X (alk. paper)
　　1. United States. Army--History--Civil War, 1861-1865. 2. Camp
Curtin (Pa.)--History. 3. Military training camps--Pennsylvania-
-Harrisburg Region--History--19th century. 4. Harrisburg Region
(Pa.)--History. 5. Pennsylvania--History--Civil War, 1861-1865.
I. Title
E491.M65　　　1990
973.7'448--dc20
　　　　　　　　　　　　　　　　　　　　　　　　　　　　　　90-31770
　　　　　　　　　　　　　　　　　　　　　　　　　　　　　　CIP

PRINTED IN THE UNITED STATES OF AMERICA

To my parents,
who gave me curiosity
and the opportunity to satisfy it.

Preface

For generations, the school children of Pennsylvania have read in textbooks and surveys of their state's history of the size and importance of Camp Curtin in Harrisburg as the state's principal Civil War rendezvous site and training camp. The name of Camp Curtin is also familiar to readers of Civil War history, for it pops up occasionally in both general and esoteric studies of the war as well as in a great many of the unit histories of Pennsylvania regiments. In 1984, therefore, when I found myself living in Harrisburg, I was curious to know more about the camp that had been of such importance 120-odd years ago. I was surprised to learn, however, that almost nothing about Camp Curtin was known. Of all the thousands of books that had been written on the Civil War, not one dealt more than passingly with Camp Curtin. More surprising was that not a single major article had been written, nor had any research been undertaken (I later learned that much of the small amount of material that had been published about the camp was erroneous). I therefore set out to learn more about Camp Curtin, and this book is the result.

In the second week of April, 1861, the United States suddenly found itself at war. Probably only then did the Lincoln administration and leaders of the loyal states realize how unprepared the republic was for armed conflict. The United States Army numbered just over 16,000 men, many of whom were from the South and would leave the Federal ranks to fight for the Confederacy. The United States Navy and Marine Corps were even smaller. On April 15, therefore, President Abraham Lincoln called upon the Northern states for 75,000 men to put down the rebellion.

Each state was given a quota of men to fill, and each of the governors of those states was charged with mobilizing his state's manpower to meet that quota. The larger, more populous states, of course, had larger quotas to fill. New York, Pennsylvania, Ohio and Illinois bore the heaviest burdens. Lincoln asked Pennsylvania for 14 regiments: the Keystone State sent 25 regiments.

Pennsylvania's governor, both in those hectic days and throughout the war was Andrew Gregg Curtin, who had been in office exactly three months when Lincoln issued his first call for volunteers. Among Curtin's many problems was finding someplace where the volunteers could be uniformed, equipped, armed, trained, organized into companies and regiments, and generally turned into something that resembled soldiers before they went off to the front. This was no small task considering that Pennsylvania would have to provide thousands of men at any one time.

In the Civil War, there were no such things as "training camps" as we know them today, where a soldier, sailor or marine is sent to a permanent military base to go through a prescribed number of weeks of basic training before being shipped out. The soldier of the Civil War received a more haphazard training. Many men were shipped out to the front without any formal training. The camps, too, were less organized, and few remained in operation longer than a few weeks or months. In the days after Lincoln's call, camps sprang up on fairgrounds, vacant lots, train yards, parks, village greens and town commons all across the North, and the South for that matter. State authorities officially designated some of these camps, the larger ones in principal cities, as Camps of Rendezvous. There, volunteers from that portion of the state would be brought together and organized into regiments. Later, some camps had their designations changed to Camp of Instruction, but the training given there was still sketchy, and the length of the instruction depended upon the exigencies facing the armies in the field. These camps were the Civil War equivalent of modern boot camps, perhaps the principal difference being that the emphasis was on organizing the volunteers into companies and the companies into regiments rather than training them individually to be soldiers or preparing them, physically and otherwise, for combat. Training was almost an afterthought to occupy the time between the volunteers' arrival in camp and when they were organized into regiments and shipped out. There was no prescribed length of training; some men were in camp for mere hours, some for months.

Governor Curtin established a Camp of Rendezvous on the fairgrounds of the Dauphin County Agricultural Society about a mile north of Harrisburg, the state capital. On April 18th, Pennsylvania militia officers assumed control of the fairgrounds and named the camp Camp Curtin.

The proximity of Harrisburg to Washington and Harper's Ferry, the two principal staging areas for operations in the eastern theatre early in the war, gave Camp Curtin an importance second to no other Camp of Rendezvous or Instruction in the North. Harrisburg was not only closer to Washington than any other capital or major city in the Northern states, even closer than Philadelphia, but it was centrally-located and was served by no fewer than four railroads. Camp Curtin became the most important military post in what was arguably the state most important to the North's war effort.

The story of Camp Curtin is far more complex and wide-reaching than what went on within its gates. The events at Camp Curtin and the camp's importance can not be fully understood without knowing the successes and failures of the Union armies—particularly the Army of the Potomac, to which most of the regiments formed in Camp Curtin went. If the Union armies met with misfortune and more men were needed, Camp Curtin would spring to life and be crowded with recruits and volunteers. If the army fought a major battle, the camp hospital, the barracks and even the schools and churches of Harrisburg would be flooded with wounded fresh from the battlefield.

I have made no attempt to disentangle the story of the camp from that of the Army of the Potomac, but have tried to present them as they relate to one another. Where I have omitted detail, I have done so from the army's story, elaborating on details of life in the camp wherever possible.

The fibers of these entangled histories, of course, are the stories of the men of Camp Curtin. If, as Thomas Carlyle said, there is no history, only biography, then the story of the camp can be told through the lives of the men who served there. The commandants, the drill masters, the company officers and the rank and file made Camp Curtin what it was. Their characters, their temperaments, their intelligence or stupidity, their inflexibility, their inattention or devotion to duty defined the character, atmosphere and appearance of the camp, so no history of the place could ignore these common men. To tell this aspect of the story, I have introduced both key figures in the running of the camp—commandants and other officers—as well as representative men of the ranks. I have followed these men from their pre-war lives into the camp then out to the battlefields and back again, for only in that way can the reader truly begin to understand the innocence and unruliness of the recruits of 1861 and 1862 or the sadness and anxiety of the returned veterans in 1864 and 1865 waiting to be mustered out and sent home.

This is not a history of Pennsylvania's participation in the Civil War, nor of Harrisburg's role, nor of the campaigns of the Army of the Potomac, nor of the life of the common soldier, though it contains elements of all these. It is rather the story of obscure men who left their homes and families and went off to war. It is the story of a place where many of those men began and ended their service, where some fell ill and died, where others recuperated from wounds received in battle and where hundreds of thousands of men first experienced the life of a soldier. One man who lived in the camp wrote of its importance to the common volunteer:

> Camp Curtin was his first and last camp. Here he underwent a physical examination; it was here where he first slept in his blanket upon some meagre straw, or on the bare hard ground; it was here where he first learned to take a meal in a primitive fashion; where he received his first training in the manual of arms; and where he became isolated from his friends, his family and his old associates...he had plenty of time to think of the dear ones he had left behind him, and it was these thoughts which frequently produced "home sickness," and made him feel that "life was not worth living."

It was in Camp Curtin that volunteers learned that the life of a soldier was one of discomfort and frustration. There, amid the disease and discomfort, in leaky tents. and on the sun-baked parade ground, boyish illusions died. Men learned to tolerate and work with other men. They made strong friendships, some of which ended on battlefields, some of which survived and endured for decades. There, also, they said farewell, often tearfully, to friends and comrades and to the life of extreme excitement, danger and boredom they had lived in the army. For these men, Camp Curtin was as much a part of their war experience as were the marches, battlefields and hospitals. Regardless of how Camp Curtin was remembered by the men who moved through it, remembered it was.

W.J.M.
Alexandria, Virginia, 1989

Table Of Contents

PROLOGUE

Though the night had been full of snow and wind, January 15, 1861, dawned clear and calm. The people of Harrisburg, Pennsylvania awoke to see that the charcoal-smudged clouds laden with snow that had swept low over their spires and rooftops for a week or more had blown away. The city lay on the eastern bank of the Susquehanna River, and despite the clearing of the skies, a stabbing wind lifted off the gray, icy waters and slashed through the town, forcing gentlemen to walk briskly with upturned collars and discouraging ladies from going out at all.

Notwithstanding the raw weather, the sidewalks and streets of the city were unusally crowded. Dozens of sleighs pulled by snorting sorrels and chestnuts glided over the white streets, and throngs of men picked their way carefully over the slippery, rutted sidewalks. Marching bands and smartly-uniformed companies tramped through the snow and drew crowds wherever they went. It was inauguration day in the capital city of Pennsylvania, and Harrisburg's little population of about 16,000 swelled to include wealthy, powerful, and respected men, and their ladies, from all over Pennsylvania. Men in silk vests and broadcloth suits and women in lace and plumes made their way to the capitol building to begin the ritual of welcoming to office a new governor.[1]

The new chief executive was 45-year-old Andrew Gregg Curtin, a lawyer from the town of Bellefonte, Centre County—in heartland of the Commonwealth. Of average height and proportions, with longish, thinning brown hair that was allowed to curl in compliance with the fashion of the day, Curtin, like many of his constituents, was Scotch-Irish. His father, Roland, had been born and raised in Ireland. His mother, Jean Gregg, was the daughter of Andrew Gregg—soldier of the Revolution, and member of the United States House of Representatives for sixteen years, and of the United States Senate for four. When Jean Gregg Curtin had given birth to her first son on April 15, 1815, she and Roland had promptly named the boy after her illustrious father.[2]

Andrew Gregg Curtin had attended a number of prestigious private academies while growing up, and, like all well-educated young men of his day, was versed in both mathematics and the classics. He eventually turned his attention to the study of the law, reading at the Law School of Dickinson College in Carlisle, Pennsylvania. In 1839, he had been admitted to the Centre County Bar and become a partner of future Congressman John Blanchard.[3]

Curtin's promise and eventual success as an attorney was due in part to his ability as an orator. He found his ability to move an audience suited him to public service as well, and, at 25 he entered his grandfather's old realm and began working in local politics. In 1844, he campaigned for candidate Henry Clay. Four years later, he canvassed the commonwealth for Whig General Zachary Taylor. His devotion to the party and his speaking ability marked him as a man on the rise among the Whigs in Pennsylvania, and, by 1848, when he spoke on behalf of another general, Winfield Scott, Curtin had established himself, at the age of 33, as a force in Pennsylvania politics.[4]

In 1854, the party offered him the gubernatorial nomination. He declined, however, perhaps not wishing to make a premature move or out of deference to the man who eventually received the nomination, James Pollock. Pollock prevailed easily in the vote and rewarded Curtin with an appointment as secretary of the commonwealth. It was in this office that Curtin began making his first important contributions to his state. His title made him ex-officio superintendent of the Common School System in the commonwealth, and he devoted much of his time to functioning in that capacity. Curtin was a patriotic Pennsylvanian, and he, like his parents, recognized the importance of education to both the individual and the community. The quality of life in Pennsylvania could only be bettered by educating its people, and it was a better, stronger Pennsylvania that Curtin sought. At the same time, however, Curtin had a genuine concern for the people. He was a politician of unusual compassion. It was this concern for the condition of the average Pennsylvanian and his willingness to work to improve that condition that made Curtin popular among the people of the Old Keystone State.

The peace and prosperity of the 1850s had enabled Curtin to devote himself to the betterment of life for Pennsylvanians, but by 1860, matters had grown more complex. The country was in a state of civil unrest. Throughout the fall and winter, the states of the deep south threatened to secede from the Union, and, in fact, several of them had already done so as a result of the election of Abraham Lincoln, the "Northern" candidate, to the presidency. The country seemed headed for a civil war and the outlook for a restoration of good relations between sections of the country seemed bleak. Pennsylvania's position on the issues involved was, of course, never in doubt; she was for the preservation of the Union. But as a very large, wealthy, and powerful state, the *degree* of her commitment to the federal government—more specifically to the policies of Lincoln's administration—would matter very much when war came. Curtin had been a "party man," as a Whig and as a Republican, for more than twenty years, so he was expected to support Lincoln. But even had he not been so devout in his support of the party, he was personally pro-Union, and he saw the actions of the Southern states as madness. He had supported, heart and mind, Lincoln's cause: preservation of the Union at all costs. He had made no secret of his views during the gubernatorial campaign in the autumn of 1860, and the election therefore became a referendum. The question to the voters was: would Pennsylvania's public commitment to the president and his efforts to preserve the Union be wholehearted and unquestioning? The people of the Commonwealth responded affirmatively, electing Curtin by a majority of 32,000 votes.[5]

By inauguration day, South Carolina, Mississippi, Florida and Alabama had declared themselves out of the Union. Curtin had no doubt that secession was not only illegal but immoral. Secessionists were assaulting nothing less than a government with divine blessing—a holy Union of free people. In his inaugural address, therefore, Curtin proclaimed that, as the elected representative of the people of Pennsylvania, he would do all in his power to aid the government of the United States in its efforts to preserve the Union. "I assume the duties of this high office at the most trying period of our national history," he declared. "The public mind is agitated by fears, suspicions and jealousies. Serious apprehensions of the future pervade the people. A preconcerted and organized effort has been made to disturb the stability of the government, dissolve the union of the States and mar the symmetry and order of the noblest political structure ever devised and enacted by human wisdom,...[but] the people mean to preserve the intregrity of the National Union at every hazard."[6]

Curtin was making it clear that doubt and equivocation would not play a part in his direction of the commonwealth. He was serving notice to all who listened—Northerner and Southerner—that when war came, Pennsylvania would be committed to executing the policies and orders of the president and Congress of the United States.

Despite their admiration of him and their generally pro-Union sentiments, many Pennsylvanians did not share Curtin's outrage or sense of sacrilege over the actions of the secessionists. Most Pennsylvanians were more occupied with other matters of more immediate importance. Some of the richest, most fertile farmland in the world, for example, lay in the Susquehanna Valley, and the people who lived there struggled to pull from the earth everything it could give. A great many of the farmers did not even speak English, or spoke it only badly. Their fathers and grandfathers, or they themselves, were immigrants from Ireland, Scotland, or, more commonly, Germany, and had come to America seeking just two things: good land by which to support their families and to be left alone. Often, they lived out their lives without ever traveling ten miles from the land they toiled over and sweated into. Sometimes, if they needed help during busy seasons, there might be brothers, nephews, or cousins nearby to lend a hand, but they mostly worked alone. Around these farmers grew small communities of similar people who served as smiths, mechanics, carpenters, millers, grocers and teachers. Their industry was their morality, and they all strove to keep their houses painted and their fences straight.

Throughout the long winter, these common people had read in their community newspapers much talk of war and had watched as states seceded from the Union. Interest in the issues had peaked during the gubernatorial elections, when Curtin focused attention squarely on them by campaigning on his dedication to the Union. Though the people had agreed with him, and sent him to the capitol in Harrisburg, they quickly turned their attention to other matters once the election was over. The haggling over the legality of secession or the constitutional responsibilities of states was, after all, very far away from the peaceful world of grist mills, dairy yards, fallow fields and factories in which the majority of Pennsylvanians spent their lives. The bewildering swirl of national politics had provided an interesting diversion during the idle winter months, but in the weeks and months after Curtin's inauguration, as the air warmed and the earth softened, the time for diffusing energies had passed for many of the people of the Keystone State. It was spring in farm country, and these practical people went about their business, knowing that war could come any day, but knowing as well that corn and beans had to be planted.

XIV

Curtin, though, could not afford to disregard national events. After taking office, he maintained continual communication with the White House, and Lincoln came to trust him as an astute observer and intelligent advisor. On April 8, 1861, Curtin met with the president in Washington. Both men knew then that war was not very far off, and it is likely that the president asked the governor to hasten preparations already underway in his state. The next day, with all the states of the deep South in rebellion and eighty-three United States soldiers besieged in Fort Sumter, in Charleston harbor, South Carolina, Curtin addressed Pennsylvania's legislature and urged the members to prepare for the hostilities that could be just hours away. "It is scarcely necessary to say more than that the militia system of the State, during a long period distinguished by pursuits of peaceful industry exclusively, has become wholly inefficient, and the interference of the Legislature is required to remove its deficits, and to render it useful and available to the public service."[7] A great many volunteer militia companies, he noted, were understrength and ill-equipped; their weapons were outdated, in disrepair, and few. He recommended the creation of a military bureau at Harrisburg and the modification of laws to restore to the commonwealth's military system "the vitality and energy essential to its practical value and usefulness."[8] The Legislature responded quickly and fully to Curtin's appeal, moving on legislation that would rejuvenate the militia. Just four days later, on April 12, 1861, Fort Sumter was fired upon by Confederates in Charleston and bombarded into submission. Pennsylvania, along with the rest of the nation, was at war.

CHAPTER ONE

"Reveille at the Dawn of Day"

APRIL 13 — APRIL 19, 1861

As soon as the news of the firing on Sumter reached Washington, Lincoln sent for Curtin again. On his birthday, Monday, the 15th of April, Curtin arrived at the White House. Lincoln explained that, in the interest of expediency in this emergency, he and Secretary of War Simon Cameron, another Pennsylvanian Republican and the architect of one of the more powerful political machines in American history, had already discussed much of that for which Curtin had been summoned. The president needed help from all the Northern states, but especially from Pennsylvania because she might be able to provide men for the defense of the capital most rapidly. Cameron, knowing well the circumstances that existed in his native state, told the president just what he could expect from Pennsylvania. When Curtin arrived, he was able to officially sanction Cameron's promises for men. Lincoln said that later that day, 75,000 volunteers were to be called for from all loyal states. Pennsylvania would be asked to provide about one-sixth of them. The volunteers would be armed and equipped at the expense of the federal government, but, as few preparations had been made, the state should provide for the men and submit a bill to Washington. The volunteers would be needed immediately—within days—and would be asked to serve for three months. The president could not call out troops for service any longer than three months without the consent of Congress, and Congress was not in session. Besides, ninety days was generally thought to be ample time to repress the rebellion.[1]

1

In Harrisburg, it was becoming evident that the people of Pennsylvania, who had been slumbering in preoccupation throughout the early spring, were awaking. Although the president had not yet publicly called upon the northern states to furnish troops, Secretary of the Commonwealth Eli Slifer began receiving telegraph dispatches in Harrisburg on the morning of April 15th from men offering their services:

Philadelphia, April 15, 1861

To his Excellency A. G. Curtin:

I respectfully offer you the services of my company, the Washington Blues of Philadelphia.

Captain J. M. Gasline

Pittsburgh, April 15, 1861

To Governor A. G. Curtin:

In the absence of the captain, R. P. McDowell, I, the first lieutenant of the company, report said company ready to march.

G. W. Dawson, First Lieutenant State Guards, Allegheny City

Chambersburg, April 15, 1861

To Eli Slifer:

If aided in uniforms, eight hundred to one thousand men, I will report in person to-morrow evening.

F. S. Stambaugh, Colonel First Regiment

Philadelphia, April 15, 1861

To his Excellency, A. G. Curtin, Governor of Pennsylvania:

Will you accept a company of horse to be raised by me in Elk and McKean counties? I can leave here tonight and bring down my men in a week. My offer of service is unconditional.

Thomas L. Kane[2]

Dozens of such dispatches came to the capital, promising thousands of men. By the time the president did officially call upon Pennsylvania for 13,000 men, 2,000 within three days, more than enough men than were immediately needed had already offered their services. Pennsylvania was mobilizing.[3]

While there was no shortage of men, there was a question as to where the state could gather and organize them into regiments. Harrisburg was the logical place to consolidate the volunteers. Not only was it the state capital and seat of government, but it was centrally located and for that reason had grown into a major transportation center. The principal means of transportation over long distances was the railroads, and no fewer than four railroads passed through Harrisburg: the Pennsylvania Railroad, The Lebanon Valley Railroad, the Northern Central Railroad and the Cumberland Valley Railroad. In addition to the railroads, the relatively new and only moderately successful Pennsylvania Canal ran through Harrisburg on its way from Philadelphia to Pittsburgh and Erie. The Susquehanna also served as a main commercial route, principally for shallow-draft vessels carrying coal or lumber. A great many men and materials could be concentrated in Harrisburg very quickly. Perhaps more important, they could be dispatched just as quickly to Washington. Harrisburg was an ideal jumping-off point.

Upon his return from Washington, the governor set to the task of organizing an army. Hundreds of men were known to be enroute to the state capital, and no doubt hundreds more coming who had not wired ahead. The city did not contain accommodations for these hundreds, perhaps thousands, of men, yet they had to be put someplace. When faced with the sudden influx into the capital of hundreds of amateur soldiers and dozens of quasi-military groups in need of organization, Curtin wasted no time in calling upon the local military authorities for assistance. He summoned Brigadier General Edward C. Williams, commander of the local, peacetime militia. Williams was a burly, round-faced man with a habitual squint, a shiny, bald pate, and a thick, dark moustache that drooped over his upper lip to almost cover his mouth. He had considerable military experience and therefore was in high demand in those hectic days after the firing on Sumter.

COLONEL EDWARD C. WILLIAMS
9th Pennsylvania Cavalry.
The founder of Camp Curtin and a key man in Pennsylvania's mobilization early in the war.
(Dauphin County Historical Society)

Born in Philadelphia on February 10, 1819, Williams was what might be called a professional militiaman. His military dossier included very nearly twenty years of service to his state as a member of militia organizations as well as combat experience in the war with Mexico. As a 26-year-old in December, 1846, he raised a company of volunteers to serve in Mexico. As its captain, he brought himself to the attention of state authorities by coaxing, encouraging and threatening his infantrymen through 150 miles of snow-filled forests and icy mountains between Chambersburg and Pittsburgh in four days.[4] Once in Mexico, Williams, as a member of the 2nd Pennsylvania Regiment, served with distinction at Vera Cruz, Cerro Gordo, and Chapultepec, where he was wounded. When the conflict ended, he returned to Harrisburg, where he and his wife, Salima, had made their home, and once again took up his craft of bookbinding. In 1850, he was elected sheriff of Dauphin County but continued to participate actively in the state militia. On June 6, 1859, he had been commissioned brigadier general of militia and given command of the Third Brigade, Fifth Division Pennsylvania Militia. In April, 1861, the 42-year-old Williams had no reputation as a soldier beyond the borders of Pennsylvania, but he was a good organizer and his experience commanded respect. Curtin knew Williams was a good man to have on hand, so, on the afternoon of April 18, the governor and the general met in the capitol.[5]

Walking with Williams as he climbed the granite steps of the capitol that day was another Mexican War veteran, Major Joseph Farmer Knipe. Knipe was born March 30, 1823, in Mount Joy, Pennsylvania, the fourth of blacksmith Henry Knipe's ten children. Educated in the local public schools and apprenticed to a shoemaker in Philadelphia, Knipe soon longed for more excitement than cobbling could offer, and, in 1842 at the age of 19, he had enlisted for five years in Company I, 2nd United States Artillery. Three years later, Knipe had all the excitement he could hope for as he marched through Texas and Mexico under General Winfield Scott. After duty in Mexico, Knipe was discharged from the 2nd Artillery as a sergeant. He returned from the war and settled in Harrisburg, where he became associated with the Pennsylvania Railroad, eventually rising to become the company's Harrisburg mail agent.[6] In June, 1859, when his friend, Edward C. Williams, was made a brigadier general of militia, Knipe was given the position of aide-de-camp on the brigade staff.

It was Williams, however, who held Curtin's attention that afternoon. Volunteers were already arriving in the city, and there was no place to put them. Five companies of volunteers, in fact, had not only already arrived, but had departed that morning. The Ringgold Light Artillery, a company from Reading, and the first military unit in the commonwealth to mobilize, came into town on the night of the 16th. On the morning of the 17th, the Logan Guards of Lewistown arrived by train. The Allen Guards of Allentown and the National Light Infantry and the Washington Artillery, both of Pottsville, followed that night. All five companies were quartered in hotels and meeting halls within the city.[7]

Two hundred men of Company H, 4th United States Artillery, had also arrived in Harrisburg on the 17th. The regulars had come from garrison duty on the western plains following the news of Sumter and were on their way to Fort McHenry in

Baltimore. In command of Company H was an undistinguished 44-year-old captain, a West Pointer and a Philadelphian, who was wrestling inwardly with a difficult decision. Six days later, the captain would resign his commission in the United States Army and head south to join the Confederate Army. His name was John C. Pemberton.[8]

Captain Seneca G. Simmons, 7th United States Infantry and United States mustering officer in Harrisburg, mustered into Federal service the five companies of volunteers drawn up at the Pennsylvania Railroad station on the morning of the 18th. In the months to come, Captain Simmons, aided by Captain D. H. Hastings, 1st U.S. Dragoons, was to swear in nearly 15,000 volunteers at Harrisburg.[9] After being mustered in for three months and given a few hearty cheers by the crowd at the station, the five companies, numbering about 460 men, had boarded a train with the Regulars and set off for Washington via Baltimore.[10] The five companies of volunteers were the first Northern volunteers to arrive at Washington. Anxious members of the administration and Congress greeted them gratefully, with the president himself thanking them. The men were not unjustly proud of their promptness and patriotism and even still, they are paid tribute by being referred to as the "First Defenders."

Even as the First Defenders were leaving Harrisburg on the morning of the 18th, other companies were continuously arriving. All through the morning and into the afternoon they detrained at the railroad station and poured into the city, swarming through the streets and parks and taverns of the city by the hundreds. Curtin knew that these men had to be organized quickly, for they had to be fed and given places to stay. Dauphin County officials had already offered the use of the County Agricultural Fairgrounds and the governor had accepted. Williams was to take possession of the fairgrounds, which lay north of the city, and put the place in order to serve as the point of rendezvous for volunteers where they could be quartered and confined. Two companies, the Johnstown Infantry and the Johnstown Zouave Cadets, had, in fact, been sent that afternoon to the fairgrounds and had already bivouacked there.[11] Other companies, ranging from sixty to 120 men, were quartered in hotels and halls throughout the city just as the First Defenders had been.[12] Curtin wanted all of them moved to the new camp. With his orders complete, Williams prepared to go, but, before the meeting ended, someone suggested that the camp should have a name. "Camp Union" was proposed and agreed to, and Williams and Knipe departed to get to work.[13]

As the militia officers proceeded north out of the city to inspect the fairgrounds, they attracted a fairly large group of curious citizens and disorganized volunteers. The assemblage of militiamen, citizens and citizen-soldiers headed out the Ridge Road, the principal road leading north from Harrisburg. It was a long, straight thoroughfare that rose out of the city to the crest of a ridge that gave it its name. Once the crest was reached, the high, board fence that surrounded the fairgrounds could be seen between the trees at some distance. As the officers and citizens proceeded cheerfully down the pleasant avenue lined by maples and cherry trees, the movement took on something of the atmosphere of a parade.

Williams and Knipe, as Harrisburg residents, were undoubtedly familiar with
the fairgrounds, but, on this day, once within the enclosure, the men surveyed the
familiar place as they never had, with an eye toward castramentation. A large, fairly
new, two-story wooden structure sat on the infield of the racetrack and dominated
the grassy park. Called "Floral Hall" or "The Park House," it had been used to house
the horticultural and other indoor exhibits during the fairs. Scattered around the grass-
covered field, especially along the eastern side of the fairgrounds, were long, simply
constructed, one-story buildings filled with stalls that sheltered the livestock brought
to the fairs. Along the western fence of the fairgrounds was a row of sheds in which
hay and feed for the livestock had been stored. A few other large buildings, like Floral
Hall, stood around the park and housed machinery exhibits and crafts. With the exception of Floral Hall, all of these sheds and buildings sat in various degrees of
dilapidation after being inexpensively built and continuously exposed to the weather.[14]

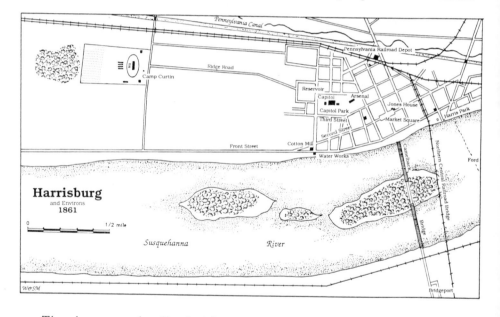

The place seemed well suited for a camp. A well and a good strong pump provided plenty of fresh water, and the river was just a few hundred yards to the west,
providing a place for bathing and relaxing. Transportation was available over the Pennsylvania Canal, which lay just a few feet from the camp's eastern fence, and the Pennsylvania Railroad, which passed by just yards beyond the canal. There seemed to
be an abundance of room in the 80-square-acre park, and the buildings, decaying as
they were, could be repaired at little expense and put in condition to serve as barracks to shelter at least some of the men. Volunteers could erect tents in the broad
open areas in the park to quarter thousands of men.[15]

But in truth, the fairgrounds had a serious shortcoming as a campground. The ground was far from level, sloping off in both directions from the crest of the ridge. Viewed from the main gate, which was on the Ridge Road at the south side of the fairgrounds, the terrain within the enclosure sloped gently off to the left for just over 100 yards before it dipped suddenly and declined to a plain several hundred yards wide that led to the bank of the river. The western fence of the camp was on the slope. To the right of the main gate, the eastern side of fairgrounds, the crest of the ridge extended a bit to form a narrow plateau, but the ground dropped sharply off the edge of the ridge toward the canal and the railroad tracks. There was, perhaps, enough good, level ground for drilling and parading, but the sloping ground might cause problems for those encamped in low-lying areas when rain water drained away from the high ground. In any event, Williams believed the camp was intended to serve only as a central location where volunteer companies and battalions traveling from various parts of the commonwealth could meet. It was a place of rendezvous, and for that reason was officially called just that—a Camp of Rendezvous. Whatever its faults, it was a far more suitable place for thousands of volunteers to stay for a few days than the Jones House or Bryant's Hall or any of the other hotels or halls within the city.

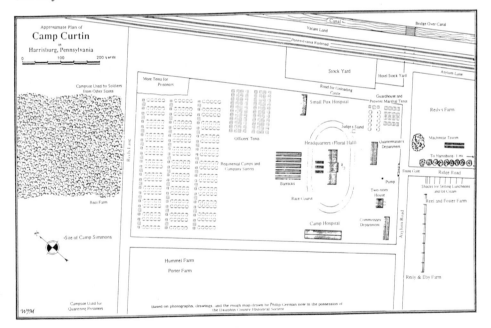

As General Williams and Major Knipe surveyed the camp, hundreds of flannel-, wool-, and homespun-clad volunteers, all members of the companies that had been quartered downtown, continued to arrive and mill curiously about the uniformed officers. They were but boys, most of them. Seventeen, 18, 19 years old they were, with smooth faces and bright eyes. They stood with slack jaws, totally unconscious of themselves, and watched the men in uniform. There were, of course, a good number of older men, 25 or 30 year olds or even older, but the boys were far and away the majority. They had come from all across the commonwealth, from Pittsburgh to Easton, and had given themselves names intended to show their fighting spirit: "The Turner Riflemen" and "The Union State Guards" from Pittsburgh, "The Zouave Cadets" from Johnstown, "The Juniata Rifles" from Altoona, and "The Wyoming Artillery" from Wilkes-Barre. There seemed to be no end to the stream of men coming through the gate: two companies from Pottsville, two from Easton, another from Pittsburgh, and two more from Mauch Chunk. Hundreds of men of all shapes, sizes, and descriptions, more men than most of the country boys had ever seen in one place.

One of the volunteers in camp that first afternoon came as first lieutenant of a local militia company from the governor's hometown of Bellefonte. James Addams Beaver was tall, hale, handsome, and 23 years old. His father had died when the boy was only three, and he had been raised by his mother and, later, a stepfather, a Presbyterian clergyman. Exceptionally intelligent, Beaver was already an attorney and a partner in one of the more prominent and successful law firms in the commonwealth. His friends at Jefferson College in Canonsburg, Pennsylvania, from which he had been graduated at the tender age of 18, remembered him as "Jim Beaver...a little bit of an enthusiastic fellow, full of fun and pun and pluck and frolic, who never did anything bad and always looked glad." He had finished his study of the law so young that he had to wait to be admitted to the bar until he reached voting age.[16]

Beaver's outfit, the Bellefonte Fencibles, had been captained by none other than Andrew G. Curtin until shortly before he had been elected chief executive. Beaver, ambitious-young-man-on-the-rise that he was, knew that associations with men like Curtin would not hurt him and, of a military bent anyway, he joined the company and was elected second lieutenant. He and Curtin became well acquainted and, even after Curtin left for the Executive Mansion, Beaver remained as second lieutenant in the Fencibles. The company mobilized immediately upon Lincoln's call. After a reorganization, in which Beaver was promoted to first lieutenant, it proceeded to Harrisburg under Captain John B. Mitchell, with Beaver second in command.[17]

Even the city dwellers of Harrisburg, many of whom had gathered out at the fairgrounds, were impressed by the number of men arriving. "We had a fine time watching the soldiers," recalled Teresa Knipe, one of Major Knipe's daughters, who had accompanied her father to the camp in a large open carriage. "When father led some soldiers toward one of the buildings," remembered Miss Knipe later, "we drove over to see what he was going to do." Major Knipe, apparently a man with a good sense of drama, climbed a ladder and appeared on the roof of the building clutching a national flag. He wrestled with the halyards on the flag pole for a few moments, but soon had the flag attached to the ropes. He turned to the crowd below and shouted, "What shall we name the camp? I propose the name of Governor Curtin!"[18] The suggestion was a popular one. While Knipe ran the colors up the pole, the growing crowd cheered and sent hats sailing into the early twilight sky of that Thursday, April 18. Camp Curtin was born.

*   *   *

COLONEL JOSEPH F. KNIPE
46th Pennsylvania Volunteers.
The Harrisburg native who named Camp Curtin. He was wounded at Cedar Mountain, was promoted to brigadier general and led militia in the Gettysburg Campaign.
(Dauphin County Historical Society)

The commonwealth had provided 200 Sibley tents for Williams's use at Camp Curtin. Sibleys, sometimes called Bell tents because of their shape, bore a great resemblance to Indian tepees, and had, in fact, been invented by an army officer who had served on the western plains. The tents were 18 feet in diameter at the base. In the center of the tent's interior was a stove that was supposed to heat the entire enclosure. Twelve men could be comfortably accommodated in each tent.[19] The volunteers already in camp were set to work erecting these tents, and Williams hoped that the tents, together with the long animal sheds that were to serve as barracks, would provide shelter for most of the volunteers expected to arrive within the next few days.

All through the afternoon and far into the night, the engines of the Pennsylvania Railroad, snorting great swirling clouds of steam, pitched and rolled and squeaked over the tracks just yards from the camp, bringing carload after carload of volunteers from all over the state. As the night wore on, some of the newly arrived companies remained at the depot in Harrisburg and reposed on the brick pavement, others tried to find berths in one of the city's hotels, but many undertook the mile-long walk out to Camp Curtin. These men were guided through the camp to where whey were to spend the remainder of the night. The slow, ceaseless shuffling of these hundreds of tired men, the shouts of impatient officers, and the wailing whistles of the locomotives made sleep a rare and precious thing that night.

To make matters worse, the mid-April air was exceptionally damp and cold. Water in buckets by officers' tents froze solid, and the men, wrapped in what few blankets could be found, clustered around smoky fires that sent sparks winding aimlessly up into the cold black sky. The stars were hidden by thick clouds that threatened rain. The old fairgrounds offered no comfort for a man accustomed to the warm second story bedroom at home. "As the boys lay down in the clean straw to sleep off the fatigues of the day," remembered one tired volunteer, "they not only thought of the girls they had left behind them, but of their mothers' soft beds they had exchanged for the 'cold, cold ground.' "[20] They were fighting a soldier's first battle: the nightlong campaign of a tired man against noise, excitement, cold air, and damp ground. Camp Curtin's first night was not a restful one.

Dawn came at last when the sky in the east grew pink and the countryside beyond the railroad and camp fences gradually turned a moist gray. Ravens, barking harshly, sailed through the mists and swooped to the tops of the chestnut and maple trees around the camp, thrashing the heavy air with their glossy black wings and lurching about crazily as they settled on the slender swaying branches uppermost on the trees. There they surveyed the smoking city of white canvas that had grown up below them. The long thumping rattle of a drum suddenly brought the peaceful city to life. Languid volunteers gratefully rose from their dewy blankets in the stable-barracks and left the imperfect slumbers of the long, cold, noisy night behind. Canvas tent flaps flew open and bleary-eyed men emerged into the streets between the tents and milled about in disorganization. Officers moved through the crowds trying to get men into a line, gently pushing, prodding, and gesturing.[21]

The men in camp were from all walks of life: carpenters, coopers, miners, lumbermen, rail hands, longshoremen, fishermen, sailors, clerks, machinists, teachers, lawyers, farmers, and general laborers. Companies were sometimes formed along occupational lines. Whole companies of railroaders, glassblowers, and iron workers came from Pittsburgh. A company of blacksmiths was raised in Phoenixville, Pennsylvania.[22] The canal boatmen and their co-workers, the mule drivers, left their jobs and "joined up to the Army."[23] The small county of Schuylkill contributed twenty-two companies in the first several weeks of the war. Most of those 1,860 men were miners. This was the best effort made by any county and nearly depopulated some of the county's mining districts.[24] Usually, however, the men of a company did not share a common occupation and had nothing more in common than that they were from the same portion of the state, and sometimes not even that.

Exactly eighty-six years before that first morning in Camp Curtin, queued minutemen were leaping from their beds and assembling on village greens throughout eastern Massachusetts preparatory to meeting the British at Lexington and Concord. The minuteman of 1861 was no better trained as a soldier than had been the 1775 version, a fact the latter-day patriots would have readily admitted. The rag-tag, citizen-soldiers of the revolution had waged and won a war against a superbly trained, equipped, and led enemy and had thereby set a dangerous precedent. The boys of '61 were well aware of the military accomplishments of the soldiers of the Revolution, and reasoned that if it could be done once, it could be done again, the enemy this time, though fighting closer to home was not nearly as well trained, led, or equipped. The farmers and tradesmen in Camp Curtin on that April 19th were perfectly willing, even anxious, to march down South that very day and whip the hell out of the rebels and get it all over with. General Williams, however, knew that they had much to learn before they would be allowed to go down to Dixie and quash the rebellion. Williams determined that their education should begin at dawn, an hour with which all men wishing to be soldiers must become well familiar.

After the officers lined up the men of their companies, the volunteers were given instruction in posture, facings and foot movement. An hour of this gave the men a healthy appetite, and they were allowed to have their breakfast. The Camp Commissary and Quartermaster's Departments had been set up in Floral Hall, and rations, consisting mainly of raw beef and bread, were distributed to all the men. The hungry volunteers then returned to their tents to cook their own meals in small groups, or messes, of four or five men or even more. That first breakfast in the still-cool morning at Camp Curtin was a good one. "Butter, molasses + other little luxuries were missed by several," remembered one lad, "but still all were in good spirits + made way with the first soldier's meal, with a true soldiers appetite."[25] After the long, cold, sometimes lonesome night, the men welcomed the pots of hot coffee and the warm fires and camp stoves. Just as welcome was the companionship of their messmates, the quality of which had been strengthened by the night's ordeal.

When the meal was over about nine o'clock, the men were hastily called again into line, this time on the open expanse of the fairgrounds racecourse. Williams had established Camp Headquarters in Floral Hall as well, and there the men witnessed the first of many military ceremonies: the mounting of the first guard at Camp Curtin. Captain William H. Ganzler of Allentown was officer of the day, and Captain Henry A. Hambright of Lancaster and Major Knipe supervised the ceremony. The Lancaster Band played as stirringly and as martially as it could, but the brevity of the ceremony left little opportunity for music. The gathering also enabled Williams to distribute general orders, which would affect every man in camp. Williams's orders detailed the schedule on which the camp would be run and defined the behavior that would be expected of the volunteers. Company officers read the orders to their men.

General Orders, No. 2
HEADQUARTERS
CAMP CURTIN, April 19, 1861

The following orders will be observed by the troops while in camp at Camp Curtin:

1. The Reveille will be sounded at the dawn of day, and companies will form on the parade grounds, and as soon as the Reveille ceases, the rolls will be called by the Orderly Sergeants, superintended by a commissioned officer, and immediately after roll call the companies will drill for one hour.

2. Immediately after company drill, the tents will be put in order by the men of the companies, superintended by chiefs of squads; the parades, streets of the camp, &c., will be cleaned by the police party of the day, in charge of a non-commissioned officer, superintended by the officer of the guard.

3. Breakfast call will be sounded at 7 o'clock.

4. The Troop will sound at half-past nine, a.m., for the purpose of guard mounting.

5. The first Sergeants will make their reports at Headquarters every morning, at 10 o'clock.

6. Captains will be required to drill their companies from half-past ten to half-past eleven, a.m., and from four to five, p.m.

7. The dinner call will be sounded at twelve o'clock.

8. The Retreat will be sounded at sunset, when the rolls will be called and the orders of the day read.

9. The Tatoo will be sounded at nine o'clock in the evening, when the rolls will be called; and no soldier will be allowed to be out of his tent after this hour without special permission, and all lights will be extinguished at the tap of the drum.

10. Any soldier coming into camp intoxicated or bringing liquor in, will be immediately placed under arrest by the officer of the guard.

11. Any person selling liquor within the bounds prescribed by law will be dealt with according to law in such cases made and prescribed.

Captains of Companies will be held responsible for a strict observance of the above orders.

By order of

E. C. Williams
Brig. Gen. Commanding
Joseph F. Knipe, Aid de Camp[26]

The reveille at dawn probably didn't bother the farm boys in the ranks as much as it did the clerks and the mechanics, but the three hours of drill each day and the policing of tents and messes while under constant supervision likely grated on everyone. Nevertheless, every man in camp would soon find himself up at the day's first blush for exercises and drills before breakfast.

The company officers, the men charged with executing these orders, had in many cases to make adjustments as well. Since company officers were elected by the rest of the men in the company, the officers tended to be either popular or intelligent, professional men respected in their communities. The physicians, lawyers and even clergymen who very often wound up as officers certainly were not accustomed to turning out at dawn to count heads and exercise. Furthermore, many of these men were not qualified to drill their companies at any time of the day. One of the companies that arrived from Pittsburgh that on the afternoon of the 19th, the Zouave Cadets, was led by a professional man typical of the type of man who often led companies in those early days of the war. Captain R. Biddle Roberts was a well-heeled Pittsburgh lawyer, and recently a member of the Duquesne Grays. He had keen political ambitions. At 35, he had already been a local district attorney and a Federal prosecutor appointed by President James Buchanan, none of which qualified him to be a captain of volunteers. Aside from his being a lieutenant in the Duquesne Grays, which in peacetime was little more than a social organization, Roberts's only military experience had been at his father's knee listening to the old man's stories of his service in the War of 1812. But polished, educated, and, above all, socially prominent as he was, Roberts was in high demand as a military commander. He was exactly the type of man with whom other ambitious young men wished to associate themselves. So, when a company of such young men in the Zouave Cadets planned to march off to glory, they clamored loudly to have Roberts serve as their captain and to lead them into battle.

But Roberts was first and foremost a politician, even in uniform, and the degree of his devotion to his new command became clear just after they arrived in Harrisburg. Roberts led his company to the capitol to pay respects to the governor, and during the idle chatting that followed, Curtin mentioned that he needed an aide to assist him in attending to military matters in the capitol and ultimately asked Roberts if he were interested. The two were known to one another, of course, because of prewar politics, and Roberts, though a Democrat, was very interested in working for the governor, for he, too, sought to associate himself with influential men. After what must have been a very small amount of soul searching, the captain left his company of volunteers for the company of the chief executive, who gave him the rank of lieutenant colonel.[27] The brash young men of the Zouave Cadets were forced to find another captain.

CHAPTER TWO

"The Madness That Rules the Hour"

APRIL 20 — JULY, 1861

After establishing Camp Curtin, General Williams was ordered to proceed to York, Pennsylvania, to establish another Camp of Rendezvous.[1] Finding someone to command Camp Curtin after Williams departed on April 20 was no easy matter. Army regulations of 1860 provided that the senior officer present in an encampment would command the entire encampment. As commandant, he would be responsible for the health and safety of the men in the camp as well as ensuring that their basic needs were satisfied. Determining the seniority of officers in those early days of the war, however, was difficult at best. Only five days had elapsed since Lincoln's call, and most officers had been elected by their men at about the same time. By April 20, the 1st, 2nd, and 3rd regiments of Pennsylvania Volunteers had already been organized and equipped in Camp Curtin and dispatched to Washington, and the 4th regiment was enroute to Harrisburg. Of the assorted company and field officers in camp, no one seemed willing to claim seniority. Finally the lot fell to Mr. Washington H. R. Hangen of Allentown, lately elected lieutenant colonel of what would be the 9th regiment. The officers of the 9th had elected Henry C. Longnecker their colonel, but he had been absent in New York at the time and was still somewhere enroute to Harrisburg. Hangen, then, who had begun as captain of a company in the 9th, became the first commandant of Camp Curtin, excluding Williams.[2]

Hangen remains a mysterious figure. He left virtually no record of his life or accomplishments. It seems he had not been especially successful in his community,

14

although he was popular enough to have been elected captain of a company and later to the lieutenant colonelcy of his regiment. He seemed unremarkable, undistinguished, almost nondescript when he arrived at Camp Curtin, and he did little in camp to alter that. The daily duties he assumed as commandant consisted mainly of authorizing requisitions and other tedious administrative duties. Later commandants would take complete control of all functions in the camp, from drilling and policing to organizing the companies into regiments in time for them to be shipped out.

So complete and sudden had been the response of the men of Pennsylvania to the firing on Sumter that within ten days of Lincoln's call on April 15 for 75,000 men from the northern states, nearly 21,000 volunteers were organized, equipped and armed at camps within the commonwealth alone. In all, 25 regiments had been formed in those ten days (Lincoln had called upon Pennsylvania to furnish 13, then changed that number to 14) and of those 25, 16 had been formed at Camp Curtin.[3] Those 16 regiments constituted 9,538 men.[4]

No system existed in camp for providing daily rations for these thousands of men, and the amount of food needed was staggering. During the week of May 1, 1861 for example, approximately 5,000 men were quartered in Camp Curtin. *Each day*, those 5,000 men consumed 6,500 pounds of fresh beef, an equal amount of soft bread, 600 pounds of sugar, 300 of coffee, four bushels of salt, and 13 bushels of beans. For that week, a week that was to be by no means extraordinary as the war went on, nearly 23 tons of fresh beef were distributed at the camp, an equal amount of fresh bread, and more than two tons of coffee. In addition, in the first three weeks of the camp's operation, 15 barrels of salt pork were served as a variant to beef.[5] On hand to assist in the organization of the Camp Commissary was Captain Parmenas T. Turnley, Assistant U.S. Quartermaster. Captain Turnley, West

LIEUTENANT COLONEL WASHINGTON H. R. HANGEN, 9th Pennsylvania Volunteers. Camp Curtin's first commandant (serving as such in April and May, 1961) was later embroiled in controversy. While serving as adjutant of the 47th Pennsylvania Volunteers in 1864, he was dismissed for cowardice. *(Massachusetts Commandery Military Order of the Loyal Legion Collection, U.S. Army Military History Institute)*

Point class of 1846, had happened to be enroute to Washington from the west when he arrived in Harrisburg. He was known as an experienced officer and was prevailed upon to remain and develop a system by which the commissary could feed the volunteers.[6]

All of Turnley's expertise would be needed, for the militia and volunteer officers at the Commissary Department had their work cut out for them. The farmers of the valley were urged to plant abundantly and fatten their hogs and cattle, for much food would be needed, but such foresight did little to feed the men then in camp.[7] Even in farm country, obtaining enough fresh food every day for thousands of hungry men was a monumental task. Contracts were given out to local butchers and bakers as rapidly as possible, and they in turn gave out subcontracts. The ovens in the bakeries of the city never grew cold as bakers worked in shifts around the clock to provide enough bread.[8] The Roumfort Brothers Bakery, for example, employed about twenty men as bakers, and produced an average of about 4,000 loaves of fresh bread a day for Camp Curtin and for regiments passing through the city and temporarily encamped nearby. The Roumforts used between 170 and 200 barrels of flour each week in their efforts to keep Camp Curtin supplied, and in doing so might have become the largest baking operation in the country for those first few months of the war.[9] The large kitchens of the Harrisburg Insane Asylum, which were not far, also were used to prepare food to be brought to camp.

All this contracting and subcontracting led to inconsistency in the quality and irregularity in the delivery of food. Sometimes the beef ration was given to the soldiers raw, other times it was served already cooked, and was distributed directly to the hungry men by the contractor.[10] Drove yards were constructed where the carloads of cattle that arrived steadily from the west were confined and readily available to the contract butchers.[11] As a substitute for soft bread, Army crackers or hardtack was frequently issued. The Roumfort Brothers turned out about 100 barrels of the floury wafers each week in addition to the soft bread, but much of what was given to the volunteers, especially at first, was anything but fresh.[12] The hardtack was indeed very hard, and the older stuff was in many cases moldy and worm-infested as well, having been stored in warehouses around the commonwealth for many years. Some of the volunteers thought them old enough to be Mexican War surplus. One volunteer found himself unable to properly describe the things in a letter home and decided to send one to his friends so they could experience it for themselves. "Bite steady," he wrote, "as there is a great danger of breaking teeth."[13] In any event, the "ironclads" as they came to be known, were unsavory at best and only became edible after a great deal of soaking, frying, seasoning and other preparation.

Complaints about the indifferent quality of the food filtered out to the corners of the commonwealth. Local officials and parents of boys in the camp grumbled about why the state could not do better by its charges, but the citizens of Berks County acted on the problem. Concerned for the welfare of their native sons, the good people of Berks donated 15 tons of hams, beans, and crackers and shipped it all to Harrisburg for distribution at Camp Curtin.

Obtaining good food was only part of the problem. Because troops came and went almost constantly, determining just how many would have to be fed during a given week was a difficult task. The officers at the commissary had not yet had enough experience to make accurate estimates, and the result was that there was sometimes too little or even too much food on hand. Late in May, for example, coffee and pork were piled so high in the warehouse that some officers became concerned that it would spoil before it could all be used.[14] With such large amounts of foodstuffs being delivered to the camp and passing through so many hands before finally reaching the hungry soldiers for whom it was intended, opportunities for dishonest dealings were abundant. Some clerks and other subordinates began to issue short rations so that they might sell the "surplus" for personal profit. That trick was not run long, however, and generally ceased as soon as the men figured out what was happening and could send a delegation of burly diplomats to discuss the matter with the enterprising thief.[15]

Uniforms presented another problem. The volunteers certainly had to be given uniforms, but very few suits of any kind were on hand. The men were generally unhappy because they had expected to be uniformed immediately, so they could send their own clothes, the ones they had been wearing since they enlisted, home for safekeeping. The volunteers were, for the most part, not wealthy, and a suit of clothes was an important possession. Many enlisted because they were impoverished and had only bad clothing and shoes. Barefoot men were not uncommon. The Quartermaster's Department did not have enough uniforms to issue. Complete, regulation outfits of blue were difficult to provide. They could not simply be found someplace, like cattle, for instance; they had to be made, and that took time. By the first of May, the only company in camp with uniforms was the Doylestown Guards, and they had brought their own suits from home.[16]

Given the speed with which the volunteers came forward, and given the urgent need for proper clothing in the still cool weather of April, there was clearly not enough time for the proper government procedures to be followed in bidding on and awarding contracts for such things as shoes and uniforms. Governor Curtin, therefore, took steps to provide what was needed in whatever way possible. He appointed a committee to work with the army in producing uniforms for the Pennsylvania troops.[17] The committee decided that, to save time, no jackets would be made for the volunteers. The planners hoped that the unseasonably cold weather would soon give way to balmy spring sunshine, so simple blue blouses were the only upper garments manufactured. It was, after all, just springtime, and most felt hostilities might be over well before the first frost of autumn, still six months away.[18] Although many of the uniforms manufactured quickly at the beginning of the war were satisfactorily made and proved adequate, many others were not. Pennsylvania ordered about 7,000 uniforms from a New York contractor, who provided them promptly and just as promptly received payment from the commonwealth. Just weeks later, however, the luckless volunteers to which these suits were issued found them coming apart at the seams and unraveling at almost every point. The material was shoddy and the trousers especially often fell apart in less than a fortnight.[19]

The greatest shortage at Camp Curtin in those early days, however, was of blankets. The weather was terrible—on the 4th of May, six inches of crusty snow still covered the ground, and cold winds and rain lashed off the river and through the camp. Everyone had been caught unprepared, and nowhere near the necessary number of blankets were available. Someone, it was never learned who, decided that half a blanket was better than none for a cold soldier, and all the available blankets were cut in half. Whoever had made the foolish decision must have slept in a warm bed with clean counterpane and a heavy quilt, for no one who had ever slept on the cold, wet ground in temperatures near freezing could ever suppose that half an army blanket would be of any use at all. Fortunately for the sufferers, an unidentified soldier took it upon himself to let the state of things be known, and he wrote a letter to the editor of one of the Harrisburg dailies:

> "Can anyone interested in furnishing the blankets for the volunteers give the cause of the original blankets being cut in two; for we are freezing, with only a half blanket to shield us from the cold and damp...[signed a Soldier]."[20]

The people were outraged and were quick to move toward rectifying the problem. Scores of citizens carried extra blankets and quilts to camp and donated them to help ease the discomfort of the men. No lesser body than the Pennsylvania House of Representatives took up the matter of the blanket shortage during its regular session and "strong insinuations were made that money had been used for purposes not contemplated" when the legislators had appropriated half a million dollars to equip the volunteers.[21]

*   *   *

Not all the camp's problems were centered at the Quartermaster's and Commissary Departments, however. The problem of feeding and clothing the thousands of men proved to be less difficult as time went on and was relatively minor in comparison with the task of maintaining some sort of control over the men. Williams's orders had been explicit in setting the daily routine to be followed in camp and prescribing the hours of drill and police duty to be spent by the volunteers. But those orders were based upon a faulty assumption: they assumed that the inexperienced officers would or could enforce them. The company officers had little control over their men at this early juncture, and this was well illustrated by an incident that occurred on Capitol Hill on April 19.

The Duquesne Grays, one of the oldest military organizations in Pittsburgh, fancied themselves well prepared for war. They were a "regular" militia unit, a military club that met often for drills and parades. They were well drilled, had some grasp of discipline, were fully armed and well equipped, and, to the envy of virtually every other volunteer they passed, were resplendent in beautiful, tailor-made gray uniforms. Before the company had left Pittsburgh, it had been attached to a regiment soon to be designated the 12th Pennsylvania Volunteer Infantry and commanded by Colonel Charles Campbell. The Grays became Company B. Private John Donaghy was from Pittsburgh and had arrived in Harrisburg on April 18th with the Grays. Donaghy was not an original member of the company and had only been admitted to the "elite" group recently, and then only by special application. Not only did Donaghy have no military experience, but he had not much interest in being a soldier either. He was an artist, and planned to make sketches of army life and sell them to the newpapers.

On the morning of the 19th, having spent the night on the carpet and benches of the Senate Chamber, the Grays were drawn up in formation outside the capitol and given bad news. At that time, the maximum number of men that could be enrolled in any company was 77 (this was later raised to 101 men), and the officers had mistakenly enrolled too many men; some men would have to be transferred to other companies in the regiment. Captain Joseph Kennedy, therefore, stood before the Grays and read the names of the men who would be terminating their association with the outfit. Donaghy's name was on the list, "doubtless because I was a stranger to the captain who had not been consulted in regard to my joining the company," he later wrote. The private had strong feelings on this matter, however, and not being a regular member of the Grays, and not possessing as clear an understanding of military subordination as perhaps some of the other men, he decided to let the captain know of his feelings. "The company was in line at the time, and I was in the rear rank; I came round to the front, threw down my musket and told the captain he could not transfer me as he pleased; that I had enlisted to go with the Grays, and if I could not go with them I would go where I pleased. I demanded to see Col. [Charles] Campbell, who had put me in the company. I...defiantly told the officers that I was as good a man as they had." Captain Kennedy and the other company officers were nonplussed, not immediately knowing what to do after the outburst by the unfamiliar private. Several other soldiers in the ranks, though strangers to Donaghy, admired his pluck and threw down their arms out of sympathy and in support for him declaring they would not serve if he were transferred. Later in the war, Donaghy and even his supporters would likely have been thrown in the guardhouse after such a performance, but Kennedy and his officers were just as unfamiliar with military discipline as were their men. The officers withdrew, consulted and presently returned to the formation having resolved the issue. "I was ordered to resume my place in the ranks," boasted Donaghy, the victorious insubordinate, "some other man was transferred."[22]

Until the new officers learned for themselves how to command respect and obedience, the senior officers could not compel them to be more conscientious in disciplining their troops. Hangen, the Commissary General, and the others running the camp had too much to do in trying to feed and clothe the men without worrying about training and disciplining them as well. Their camp, after all, had been official-ly designated a Camp of Rendezvous, not a Camp of Instruction (though the designa-tion would later be changed), and the general attitude among the officers seemed to be that there would be plenty of time for instilling discipline later. The immediate result of this attitude was very much like chaos.

Admission to the camp was ridiculously easy to obtain. A pass system was in effect, meaning that anyone entering or leaving the compound needed a pass signed by an officer, but the system was very loose. Officers would sign passes for almost anyone. Women, it seems, could come and go as they pleased; any woman, of any sort, could get into camp, pass or no pass, if she had so much as a smile for the guard at the gate. Many, many civilians, therefore, all interested in the novelty of the huge encampment, roamed freely about distracting guards, tempting young privates, sell-ing liquor and other unauthorized goods and generally getting underfoot.

The absence of good military discipline took a more tangible form within the various company encampments. The tents were not kept orderly, the company streets were not policed thoroughly, uneaten and left-over food was not disposed of proper-ly, simply being piled in an "open lot" where the sun and the flies had easy work in making it nauseous. There were a thousand other seemingly minor infractions of the rules of good sanitation that seemed to have little to do with fighting a war. But, filthy camps invariably led to sick soldiers and sick soldiers could not fight. Maintaining cleanliness and sanitation in camp, thereby keeping the fighters healthy, had everything to do with fighting a war. Few of the officers and even fewer of the men realized this at first, so they did not even recognize that they had a problem. This was not surprising considering the inexperience of the officers in command; few had any military experience at all. The few soldiers in camp who did have experience—West Pointers or regular army men—were so busy performing other duties, such as organizing regiments and completing the mountain of paperwork that went along with that task, that they had no time to instruct green officers and men in good discipline and the importance of cleanliness and hygiene.[23]

The lack of discipline in camp was, of course, the fault of the officers, not the men. Most of the enlisted volunteers were accustomed to nothing more exciting than the events and minor problems of their homes and trades. Suddenly being thrust into an entirely different world and being called upon to eat with, sleep with, work with, and befriend scores of men they had never seen was enough to give even the most rational and intelligent among them a few giddy moments of irresponsibility. The officers, however, had accepted a trust. They had been respected enough, though not always for the right reasons, to be given the responsibility to refrain from any giddiness and to attend to business—to help the men of the company and to see that they, too, attended to the business of being soldiers. Many of the officers, however, took their trust lightly. They took advantage of the privileges given them by rank, as well as some privileges not given them by rank. They would frequently leave a subaltern in charge of the sometimes menial chores of running a company or a regiment and would leave camp to attend to dinner, drinking, and the ladies of Harrisburg. Some of the "shoulder straps" even went so far as to move their quarters from a cold, leaky canvas tent in camp to a dry hotel room in the city. None of these officers retained the respect of their men for very long. But to make matters worse, the enlisted men—all with a strong sense of democracy—saw no reason that the men they had elected to command should enjoy soft, warm featherbeds and female companionship while they, the electors, lay in verminous blankets on ground softened only by the water that seemed to be constantly seeping into it. So, they did what soldiers had been doing for centuries when life in camp did not quite suit them: they broke guard.

The volunteers spent 16 hours a day in "Uncle Sam's pig-pen," as they called it, and they didn't see why they should not have the other eight to themselves.[24] Furthermore, sneaking past a camp guard was considered a challenge, an adventure. It would have been no easy trick if the guards and the officers who supervised them had been conscientious and alert, but the guards and the officers at Camp Curtin in those early days were neither. The guard details were composed of soldiers from the companies in camp at the time, and these sentries knew how tedious camp life could be. They themselves would be forced to return to that tedium when their watch was over and might even feel the urge to slip out past the new guard line themselves; they were generally sympathetic, therefore, to the men trying to get out for a few hours and were sometimes willing to look the other way. Even while on duty, the guards had a tendency to congregate near the front gate and neglect the other portions of the boundary. While less than vigilant about watching for guard-breaking soldiers, the guards were quick to recognize a slow-witted officer of the guard and to "take some liberties" with him—perhaps duck into a shed or behind a tree for a few quiet moments with a pipe or for a doze or even a nip from a flask.[25] The result of all this was that going absent without leave for a few hours soon became something like the official camp pastime.

The camp was bounded by a high board fence, but all along the southern and eastern sides, small, three-walled sheds had been erected, of which the wooden fence served as the fourth wall. These sheds were used for storage, but were also commonly used as shielded avenues to freedom. The men wishing to go absent without leave would usually wait until dark, then duck into one of the sheds, knock off at the lower end one of the fence boards, swing it to one side, and squeeze through the opening. The officers of the guard routinely placed their sentinels inside the enclosure instead of outside, so once a soldier made it into one of the sheds and was hidden from view, he was all but home free. Whole companies and even entire regiments were on were on occasion known to filter through the sheds, and the men would then make their way through the mile or so of pastures and woodlots to the city, laughing at the dim officers the whole way.[26]

With thousands of men, most of them young, inexperienced country boys, being quartered near the city, it was only a matter of time before prostitution reached the status of local industry. When it was learned that a penny or two could be turned in Harrisburg, women of the inclination began arriving from all over the common-wealth and began setting up shop. Harrisburg was seriously afflicted, but it was not the only city with the problem. In Easton, where a camp much smaller than Camp Curtin had been established, residents were outraged by a report in the Easton *Daily Express* that certain members of the community, "to the scandal of decent people and the disgrace of genteel vicinities, were renting horses to prostitutes." A Harrisburg editor responded that while the renting of horses to prostitutes might be a grave of-fense in Easton, many of the "strict moral and religious citizens" of Harrisburg were turning a profit by renting *houses* to the "same disreputable class, some of them located in the very heart of the city." The business was officially looked upon as an unavoidable evil and the women were generally not bothered as they went about plying their ser-vices. The number of "houses" in and about Harrisburg grew unabated until later in the war, when popular outcry moved officials to action and attempts to curb, if not their success, at least their number.[27]

Once out of camp, a soldier had only to remain inconspicuous to avoid trouble with officers or the police. Staying out of trouble was sometimes too much for the volunteers to handle, however, and the daily list of soldiers who had gotten drunk or into fights in town was usually a long one. Guard details were often sent out from camp to round up deserters and others who had found their way into town without first obtaining a pass. This task provided the men of the detail with a break from the monotony of camp and allowed them to get into town for awhile. Going on detail into town could even be as much fun as breaking guard. Four soldiers of the Biddle Guards of Carlisle, for example, welcomed the chance to get out of camp when they were sent into the city in search of a deserter. They did not find the man, but in their travels, they did find the Fifth Ward House, a tavern that became something of a favorite with the volunteers. The detail drank so much that they were themselves arrested for disorderliness.[28]

Rounding up stragglers in town was not by any means a lark, however, and was usually undertaken with a good deal more seriousness. Sergeant John Corcoran of the Richmond Artillerists was a member of a detail that collared a group of A.W.O.L. men in town. One of the delinquents, Private John Harris, was irate at having been caught and swore he would have revenge upon Corcoran. In camp a few days later, Harris, not a man to forget a grudge, came after the sergeant and clubbed him with a musket. Corcoran died in a hospital that afternoon. There was little doubt about the murder, and Harris was quickly tried and convicted by civil authorities.[29]

What discipline there was in camp was of a reactionary sort. Breaches were punished, but few precautions were taken to ensure that such breaches did not happen in the first place. One of the most common methods of punishment was to publicly humiliate the offender. When one wild private, a Pittsburgher named Ritter, lost his temper and knocked down an officer, he was thrown in the guardhouse and put on bread and water for a few days. It was determined that the public punishment of this insubordinate would help prevent like incidents in the future, so Ritter's head was shaved, and, at dusk, in the presence of the entire camp, he was drummed out of the camp and the army at the point of the bayonet while the bands played the "Rogue's March."[30] It was a solemn and affecting ceremony, but even if none of the thousands of spectators was impressed by the shame cast upon the private, Ritter himself was. Upon exiting the camp, he immediately turned to the right and proceeded to the bank of the river. Apparently not a good swimmer and knowing it, Ritter threw himself into the water intent on letting himself drown. He floundered about for only a few minutes before being pulled out by someone who, knowingly or unknowingly, would not allow him to be so quickly rid of his shame. Ritter disappeared after his rescue, and the officers who had written the script and staged the show thought a good thing had been done and let the curtain fall on the little drama. But Ritter would not let them so easily rid themselves of his spectre. He made his way upriver through the dark woods and windy fields a few miles to the little hamlet of Dauphin and wrote his own ending to the drama in which he had played an unwanted part. A few days later, he was found dead, hanging from a tree by his leather belt. A diary was found on his person, and in it was written, "Adieu, lovely world. This is the last departure in June, 1861. Harrisburg, Pennsylvania."[31]

The poor discipline in camp probably was owed to the presence of 500 men from the wooded, mountainous regions of north central Pennsylvania. They were mostly lumbermen, trappers, woodsmen, and river raftsmen who were far more acquainted with animal pelts and whiskey than the polite streets of Harrisburg and the neat wool uniforms of officers. They were led by a truly remarkable man, a unique individual who had been educated as a gentleman but had spurned the civility of some of the world's great cities for the wilderness of McKean County, Pennsylvania, and the society of lumbermen and laborers.

Thomas Leiper Kane was a romantic idealist in the strictest nineteenth-century sense. Born in Philadelphia on February 27, 1822, he had spent his teenage years in school in Paris, where he identified himself with local extremist groups that occasionally occupied themselves with street fights and riots against government forces. After his studies in France, Kane had returned to Pennsylvania to begin reading law under his father, a federal judge. But young Kane did not share his father's reverence for the law, and had become involved in causes that had seemed to him to be right, but were clearly illegal. A avowed abolitionist, he had served as an agent on the Underground Railroad. When Judge Kane had discovered his son's activities, he had thrown the young bounder into jail for violation of the fugitive slave law.

COLONEL THOMAS LEIPER KANE
13th Pennsylvania Reserves (Bucktails).
Among the first to volunteer after Sumter, this
adventurer became colonel of the Bucktails
after C. J. Biddle resigned. Kane went on to
become a brigadier general.
(Library of Congress)

In 1858, he had settled in McKean County and worked for the Erie and Sunbury Railroad, assisting in locating a pass over the mountains east of Erie through which the rails could be run. He had built a home and a sawmill on the proposed route of the road and encouraged others to settle nearby. A small village sprang up, which was later named Kane.

When the war came, Kane had immediately set about raising men for a company. He was a small, slight man, only 5 feet 4, with long, dark, wild hair, a full beard, and one eye that appeared perpetually half-closed. He possessed tremendous energy, however, and had the gift of being able to make other men like him. He had no trouble raising more than 300 men for service within four days of the firing on Fort Sumter. This was no small accomplishment given the sparse population of that mountainous portion of the commonwealth.[32]

Kane was one of the many to wire Governor Curtin to offer troops even before Lincoln had called for volunteers. So impatient had he been to get to Harrisburg and into the war that he had not even waited for Curtin's response before he started with three companies of woodsmen. Before departing, however, the men had already adopted a uniform of sorts and a name to go with it. On the way to Harrisburg, some of the companies had spent a few days in the town of Smethport. Outside a butcher shop hung the carcass of a white-tailed deer. One of the boys with a flair for outrageous fashion cut off the animal's tail and attached it to the front of his hat. Kane was apparently an early marketing genius and recognized a good gimmick when he saw one. Knowing that most of the men had lived in the wild regions of the state all their lives and were experienced hunters very proud of their prowess with a rifle, Kane henceforth advertised the regiment as the "Pennsylvania Bucktails," and the men all tried to sport a tail or hank of deer fur on their caps.[33]

An observer in the capital remembered the appearance of the Bucktails as they disembarked at the train depot and stalked into the city. They wore "high-topped boots, pants tucked inside the boots, a woolen shirt (usually red), a large back neckerchief loosely tied, a loose blouse, and a soft felt hat often so misshapen that the crown was peaked...[they were] ragged, undisciplined, ununiformed save in the singular ornament that surmounts their head gear."[34] Some of the men had been to Harrisburg before bringing shipments of lumber downriver, and the saloons of the capital were familiar to at least some of them. The portion of the commonwealth from which the men came was referred to by many as the "Wild Cat" region, so at Harrisburg, the loggers were commonly referred to as "Wild Cats." This tag seemed particularly apt in light of the usual behavior of the men in the city's taverns.[35]

The Bucktails proved themselves especially adept at locating adventure. On May 5, in fact, a number of them managed to break guard and wander into town long enough to stage a riot. A lone Bucktail, apparently drunk, appeared on one of the city's streets noisy and boisterous. A policeman, accustomed to loud soldiers, had encountered him at least once before that evening and cautioned him about creating such a disturbance. The advice was not heeded, and the policeman finally decided to arrest the man. No sooner had he done so, than five or six other Bucktails arrived on the scene and were angered by the policeman's rough handling of their comrade. They descended upon the captor and wrenched their friend free. The policeman had no opportunity to call for assistance and responded by lashing out and striking one of the rescuers with his billy club. The Bucktail's head was gashed open and the blood flowed freely. Enraged, the stricken man's friends went after the overmatched policeman, who began crying loudly for help. But rather than receiving assistance, the constable got more trouble—about forty other Bucktails appeared and joined the fracas. A large crowd had by this time gathered and was blocking up a main street. Finally, some other police officers arrived and the mayor himself was sent for. Immediately upon his arrival, Mayor William H. Kepner ordered the crowd to disperse and threatened the Bucktails with the loaded muskets of fifty members of the "Home Guard," a sort of unofficial police auxiliary force. The Bucktails remained defiant, however, more out of principle or disposition than of wisdom, and the stalemate continued. The tense situation was ended when three companies of armed men came in from Camp Curtin on the double quick, surrounded the Bucktails, and marched them back out to the camp.[36] Mayor Kepner was not entirely satisfied with the resolution, and took steps to ensure that similar incidents would not occur in the future. The next day, noting that "the peace of this community had been greatly disturbed by the disorderly and riotous conduct of drunken men," he forbade the sale of liquor on Sunday and warned that no leniency would be shown violators.[37]

But subverting authority and its rules was just another challenge for the Bucktails. Three of them found themselves in the camp guardhouse one evening and decided that they had been punished enough and broke out of the place. They then slipped past the camp guard line and scampered into town and the first tavern they came upon. It was not long before Thomas Kane and a squad from camp came looking for them.[38] Henceforth, Kane tried to keep a tighter rein on his men in camp, making it a bit more difficult for them to slip away. But, once again, the Bucktails were equal to the challenge and managed to find a way around the problem. If they could not get out of camp long enough to find and enjoy the liquor they longed for, they would simply bring the liquor into the camp and enjoy it there. So common was the stuff in camp that one visitor, undoubtedly an Irishman, wrote a bit of doggerel about it:

> "Oh there's whiskey 'tis certain, all over Camp Curtin
> In ilegant bottle, wid niver a flaw.
> A'most everybody has plenty of toddy
> Hid round in the corners, dape under the straw
>
> Oh the Guards they turn out, wid a terrible rout,
> Wid their guns on their shoulders, they make a great show;
> But the Wild Cats make fun o' them, divil a wan a them,
> Find out at all where the whiskey does go."[39]

Perhaps not everybody had "plenty of toddy," but it is not difficult to believe that bottles were hidden "dape under the straw" all over camp. A great deal of liquor was available to the men in camp, and much of it came from a black man named Jack Smith. Smith operated a still in the woods not very far from camp and reportedly did a thriving business among the soldiers.[40]

Wild though they were, the Bucktails were of good material, and if they could be kept under control, they could become good infantrymen. Fortunately, the officers were made of as good a stuff as the enlisted men and several even went on to command regiments later in the war. One such officer was Captain Charles Frederick Taylor of the Wayne Independent Rifles. Taylor and his men were not from the rugged regions upstate but the gentle farmlands of southeastern Pennsylvania just west of Philadelphia. They were thrown in with the Bucktails by chance in Camp Curtin. But the officers and men of the different companies got along so well that when the upstate companies were organized into a regiment, Taylor's men were made Company H.

Born February 6, 1840 in West Chester, Pennsylvania, Taylor grew up in Kennett Square, near the Brandywine River—about 25 miles west of Philadelphia. The low, wooded hills, small, neat meadows and clear brooks made the Brandywine Valley a fine place for a boy to grow up, but there was more to the area than the picturesque. Just a morning's walk from the Taylor farm lay the battlefield on the banks of the Brandywine where Cornwallis had defeated Washington in 1777. Young Fred grew up with tales of the valor of Nathanael Greene and Light Horse Harry Lee ringing in his ears and could even see the tree under which, as local legend had it, the wounded Lafayette, weak from loss of blood, had been lain to rest and have his wounds dressed. Valor was a part of young Taylor's life even then; the very earth was soaked with the blood of patriots and heroes.

By age 18, Taylor had already completed two years at the University of Michigan and had spent a year traveling in Europe, where he had become fluent in French and nearly-so in German. Want of money forced him to leave the university after his sophomore year, however, so he went home to Kennett Square. Rheumatism had disabled his father, and the family farm, Hazeldell, had suffered. So Fred immediately took control of things and tried to get the farm back into profitability. "I believe that it will only depend on myself whether this farm carried on properly will be self-sustaining," he wrote to his brother in January, 1861, "...and I am desirous of testing my own capabilities...I have a heart for the work and I think I have energy enough to carry it through." He was, above all, sure of himself and his abilities and hesitancy was nowhere in his character.

When war came, in April, 1861, Taylor, though only 21 years old, took a leading role in organizing a company from the neighboring countryside. He called a meeting and enlisted men to serve with him. At 5'10", the fair-skinned, dark-haired Taylor stood a good half a head above most of the men at the meeting, and his sharp hazel eyes helped give him a look of easy authority. The men, many of whom were much older than he, admired his vigor and initiative and elected him their captain. Soon thereafter, they were all in Camp Curtin where they were introduced to the Bucktails.[41]

Despite his youth, Fred Taylor already had the potential to be a fine officer. He was aggressive, ardent, dedicated and intelligent. Most of all, however, he had an intense desire to succeed—to perform his duty well. He craved the high opinion of both his men and his superiors. "I am not unduly ambitious of promotion," he wrote to his sister, "...but I am ambitious of a high reputation as an officer in the Army, and, in order to deserve that my utmost energies and whatever ability I may have will be required."[42] He began working toward the high reputation he craved in Camp Curtin in May, 1861, by attempting to keep his men sober, in camp, and out of trouble while they, and he, learned the trade of the soldier.

*   *   *

While the administrators in camp were attempting to organize a system by which to feed, clothe and discipline the troops, the civilian population of the commonwealth was organizing as well. The women of the city of Lancaster, for example, formed a society to provide clothing and support for the volunteers and to act as a corps of nurses for the sick and wounded. The members called themselves the Patriot Daughters of Lancaster and among their first acts was to provide overcoats and blankets for two companies being formed in Lancaster.[43] Women formed similar groups of varying sizes in Reading and Philadelphia, and innumerable larger charitable organizations sprang up for the relief of both the volunteers and their families. On the day after Lincoln's call for troops, the people of Harrisburg held the first meeting to establish what they would call the Volunteer Relief Fund. The fund, to be raised through donations and subscriptions, would benefit dependents of men who had entered the service.[44] Within ten days of the first meeting, $12,620 had been raised for the relief of families, and weekly payments were begun, prorated according to the size of the family.[45]

Captain William B. Sipes, a Harrisburg native in command of the "State Capital Guards," assisted in the identification of some of the needy families by publishing a brief list of the names and addresses of Harrisburg residents in his company who would be leaving behind wives and children. "Some of these families are not asking for charity," wrote Captain Sipes, "but it could make a soldier's heart lighter to know that, come what may, those left behind would be cared for...I make no appeal for these persons who are now left without protection, because none is necessary. It will be enough for the people of Harrisburg to know who and where they are, and they will have many true friends."[46]

The women of Harrisburg, while taking an active role in the organization of the Volunteer Fund to benefit the wives and children of the volunteers, also provided for the health and comfort of the soldiers themselves. In the first week in May, a large wooden building was completed in Camp Curtin and opened as the Camp Hospital. This provided the women of the city with a perfect outlet for their compassion, and many volunteered to serve as nurses. Some even took such a personal interest in the welfare of ill soldiers that they removed them from the hospital and brought them to their houses so they might receive more thorough and constant care.[47]

The wealthy gentlemen of Harrisburg, Philadelphia and some of the other larger towns in the commonwealth were also generous, often favoring a company or regiment with a large donation of equipment or weapons. A Philadelphia man, for example, financed a plan to equip each member of the Lochiel Greys, a company from Harrisburg with, "a most excellent and serviceable silk oiled-cloth covering for head and shoulders." Such havelocks were worn at various times by European armies and were therefore considered part of the military fashion. Many companies and regiments from both the North and the South went off to the war wearing them, believing they would provide protection from the harsh sun.[48] In actuality, they worked a good deal the opposite, decreasing the free circulation of air around the back of the neck and flapping about annoyingly at the wearer's ears and cheeks interfering with his aim or his hearing of orders. Notwithstanding the good Philadelphian's benevolence, the men usually ripped the havelocks from their headgear and discarded them of the first march in a hot sun.[49] A Harrisburg gentleman developed the scheme of providing each man of another local company, the Cameron Guard, with a Colt's revolver. A revolver was not a regulation piece of equipment for an infantryman, but every volunteer, of course, wished to go off to war armed to the teeth. It was common to see privates buying and carrying pistols, knives, and even swords in the spring of 1861.[50]

In all, Pennsylvanians, the people of Harrisburg in particular, were in those early days of the war exceedingly generous in giving of themselves and their possessions. Merchants donated food and goods, and the ladies provided soldiers with cakes, pies, and coffee to make them more comfortable. And this kindness was not restricted merely to Pennsylvanian volunteers, but was lavished upon Ohioans, Michiganders, Wisconsinites, Bay Staters, and men from anywhere who were going off to fight the rebellion.[51] The 1st Ohio arrived in town on April 21, and was quartered first in the Senate Chamber and later on the grounds around the capitol.[52] At the end of the regiment's brief stay it published in a Harrisburg newspaper a card of thanks to the people of the city for their graciousness and hospitality.[53] Later, the 3rd Michigan was given coffee (reportedly more than 100 gallons), bread and butter, lemonade, ice water and even oranges by people living in the vicinity of their camp in downtown Harrisburg.[54] The 1st Minnesota also received kind treatment in Harrisburg, but as far as one young soldier was concerned, the sweetness and generosity of the women of Huntingdon, Pennsylvania, a small town in the mountains west of Harrisburg and a regular stop for most trains coming east, could not be surpassed. "About sunrise," the Minnesotan wrote, "the train stopped about fifteen minutes...." The hungry, travel-weary soldiers had no right to expect anything at a dawn rest stop at Huntingdon but a few moments respite from the ceaseless pitching and squeaking of the train. To their complete surprise, however, they saw the train "at once boarded by the ladies of the place, loaded with delicious coffee, sandwiches, doughnuts, etc., giving an abundant and most acceptable breakfast to all." Those men never forgot the simple thoughtfulness of those women who rose before the sun that they might feed some hungry volunteers.[55]

Just as a majority of the citizens had welcomed the opportunity to do their bit for the volunteers, a segment of the population saw the excitement and the circumstances as an opportunity to make some money. Many Harrisburg residents, of course, made an honest living and a fair profit from the increased demand for goods and services, like the butchers and bakers who contracted to supply the wants of the Camp Commissary. Others contracted to provide the army with mules and wagons, and as a sign of the times, the usual advertisements in the newspapers for tonics and elixirs were replaced by those for caskets and DuPont gunpowder. But some residents let their hunger for the dollar get the better of them.[56] The people of the city were insatiable in their appetite for the interest and excitement of Camp Curtin. Everyone, it seemed, wished to go out and have a look at the camp and the truly incredible number of men there. In response, hack drivers began running a regular route from downtown out to the camp, and businessmen for the surrounding country-side were quick to lease horses to the drivers while the demand for them was strong. So good was business that drivers and gigs came from as far away as Carlisle, 25 miles, to run the loop between Market Square in downtown Harrisburg and camp.[57] The standard fare was 25 cents each way, and naturally the faster the hackmen could get out to camp and then back to the city, the more trips they could make. This simple mathematics was not lost on any of the drivers, and they were not bashful about putting the whip to their horses. They made a killing, but in doing so they ultimately hurt their business. In three weeks time they had so badly worn out the horses that the lessors began to withdraw their animals before they were ruined, and some of the harder-driving hacks were left with nothing to pull their omnibuses.[58]

As blinded by the dollar and as unkind as the hacks were to their four-legged partners, they were still earning an honest living by providing a valuable service. There were others, though, that were far less scrupulous. Some merchants attempted to charge citizens more for groceries under the pretext that the influx of volunteers into the city had caused a shortness of supplies (it had not).[59] Two men of the city did a very good business by going to Camp Curtin and making deals with soldiers. The soldiers were issued daily rations of coffee by the government. After the soldiers had used the coffee grounds and enjoyed their coffee, they had only to save the grounds for these two men, who would gather up the old coffee grounds, dry them and sell them to people in the city for 25 cents a pound. On their return trips for more coffee, they would smuggle in whiskey with which they paid the soldiers for their help.[60] Worse was the man who regularly visited the camp and made money by charging soldiers five cents for a peek at his "cosmoramic views in a box." He always attracted large crowds of men, usually young ones, eager to pay their nickel for a look in his box. This made the officers curious, and one lieutenant finally got a look at the pictures. He was shocked to find that they were not "mere ordinary pictures," but "a series of the most disgustingly filthy and obscene pictures probably ever manufactured...." The game was up for the "Hoary Headed Scoundrel," and a city policeman arrested him and confiscated the box.[61]

Undoubtedly lowest of all these greedy souls were the heartless men who walked about the city posing as agents for the Volunteer Relief Fund and soliciting donations. They preyed upon the charitable, the compassionate, and the generous, and then absconded with whatever they had managed to collect.[62]

*   *   *

An Artist's View of Camp Curtin. Floral Hall stands at center, barracks and tents at left and the Harrisburg Lunatic Asylum sits on the hill in the far right distance.   *(Harper's Weekly, May 11, 1861)*

While the regiments were being organized and outfitted, Governor Curtin wrestled with problems of sending more than 21,000 men off to war within two months. Chief among these dilemmas was how to pay for it all. The feeding, sheltering, clothing, arming, and equipping of the volunteers required money and lots of it. Immediately after Fort Sumter, a great deal of money was put at the disposal of the state government by private corporations and individuals throughout Pennsylvania. Accepting such offers was not for the governor alone to do. The need for funding had to be properly addressed by the state legislature, without which public funds could not be legally appropriated. The Pennsylvania House and Senate were, however, in recess in April, 1861, so Curtin had to call them into emergency session. He sent a special message to all state senators and representatives, "Adequate provision does not exist by law to enable the Executive to make the military power of the State as available and efficient as it should be for the common defence of the State and the General Government," the message read, and, therefore, "a prompt exercise of the Legislative power of the State," was needed.[63]

On April 30, a joint session of the legislature convened in the House of Representatives and was read a message from the governor:

"It is impossible to predict," the message read, "the length to which the madness that rules the hour in the rebellious States shall lead us, or when the calamities which threaten our hitherto happy country shall terminate. We know that many of the people have already left the State in the service of the General Government, and that many more must follow. We have a long line of border on States seriously disaffected, which should be protected. To furnish ready support to those who have gone out, and to protect our borders, we should have a well-regulated military force. I therefore, recommend the immediate organization, disciplining, and arming of at least fifteen regiments of cavalry and infantry, exclusive of those called into the service of the United States; as we have already ample warning of the necessity of being prepared for any sudden exigency that may arise, I cannot too much impress this upon you."[64]

Curtin and the people of Pennsylvania had already done much more than what had been asked of them. Nearly 25,000 Pennsylvanians answered the federal request for 14,000 men. The people of the Keystone State deserved well the thanks of the president. But Curtin would not let his people rest. He felt that the vastly powerful machine that was Pennsylvania could not be allowed to lie idle even for a moment. It must not simply serve faithfully and capably. It must take a leading role in resolving the conflict. It must exert itself fully. Curtin saw it as his duty to coax such leadership and exertions out of his state and people. His solution came in bringing more men under arms. He knew that when the three-month men came home and the nation's army was dissolved almost overnight, Pennsylvania, a powerful state in a vulnerable geographic position, could best serve the cause of the Union by protecting itself, and it was just that which Curtin wished to do. In planning for this contingency, Curtin might have achieved his greatest success as a great war governor.

Curtin was looking ahead and anticipating what would be needed, both by the commonwealth, and the federal government. He said that he did not know how long madness would rule , but he was certain that it would reign longer than three months. He advocated, therefore, the creation of a reserve force that could be thrust into the breach in times of trouble, such as, perhaps, at the end of July, when the terms of the three-month men would expire. The project would require an enormous appropriation and would require that innumerable questions be answered. How long would these regiments be required to serve? From where would come all the food, uniforms, wagons, horses, saddles, camp kettles and other materiel required to properly outfit the 15,000 men of all arms the governor was calling for? Where would these men be quartered? Curtin could provide few answers to those questions. The details were to be worked out by the legislative committees whose work would make the creation of a "well-regulated military force" possible.

The legislators were equal to the enormous task and in just 16 days had a bill on the governor's desk. The force was to be called the Pennsylvania Reserve Corps, and the lawmakers had appropriated funding sufficient to raise and equip its 15 regiments. Furthermore, they determined that the Reserve regiments should be gathered at four points throughout the commonwealth. One camp would be in West Chester, near Philadelphia, one in Easton, on the Delaware River above Bethlehem and below Scranton, one just outside Pittsburgh, and the fourth at Camp Curtin.

Curtin promptly signed the bill creating the Pennsylvania Reserve Corps and recruiting began at once. The task was not difficult. Many of the companies that had volunteered in mid April at the first call for troops were still willing and anxious to serve, some of them had even continued to meet regularly to drill and complete their organization. The governor authorized men to recruit companies with the understanding that they would be rewarded for their efforts with a commission of some sort. Often these men merely gathered already filled companies and organized them into a regiment, after which they would be elected colonel or to some other field grade. In any event, the ranks of the Reserve Corps filled quickly, even after it was learned that the men would be required to serve not three months but three years or the duration of the war.

The bill creating the Reserves Corps called for twelve regiments of infantry, one rifle regiment, one of cavalry, and one of artillery. Several of the new regiments were to be formed in Camp Curtin, both from troops already there and from new arrivals. The Bucktails were designated the 1st Pennsylvania Rifle Regiment, but were also officially called the 13th Regiment of the Pennsylvania Reserve Corps and the 42nd Pennsylvania Volunteer Infantry. The company officers elected Thomas Kane colonel of the regiment and Charles J. Biddle of Philadelphia lieutenant colonel. Kane was somewhat embarrassed by this because, well-educated and experienced in other areas as he was, he had no military experience and questioned his own ability to lead a regiment. Biddle, on the other hand, had served as a captain in the Mexican War and had been commended for bravery in the official reports of several general officers, including Winfield Scott and John Wool. Biddle had been brevetted major for "gallant and meritorious services" and was made an aide to General Stephen W. Kearney. It was obvious, especially to Kane, that Biddle was much better qualified to command the regiment than he. He resigned his position, therefore in favor of Biddle, who immediately accepted the colonelcy. Kane filled the vacancy at lieutenant colonel. The switch pleased everyone involved.

At 42, Biddle had already been a successful member of the Philadelphia bar for more than 20 years. He was married, an alumnus of Princeton, and prospering financially and socially. Like Kane, he was diminutive, weighing just slightly more than 100 pounds, with dark, sad eyes, a high forehead and close-cropped whiskers running along his lower jaw and flourishing into a wiry beard protruding from his chin.[65] At least one private did not like his looks, calling him an "old prissy little man with grey hair + few teeth, having on the latter account some difficulty in speaking."[66] Biddle was a natural leader, however, and knew exactly what he was doing in spending long hours with his men on the drill field. He was a strict disciplinarian and was relentless in demanding perfection. His precepts of discipline were not popular, but he eventually won the grudging respect of the men in the ranks. "His manner of delivering commands, or...of explaining intended movements," wrote one, "is slow + hesitating, but he does not make mistakes + appears to be master of the battalion drill."[67]

Another Reserve regiment formed in camp was designated the 5th Reserve regiment and was to be led by Seneca G. Simmons, who resigned his post as United States mustering officer to accept the colonelcy. Simmons's life had been quite different from Biddle's. Exceedingly unremarkable, he was capable, but not extraordinarily so. He was neither an underachiever, for he never had the benefit of advantageous circumstances, nor an overachiever, for he seemed to have very little ambition. In 1861, he was 52, and the one interesting aspect of his career was that he had served in the United States Army for more than 30 years, beginning as a plebe at West Point, and was still only a captain of infantry.

He began his life near the town of Woodstock in the small, snowy county of Windsor, Vermont. When he was 14, he was sent off to Captain Alden Partridge's Military School in Middletown, Connecticut. Financial reasons forced the small institution to move to Georgetown in the District of Columbia, and Simmons went with it. He found the school work exceptionally difficult at the academy, and he struggled to maintain pace with his classmates. But even then, in his mid teens, he looked like a soldier. He was tall, nearly six feet, and erect, and truly enjoyed the military life. He determined then that he should like to become a soldier for the rest of his life and sought an appointment to the United States Military Academy at West Point.[68]

COLONEL CHARLES J. BIDDLE
13th Pennsylvania Reserves (Bucktails).
A disciplinarian with prior military experience,
Biddle took command of Camp Curtin in
June, 1861. His attention for regulations and
procedures made him unpopular with the rank
and file. He later resigned to assume a seat in
Congress.

(Library of Congress)

COLONEL SENECA G. SIMMONS
5th Pennsylvania Reserves.
A West Pointer with more than 30 years experience, this Harrisburg resident served as
mustering officer at Camp Curtin. He was killed at the battle of Glendale on the last day of
June, 1862.

(Dauphin County Historical Society)

The young Vermonter arrived on the Plain at West Point in July, 1829. Just weeks earlier, First Classman Robert E. Lee had received his commission as second lieutenant, United States Engineers and had triumphantly departed the vaunted halls and fields of the academy. Plebe Simmons was 20 years old, less than two years younger than Lieutenant Lee. In a time when cadets came to the Point at a young age—Lee, for instance, had been 18 when he entered and many others were even younger—Simmons was exceptionally old to be starting the rigorous four-year program.

But his age gave him none of the advantage that might have been expected. He found the work at the academy every bit as taxing as his preparatory work at Captain Partridge's, and more so. He foundered, and the end of his first year found him confronted with every plebe's nightmare: he was deficient in his studies, and, if he were to continue at West Point, he would be required to repeat his entire first year. To his everlasting credit, Simmons opted to stay. He was set back a class and began all over again, a 21-year-old plebe.[69]

That was the last of his serious trouble with grades, however, and he was a good cadet otherwise. He finished his five-year stint at West Point in 1834 and was graduated 22nd in a class of 36. Simmons was posted to the 7th U.S. Infantry and immediately detached for topographical survey duty in Florida. Before he left for the South, however, he married a Harrisburg girl.

In 1835, Lieutenant Simmons began a trek to posts all over the country. First to Florida for service against hostile Indians, then to Fort Pike, Louisiana, from 1842 to 1844, where his fourth and last child, Elmira Adelaide, was born on her father's birthday, 1842. In 1844, Simmons began three years on recruiting duty in Syracuse, New York. He then went to war in Mexico, was promoted to captain, and fought without distinction in the battle at Huamantla. After the war he resumed his post-hopping tour of America, seeing duty at Jefferson Barracks in St. Louis; Florida once again; Fort Leavenworth, Kansas; Pottsville, Pennsylvania; the Indian Territory again, this time at Fort Arbuckle; Fort Smith in Arkansas; back to Jefferson Barracks, then to Newport Barracks in Kentucky. While at Fort Leavenworth in 1850, Simmons sustained a mysterious injury to his leg, one knee being badly smashed. So serious was the injury that, for a time, his life seemed to be in danger, but he recovered sufficiently to return to duty. His assignment to recruiting duty at Pottsville for three years was a direct result of the leg injury, and he was never again to have the vigor that was required of a junior officer in active service. In 1859, in fact, he took sick leave that would last the better part of two years. He returned to Harrisburg and took up residence with his wife and children in a quaint house on Front Street. He remained there until the war came. He was showing his age by then. No longer the tall, slim cadet who had entered West Point as a man among boys, he walked with a limp, was tending toward paunchiness, and his dark, breast-length beard was grizzled with gray. But, as the ranking officer in Harrisburg, he was detailed as the United States mustering officer in the city.[70]

During his service as mustering officer at Camp Curtin, he possibly mustered more volunteers into the service of the United States than any other man in the North. When the officers of what was to be the 5th Reserve Regiment proffered him the colonelcy of the regiment, Simmons accepted after very little consideration. After 32 years in the army as a nondescript junior officer, Simmons had suddenly become important. Because of his great experience as a soldier, his opinions were valued by the citizen soldiers in Harrisburg trying to organize themselves. The opportunity to achieve greatness was being thrust upon him.

On June 17, the governor directed Colonel Biddle to replace Colonel George A. C. Seiler as commandant of Camp Curtin. Seiler, a prominent Harrisburg lawyer and a member of the governor's extended staff, had been serving as acting commandant since May 10, Lieutenant Colonel Hangen having relinquished command several days before that when his regiment had departed for Washington. Seiler had been popular among the officers and men (one officer warmly described him as a "Damned clever fellow"),[71] but Biddle was tougher, more vigorous, a different kind of officer altogether. As soon as he took command, he set about straightening out the various problems that had been plaguing the camp and its administrators. High on his list was improving discipline in the ranks of all the companies and regiments, not just his own, which did little to make him popular with either the officers or the men.[72] He was also concerned about the uncleanliness and poor sanitation there. Accordingly, he put squads of men to work in scrubbing and painting buildings, moving and airing tents, thoroughly policing and cleaning company streets and disposing of waste and garbage.[73]

*   *   *

On the 21st of June, the War Department asked Governor Curtin to immediately send two regiments to Cumberland, Maryland, where Federal troops were anticipating stiff resistance from Confederate troops and were in need of reinforcements. Curtin sent orders to Camp Curtin instructing Colonel Biddle to prepare his regiment, Colonel Simmons's 5th Reserves, and Battery A of the 1st Pennsylvania Artillery, to move south to Cumberland. Biddle promptly began arming and equipping the two regiments and the battery, hoping to start the expedition the next morning. Preparations did not proceed as smoothly as hoped, however, and trouble loomed with the difficult Bucktails. Biddle found himself having to play the role of diplomat in appeasing his men.

The legislation that had created the Reserves called for all the regiments of the corps to receive "the most approved style of arms." The requisite number of quality weapons were not always immediately available, however, so many regiments were temporarily armed with older guns. When the Bucktails found themselves ready to be armed and shipped out to Maryland, they were shocked when the weapons put in their hands were not new Springfields or Sharps, but 1837 Harper's Ferry muskets.

The men had all enlisted under the impression that they would be formed into a Rifle regiment and indeed had been designated the First Pennsylvania Rifle Regiment. The concept of a rifle regiment was left over from earlier wars when rifled guns were rare and only the best marksmen would be armed with the advanced weapons. By the time of the Civil War, rifles were much more common and most of the men in all the armies would eventually be armed with them. Nevertheless, the law creating the Reserves had called for one rifle regiment and the Bucktails had been given the honor. Now, they were not only given muskets, but the weapons they were given were almost a quarter of a century old. The Wild Cats then did what they had always done when things displeased them, they threatened to riot.[74] The men did a great deal of angry and mutinous shouting before Colonel Biddle succeeded in calming them by explaining that the issue of the muskets was only temporary, and that he was no happier about it than they were. He promised he would not rest until they received the modern rifles they had been promised. He was as good as his word, for later in the war, the Bucktails received Sharps breech-loading carbines, which were then among the finest weapons made.[75]

Despite all the excitement, the Bucktails, Simmons's 5th Reserves and Battery A, all departed for Cumberland on schedule early on the morning of June 22. They knew not what awaited them, but everyone on the expedition—from Biddle to drummer boy—was excited to finally be out of the camp and in motion toward the enemy.

*   *   *

Life in the camp was certainly not comfortable, but it had come a long way during Biddle's four days as commandant. As sanitation improved, efforts were made to "civilize" the place, and improvements were always underway. Carpenters erected makeshift frame barracks all around the entire enclosure. Between 500 and 600 tents were up and in use, but attempts were being made to house as many men as possible in the more permanent and comfortable wooden barracks. All the stalls where the animals had been penned during the fairs, for example, had been boarded up on all sides and turned into shelters.[76] For the time being, however, the majority of the men would live in the Sibley tents.

The canvas tents served as more than just shelter, they became easels for the artistically inclined, and nearly all of them had charcoal sketches upon them. The inhabitants of each tent, the number of which varied according to whether the tents were "wedge" tents or Sibleys, would exercise their creativity and name or decorate their abodes with whatever struck their fancy. One tent was labeled "Fort Pickens," after the Federal stronghold in Pensacola Bay, Florida, another the "Lazy Club." The more conservative men simply wrote the names of their company on their tents, but some of the more outgoing made elaborate drawings. One tent, for example, was decorated with a life-size caricature of Confederate President Jefferson Davis.[77]

One of the soldiers who had lived in a tent recalled some of the many ways the men would spend their time. "Those familiar with the art of writing domestic letters found ample employment, and were sought by those...who had not had training in this department...artists did sketching; poets wrote poems; journalists kept diaries....Washday was indefinitely deferred. Some had brought with them text books for College preparatory work; some had Institutes of theology; Usually there was an accumulation of enough books to fit out a small library."[78] Another man remembered that they had very few duties to perform, "hardly more than two or three hours per day were devoted to drilling, [and] there remained ample time for jollification...." Such "jollification" took numerous forms, but there was usually "a party at play with bat and ball...[or] parties who, despising noisy violent pastimes, quietly practiced with the ace of spades and consorts."[79] The men had fun in other ways, too, and jokes and riddles were popular ways to help pass the time. One puzzle that made the rounds for awhile was: "What is the difference between a good soldier and a fashionable young lady? One faces the powder, and the other powders the face."[80] Another joke making the rounds was about the Union Necktie, a red, white and blue silk cravat that was being extensively worn in Harrisburg. The men laughed that the secession necktie, on the other hand, was manufactured of hemp, and was to be worn with a choker collar. It was not as handsome as the Union tie, but it was generally considered more useful than ornamental.[81]

*   *   *

The Battery under Colonel Charles Campbell that had accompanied the infantry on the expedition to Cumberland returned to Camp Curtin on the afternoon of July 2.[82] The men were given no time to rest, however, and were set to drilling in earnest, not with an eye toward serving in combat, but with the much more shortsighted view of looking good during the Independence Day ceremonies. The artillery units were to fire salutes from Capitol Hill while the infantry paraded through the city.

If a man knew not what he was doing, if he were careless or inattentive, even for just a moment, or if he had just plain bad luck, the artillery was by far a more dangerous branch of the service in which to serve than either the infantry or the cavalry. Tremendously heavy guns or cassions could roll over hands or feet, horses, often just as new to artillery service as were the men, could kick or rear and knock men about at any time, and firing the guns themselves was a far more dangerous operation than anything either an infantryman or cavalryman was called upon to do. A young private from Philadelphia, and all those around him, found this out on the Independence Day.

Private Henry Welsh of Captain J. G. Simpson's company, designated Battery C, 1st Pennsylvania Artillery, was among those detailed to serve the guns that were to fire the salute from beside the Arsenal on the hill.[83] Eighteen-hundred men from Camp Curtin, all unarmed, marched in through Harrisburg, with the city's veterans of the war of 1812 leading the way. Welsh's position on his gun crew was that of rammer, which meant that after one man placed into the mouth of the cannon the charge to be fired, Welsh would ram the charge down through the barrel of the gun with a long, swab-tipped staff. James McKnight, a veteran of the Mexican War and a friend of Welsh, stood behind the gun tending the vent, which meant that he kept his thumb over the small hole through which the powder inside the gun was ignited when the gun was to be fired. By keeping his thumb over the hole, McKnight was reducing the risk of a stray spark reaching the powder and setting off the charge and the gun prematurely. Unfortunately, McKnight's thumb was not sufficient. The powder in the blank round that Welsh was ramming home ignited while he was still in the act and standing full in front of the gun's muzzle. The explosion carried away both of the young man's arms from below the elbows. Bleeding terribly, Welsh was immediately taken to a nearby home where he was cared for. The festivities, of course, came to an abrupt and unhappy stop. A few days later, his condition stabilized, Welsh was moved to the Camp Curtin Hospital. By mid-August, Welsh's condition had improved greatly, though he still suffered from poor eyesight—the result of powder burns. His mates in the battery had taken up a collection for his benefit, but had raised only $46. Months later, however, by special direction of Governor Curtin, Welsh was fitted with two artificial limbs.[84]

After the excitement on Independence Day, life in Camp Curtin and Harrisburg in general seemed to settle into a lull. With the Bucktails and the 5th Reserves still in the field in Maryland, only about 5,000 men remained in camp, most belonging to either the 6th or 12th Reserve regiments, the 1st Pennsylvania Artillery, or the 1st Pennsylvania Cavalry. Colonel John Henry Taggart of the 12th Reserves was in command and had been since Biddle had left for Cumberland. A general lull in activity pervaded in Harrisburg as well, where the economic ramifications of the war were already being felt. A principal employer in the city had been a cotton mill on the banks of the river on Front Street at the corner of North Street. Hostilities made it impossible for the mill to obtain raw cotton from suppliers in the deep South. On the 9th of July, the mill was forced to close for lack of cotton and great many citizens found themselves without jobs. Fortunately, wheat was in season and there was much harvesting to do in the countryside around the city. Many of the displaced workers from the mill went out to the farms to find work. Many others found one of the recruiting offices in the city, enlisted and moved to Camp Curtin. The result was that Harrisburg was for a time fairly stripped of its young, working-age males. Life in the bare streets of the town was dull, duller than it would be for many months.[85]

But, for the perceptive, there were signs to indicate that the quiet would not last long. For example, 31 freight cars fitted up with seats sat on the tracks of the Northern Central Railroad just across the river from the camp, and 22 more cars were down at York. The Reserve regiments around the state had all been uniformed and equipped, and there had been an increase in the southward movement of troops from other Northern states over the railroads of Pennsylvania. Portions of the 1st and 4th Michigan regiments passed through in mid-July on the way to Washington, and, on the afternoon of July 13, the 13th Massachusetts pulled in from Philadelphia.[86] The Bay Staters had enjoyed to the fullest the privilege of being soldiers and patriots. Since they had left home, socks and shirts, Bibles and meals, and bully cheers had been lavished upon them by virtually everyone they met between Boston and Philadelphia. By the time they reached Harrisburg, they were coming to expect such favors as their due, and, as it happened they were just then hungry. The instant the train stopped moving, "a grand rush was made for the nearest restaurants." Time was short, however, and the officers were not long in rounding up the boys and putting them back on the train for Hagerstown. "Those who got anything [to eat] were lucky," one of the Massachusetts boys recalled, "and those who were paid for what was eaten were also lucky."[89]

With regiments being moved in such force to the nation's capital and other forward points, it was not difficult to deduce that something was in the works. In little more than a week, the terms of enlistment of the three-month volunteers would expire and little of any military importance had been accomplished with these men. They had, for the most part, sat around Washington and Harpers Ferry performing guard duty at various bridges or forts. The newly-organized regiments from all across the North, which had enlisted for longer terms of service, were being hurried forward to replace the soon-to-depart three-month regiments. These new regiments were few, however, perhaps not even enough to protect the capital, and Lincoln and his administrators were genuinely concerned for the safety of Washington and other cities, such as Philadelphia and even Harrisburg. While the regiments from other states hurried through Harrisburg, Curtin sat in his office and realized that events were proving that he had been correct in his anticipation of the untimely expiration of the three-month terms and justified in initiating the formation of the Reserve Corps. The flurry of troop movements was evidence that the War Department had also recognized, albeit too late, that Curtin had been correct and had shown great foresight. On July 13, Secretary of War Simon Cameron finally asked the governor for assistance.

Washington July 13, 1861

His Excellency Governor Curtin,
                Governor of Pennsylvania:

SIR: I respectfully request your excellency to send five of the long term regiments of Pennsylvania Volunteers, in addition to the two at Cumberland, to report to Major-General Patterson, say at Harper's Ferry, and the remainder of the long-term regiments to report to Lieutenant-General Scott in this city.

I am, sir, very respectfully, your obedient servant.

Simon Cameron
Secretary of War[88]

The "long-term" regiments Cameron was referring to were, of course, the Pennsylvania Reserves. It had not been very long ago that Washington had been telling Curtin that no more troops were needed, none could be used, it would be too expensive for the government to feed and clothe the men, and that if Curtin wished to keep them together and organized he would have to do so at the commonwealth's expense. Now, Cameron and the others in Washington, realizing that more men were needed, had considerably more interest in Curtin's men. His perfectly organized and completely equipped corps was the only such body of troops readily available. The governor might have been excused a twinge of smug satisfaction at the irony.

Some of the interested observers in Camp Curtin, however, thought that there was more to the hurried movements than just the replacement of the three-month men in the defenses of Washington. It was entirely possible that an offensive was being planned, and the additional "long-term" regiments were to immediately join in an invasion of Virginia. To the officers and men of the Reserves, it mattered not so much *what* was happening, only that something *was* happening and they might not be a part of it. The uncertainty—the fear—of missing what might be the crucial event of the war was gnawing at every man there. As one remembered, "In those days of intense excitement, 24 hours in camp reached the limit of any one man's patience. Officers and men were alike clamorous to be sent to Washington or anywhere else out of the state that danger threatened. Each one acted as though in fear that the rebellion might be ended without giving him the opportunity of striking a single blow for the Union."[89]

They had little to fear on that account, of course, and on the evening of what had been a hot July Sunday they found out. Assistant Secretary of War Thomas A. Scott sent a message to the Governor:

[July 21, 1861]

Hon. A. G. Curtin, Harrisburg:

Get your regiments at Harrisburg, Easton, and other points ready for immediate shipment. Lose no time preparing.

Make things move to the utmost.

Thomas A. Scott

To operator:

Under no circumstances let this message be made public.

Thomas A. Scott
reply[90]

No reason was given for the haste, but the postscript to the telegraph operator gave an indication that there was good reason for concern. The Union army had advanced into Virginia without waiting for the Reserve regiments, and the Battle of Bull Run had been fought near Manassas, Virginia, just about 30 miles southwest of Washington. The Federals, under Brigadier General Irvin McDowell, had been badly beaten and thrown back into Washington, stunned. Fear in the capital city reached its peak as an attack by the victorious Confederates seemed a certainty. Fresh men were needed who had neither been beaten nor were clamorous to go home precisely as their enlistments ran out. Harrisburg and Philadelphia were the nearest sources of fresh troops and Assistant Secretary Scott, until lately president of the Pennsylvania Railroad, knew that Curtin could be counted on to quickly push forward all available men. His Pennsylvanians might mean the difference between the survival or fall of the capital of the United States.

In response to Scott's dispatch, Curtin sent orders out to the colonels of the Reserve regiments around the commonwealth to proceed immediately to Harrisburg with their commands and to be receive arms at the State Arsenal. Among the first of the Reserve regiments to arrive at Harrisburg was, appropriately, the 1st Pennsylvania Reserves, under R. Biddle Roberts. After the inexperienced Roberts had given up command of Company B of the 12th regiment and accepted a position on the governor's staff, he became dissatisfied with the dull statehouse duty and longed for action. It took him a few weeks, but he somehow convinced the governor to give him the colonelcy of one of the new Reserve regiments then being formed. He took command of the 1st Pennsylvania Reserves early in June, at Camp Wayne in West Chester, Pennsylvania.

The 1st left Camp Wayne on Sunday, July 21, 1861, and proceeded to Harrisburg to be armed at the State Arsenal. Arriving after nightfall, the regiment was issued Harpers Ferry muskets and marched out to Camp Curtin, where the men pitched their tents in the darkness. Once there, a witty, intelligent and slightly smug private named William Henry Darlington, Company A, learned that life in the army was going to be what could best be described as hurry up and wait. "Getting to bed about 12 [midnight]," wrote Private Darlington to his mother, "we were soon asleep. At ½ past 3 next morning, we were ordered to strike tents + fall in ranks. In the darkness we did so + were soon standing with our knapsacks on our backs leaning upon our guns, + watching the first faint streaks of light in the east." It was in that position that Darlington and his comrades remained for about four hours. "We were alternately at shoulder arms, order arms, parade rest, or rest," he wrote, " + during intervals of the latter, I seated myself on a broad board + lay back upon my knapsack which then served as a pillow + took an excellent nap of more than an hour." Not until after 8 o'clock was the regiment marched out of Camp Curtin. The boys were happy to finally be underway and looked well as they filed toward the depot to the raucous strains of "Dixie Land".[91]

Darlington and his mates knew not what to expect of the train ride south but found that accommodations would be less than comfortable. They boarded open cars with rough planks placed crosswise for seats. They would be exposed to the wind and the weather throughout the whole ride. The train pulled out of Harrisburg and proceeded across the river then southward on the Northern Central Railroad. A long delay at York enabled a number of the less ethical companies of the 1st to begin taking advantage of their position as defenders of the Union, "some companies," reported the observant and upright Private Darlington, "particularly the Archie Dicks behaved badly."[92] Many of the men jumped off the idle train and stole a quantity of liquor from a nearby tavern. One company, the oddly-named Archy Dick Rifles, managed to smuggle an untapped keg of beer into one of their cars. Darlington's company, the Brandywine Guards from West Chester, was in the car immediately behind the Archy Dicks. The Brandywine Guards apparently was well stocked with high-bred, morality-conscious young men, for Darlington and many of the other privates looked upon the uncouth men of the Archy Dicks with distain and did all they could to disassociate themselves from them. "We called all the Brandywine Guards away from them," wrote Darlington to his mother.

Stealing the beer was only part of the challenge the Archy Dicks faced, for, as Darlington reported somewhat gloatingly, "They did not know how to open their barrel." The thirsty boys crowded around the keg and fussed and hypothesized for a time until some one of them lost patience and stove the cask's head in with the butt of his musket. Darlington gleefully recorded what happened next, "The beer shot up into the air 15 feet like a fountain + fell foaming on every person + thing in their car. Very little of the beer was left + every thing in the car was deluged. It was amusing to see them all trying to get out of the way."[93]

From York, the train moved through the sunny farms of Southern Pennsylvania with its great, fat barns and its fields of rich red earth and knee-high green corn. Around five o'clock it began to rain and the men put on their great coats as their train sped into Maryland under a black and turbulent sky. Most of the bridges over which the railroad passed in Maryland were guarded by Federal troops as a precaution against Confederate cavalry raids, which were not likely, or acts of sabotage by southern-sympathizing Marylanders, which were a somewhat greater possibility. The guards cheered as the Reserves passed, as did the Marylanders living in nearby houses.

*   *   *

While the 1st Reserves headed for Washington, regiments of the Reserve Corps continued to arrive at Camp Curtin. The 2nd Reserves from Easton arrived on July 24 after having received a tremendous send off from the people of that town on the Delaware River. The boys paraded through the streets of Easton to the train depot, escorted by a cornet band, and pulled out of the station amid waving handkerchiefs, ringing bells and cascading cheers. The traveling was not comfortable in the cars, however, for the day was excessively hot and the inside of the enclosed cars quite stuffy. The men took matters into their own hands and many climbed out of the boxes and sat on the tops of the cars. Others ventilated the cars by knocking the sides out with the butts of their muskets. The trip was long and fatiguing, and when the regiment finally arrived at Camp Curtin, the men fell down on the grass and went to sleep, too tired even to pitch their tents. One of them remembered later that the men found they "enjoyed the novelty and romance of sleeping...with nothing but the vault of heaven above." They were sorry later in the night, however, when the heavens opened and poured a drenching rain upon them.[94]

The 5th Wisconsin arrived in Harrisburg two nights later, and immediately pitched their tents on an empty lot by the Pennsylvania Railroad's Round House near the heart of the city. They had been in camp in Madison for about four weeks, and had been traveling in wildly rocking boxcars, through steep, forested mountains for two solid days. They had seen Chicago, Toledo, Cleveland, and Pittsburgh along the way and now, just a few hours ride from their destination, were ordered to rest in Harrisburg until they were given their arms from Pennsylvania's Arsenal.[95]

But, the "emergency" at Cumberland had not been as urgent as Colonel Wallace had led everyone in Washington and Harrisburg to believe, and the two Reserve regiments returned on the last day of July a bit disappointed. Although they had done some marching and had seen some real Rebels, not much else had come of all the bother. The men came home a bit dirtier and with a few stories to tell, but still unbloodied.

As the Reserves and other regiments were being rushed forward, the three-month regiments slowly began to arrive in Harrisburg from their campaign in Virginia. The first two regiments arrived on Sunday, the 21st, and went into bivouac in and around the capitol. In the days to follow regiments arrived in what seemed an endless stream. The streets were again choked with soldiers, and the hack drivers again began doing a great business between the city and Camp Curtin.[96]

The returning volunteers were markedly different from the clean, shiny type of soldier to which the city was accustomed. These soldiers wore dirty, sweat-stained uniforms of faded blue with rents and tears and split seams. Some of them wore scraggly beards and long, oily hair. They walked with a swagger, for they had "seen service" and were proud of it. Their filthy outfits were badges of patriotism and experience, and therefore the filthier they were the better.[97]

Those who had stories to tell found willing audiences in the people of Harrisburg. Some had seen the enemy, others had a chance to fire a shot or two at a Rebel picket or perhaps a skirmisher. A very few had actually been in what they called a "battle." The 11th Regiment had run into some Rebels at Hoke's Run, near Martinsburg, Virginia. A short, quick ruckus ensued and ten men of the regiment were hurt—one killed. Sergeant William Sees of Company E had told of this part in the contest and carried with him a relic of war to go along with it. Private John Snyder, also of Company E, was advancing with the regiment when the enemy began firing in earnest. A rifle ball struck Snyder's musket and bored clean through the barrel. The private halted, cooly examined his now useless weapon, discarded it, and walked to the rear of the fighting until he found a wounded man who would give up his musket. Snyder then turned and walked forward again into the fray. Sergeant Sees picked up Snyder's ruined musket and returned with it to feed the hungry eyes of the folks at home.[98]

Both the stories and the appetite for them eventually petered out, however, and the volunteers began a new and unhappy chapter of their service. Having been under military discipline for three months and having during that period been usually encamped in rural areas, the men were anxious to kick up their heels in Harrisburg and enjoy their imminent freedom. This they were unable to do, however, each and every one of them was broke. Many of them had not been paid even once in the three months they had been in service. Even those who had been paid had not received all that was due them and had no money left by the time they reached Harrisburg.

It was in this penniless condition that the government decided to discharge the returned volunteers. To keep paying and feeding thousands of men after all their practical usefulness was gone was, of course, very expensive, so the War Department determined that the three-month veterans should be mustered out as soon as possible. The men returned their arms and all their equipment, including tents, blankets, and cooking and eating utensils, to the authorities in Harrisburg. They were then mustered out of service and there was nothing to stop them from going home, which all ardently wished to do. The one catch, however, was that none of them had been paid, and no one in his right mind would leave without collecting what was due him. So they waited. They were issued no more rations. They were not quartered either in Camp Curtin or in any of the city's hotels as they had been a few months ago. They were allowed to sleep anyplace they had a mind to. In short, the government discharged them from its service and immediately ceased to care for them. They were no longer soldiers of the United States and were, therefore, no longer the responsibility of the Federal government. This was callous treatment, to be sure, but it would not be too hard on the volunteers if the army paymasters made quick work of disbursing their gold and silver. They did not.[99]

One paymaster was in Harrisburg to face the deluge of dirty, hairy, hungry veterans. The money required to pay off a regiment for three months was very nearly $50,000, and all payments were made in gold and silver.[100] It was exceptionally difficult to move that much coin from one place to another, and the result was that paymasters frequently could not carry with them as much money as they needed. The paymaster in Harrisburg, for example, had barely enough with him to pay two regiments, but 16 regiments were in the city during that last week in July—all of them awaiting payment. In all, about 30,000 volunteers jammed Harrisburg, and the paymaster wired Washington for help; two more paymasters were dispatched, though not immediately, with what was thought to be the needed amount of currency. In paying two regiments on the 24th, the one, very unpopular paymaster in town used all his available cash, and he could then only anxiously await the promised help from Washington.

The volunteers had a difficult wait. They were hungry and dirty and, as the days passed, many were becoming ill. Produce in the city's public market was abundant. A tremendous variety of meat, fish, poultry, and fruits and vegetables graced the stalls, and the plenty made the prices low.[101] But the bargains were of no good to the soldiers, for they had nothing to bargain with. So hungry were the men that some turned to stealing, or "foraging" as they preferred to call it. Mr. John Loban, a farmer near Camp Curtin, claimed soldiers stole 600 heads of his cabbage and most of his strawberry crop, and what they did not take they thoughtlessly destroyed. Apparently the hungry men had been in such a hurry to scoop the cabbage and the strawberries that they trampled right over his tomatoes.[102]

Such depredations upon private property were shameless, but the famished soldiers, some of whom had not eaten in days, could hardly be blamed. Some were so bad off that they turned to begging in the streets, and the people of the city were outraged that a soldier of the United States was not better attended to by his government.[103] The Reverend Mr. Hunt, chaplain of the 8th regiment, fanned the flames when he took the pulpit at Sunday service in one of the city's churches and ardently damned whomever was responsible. The returned men had "been treated like hogs," he proclaimed, and the people of Harrisburg agreed.[104] They did not wait for the government to make restitution, for all realized that might take forever. Instead, they immediately went to the soldiers' relief. They opened their homes and took in the sick to be cared for. They carried baskets of food and blankets to Capitol Hill, where thousands of men were sleeping in the open.[105]

The legislature was not in session inside the capitol, but the governor and his staff finally realized, after the men sleeping on the capitol lawn had been three days without food, that something had to be done for the volunteers until they were paid and could fend for themselves. Cattle were slaughtered at the order of the governor and the hungry men were given rations, but they were even then little better off than before, for they were without pots, kettles, or frying pans, all of which had been turned in to the quartermaster almost immediately upon their return. Even if the men did manage to cook the beef, perhaps roasting it on a stick over an open fire, they had no plates, knives or forks with which to eat the hot meat.

Even the weather seemed to be conspiring against the returned men. It was rare for the heat to grow oppressive in Harrisburg, as cooling breezes from the river helped keep the temperature down, but the breezes would not blow in that last week of July, 1861. The hungry, dirty men were made to swelter in addition to their other woes

Some of the returned soldiers declared that they felt the heat more that week then they had in Virginia.[106] One put it this way, "weather never so hot, dust never so deep, shade trees never so scarce as at present."[107] Quite logically, they sought to escape the heat, and some of their uncleanliness, by taking refreshing dips in the river and the nearby Pennsylvania Canal. This gave them some relief, but caused a minor uproar among some of the people of finer sensibilities. The spectacle presented by hundreds, perhaps thousands, of naked men bathing and playing in the river in full view of the homes and traffic on Front Street is one that must have given morally-stringent victorian observers nightmares. "From early morning until sundown," complained one upright citizen, "those who live on Front Street, and the strangers in our large boarding houses on that street, are continually annoyed by these filthy exhibitions, while their ears are stunned by the oaths and the blasphemies, intermingled with the most impure and licentious language that a reckless and shameful depravity can invent."[108] Even bathing in the more remote canal out toward the camp was unacceptable to the people of the city, for ladies passing over the canal en route to the Lunatic Asylum on the hills behind Camp Curtin would be subjected to the nakedness of the soldiers.[109]

The complaints of the citizenry were just one more indignity for the volunteers to bear. Those poor men were very nearly at the end of their patience. To them, the situation seemed to be getting worse instead of better. Some had been in Harrisburg without shelter or regular food for more than a week and there was still no sign of the paymasters reported to be en route from Washington. The situation was not a good one and city officials began to worry. Mayor Kepner knew a boiling pot when he saw one, and he acted quickly to stop trouble before it started. He issued an ordinance that no soldier would be allowed to carry a firearm into the city unless he were responding to an emergency of some sort.[110] The police were directed to close all saloons, taverns, inns, and any establishment that sold liquor of any kind.[111] And old Jack Smith's whiskey still out near Camp Curtin was closed down.[112] The volunteers needed no artificial stimulants, anyway, for they were already more than amply aroused. They decided to endure no more abuse at the hands of the government they had sworn to protect. The time had come to take matters into their own hands.

The additional paymasters had finally arrived from Washington, but they did little to pay anybody. They were staying at the Jones House on Market Square, just a few blocks from the capitol grounds, where most of the volunteers had been living. About 4 p.m. on Saturday, July 27, a large number of the volunteers met in Market Square in front of the Jones House. The hotel operators themselves had a legitimate complaint about the payment policies of the government. The hotel had been filled to capacity since the beginning of the war, especially in the very early days before Camp Curtin was opened. Companies of volunteers who arrived in the city then were put up in hotels at the government's expense. In those few days quite a bill was run up. Some of the places had submitted to the government bills for over $1,000, making them very expensive barracks. By the end of July, the government had not yet remitted payment, and the hotel operators were not pleased. So when the crowd of unpaid volunteers showed up outside the Jones House they had sympathizers in the hotel's management. This is not to say that Mr. William Reed, clerk of the establishment, and his colleague, D. H. Hutchinson, were pleased to look out their door and see a distraught mob of hungry, bearded men congregated there, nor did they look upon those men as allies. Messrs. Reed and Hutchinson were concerned for the safety of the house, especially after the mob began shouting and threatening violence upon the paymasters. Suddenly, an effigy labelled "Paymaster" was hoisted upon a lamppost and set afire. The mob cheered crazily and seemed to gain strength and momentum from the flames that engulfed the figure. Their lust for action or violence seemed merely whetted by the fire rather than sated. The situation began to look very serious.[113]

Meanwhile, word of the riot had reached Camp Curtin, and the 12th Pennsylvania Reserve regiment was quickly assembled, armed and started off toward the city at the double-quick. Colonel John Henry Taggart, a 40-year-old newspaper editor and publisher from Philadelphia, was in command of the regiment. Someone, it is not quite clear who, the governor perhaps, had shown some foresight when the returned men had begun getting restless earlier in the week. The 12th Regiment had not been shipped out from Camp Curtin with the other regiments of the Reserve Corps, but had remained awaiting just such a contingency. Taggart had served as camp commandant for about five weeks, succeeding Biddle and remaining in command until July 17, at which time preparations were being made to ship all the Reserve regiments to Washington or Harpers Ferry. In preparation for the move, Taggart relinquished command to Colonel Seiler, but then his regiment was not moved after all.[114]

Colonel Taggart led his regiment straight down Second Street and boldly into the heart of the Square. He saw the burning effigy and heard the jeers and threats aimed at the paymaster, so he wasted no time in issuing orders to the rioters to disperse. The situation was out of control and emotions were running high. He therefore simply gave the order to charge the rioters. The mob was surprised and, being unarmed, retreated. The rioters were not ready to give up their cause entirely, however, and had enough spirit to counterattack. One of them decided that weapons would be needed to continue and called out, "To the Arsenal for your arms!" The crowd surged toward Capitol Hill and the State Arsenal there. Taggart and his men were alert and immediately about faced and sprinted for the Arsenal. The 12th was closer to the destination and won the race, quickly surrounding the Arsenal with loaded muskets. The mob was frustrated and shouted angrily at the men of the 12th, but the loud talk was not itself dangerous and the situation seemed at last under control.[115]

But the three-month men had pluck and refused to knuckle under. More out of spite than anything else, they seized an old dismounted cannon that had been lying about outside the Arsenal and proceeded back to Market Square, dragging the useless tube on a dray. What they were going to do with it once they got it there was unclear, but they were shouting something about "blowing up the paymaster." They did not get far before realizing the futility of their mission, however, and returned the cannon without having done any damage. Men of the 12th served as a guard at the Jones House as the crowd dispersed and the excitement died down.

The riot, however, was not without effect. The paymaster related the condition of affairs to Washington, and some gold was immediately sent—but not much. Just eight companies were paid on the day following the riot, and no one was paid on the day following that. The paymaster general of the United States Army did come up from Washington to assess the situation and to smooth what rumpled feathers he could but what was really needed was more money.[116]

Finally, on the 30th, the paying of the men began in earnest. Four payment offices were established at widely separated points around the city and by the end of the day about half of the men in town had received their due. All ill feeling disappeared, temporarily, when the boys were handed their gold and silver. The privates in the 3rd Regiment had not been paid in their entire three months of service and received $39.95, including $6.95 for time over the three months, mileage to their homes, and commutation for their rations since they had arrived in Harrisburg.

Once they had money, the volunteers stampeded the haberdasheries of the city and purchased new clothing, finally ridding themselves of the tattered blue woolen they had been wearing for three months.[119]

CHAPTER THREE

"The Colonel Seems to be Boss"

JULY, 1861 — MARCH, 1862

The results of Bull Run had convinced people of the North that the war was not to end quickly. After a brief lull in Harrisburg following the departure of the three-month men, the crush of arriving volunteers began all over again, and Camp Curtin was once again packed. It would remain so until the end of October.

The demand for and supply of men were both great, but raising and organizing a regiment was no simple matter. Not just anyone was allowed to go about recruiting. Special permission to raise a regiment for United States service had to be obtained from the War Department, that is, from Secretary of War Simon Cameron. Governor Curtin could authorize the raising of a regiment for United States service, but he had, in turn, to receive permission from Cameron in the form of a quota to be filled by Pennsylvania, and he could use whatever legal means he liked to fill that quota.

Cameron could not indiscriminately accept every regiment that was offered to him because the government could not afford the tremendous expense of providing for them. The Pennsylvania Reserves were not immediately accepted for this very reason. The War Department did not think the 15 Reserve regiments were needed and therefore did not consent to providing for them. Pennsylvania took care of her own in that instance. Permission to raise regiments was given carefully, and often only to politically influential men known to Cameron or to others in his powerful political machine.

On the day after the disaster at Bull Run, a young man in uniform appeared at Cameron's Washington home to ask permission to raise a regiment in Pennsylvania. First Lieutenant James A. Beaver of the 2nd Pennsylvania Volunteers was a rarity among those coming to see Cameron in that he had already served as a junior officer and had proved he had the makings of a good soldier. His present regiment was, even then, enroute to Harrisburg without him to be mustered out. Beaver would join them after his errand to Cameron.

Cameron was the man in Washington upon whom the burden of the recent defeat fell most heavily. Many in the capital feared the city would be attacked at any moment, and few of the regiments called upon for help from the North, including the Pennsylvania Reserves, had arrived. Panic again reigned in the streets of Washington. Added to these official concerns for Cameron was the personal grief of the death of his brother, Colonel James Cameron of the 79th New York, who had fallen on Henry House hill at Bull Run. Despite all this, Cameron greeted Beaver cordially.

The two Pennsylvanians, acquainted from pre-war politics in the commonwealth, spoke freely. The young lieutenant explained the purpose of his visit and stated that he already had a good start in recruiting a new regiment. The 2nd's lieutenant colonel, Thomas Welsh of Columbia, Pennsylvania, had already lined up a number of men who would help raise companies and serve as the company officers, and a large number of the men of the 2nd, including, according to Beaver, every last man of his Company H, had already volunteered to reenlist to serve in the new regiment. Welsh and Beaver would, of course, like to serve as the principal field officers.[1] Cameron did not hesitate to give his sanction to Beaver and Welsh, and Beaver quickly returned to Harrisburg to tell Welsh of his success. They were mustered out of the 2nd and parted, each going home to recruit.

They had plenty of company on the recruiting circuits; scores of men were swarming through the villages and hamlets of Pennsylvania trying to induce men to enlist. Many of the recruiters were from out of state. Men from New Jersey, Ohio and especially New York came into the Keystone State to tap the vast resources of manpower. One of these men was Captain J. W. Dewey, who was in Harrisburg recruiting not for a volunteer regiment but for a Regular Army unit just being formed. The regiment was to be composed of just sharpshooters, and, although it would later be designated the 1st United States Sharpshooters, everyone simply referred to it as "Berdan's Sharpshooters," after its colonel, Hiram Berdan of New York. Only marksmen were recruited, and, before actually enlisted, each man had to prove he could shoot. Every man had to put ten shots into a ten-inch circle at a distance of 200 yards. By mid-August, Captain Dewey had found fifty "old deer hunters from Potter, McKean, and Tioga counties" who qualified for enlistment.[2]

Companies began arriving in great number at Camp Curtin in mid-August. Some of these companies were "claimed," meaning they were already slated to become a part of a certain regiment being formed. Other companies were independent in that they had been formed without an eye toward joining any particular regiment. Recruiters, like Welsh and Beaver, scrambled madly to enlist these entire companies in their regiments. The scrambling and bargaining did not always stop with the unattached companies, however, and a good number of the "claimed" companies were persuaded away to other regiments.

With all these companies arriving in Harrisburg, Camp Curtin soon became seriously overcrowded. Efforts were made to organize and dispatch regiments as quickly as possible so room could be made for others. Even these efforts were not enough as arrivals outstripped departures. Out of necessity, a new camp was formed. In establishing Harrisburg's second Camp of Rendezvous, there was none of the ceremony and excitement that attended the opening of Camp Curtin. A regiment arrived from Pittsburgh on July 24, when Harrisburg and Camp Curtin were full of returned three-month men. Since no room was available there, Colonel Samuel W. Black and his men found a place on a vacant lot in the city and remained there for about a week. In that time Black learned that because his regiment was not quite full it would remain in Harrisburg until it could be brought up to full strength. Black then wished to quarter his men in a more comfortable place with fewer distractions, so he led his outfit about a mile and a half east of the city.[3] Black's regiment, eventually designated the 62nd, was later joined by a few other regiments, and the campsite was named Camp Cameron, in honor of the secretary of war.[4] Black's regiment departed from the camp in mid-August, and Major Thomas Williams, 5th U.S. Artillery, took command of Camp Cameron. He departed very early in September, however, and was later in the month appointed brigadier general. Captain Daniel Hastings, who had assisted Captain Simmons in the mustering of volunteers in the early weeks of Camp Curtin, suceeded Williams as commandant of the new camp.[5]

In mid-August, Colonel Seiler was again serving as commandant at Camp Curtin. As new companies began coming in later in the month, the duties of the commandant became necessarily more strenuous. Governor Curtin, remembering the chaos in camp back in April and May, wished for a strong hand to direct things. In the third week of August, Curtin called for Thomas Welsh and ordered him immediately to Camp Curtin to assume command. Welsh was in Lancaster County recruiting his regiment and had been home only three weeks. He had not had much opportunity to fill his new regiment, but he followed orders and returned to Harrisburg.[6]

Curtin had chosen a good man. As he arrived at Camp Curtin about the 20th of August, Welsh was the picture of youthful vigor and exuded strength and competence. He was the father of four, soon to be five, and had been a canal supervisor and justice of the peace in Columbia before the war. He was an exceptionally tough man for having had such docile occupations. At age 23, he had enlisted as a private and gone off to the Mexican War. Promoted to sergeant and later grievously wounded in the leg at Buena Vista, he had been discharged and sent home. He had not had enough of that war, however, and after recovering for several months late in 1847, he returned to Mexico as a lieutenant in the 11th United States Infantry. In April of 1861, he had raised a company and taken it to Harrisburg, where it had joined the 2nd Regiment. Welsh was elected lieutenant colonel. In an age of long flowing hair and sometimes outlandish whiskers, Welsh wore his hair closely cropped and kept his full beard neatly trimmed. His eyes were deep set and were bright and fierce. A small, tight mouth was mostly hidden by the beard but contributed greatly to giving Welsh the look of a serious man, intolerant of nonsense. He had a commanding presence, and he knew it. Better still, he knew how to take advantage of it.[7]

COLONEL THOMAS WELSH
45th Pennsylvania Volunteers.
Perhaps Camp Curtin's best commandant, Welsh was in charge from August to October, 1861. He rose to the rank of brigadier general in the Ninth Corps.
(Library of Congress)

As a captain and lieutenant colonel in the 2nd, Welsh had seen the mismanagement that had dominated the camp in its early days and, as he began his tenure as commandant, the errors of his predecessors were in the forefront of his mind. The frequent disturbances the volunteers caused in the city were the first things he moved to eliminate. He offered troops to the mayor to augment the police force in times of difficulty. He attempted to reduce the number of trouble-making men in town by eliminating the pass system, and he went one step further by disallowing passes to visitors wishing to enter Camp Curtin. He took steps to ensure that the camp, which was again becoming notoriously unclean and unhealthy, would be frequently and properly policed. Finally, he moved to improve the cleanliness and efficiency of its hospital, which had been such a bad place in which to be sick that the men were afraid of going there for fear their illnesses would worsen. Welsh impressed his own no-nonsense attitude upon the entire camp. As he saw it, Camp Curtin was a place for volunteers to learn what soldiers must know, it was not a base of operation from which to run nightly sorties past the guard to the saloons of the city. If C. J. Biddle had been tough with the volunteers, Welsh was nearly a tyrant. Welsh knew, however, as all good soldiers knew, that good discipline would save lives, and an officer's job was to save lives.[8]

In the first week of September, James Beaver was called to the camp to assist his new colonel. He was installed as second in command on September 9, and his duties were to assist in the mustering in of troops, to frank soldiers' letters and to take command in the absence of Welsh. About 5,000 men were quartered there with the number growing daily, and the full efforts of both Welsh and Beaver were required to keep things running smoothly. Yet the two were still trying to fill their own regiment and their success there was not as complete. They had had some companies lured away to other regiments that were forming and presented a better prospect of getting to the action more quickly. Above all else, the goal of the men in camp was to "get into the war" before it was over.[9]

Some familiar faces returned to Camp Curtin in August and September. Joseph F. Knipe, the man who had raised the colors back on that first afternoon and given Camp Curtin its name, had returned. He was no longer a militia major on E. C. Williams's staff, for he had been given a colonel's commission. Knipe was in camp trying to fill his regiment, which would become the 46th Pennsylvania Volunteers.

Back as well was the first commandant, Washington H. R. Hangen. Although he had been lieutenant colonel of the 9th regiment, he was now just a lieutenant and would be content to remain as such for awhile and serve as adjutant of his new outfit, the 47th Pennsylvania. The 47th's lieutenant colonel was George Washington Alexander, a 31-year-old giant from Reading, Pennsylvania. Standing six feet tall and weighing over 200 pounds, Alexander towered over most of the men, and his physical presence no doubt had something to do with his having been elected lieutenant colonel. Though still young, he had already been married twice, his first wife dying while he was still a teenager, and was the father of two. Though he had no prior military experience, Alexander would prove himself a good officer and would figure in the history of the Camp Curtin later in the war.

A portion of the 47th had been raised in Harrisburg and one of the local boys who had enlisted was, like Alexander, a newcomer to the camp. William Wallace Geety was from a prominent family of the Harrisburg area and married a local girl, Miss Henrietta Thompson, in 1857. Geety left his childless wife in August, 1861 and enlisted in what was to become Company H of the 47th. The men of the company thought Geety vigorous and intelligent enough to command their continued respect and elected him first lieutenant, a post he would hold for three years.

Among the many veterans of three-month service returning as members of other regiments were two who had served together in the 4th Pennsylvania. John Frederic Hartranft had been colonel of the regiment, and John Rutter Brooke had been captain of Company C. Both men were now busy filling new regiments and both had been given commissions as colonel. Brooke would lead the 53rd regiment, and Hartranft the 51st. Hartranft thus became the first man to serve as colonel of two Pennsylvania regiments.

Hartranft had led the 4th Regiment into Camp Curtin on April 20, 1861. He was trim, above average height and looked very much like a soldier, with flowing hair and a long, sweeping mustache. He came from a long line of Germans, and his features—the large broad nose and the ample eyebrows over wide-set eyes showed that the European blood still coursed thickly through his veins. He was a college man—Union of Schenectady, New York—and was a civil engineer of some experience, having helped lay a railroad through the lower Pocono mountains from Mauch Chunk to White Haven. His home was in Norristown, Montgomery County, just northwest of Philadelphia. He had served as deputy county sheriff in Montgomery County there for five years, studying law at the same time and finally passing the county bar in 1860. He was practicing law there when hostilities opened.[10]

Hartranft had been active in the local militia company—the Norris City Rifles—for a number of years. The men had elected him lieutenant and later captain. Shortly before the war broke out, the militia companies in the county had elected Hartranft colonel, so, when Lincoln called for volunteers, Hartranft had immediately gone to Harrisburg to offer the services of all the organized militia of Montgomery County. All the companies were accepted, of course, and had been designated the 4th Pennsylvania with Hartranft as colonel. He was 30 years old, married and a father when he left Norristown for Camp Curtin.[11]

Captain Simmons had mustered the 4th into service for three months on April 21. The men of the regiment had not enjoyed those months. Most of their tenure had been spent in camp outside Washington amid boredom and sickness. They were thoroughly dissatisfied with the army and wanted out as soon as possible. On July 21, therefore, the day their enlistment was up, the men of the 4th had had their gear packed and had been ready to take the next train home. Unfortunately, that was also the day General McDowell had selected to mount the Union offensive against the Confederates at Manassas. As the army had moved out to the south, the men of the 4th, despite Hartranft's protestations, had moved out to the north, glad to be done with the army. Mortified, but still eager to get into the fight, Hartranft volunteered to serve as an aide to General William Franklin, and had subsequently seen the Battle of Bull Run.

COLONEL JOHN F. HARTRANFT
51st Pennsylvania Volunteers.
One of the finest volunteer officers in the Union Army, he rose to the rank of major general.
(from Parker's History of the Fifty-First Pennsylvania)

Upon his return home after the battle, Hartranft had received permission to recruit a three-year regiment. He had traveled about recruiting and found how eager men were to serve. Even some of the men of the 4th, having had some time at home to recoup their tempers and view things with a broader perspective, recognized that there might be a real danger to the Union. When Hartranft had gone recruiting in Montgomery County, a number of the veterans of the 4th had come forward again and enlisted in his regiment. Hartranft had had little trouble filling his new regiment and brought his companies to Camp Curtin in September. There, they were designated the 51st Pennsylvania Volunteers.

The 51st was a mixed lot. Half of the companies came from Montgomery County and the other half came from counties in the center of the state just upriver from Harrisburg. As a group, they were a bit wild; not quite having the insatiable thirst for illegal adventures that the Bucktails did, but liking to have their fun—even if that meant breaking the rules. If Camp Curtin had been a schoolroom, and all the regiments within it pupils, the 51st might have been the incorrigible student—the class clown— needful of an extra measure of the schoolmaster's attention.

The comings and goings through Harrisburg of companies and regiments, like the 51st, was naturally a matter of great interest to the residents of the city. The Harrisburg newspapers were diligent in learning the facts about each of the outfits in town and in camp and regularly reported the details in their daily editions. In this, the papers were no different from the papers in any city, North or South, through which large numbers of troops passed. After several months, however, the War Department realized that this practice might in some way be helping the enemy, as the flow of newspapers across the lines was not as restricted as might be thought. Late in August, therefore, a number of editors of papers in large cities decided to stop reporting on troop movements "in order that the rebels may be deprived of one of the means of obtaining information concerning the strength and operations of our army."[12] The War Department apparently issued an order in September forbidding newspapers from printing any information about troops. The order was heeded for a few weeks, but the editors, needing copy, could not restrain themselves and began again. The War Department did not generally enforce the order.[13]

All the fuss with the papers meant very little to the volunteers themselves. They simply came and went as they were told and passed the time as best they could. Many of the men could not read, but for those who were literate, writing home was a common and important exercise. Men away from home for the first time, and there were many, had a compelling desire—a need—to communicate with family. All was alien in Harrisburg, and although it was truly exciting to be on one's own, as it were, in the state capital, and in the company of thousands of men of all appearances, inclinations and even nationalities, that excitement itself, was alien and made the compulsion to remember and communicate with the familiar that much stronger. The men wrote home to reassure, to inform about things such as their health and the addresses at which equally compulsory letters could be sent to them. But they wrote mostly to share the excitement and the stories of the journey from home and sights of the capital. They wrote to remember from where they had come and to keep a little bit of it with them.

Coming to Camp Curtin from their homes had been no simple matter. The journey, more often than not, began with an emotional trial when the young men who had enlisted would gather at an appointed time on shade-mottled village squares or court-house lawns. They met under the same huge oaks and fragrant basswoods that perhaps some of their fathers and grandfathers had gathered under when going off to other wars. There, goodbyes were said and resaid as mothers, wives and sisters came to cry, fathers to worry, and perhaps envy, and younger brothers to idolize. The sons and brothers and nephews would then be put in ranks by their captain and marched out of town to a dusty highway or distant railway station. Sometimes there would be bands playing, but usually not. Everpresent were the forever-haunting figures of certain blonde- or brown- or red-haired girls peering anxiously from behind hedges or over fences or out of upper-story windows as the boys and young men marched away. They peered furtively, not wanting to be seen, and they watched for a certain one to pass—the young man to whom they had not wanted to say goodbye but whom they now wished fervently would not go. Despite their efforts at inconspicuity, these girls at their hedges or windows would be seen by the searching eyes of the boys in the ranks, and the image of them would be seen again and again for months and years to come on cold, lonely nights while on picket duty, on long and dusty marches, in rain-soaked blankets, and camp fires and hospital beds.[14]

Some volunteer companies had long marches or wagon rides to endure before reaching a station or a railroad. Others did not and the tears of wives and mothers would fall on depot floors and train sidings instead of village squares. The simple act of boarding a train was novel for the young men. Trains, although not new by any means, were a part of the life of the average young man of the 1860s only as a feature of the landscape, and many did not even have that acquaintance with the iron horse. "Unfortunately," recalled one future cavalryman, "a few of us had grown up in the country, where the locomotive whistle was not heard, where the noise most familiar to our ears was the old dinner-horn."[15] Few of the recruits had actually traveled on a train, so this first adventure in the army was for many the crowning excitement of their lives. The ride to Camp Curtin was a heart-pounding, head-lightening experience few would ever forget. One excited private wrote in his diary an account of what a ride over the rails could be like for several hundred or more adrenaline-crazed young men.

"Sept 25...At 10½ o'clock left for Harrisburg in a train of 25 cars, amid the waving of ladies handkerchiefs and shouts of Union throats. New Bethlehem a man fell off the cars. Train stopped at Allentown, where a fellow accused a soldier of stealing his watch. The soldier struck him with his fist—and knocked him down. A regular fuss immediately ensued. The man jumped up and threw a stone at the soldier (but missed him) he then run in his house, the soldier followed him, knocked in the door, jerked the wite wash-brush out of the fellow's wife's hand and broke it up on her head, he then slamed his fist threw the window + here the other soldiers interfered. So you see we had the first fight at Allentown. On our road to Harrisburg, we passed some very fine land. An old lady in a dung-yard swung a pitch-fork + cheered, the boys all roared and laughed. All along the road old men, old women, old maids, old bachelors, young men, young women, big boys, little boys, little girls, big girls, ugly girls, pritty girls, girls of all descriptions all sizes, all shapes + all colors cheered us on to Dixie. Between Allentown and Reading a man put his head out of a window of the cars, + got it knocked against some wood that was piled up along the track. The cars stoped along the road, the engine unhooked as if going to let us stand. The boys jumped off and entered an apple orchard and commenced shaking the trees and knocking the apples. I got a couple, was sitting on the fence eating one. There came a ground squirl along. I threw the apple at the squirl + come pretty near hitting it. Got aboard the cars. Commenced eating the other apple, gave part of it to John Bruce...Cars stoped at Reading. No blood shed between Reading and Harrisburg except Theodore Hester's nose bled. Arrived at Harrisburg at 2¼ o'clock."[16]

The system in Harrisburg of providing for arriving troops had been tightened up considerably and no longer were newly-arrived companies allowed to enjoy their first meal on Uncle Sam in the poshness of the hotel dining rooms. As soon as a company or regiment arrived at the train depot, it was immediately directed to Camp Curtin. The grounds of the capitol were sometimes used as a temporary campsite, but they were used as a last option because both the terrain and location were unsuitable. If the hour were especially late and men especially tired, a company, though hungry, might defer dinner and the long, dark march out to the camp in favor of sleep. Companies often spent the night on a vacant lot near the train depot or even at the depot itself. "It was about three o'clock Saturday morning when we arrived at Harrisburg," remembered Sergeant Eugene Beague, Company G of the 45th Pennsylvania. "Then and there began our experience as soldiers. Instead of going to bed, as gentlemen who travel are supposed to do, we were told to make ourselves comfortable (?) on the pavement near the station or wherever there was room to spare."[17] The floor of the depot, or the "soft side of a brick" on the pavement outside, contrasted poorly with the feather beds they had just left, and sleep was often hard to come by that first night in the state capital.[18]

In the morning, companies like Beague's that had spent the night at the depot would be awakened, drawn up into ranks and files and marched out the Ridge Road to their camp. Corporal Thomas Dornblazer of what was to become Company E of the 7th Pennsylvania Cavalry thought this stroll a "forced march," but then cavalrymen would never be known for marching. Some of the would-be cavalrymen with Dorn-blazer considered the odd mile and a half out to Camp Cameron a bit too far to walk and the thought at least crossed their minds that they should be conveyed by hack. Most decided against it because, according to Corporal Dornblazer, to ride would have been unsoldier-like—and contrary to orders. "With a huge bundle on each shoulder, and an occasional umbrella raised to break the rays of a warm October sun, we footed it through the dusty highway to Camp Cameron...of course our bundles included only the loose baggage—the trunks and extra bedding were sent out by wagons."[19]

Once in camp, whether Camp Curtin or Cameron, the volunteer companies were provided with shelter and blankets and other camp equipage, such as kettles and tripods, brooms, rakes, tin plates, and forks and knives. If the men had not yet been mustered into United States service, they were not given uniforms. The officers, both those running the camp and those organizing the regiments, wished to muster in the companies as soon as possible, for until the ceremony, the men were technically civilians and could come and go as they wished. This technicality was not generally understood by many of the volunteers, but most were eager to get into action anyway and would not have left their camps even had they been given the choice.

For each of the men, one obstacle had to be overcome before he could fulfill his wish to get into the war. One man stood between each volunteer and the glory each was sure awaited him on the battlefield. In that being rejected for service was the principal fear of every recruit, the examining surgeon scared more Federal soldiers than the strongest Confederate brigade ever would.

The examining surgeons were not popular men. The modesty of those nineteenth century recruits kept them from especially enjoying having to appear before total strangers "just as Ham saw his father...." Nothing could have been more embarrassing than such an examination. "We were stripped," one soldier wrote home, "and brought out simply into an open tent in view of the whole company and we were felt and fingered all over, though he left me off very easy...I would have given five dollars to gave gotten clear...."[20] To some, the doctors seemed "heartless and rude," in demanding that every man strip and submit to a thorough prodding and feeling. Some of the examiners had the men "perform certain gymnastic stunts to test his arms and legs" but having to pass through such "wonderful evolutions" was rare. The great crush for time led most surgeons to give just a cursory examination, which led to a great deal of error in the classification of the recruits.[21] Late in August, Company D of the 141st Pennsylvania had the extraordinarily high number of 19 men rejected by the medical officer. Discouraged, but not defeated, and knowing full well there was nothing much wrong with them, the men simply attached themselves to other companies and underwent examination the next day by the very same surgeon. All 19 went unrecognized and were passed and mustered in.[22]

For the most part the men had little to fear, for the chance of rejection was slight.

Although most examining officers were capable enough—each being required to pass an examination by the surgeon general and a board of officers—many, especially as the war progressed, were less than thorough in examining volunteers.[23] Often a quick look into a man's eyes and mouth and a hearty thump or two on his chest were sufficient to determine the man's fitness, and stories abound that show the inefficiency of the surgeons' method.

Lieutenant Oliver Christian Bosbyshell of Company G of the 48th remembered that, after the regiment departed Camp Curtin, where the men had been examined and mustered in, one of the men of his company got himself into trouble as he was standing guard at Camp Hamilton near Fort Monroe, Virginia.

"One dark, blustery night, and this camp was prolific of such kind of nights," wrote Bosbyshell, "Jake Haines let General Mansfield [John K. Mansfield, commandant of Camp Hamilton] slip through the camp guard without a challenge. Jake was as deaf as a post, and besides was walking [away] from him when the general entered. The general notified the officer of the guard to have the offender reprimanded the next morning at guard-mount, and then attempted to pass out of camp on the opposite side, but Rogers [probably John Rogers of Co. G, who was later wounded at Antietam and discharged] was there and his 'halt, or I'll prog ye' brought him up a-standing. Colonel Nagle [Colonel James Nagle of the 48th] reprimanded Haines the next morning, but it was done in the low squeaking voice which the colonel sometimes adopted, so that when it was over Haines inquired, 'What did he say?' "[24]

The most spectacular illustration of the inattention to detail paid by the surgeons was also the most infrequent. Occasionally, a woman, with close-cropped hair and a face that appeared youthful and masculine, would be passed by a surgeon. Elvira Ibecker from Northumberland County found her way into Captain George A. Brooks's Company D of Colonel Knipe's 46th. She remained in the service for about six weeks, but whether she fooled everyone or had a few confidants within the company is unclear. She had little physical appeal, according to one observer, who noted that while she was "by no means ill-looking...the indications that she chews tobacco and drinks 'whicky' [are] unmistakeably strong."[25]

In early September, "a plump lass of only sixteen" joined Captain Christian Kuhn's Sumner Rifles of Carlisle, Pennsylvania, later Company A of the 11th Pennsylvania. The girl remained in the company for more than a week before being found out, and she was discovered only because some gentleman from Carlisle who was visiting Camp Curtin recognized her as she was standing guard. Sophia Cryder was her name, and the Harrisburg *Patriot and Union* reported that although she was "a girl of unblemished reputation, and did not, as generally happens in such cases, enlist to be near the object of her affections, but merely in a wild spirit of adventure...It does not speak well for the modesty of Miss Sophia...to say, that she was in the habit of accompanying the men on their excursions to the river to bathe." The editor was generous in his judgment of Sophia, proposing that her trips to the river were undertaken only "to ward off suspicion; especially as she took precious good care to keep out of the water herself." Sophia was taken home to Carlisle, "where she [could] reflect over what she did see, as well what she did not see."[26]

A bit less than a year later, in the summer of 1862, a Frank Mayne enlisted in Company F of the 126th Pennsylvania.[27] None or almost none of the men in the company knew Mayne, but they liked and respected him enough to elect him sergeant. Mayne served with that rank until late August, 1862, when he mysteriously deserted and was never heard of again—not by the company, not by anyone in the Juniata Valley, where Mayne had enlisted, nor in Chambersburg, where much of the regiment had been raised. Months later, however, a Federal surgeon in the Western theatre was treating the wounded after a battle when one of the soldiers brought before him proved to be a woman. She told her story, and it was learned that her name was Frances Day. In August, 1862, she had enlisted in Company F of the 126th Pennsylvania under the name Frank Mayne to be with her lover, William Fitzpatrick, a private in that company. Her scheme had developed complications when she had been elected sergeant while Fitzpatrick remained a private. After the regiment left Camp Curtin, Fitzpatrick had fallen ill and was removed to a hospital in Alexandria, Virginia, where he died a few days later. When the news of Fitzpatrick's death reached the company on August 24, 1862, Frances, no longer with any reason or desire to stay, had deserted. She could not go home, for there would be too many questions and too much sadness. In despair, she had gone west, enlisted again under another name and served until wounded. She died of her wounds.[28]

Once past the horrors of the examining surgeon, the volunteers could settle down into their daily routine without the distraction of fear of rejection. They could settle down, but they could not relax, for the life of a soldier was not a comfortable one. Some of the volunteers were, at first, naively indignant over the discomforts they were expected to endure. They were patriots, they reasoned, and were entitled to be treated commensurate with the nobility of their motives. For the government, however, patriots were a penny a peck in 1861 and could be abused and cheaply spent without fear of running short.

One of the "abuses" to which the volunteers were subjected was exposure to some remarkably miserable weather in August and September. The unseasonable cold and continual rain contributed greatly to general poor health in camp. The suddenness with which the men made the change from their comfortable homes to the continuous exposure to the elements exploited even the slightest infirmity of constitution. The rapid change in diet and the sometimes questionable quality of rations also sent a good many men to the camp hospital. Dysentery and diarrhea were the most common afflictions, but typhoid, assorted fevers and respiratory ailments all claimed their share of victims. The situation was intensified by the circumstances under which the men lived within their tents. The cold and inadequate blankets forced those living in the small "A" or wedge tents to sleep huddled together "spoon fashion" to make use of one another's body heat. One sick man in a tent could infect every one of his bunkmates, or blanketmates in a single night.[29]

Camp Curtin was a depressing place for a soldier that autumn. Untrained and undisciplined as they were, the volunteers decided that they had not to put up with the dangers and discomforts of camp life. Quietly, they began to break guard and disappear. The desertions multiplied as the weather worsened and particularly hard hit was the 51st. On September 16, Captain George Pechin's company from Montgomery County arrived at Camp Curtin. Captain Pechin was told to have his men set up company streets in the lower end of the camp closest to the Susquehanna. It was common practice among the volunteers to move their campsites about within Camp Curtin for sanitary reasons, sometimes so the ground could be properly cleaned and aired with the tents removed, but also to take advantage of a sudden vacancy on ground that was considered a better spot on which to settle. If a company or an entire regiment struck tents to be shipped out, its campsite would become available. Such sites were often highly desirable, perhaps for their sunniness or shadiness or some other reason, and captains were quick to put in a claim for such spots as soon as they became vacant.

Conversely, certain places were horribly unsuited to serve as campsites. Those sites were almost exclusively located in the lower end of Camp Curtin, toward which Captain Pechin and his men had been directed. These lowlands were swamps during rainy periods, as all the water that fell on the broad western slope of the ridge that ran across the middle of the camp would drain toward the river and collect in puddles on the plain at the bottom of the slope. This area was always evacuated by companies as soon as campsites further up the slope or on the ridge were available. The low ground was therefore almost always the area vacant when new companies arrived. The veterans would stand by, much to the bewilderment of the rookies, and guffaw heartily as the new men took up residence. The first good rain relieved the greenhorns of their bewilderment and sent them searching for drier ground.

Captain Pechin and his 81 men learned the reason for the snickering just two days after their arrival. Rain fell so hard on the night of September 17 that men were driven out of their tents by freely rushing water. The storm continued well into the 18th and by the time it finally abated, a serious disaffection for soldiering had grown up within Pechin's company. As the men stood in the camp streets amid puddles and buffeting gusts of raw wind, they began to reassess their respective individual worths to the cause of the Union. They weighed wet trouser seats and muddied blankets against the need for their services by the government. Somehow the situation in which the country was embroiled seemed considerably less perilous when viewed from the quagmire that the lower end of Camp Curtin had become. At reveille on the 19th, just 54 of the original 81 men answered to their names at roll call.[30]

One of the 54 was a gray-eyed, black-haired, 5' 9½" cordwainer from Norristown named Thomas H. Parker. At 37, Private Parker was considerably older than most of the other privates in any company in the camp. He was considerably more experienced as well, having been twice married. His first wife had died in 1849, but just over a year later he had remarried. His new wife, Clara, had also lost a spouse. Her husband had been a captain in the Merchant Marine and had been lost at sea when his ship went down off Cape Hatteras two days after Christmas 1847. She had been married less than a year. Parker and his new wife had three children before the war came, two sons and a daughter, none of whom were yet in their teens. In September, 1861, the head of the house elected to leave the family and go off to war. Parker had been away from his home and family for less than a week when he and the rest of Pechin's company were washed out of their tents at Camp Curtin.[31]

Desertion was not as bad in the other companies, but it was still a serious problem. Recruits were always arriving in small groups, but, as Private Parker claimed, "if two were added in daytime, two would desert at night"[32] A terrible cycle was begun in that as more men deserted, companies and regiments would take much longer to fill to regulation size. The longer they took to fill, the longer the men who had already enlisted were made to remain exposed to bad weather and disease, which, in turn, put even more men out of the ranks and the regiment further from its required number of men.

In response to the epidemic, Colonel Welsh adopted a policy that was continued even after his departure. Squads were sent after deserters, and camp guards, who were often posted in double strength, were instructed to fire on men who refused to halt when ordered to do so. Several deserters were shot outside the camp. For the deserters, though, the danger of going over the hill did not end after the guards were eluded. One man, after being denied a furlough, successfully avoided the guards only to be killed while trying to board a moving train just east of Camp Curtin. When applying for furlough, he had said that he was needed at home by his wife and four children.[33]

One thing that could be said for the deserters was that they at least temporarily lightened the burden of the company officers they left behind. Captains and lieutenants, themselves just recently converted into soldiers, were finding that attending to the wants of 50 to 100 men was much more difficult than they had expected. Many of their charges literally had no concept of how the military worked. Sergeant Robert S. Westbrook of Company B of the 49th regiment, for example, noted in his diary that one Sunday as a portion of his regiment was walking from Camp Curtin into Harrisburg to attend church, the colonel of the 49th, William H. Irwin, was met on the road returning from the city. Apparently, the colonel did not wish his men entering the city for any reason unless it was done with his approval. Irwin, remembered Westbrook, ordered the men to turn around and return to camp and stay there until ordered to do otherwise. Sergeant Westbrook did as he was told and concluded in his diary that "the Colonel seems to be boss." By the next day, Sergeant Westbrook had become sure of the colonel's supremacy and reported that his chums were even coming to grasp the principle of subordination, "some of the boys," he wrote, "are commencing to think they cannot do as they would like to do...."[34]

The boys were, of course, correct, but there were times when, with some intelligence and organization, they could create circumstances that would eventually allow them to have things as they liked. At Camp Cameron, for example, Corporal Dornblazer and his comrades of the 7th Cavalry were unhappy with their rations. While the men in Camp Curtin were rumored to be receiving regular issues of fresh, soft bread, the 7th was given hardtack. The crackers were, "stale, worm-eaten, and hard as a brick...doubtless left over as a surplus from previous wars, and...now issued by the commissary department to break in new recruits....Artificial teeth were pronounced unreliable [for use on the hardtack], and some, we know, sent theirs home for safe-keeping."[35] The men of the 7th decided that "better rations could be furnished if the officers felt so disposed," and further decided to see what they could do to so dispose those officers. One night, at an agreed upon signal, "five hundred men, more or less, rushed from their tents, each loaded down with forty rounds of ammunition, and with a concert of action that was truly wonderful, they were seen in the starlight charging with furious impetuosity upon the headquarters of the Commissary Department, fairly burying the suspected officials beneath a stormy bombardment of hard-tack." The message was not lost upon the officers, and the wormy old crackers were exchanged for fresh ones. In addition, Dornblazer proudly crowed that "a two-pound loaf of soft white bread was issued to each man every five days during our stay at Camp Cameron."[36]

The difference in rations issued at Camp Curtin and Camp Cameron was not so pronounced as Dornblazer and his mates assumed. Though the food at Camp Curtin was generally fresh, it varied little, the rations were healthful only because they were often supplemented by donations of fruits and vegetables from townspeople.[37] Even then, the men became bored with the daily repetition of hardtack, white bread, beef, saltpork and beans. For example, some members of the 51st became particularly tired of the standard fare and decided to augment the menu. They had no money, so they could not buy anything from the camp sutler or from any of the local merchants who sometimes sold goods at booths just outside the front gate. They would have to resort to "strategy," which to a private usually meant stealing. The guards had standing orders from Colonel Welsh to arrest all soldiers even suspected of foraging on the surrounding farms. Neighbors of the camp, Mr. George Reel and Mr. John Loban in particular, had been victims of hungry soldiers more than once. The men of the 51st, however, were thinking not vegetable, but animal. They had noticed a cattle train with hogs aboard had been standing on the tracks just outside for most of the day. All the men agreed "that a piece of fresh pork would eat tolerably well" especially as it would be heavily seasoned with the excitement of breaking guard and then smuggling a dead hog in past the sentries.

After dark, a group of men from the 51st, one of whom might quite likely have been Tom Parker, quietly broke guard and made its way to the cars. The guards were posted thickly, and the movement took some time, but finally a nice fat hog—a beautiful animal of about 250 pounds—was selected and quickly dispatched. That done, only the most difficult part of the expedition remained: getting back into camp with 250 pounds of undressed pork.

Colonel Welsh, the thieves found, was doing his job well. Knowing that determined men could slip by the camp guard fairly easily, he had placed a second cordon of guards farther out to apprehend the deserters, foragers, and others who made it past the first guard. These roving pickets presented the greatest danger to guard breakers, and, as Private Parker thought when later retelling the story, gave "a party of a dozen men together...small chance for being successful in the pork business."

The twelve amateur butchers loaded up the slaughtered hog in a makeshift litter of blankets and fence rails, then started back to camp. They had not gotten very far when the shout of a picket somewhere in the black night challenged them to halt and identify themselves. Twelve hearts skipped a beat apiece, but the minds stayed clear and quickly recognized the need for more "strategy," which this time meant lying. It being too dark for the sentry to see anything too clearly, one of the men went forward and began to spin a yarn. He identified himself and his comrades as railroad hands. They had found a hurt soldier on the tracks, they explained, and had taken him to the nearby house of a local doctor, who said the man was in very dangerous condition and had to be taken to the camp hospital straight away, by the shortest possible route, for he would not survive if carried around to the front gate. The story was so ridiculous it worked like a charm. The sentry didn't wish to assume personal responsibility in the matter and passed the "railroad hands."

In making that narrow escape, the park toters had used up more than all the luck they had a right to expect, but upon nearing the camp proper, they were challenged again. It would have been easy then to panic, drop the hog and scatter, trusting to luck to get back without being arrested, but all twelve stuck to their posts and the same absurd story was doled out to the camp guard when he approached. None of the dozen had any right to hope that two dull-witted guards would halt them in one night, but, miraculously, the tale worked again! It was by then well after midnight. The tired and hungry men had started their sortie more than five hours before, and they had all been wondering if their pork dinner would be worth the trouble they had already gone through to get it. Just as they were leaving the second camp guard, the officer of the day, making his rounds, spotted them on the guard line and advanced to investigate. The game was up they thought, but they would go down with their colors flying. They repeated their story a third time, at least twice more than they had ever wished to, and, as expected, the officer was skeptical. He wished to lift the blankets from the soldier-sized burden they were carrying on the litter, but he was stopped by their assurance that the doctor had told them not to allow even the slightest draft of air to blow on the poor man. They would not be responsible, they claimed, if the officer insisted on violating the doctor's orders and in so doing caused the man's death. The wrangle continued until finally the officer too relented and passed the men—and their dinner—into the compound at one o'clock in the morning.[38]

*   *   *

On September 10, Governor Curtin traveled to Tenallytown in the District of Columbia to pay an official visit to the Pennsylvania Reserves encamped there. The reason for the visit was to deliver colors to the regiments. The Reserves had been so quickly called away from Camp Curtin and the other camps around the state that the governor had been unable to give them state or national flags. Regiments routinely carried both a national flag and a version of its home state's flag, and Curtin had ordered special flags made so each regiment of the Reserves could be given one. The colors were paid for with funds given to the commonwealth by the Pennsylvania members of the Society of the Cincinnati, an organization comprised entirely of descendents of officers of the Continental Army of the Revolution. By September the flags were ready and Curtin and an official party set off to present them to the troops.

The Reserves were drawn up on the parade ground at nine a.m. A cooling breeze moved steadily across the plain where they stood in array, keeping them, in the dark woolen uniforms, from suffering under the bright September sun. Thousands of them stood at attention on the green grass, and thousands of belt buckles, and rifle barrels glinted fiercely beneath the blue sky. President Lincoln had ridden out from Washington for the occasion and had arrived first, in company with Secretary of War Cameron. Soon after came Major General George Brinton McClellan, his staff, a few other generals, and his escort, which amounted to a full troop of cavalry. The scene was one of stillness. The only sounds were those of the moving horses: the thumping of powerful hooves striking the soft earth, the barely audible rattle of tack and accoutrements, the heavy, rhythmic breathing and the occasional snort, and the crackling and moaning of saddle leather pressed between man and horse. Black horses and white, browns and chestnuts, with blazes and stockings and sleek, curried coats sheening in the sun, tossed their muscled necks and pranced beneath important men in gold braid and snowy gauntlets.

McClellan was, by far, the most splendid figure on the field that day. He was, like the men in the ranks, a Pennsylvanian, the son of a respected Philadelphia physician. Just 35 years old and already a major general, McClellan was commander of the army in the field. General Winfield Scott, in Washington, was his only military superior. But before the Reserves that day, it seemed impossible that anything in blue could be better than he was. His uniform was the neatest, his brass the most lustrous, his gloves the snowiest, and his horse the most magnificent. He was a small man with neatly trimmed hair and mustaches, but had power in his arms and chest and handled his huge mount as complete master. He was the ideal of a general.

Curtin and his party did not arrive for another half hour, but were announced by the boom of an artillery salute. The gleaming carriage rolled up to where the president sat, and all exchanged greetings in the fresh air and warm sunshine. Curtin wasted little time before proceeding directly to distribute the colors. Each banner was personally handed by the governor to the colonel of its respective regiment. The flags were something of a hybrid of the national and Pennsylvania flags. Each had 13 stripes of red and white and a field of dark blue in the upper corner and yellow fringe around the edges. In the center of the blue field, however, appeared the commonwealth coat of arms amid a shower of 34 stars. Each flag bore the name of the regiment to which it was given.

The distribution took some time, but finally Curtin returned to his carriage. He climbed upon the seat that he might better see and be seen by the assembled Pennsylvanians, and he spoke to them. Flags of red, white, and blue hung on hand-held staffs, slips of air rolling through their draped folds and silken stars and stripes carressing the stubbled, sunburned cheeks of color sergeants. The governor's prepared speech was a long one, and the size of the army before him made it impossible for all to hear him, but every soldier probably knew the essence of what he was saying. The breeze carried only isolated words and phrases like "Constitution," "Liberty, Civilization and Christianity" and "sacred fabric of the Government." He was telling them to return with their honor or not at all, and they thrilled to his words. They watched him and listened to his renowned oratory, and they thought they could not do other than what he asked. Curtin closed with a blessing. "May the God of battles in his wisdom protect your lives," he said, "and may Right, Truth, and Justice prevail."[39]

As they stood arrayed in all their splendor, the men of the Pennsylvania Reserves were quite satisfied.[40] They were seeing themselves for the first time in the way they had dreamed about when they enlisted—in immaculate blue uniforms with shining brass surrounded by sparkling, rattling sabres and burnished muskets, officers in magnificent uniforms mounted on magnificent steeds, and large, stainless banners floating above it all. This was war as they knew it, as they had come to recognize it from the stories of their youth and the newspaper illustrations of the present. The glory of war was there on the plain at Tenallytown; it was all about them, in the air, the flags, the prancing horses and in the men themselves, as they stood together straight-backed and square-shouldered. It was more than just all in and about them—it was they themselves.[41]

*   *   *

As the season progressed at Camp Curtin, the weather stayed bad. On the morning of October 3, the cold and stiff volunteers emerged from their flimsy homes to find the first frost of the year lacing the windows of headquarters and lying in a thick, icy velvet on their canvas tents. The nights would henceforth be marked by an inescapable, joint- and muscle-clenching chill creeping up from the earth and into the tents full of sleeping men. Those who had not already done so found board lumber and hastily put a rough, insulating floor in their tents in an effort to keep the cold at bay. While most of the volunteers harbored hope that the sun would return and warm the ground on which they slept, the sun shone only on the tops of the dense clouds that hung low over the hills. The soft, cool summer breezes that the river had given them turned to damp, slashing gusts, and the river itself remained gray and flowed grimly southward. Harrisburg would have no Indian Summer that year. The warmth was gone, and the sun, for the next six months, would rarely be able to out-muscle the cleaving winds that sheared in from the river through the camp tents.

Though the trees around the camp and on the mountains visible upriver stayed generally green until about the middle of October, signs of an early winter were everywhere. The early chill had caught many unprepared and men bustled about the streets with pieces of stovepipe under their arms. Apples, chestnuts and grapes made their appearance in the market, and there was a run on the coal yards.[42] Soldiers on guard at camp and at the arsenal seemed more alert and moved their rounds more briskly, more in an effort to keep warm than to please their captains. Some of the guards, less concerned with presenting a dignified or martial appearance, even hopped in place or waved their arms about, slapping them across their chests. Other men would go to any lengths to get warm. One guard at the arsenal, evidently half-frozen, was seen whirling his musket around, thrusting and lunging with his bayonet, apparently at imaginary Confederates.[43]

Despite the cold, some companies had not yet even been issued blankets. When the blankets were finally distributed, the men found, to their horror, that the things were infested with lice. The volunteers were outraged that they were being forced to choose between the cold and the lice. Most of them opted for the cold and angrily pitched the blankets into a bonfire. Had the cold volunteers known that the "grey backs" would be their near-constant companions for the duration of the war, they might have been a bit less hasty in burning the blankets. If they were to get lousy sooner or later anyway, which they were, they might as well get it sooner if it would help them get warm. As it turned out, a few of the men unwittingly accepted a few of the "guests" and before long, most of their company and regiment were "enjoying a good scratch." Private Parker of the 51st could later laugh about the problem, but, at the time, the men were all mortified. "The vermin increased with great rapidity, and each soldier looked with strong suspicion on his neighbor as being infested...yet with much pertinacity denying the existence of the insect on their persons; still they were there, which many a sly twitch of the arms or body silently indicated." It was humiliating to be the victim of another's uncleanliness, and the men would secretly try to rid themselves of the little creatures by slinking off to a deserted shed or to the surrounding fields or bushes to strip themselves and hunt through their clothing with their clumsily-tweezing fingers.[44]

The scarity of blankets was a real problem. The Quartermaster General of Pennsylvania, Reuben C. Hale, who was responsible for procuring all of the necessary equipment for the men, was caught off guard by the early arrival of autumn. He found himself in just the same position he had been in the previous spring: short of blankets. Throughout the summer, contracts had been given out to blanket manufacturers, but apparently the contractors had not been pushed to produce and the result was that few of them delivered their quotas on time.[45] At least 50 woolen mills operated in Pennsylvania, and presumably each had been running all summer, yet somehow the quartermaster did not get all that he needed.[46] Who was at fault made little difference to the volunteers, and they began to grouse and complain to anyone who would listen.

To his credit, Hale responded quickly in an unconventional but effective way. He immediately issued public appeals for donations of blankets. The coverlets were not initially to be accepted as gifts, but would be purchased or more often as it turned out, borrowed, until the army blankets contracted for came in.[47] These appeals were read in churches and printed in papers all over the commonwealth. One army man wrote for the Harrisburg *Patriot and Union* that "No one who has not made the experiment of passing a night on the ground with insufficient protection can have any true idea of the miserable discomfort, the depression of spirits, and the wretched physical disability produced by such exposure. The sufferer arises in the morning weak, unrefreshed and ill-conditioned. He is scarcely half a man; and, moreover, the pnuemonies, the pleurisies, the diarrhoeas, the rheumatisms, with all the host of other pestilences that walk in darkness often attack the ably covered soldier and strike him from the ranks. And we well know that *badly clad* soldiers are chiefly the victims of these disorders."[48]

All this was more than enough to inspire the compassion of the women of Pennsylvania, and, once again, they responded promptly and thoroughly. Blankets were donated by the thousands from all over the commonwealth and shipped to Harrisburg for distribution. The donors sent not just blankets and quilts, but all kinds of comforts and necessities poured in. Shirts, underwear, woolen socks, cushions for hurt or wounded limbs, "neck comforts," slippers, handkerchiefs, linen towels, feather pillows (with linen cases), sheets, crackers, "imperial black tea," sugar, books, magazines, jellies, jams, wines and dried fruits were all received by Quartermaster General Hale in Harrisburg and meted out to the needy men in the camps.[49] The women of Washington County were particularly generous, donating well over 1,000 pairs of socks to the state.[50] The editor of the *Patriot and Union* did his best to encourage donations. "Families," he wrote, "should now employ their leisure evenings in knitting stockings for the soldiers for the coming winter. The evenings are getting cool, and young ladies should invite their young gentlemen friends (those who have not gone off to war) into the parlor, where they can occupy themselves with winding yarn, etc. They can do all their talking, even if they are working. Beside all this, they should remember what a good and generous act they are doing, by which many a gallant heart will be comforted."[51]

Most of the donors of blankets or quilts neither expected nor wished for the items to be returned to them, especially after they learned that there hardly existed on the continent an enlisted soldier who was not home to a fair number of grayback lice. Even in that age before daily showers, people were squeamish about the body pests, and though the creatures could have been evicted from the blankets easily enough in a kettle of boiling water, most of the ladies who could do without their donations did not ask for them to be returned.

*   *   *

Though always rather tedious, life in camp took on a new monotony in the colder weather. During the summer, outdoor activities were the most popular pastimes. Foot races and arm wrestling matches were commonplace, while cartwheels, somersaults, and other gymnastical feats occupied the more nimble. Just about everyone enjoyed watching or playing a new game called "corners" or "base ball." Ball games were regularly played on the parade ground, and even the officers would let down their facade of detachment and join in. Colonel Hartranft of the 51st particularly enjoyed the games and was reportedly a talented hitter. With the advent of cold weather, however, checkers and card games by a fire generally took the place of races and base ball.

For the men of the 51st, however, the inside of a tent simply did not allow them enough room to have the kind of grand entertainment they craved. The men went back outside into the cold to play a roughhouse game that entailed tossing a man—usually a hapless stranger—into the air from a blanket. Not only did the men of the 51st enjoy participating, but large crowds of soldiers from other companies and regiments gathered to watch and, according to one observer, made this the most popular spectator sport in Camp Curtin that autumn.

After finding a good strong woolen blanket, as many men as could would grab ahold of the cloth around its edges and hold it at about waist level. The victim, not usually a member of the 51st, would be thrown upon the firmly grasped blanket and each of the holders would then pull sharply toward himself to tighten the blanket, give slack and then pull again, popping the poor man on the blanket a foot or two in the air. Over and over the operation would be repeated, the off-balance and wildly-flailing man being thrown increasingly higher. As the huge crowd laughed and cheered with the victim's every trip into the sky, the blanket holders took energy from the crowd and, as Private Parker saw it, "the boys would lend all their efforts and strength to send him up as high as they possibly could, to the height of fifteen or twenty feet; catching him again in his descent only to send him up still higher the next time, if possible, until his piteous appeals would obtain his final release from his persecutors, who would then secure another victim for the blanket."[52]

Such games and entertainments made up a large and important part of camp-life. The many long, idle hours the men spent each day did no good for a man's sanity; they needed to blow off some steam. "Having been brought up to work every day," wrote one soldier of the 45th, "I wondered how Uncle Sam could afford to feed and clothe all this crowd and not keep them busy." But after a few years of campaining and hard service with a dozen or so pitched battles thrown in, the same man "wondered that soldiers could stand so much and live."[53]

Between those idle hours, though, were long hours of industrious activity with not an idle soldier to be found. For a few hours in the morning and several more in the afternoon, every man who was not on duty someplace else was on the parade ground or in one of the open fields outside of the camp being drilled and drilled and drilled.[54] Movements by squad, company, and battalion were executed again and again and even regimental drill was practiced. The fields were alive with the shouted commands of officers, the sharply-called "left-right" cadences of sergeants, and public dressings-down of "lunkhead" privates who just could not get their facings right. Captains and majors and colonels stood bundled against the cold and squinted through the swirling, blowing dust kicked-up by thousands of shuffling feet. In the summer, the sun, sweat, and the choking, clinging dust tormented the men drilling in the ranks; in the winter, it was mud, cold, wet feet and sharp winds.[55] Whatever the season, the hours spent on the parade at Camp Curtin and in the fields nearby were, quite simply, an investment for these men and officers—an investment in their future, collective and individual. The thorough knowledge of necessary movements, the automatic, unquestioning and immediate obeyance of orders, and the unity and comradeship that grows out of shared hardships were all learned on the drilling field and all combined to save lives on the battlefield. In dozens of places they had not yet even heard of, the men in Camp Curtin and in the scores of other Camps of Instruction throughout the North would survive because of the exertions of their officers and drill sergeants on the drilling plain. In this sense, one man in Camp Curtin prepared more men for war and perhaps saved more of their lives than any officer in Pennsylvania, perhaps in all the North. His name was William A. Tarbutton, and he was camp drillmaster.

A Harrisburg resident, Tarbutton was of middle age in 1861—about the same age as the fathers of most of the 19 and 20 year olds that came into camp. He was not a professional soldier. He was not, as were so many other drillmasters, a West Pointer or a veteran of long service. He did not, in fact, at all fit the popular conception of an iron-willed "D.I." He was a devotee not of Mars, but of Terpsichore. Tarbutton had served for a number of years as the choirmaster at a Methodist church in Harrisburg and was reputedly a fine arranger of hymns and other choral pieces. One of his works, "Beyond the Smiling and the Weeping," was regularly included in Methodist hymnals of the period.[56] When the war came, he was given the rank of captain and the task of teaching farm boys, mechanics, students, lumbermen, raftsmen, railroaders, lawyers, grocery clerks and scores of others to march together as soldiers.

Once on the drilling plain, Captain Tarbutton went about coaxing the best out of the boys in the same manner he had his singers in the choir loft—gentle persuasion. He had, in fact, one of his singers with him. William Wesley Jennings, also a

Harrisburg native, was serving concurrently as the post adjutant and assistant drillmaster.[57] Tarbutton saw the futility in demanding that his charges act like soldiers right away. He was not a proponent of laxity, but neither was he a martinet. He was what one volunteer described as "a good disciplinarian, kind to all, yet resolute and exacting in his commands."[58]

A few hours on the parade ground could be a taxing experience for young men who were not accustomed to concentrating on any one thing for very long. Many of the farmboys, for example, did not know their left from their right, which made comprehension of Tarbutton's orders next to impossible. The farmers did know some things, though, and Tarbutton simply adjusted his methods to relate to their experience. All the farmers could tell hay from straw, for instance, so Tarbutton had the sergeants tie a bit of hay to a farmer's one leg and bit of straw to the other leg, and then drill him individually or in small groups of similarly perplexed men. These "awkward squads" would be marched about by a sergeant who called out the cadence, "Hay foot,...hay foot,...hay foot, straw foot, hay foot," instead of the customary "left,...left,...left, right, left."[59]

Tarbutton would lighten the burden for the men with good humor and an attention to civility.[60] It was not uncommon, for example, for the captain to reprove a private by gently mocking him. In the cool weather that fall of 1861, the men would often find the parade an uncomfortably breezy spot and would, while drilling, seek some relief from the cold by doing the sensible civilian thing of sticking their hands in their pockets. Tarbutton frowned on this as unsoldierly and politely asked the men to refrain from doing it. A few, however, would either not quite understand the captain's meaning or would find it impossible to comply. An amused Private Parker of the 51st would often be in the ranks while under the instruction of Tarbutton. Out of the corner of his eye, Parker would watch the captain walk slowly around the idle formations, carefully inspecting the men and their postures and such. When he happened upon a man with pocketed hands, Tarbutton would stand before him and look fixedly at him in silence until the man felt the weight of the gaze and removed his hands. Occasionally, the poor soldier would fail to take the captain's hint and leave his hands thrust deep into his pockets. Tarbutton, still mannerly and in control, would simply step up closer to the man and "in his kind, but gruff way, would ask...'what are you nursing?'" In response to which the flush-cheeked soldier would timidly return his bare hands to the cold and the wind without.[61]

Tarbutton's job was not to teach all the soldiers in camp how to march, his task was to teach the officers—commissioned and non-commissioned—so they in turn could teach their men. He spent most of his time teaching sergeants, lieutenants and captains in the basics of squad and company drill. These officers were as ignorant of the details of movements on the drill plain as were the privates and could seriously embarrass themselves if they tried to drill the men without knowing what orders to give. One private, for example, remembered that his colonel, who apparently did not pay as much attention to the drill manual as he should have, tried to put the men through their paces one day. The privates, who had been repeatedly drilled, were much more familiar with company and regimental movements and were laughing to themselves at the ineptitude of their commander. "The colonel", wrote the private in a letter to his mother, "took us out to the field, marching in four ranks, our company in front. He got us into the field by filing us, to the right + 'obliquing our company quietly to the right....' After this we moved forward in a straight line for some time till we came to some tomatoe [sic] vines (which the Col. took for cabbage plants) + not wanting to injure them, [he] gave the order 'Head of column to the left' (File left, it should have been) in a loud + confident tone.... Knowing what he meant, we filed left...." About half of the company had headed off to the left when the colonel decided that he did not wish the regiment to go that way after all and wanted the men who had already changed direction to straighten out the line as if they'd never turned. The problem was that the colonel did not know what order to give to straighten out the crook in the line, and no junior officer was about to help him. "Under these trying circumstances," wrote the gloating private, "he displayed military genius which may one day raise him to the command of a Brigade. He gave the order 'As you were, men...' so we went scuffling back into line as best we could, + our Colonel, having surmounted this difficulty, was once more satisfied and happy. This ended his care + trouble for the afternoon. During the remainder of it he might have been seen at a great distance from his 'command' as he calls it, sitting on his horse, whose tail was turned towards us, talking to some friend he had met, near the fence + there he remained till we were ready to return, not having seen, I verily believe, our single military movement during the whole time we were out."[62]

Other officers were more conscientious in learning how to move their men. First Lieutenant Lafayette Lord of Company F of the 45th regiment remembered being daily drilled by Tarbutton, and then just as regularly drilling the men of F Company himself.[63] Tarbutton would customarily take all willing officers—commissioned and noncommissioned—to a secluded field outside of camp, and there, away from the eyes of their men, they would learn how to move masses of men. In their private lessons, the officers would learn how to face, how to change fronts, and wheel, and dress lines. They became privates for a few hours every day and would then return to resume their mantle of authority and respectability and instruct their men in what they themselves had just learned. Later, the lessons would become more advanced, and Tarbutton would lecture on regimental movements using blocks of wood to illustrate his lessons.[64]

Despite all the hard work and the often unpleasant climatic conditions, many of the captain's pupils enjoyed the exercises. Whether working with the officers or the enlisted men, however, Tarbutton made it clear that the lessons were not for entertainment. He always acted with generosity and restraint, and his instruction usually left all with a sense of advancement and attainment. "The drills were regular and complete," remembered Chaplain William H. Locke of the 11th regiment, "discipline was the happy medium between the liberty of the citizen and the strict military rule of active service, preparing each man to gradually forget the one and submit to the other."[65] Tarbutton's method did not go unappreciated; it made him friends in every company that passed through camp, and he would be fondly remembered for long afterward. In 1863, Tom Parker, by then a sergeant, was serving with the 51st in Mississippi. The men were plodding wearily along through the heat and dust when they passed some Pennsylvania regiments sitting by the roadside resting for a few moments. A few of the resting men struck up a conversation with the passersby in the usual way. "What regiment, boys?" The response "51st Pennsylvania" drew murmurs of recognition of a "Camp Curtin regiment." Almost at once, "the question was asked simultaneously by a dozen voices of the other regiments, 'Boys, don't you wish old Tarbutton had you to-day drilling you?' " and all laughed and remembered the simpler, easier days on the Susquehanna with the gentle captain.[66]

What idle time was left to the men after they finished drilling and playing and eating was spent by many in prayer. Each man's relationship with his maker was of premium importance, for no one wished to go into battle with black marks against him in the Great Ledger. The soldiers-to-be devoted much time to strengthening ties with He Who Disposes. Many of the men were devout, and it was not unusual for prayers to be said or passages from scripture to be publicly read in the barracks or the large, 12-man Sibley tents each evening before lights out. Both Protestant and Catholic services were held each Sunday, often more frequently, and a general prayer meeting was usually held at headquarters every evening.[67] In addition to these meetings, smaller, informal "social" meetings were often held in different parts of the camp frequently. One area clergyman thought there was probably "more religious interest in Camp Curtin...than in any other community within 50 miles."[68]

But Camp Curtin was a difficult place to concentrate on anything, especially religion. The place was full of temptation, and not a few fell from grace. One man thought it "sad to witness the decline of the religious fervor of some who, before coming to the army, had been men of fine christian character at home."[69] Many were surprised to learn that Sundays, except for the services, were not very much different from other days of the week. One poor soldier was shocked when he learned that the Lord's Day was not "the serene, calm Sabbath which I have been accustomed to at home." He thought himself fallen among the Godless and wrote in his diary a simple appeal, "God help me to preserve my religious integrity in the military camp, as well as in my quiet and peaceful home."[70]

Morality was an important issue to many of the men, and they would often attend lectures on moral topics, sometimes in camp, sometimes in the city. Temperance was a popular topic.[71] In late October, the Reverend Dr. George Junkin of Virginia preached in one of the city's Presbyterian churches. Dr. Junkin had lived in Pennsylvania for a number of years and had helped found Lafayette College in Easton. More recently, however, he had been president of Washington College in Lexington, Virginia. His remarks were thoroughly enjoyed by all his audiences in Harrisburg, but his celebrity would soon pale in the eyes of the Pennsylvanians as they, and the rest of the North, and the South for that matter—would be dazzled by the terrible brilliance of his son-in-law—Stonewall Jackson.[72]

Another class of men lived in camp, however, whose only interest in morality was in tempting gullible young men away from it. These men were temptation itself as they drank and gambled and visited brothels at every opportunity. Young men from good homes and pure backgrounds suddenly found themselves sharing tents with drinkers and gamers, and more than a few succumbed to temptation and adopted these pastimes themselves.

*　　*　　*

By mid-October, most of the regiments that had been lying in camp while trying to fill their ranks had succeeded well enough for their colonels to begin thinking about leaving. The last recruits were mustered into U.S. service, elections were held in the companies, if they had not already been, to elect corporals, sergeants, lieutenants and captains. If a colonel and other field and staff officers of the regiment had not yet been selected, the company officers then voted to fill those positions.

On October 10, Colonel Welsh asked to be relieved from command of the camp so he could attend to getting his regiment ready for the field. Welsh had not been a popular commandant with the men. Discipline was too tight in the camp, as far as they were concerned, and the guards were too thick outside it. But if the colonel's all-business attitude had not sat well with the men, the officers had found it much to their liking. The knowledge that Welsh was a disciplinarian and that he would support them in their efforts to improve discipline emboldened company officers to deal more quickly and sharply with transgressors. A number of company officers were so sorry to see Welsh go that they passed a resolution of thanks and regret, stating that his resignation was "a great loss to the camp as his incumbency of the post has been a benefit."[73] And the editor of the *Patriot and Union* remarked upon the cleanliness of the camp, the orderliness of the Quartermaster Department and the great improvement in the health of the men under Welsh. "Colonel Welsh is truly worthy of the high encomiums bestowed upon him...and his removal to the field of service will be a severe loss."[74]

The men of the ranks were less concerned with what was going on with the command situation than they were with getting out of camp. They had had their fill of Camp Curtin and were anxiously looking forward to a change of scenery. Moreover, they were grateful to at last be getting into the war. Since the regiments had to await orders from Washington and could do nothing until the orders came, no one knew just when they were to leave. The suspense was agonizing to endure, and every private became obsessed with learning when the regiment would leave, where it was bound, and to which army it would be assigned. Such information came directly from the War Department and no one would know until it came over the telegraph and was given to the governor, the commandant and the specific colonel concerned. It was in Camp Curtin that the men of the ranks developed a soldierly skill that was to see no less exercise than loading, firing or forming on the colors: the passing of rumor.

Somehow, the men of the 51st found out, or guessed, when they would be leaving camp.[75] They knew not where they would be going, but they realized that it might, perhaps, be some place far away, and they were fairly certain not to have a friendly city full of saloons and brothels within a half hour's walk. They decided, therefore, to give Harrisburg a farewell performance. The night before they were to depart, about half the regiment broke guard and streamed south through the fields into the city. Once the men were discovered missing, Colonel Hartranft naturally became concerned and sent details after them. One half of the regiment was in detail to retrieve the other half that was absent without leave (A.W.O.L.). The episode ended some hours later rather unexpectedly. Most of the detailed soldiers had found their A.W.O.L. friends and had been unable to muster the rudeness to decline having just one drink. Before long, the drinks were being thrown down in quick succession and most of the detailed men—who were probably the less-experienced drinkers for want of the inclination lest they had gone A.W.O.L. with the first batch—were drunk, even more drunk than the men they had been sent after. The original soldiers then turned chaperone and escorted their sloshed comrades of the detail back to the camp.[76]

Before a regiment could leave it had to be uniformed. The men would often receive their suits of blue well before they were to ship out, but delays sometimes resulted in the men not getting their clothes until just days before they were to leave. In any case, few events proved as comical as the company trip to the Quartermaster Department to be uniformed. Each man was outfitted with a dark blue overcoat, and dresscoat, sky blue pants, a cap, two shirts, two pair of drawers, two pair of socks, a pair of shoes, and, as the men liked to joke, "rebel bullets and shells thrown in."[77] But the sizes of the coats, pants, shirts, and shoes often had little relationship to the size of the man to which they were issued. The men filed by in alphabetical order and requested particular sizes of clothing and shoes, but none of them had a guarantee that he would be given what he asked for. More often than not, the clerks simply "Took the muster roll of the companies, and, as each name was called, the bill was charged against the soldier, and the whole outfit was most unceremoniously flung at the astonished man."[78] Few of the uniforms fit. "A cap would fall to a diminutive recruit which would cover his head below the ears or shoes that were too large or too small; pantaloons that were too long or too short, and coats too wide or too narrow." After leaving the quartermaster, two hours or so of utter chaos would commence as hundreds or even thousands of men began running about attempting to find a man with whom they could switch uniforms. It was madness, but "there was no end of the merriment occasioned by the highly ridiculous (?) occurrence of that hour or two when men were uniformed."[79]

In one company, Private Andrew G. White found himself in the unenviable position of being last in line when issues were made, "White" being the last entry on the alphabetical muster roll. "It was 'Hobson's choice' as there was just one suit left." White recalled that "when the coat was tried on, the arms stood out horizontal, the pants came to a little below the knees, the cap covered the ears, whilst the shoes would not go on at all.... I presented myself to the captain, asking if this was the way that Uncle Sam fitted a fellow out to fight for his country." After a good laugh, the captain gave White a special requisition on the quartermaster, and he was able to exchange his clownish duds for "the best fitting suit of any in the company."[80]

The way the men saw the uniform situation was summed up in an anecdote that has the polished sound of having been repeated many times.

"There was another poor fellow, a very small man, who had received a very large pair of shoes, and had not yet been able to effect any exchange. One day the sergeant was drilling the company on the facings—Right face! Left face! Right and about face!—and of course watched his men's feet closely, to see that they went through the movements promptly. Observing one pair of feet down the line that never budged at the command, the sergeant, with drawn sword, rushed up the possessor of them, and, in menacing tones, demanded—

'What do you mean by not facing about when I tell you? I'll have you put in the guard-house, if you don't mind.'

'Why—I—did, sergeant,' said the trembling recruit.

'You did not, sir. Didn't I watch your feet? They never moved an inch.'

'Why you see,' said the man, 'my shoes are so big that they don't turn when I do. I go through the motions on the inside of them!' "[81]

THE PENNSYLVANIA ARSENAL on Capitol Hill in Harrisburg.
Much of Pennsylvania's punch came from within this building. Troops from all over Pennsylvania, and from other states as well, were armed here as they passed through Harrisburg.
(Dauphin County Historical Society)

Usually on the day before a regiment was to ship out, the men would turn in their camp equipage at the Quartermaster's Department and be marched down to the arsenal to receive their arms. A number of different types of weapons were used by the Union army, everything from very old, very heavy, modified muskets to modern marvels like breech-loading carbines with magazines, and the weapons issued to companies or regiments often varied greatly. Although most companies in a regiment received the same type of weapon, this was not always the case. Weapons were issued as they became available and that availability did not always coincide with the readiness of regiments. On more than one occasion, not enough weapons—rifles, bayonets, or sidearms—were on hand in the arsenal on Capitol Hill to arm newly organized regiments. Since the "Pennsylvania Reserve bill" of May 15, 1861 forbade any regiment from leaving the commonwealth before being armed, some regiments were forced to wait in Camp Curtin, sometimes for a week or more, before they could receive weapons and leave for war.

Once the men were given their guns, they were fully-equipped fighting men, and some of them were a bit surprised at their appearance. A member of the 45th was stunned when he realized what he was expected to carry off to war. "We got our military trappings as follows: Clothing—overcoat, blouse (short coat), trousers, cap, flannel shirt, two pairs cotton drawers, two pairs of socks, shoes and blanket; Camp equipage—knapsack, haversack, canteen, pint tin cup, tin plate, knife, fork and spoon. Arms and accoutrements—gun (Harper's Ferry musket), cartridge box, belt and plate." The whole would weigh nearly 50 pounds, and the men wondered if "[we] weren't so much soldiers as pack mules."[82]

Almost the last act each regiment performed in Harrisburg was to accept from the commonwealth the regimental colors. Two or three regiments that were due to depart soon would be drawn up on the parade ground in the camp, or often on the grounds behind or just east of the capitol, and the governor would usually personally deliver the flags to the regiments. The banners were symbols of the honor of the commonwealth, and Curtin entrusted that honor to each regiment, exhorting the men not to allow it to be tainted by cowardice or shame and to defend it with all their power. It was their home, their families, it was they themselves.[83]

After receiving their colors, the regiments would be marched to the railroad depot or to a siding that had been built by the tracks just outside of the camp. The troops would be loaded into boxcars and told to make themselves comfortable for the long ride. But the cars were altogether comfortless places. In the summer, the sun beat down and made them simply rolling ovens, and in the winter the freezing winds whistled through cracks and open doors to numb faces and fingers. Sometimes, a few rough planks had been nailed into the cars crosswise, providing some seating, but usually the men were crammed together so tightly that most of them had to stand the entire trip. If the men were fortunate enough to have room to sit, they would often find no seats in the boxcars, and would have to sit "turkish style" with folded legs on the floor of the car, with, perhaps other men sitting on top of them. Others would sit at the wide doors on the sides of the car and could dangle their legs off the edge of the floor, but these men would have to endure exposure to the relentless whipping of the wind, a nearly impossible task in the winter. Worst of all, the same cars that were used to transport the men were interchangeably used to transport livestock, and they were often filled with filth when the men came to use them.[84]

Above all, traveling by train was dangerous. In the Northern states in September, 1861, alone, 57 persons were killed and 224 were injured in railroad accidents.[85] At that rate the annual casualty rate of rail travel would be nearly 700 dead and almost 2,700 hurt. Soldiers and would-be soldiers were the most common victims, and accidents resulting in their death and maiming were so common that they received but passing notice in the newspapers. To the soldiers themselves, however, rail travel was still a novelty, and a wreck or the injury of a fellow soldier was newsworthy enough to be written home about.

COLONEL SULLIVAN A. MEREDITH
56th Pennsylvania Volunteers.
Assuming command after Welsh's departure, Meredith served as commandant for only a short time in the late autumn of 1861. He was severely wounded at Second Manassas and later made brigadier general.
(Library of Congress)

Late in September, the 49th regiment was involved in an accident on the Northern Central Railroad between Harrisburg and Baltimore, but most of the men on the train felt there was nothing accidental about it. Corporal John Woods of Company G wrote to his mother and explained the anger of the men. "When we were to leave Harrisburg," Woods began, "our train was to [sic] long for the locomotive and so they divided the train in two. The most of us were in the front train and our company was near the middle but the car was so crowded that some of the boys scattered off in other cars; there were some went to the back car, and two went out on the platform." The two were John Fulton and Daniel Parker, relative newcomers to the regiment, having been recruited to fill the ranks of Company G. Privates Fulton and Parker were friends; they had been mustered in together and had been in the army for 17 days.[86] The two "had their legs hanging down over the platform," Woods wrote. "Some of our fellows told them to come into the car that they would be hurt if they staid [sic] there, but they would not listen." The engineers of the two trains had apparently had cross words in Harrisburg, and the engineer of the lead train, Woods's, was evidently proceeding too slowly for the liking of the hindward engineer, who continually ran his train up close and blew long blasts from his whistle. At a stop in York, the feud reportedly continued and the engineer of the second train was heard to cuss that he would make the other "pull cotton out of his ears before he reaches Baltimore."

About five miles outside of Baltimore, the engineer made good this threat and rammed his engine into the caboose of the lead train. "He ran against us twice," remembered Corporal Woods, "the first time we hardly felt it where I was. The second time...five or six of our fellows in the car...were thrown out of the door and windows and the others knocked around through the car. The car was nearly broken to pieces." And, unfortunately, Privates Fulton and Parker were fatally injured. They "were sitting out on the platform sleeping and the locomotive ran against it and they fell down on the track," wrote Woods, "Their legs were cut off and their bodies awfully bruised." The engineer of the second train leapt from his vehicle and disappeared into the nearby woods. Daniel Parker did not live to see Baltimore, and his friend, John Fulton, lived only four days.[87]

*   *   *

After Welsh's departure with the 45th in mid-October, a new commandant was named at camp. Colonel Sullivan Amory Meredith of Philadelphia was the brother of William Meredith, a Philadelphia lawyer of repute and, coincidently, adjutant general of Pennsylvania.[88] Born on the Fourth of July, 1816, Sullivan Meredith had been a businessman in his hometown when the war came and had no military experience in the first 45 years of his life. But, perhaps through the influence of his brother, he had been given command of the 10th Pennsylvania, a three-month regiment.[89] After that unit was discharged, Meredith returned to the camp with the beginnings of a new regiment. He was there in October, 1862, trying to fill out the ranks of what would soon be numbered the 56th Pennsylvania.

He had inherited a difficult job from Welsh. Not only was Welsh's discipline and efficiency a tough act to follow, especially for an officer as inexperienced as Meredith, but the steadily lowering temperature posed a new and serious problem. The arriving volunteers were not physically or mentally prepared to make the transition from a warm bed and life spent generally indoors, to the coarse life of sleeping on hard boards in the cold tents, and they had not the toughened constitution needed to sleep night after night under canvas. Blankets were still in short supply, and donated goods were being relied upon more and more. Just as Meredith inherited the blanket shortage from Welsh, so did he reap the harvest of that shortage: widespread illness.

Every man suffered the cold and damp, the heat and dust, and few were accustomed to or prepared for the rigorous outdoor life of Camp Curtin. Even fewer were capable of enduring the close contact with thousands of other germ- and disease-carrying men. The boys from the rural regions, especially the sparsely populated mountain and forest counties upriver, were particularly vulnerable to illness, much more so than the city boys from Philadelphia or Pittsburgh, whose bodies and immune systems had been toughened against diseases through continual contact. Often, insignificant "childhood diseases," like colds, flus, and especially measles, took heavy tolls in the companies from the backwoods. As much as the men suffered physically from the measles, they were even more embarrassed by their illness. "To go a soldiering in defense of one's country," wrote one, "and be ambushed by a disease that at home was regarded as a trifling affliction of childhood, was a source of real humiliation."[90]

The influenza and dysentery common to any camp, especially a training camp, where the suddenness of the change of diet and lifestyle was most pronounced, were not themselves matters for serious concern for the surgeons, but these minor diseases weakened bodies and laid them more vulnerable to more serious diseases, like typhoid, consumption and small pox.[91] Eight men died in the camp hospital in November, but by early December the general health had stabilized. About 140 remained on the sick list at the hospital, but considering that 5,000 men lived in Camp Curtin and about that number had just departed, leaving their sick behind, the number was not high.[92] A campaign was launched in Harrisburg to improve, by what means were available, the diet and spirits of the patients at the hospital. The season for fresh fruits and vegetables had mostly passed, but that for soups, jellies and preserves was in full swing, and once again the women of the city rose to the occasion and busied themselves in their kitchens on behalf of the soldiers.

Camp Curtin was far more uncomfortable in the winter than it had been in the summer. It was a cheerless place where men huddled around stoves and open fires and bundled sentries stepped off their posts briskly, stopping now and again to stamp their feet and blow hot breath into cupped hands. Tedium worsened, and more than ever the volunteers wished to get out of the camp. The odd occasional diversion was most welcome, regardless of its nature. Farmer George Reel's outhouse caught fire one winter day just outside the camp. The shed, and perhaps the Reel house and barn as well, was saved only by the quick actions of soldiers who ran out to fight the blaze. Mr. Reel, who had more than one opportunity to complain about soldiers stealing from his fields and gardens, was forced to admit his indebtedness to the quick-minded men who saved his property.[93]

At least once that winter, the men and the citizens of Harrisburg as well were treated to an entirely too exciting break in the monotony. The government used Harrisburg as a depot for cavalry horses, and large shipments of the animals would periodically pass into or out of the city. Although most of the horses were kept in pens in or just outside the city, many of them were kept in a stock pen at Camp Curtin. Twenty or thirty of them, perhaps victims of boredom as well, broke down the fence one day and stampeded. They careened around the inside of the camp for awhile, knocking over tents and steaming kettles and scattering soldiers, then stormed the gate and charged out. They stuck to the Ridge Road and thundered the full mile or more into town "at a fearful rate...carrying everything before them." They did not stop until they got confused in the streets near the capitol. No one was hurt and the horses, having enjoyed their good run, were rounded up and sent across the river to a less populated area.[94]

A genuine curiosity came strolling into town in mid-November in the form of a company of volunteers from the mountains in the western part of the state. The men called themselves the Silver Grays and of the 78 men in the company, just two were under 30 and most were 50 years old or more. They were led by William Palmer, a 62-year-old innkeeper from Jefferson, Pennsylvania. The youngest of the Silver Grays was 15-year-old drummer Charlie Teeler. Twenty-nine-year-old Corporal Carl Schmidt, a carpenter, was the only other man under 30. The oldest was private Darius Ayers, a boat builder from Cambria County. He was 73.[95] Ordinarily, no man was accepted for United States service who was over 45, but these men wished to make a try at enlisting anyway and so had come to Harrisburg to offer their services to the governor. They would not, they were told, be accepted for United States service, but they would be allowed to serve their state, if they chose. Captain Parker agreed to have his company mustered into state service and led his men out to Camp Curtin. The Grays would remain there for well over a month before they were mustered in. They endured the harsh weather as well as men half their ages and performed guard duty at various places, especially at the state arsenal.[96]

In December, the men were provided with the most interesting diversion of all by the arrival of their most distinguished visitor. Secretary of War Cameron was in Harrisburg and was taken out to Camp Curtin for an inspection tour. After viewing the barracks, company streets, hospital, privy holes and trenches, the Secretary was reportedly impressed enough with the miserable sanitation conditions to unofficially suggest that the campsite be abandoned and operations be set up in a better spot someplace nearby. Cameron was not the first newcomer to be negatively impressed by Camp Curtin, and he would not be the last. No action had ever been taken on the suggestion of the tens of thousands of appalled volunteers who came and then recommended that the place be razed, and no action was taken on the similar suggestion of the secretary of war.[97]

*   *   *

That first winter marked the beginning of a new stage in the life of Camp Curtin, and the changes were directly related to the course the war was taking. Months had passed since the first battle at Bull Run, and still no serious offensive had been mounted by either government. But by spring, the future seemed more promising for the North. The Union armies in the Western Theatre had had some successes, where General Ulysses S. Grant had won impressive victories at Forts Henry and Donelson in Tennessee, and his men were driving the disorganized Confederates into Mississippi. Moreover, in and around Washington sat an army of incredible size— about 100,000 men—which was being prepared to drive on to Richmond and, it was hoped, end the war.

Altogether, the United States government had more than half a million men under arms, more than it had ever had at one time. It was inconceivable to those who had been raising the army that more men would be needed, and the opinion of the War

Department seemed to be that the issue would be decided by the men already in the field.

In any event, if any more regiments were to be recruited, they likely would not come from Pennsylvania. In April, 1861, when Lincoln had asked for 14 regiments for three months service, 25 regiments of Pennsylvanians had come forward. Two months after that, the 15 regiments of the Pennsylvania Reserve Corps had been called for by the Federal government, and since then, 75 more regiments from the Keystone State had been mustered in. In all 94 regiments of Pennsylvania Volunteers, exclusive of the 25 that had volunteered for three months, had come forward for service.[98] The Keystone State had done everything asked of it and much more, and if more men were needed, they might be obtained elsewhere.

All this seemed to mean that Camp Curtin had seen its day as a great rendezvous point for volunteers. No more, it was thought, would legions of Pennsylvanians be marching off to war from its gates. From now on, it was thought, Pennsylvania would only be called upon for a few recruits to fill up the ranks of its three-year regiments already in the field. This would hardly require an operation the size of that at Camp Curtin.

But the value of Harrisburg, and Camp Curtin in particular, as a staging area was not lost on the War Department. As an established place of rendezvous and instruction, Camp Curtin was of great importance to not only Pennsylvania but to the War Department as well. The secretary of war knew that the recruits procured throughout Pennsylvania and sent to Camp Curtin would be cared for by Quartermaster and Commissary Departments that had been operating efficiently for months, and the size of the operation at Camp Curtin was unmatched anywhere in the North. Between April and November, 1861, more than 50 regiments and dozens of unattached companies or well over half of all Pennsylvania Volunteers had been quartered for at least some time there and the Commissary Department had provided for them all. In those six months, the quartermasters had issued 23 tons of coffee, 43 tons of sugar and 96 tons of pork. During busy periods, more than 10½ tons of fresh beef had been distributed each week, and more than two and a quarter tons of bread every day. The officers in charge had learned from early mistakes, and procedures were ever becoming more automatic and efficient. Captain Tarbutton and his assistants continued to imbue the rudiments of drill and discipline into the volunteers, and Governor Curtin remained vigilant and energetically eager to cooperate in organizing and forwarding regiments. Despite that organization, a pressing need for the camp apparently no longer existed. But, even the Washington officials saw the wisdom in keeping Camp Curtin open.[99] For this reason, orders came from the War Department to improve Camp Curtin with an eye toward making it a more permanent post. If it were no longer to be needed by Pennsylvania for her volunteers, the United States Army would assume control and use the place as a depot for recruits.

Work had been begun in the autumn on new barracks to serve as warmer quarters for an additional 2,000 men, but the changes at camp were intended to last well beyond the end of the cold weather.[100] In late October, carpenters and other workers had begun measuring and staking an area near the middle of the camp and delivering lumber, roofing and nails. They built a large warehouse, where the Quartermaster and Commissary Departments could store the large amounts of sustinence and equipment that would be needed to supply both the men in camp and in the Army of the Potomac in Virginia. The structure was finished in November.[101]

Perhaps principal among these "permanent" improvements was the appointment of Captain Richard I. Dodge, 8th United States Infantry, as Chief Mustering and Disbursing Officer in Harrisburg.[102] Richard Dodge was regular army. He was a North Carolinian and a West Pointer, having been graduated 19th in the class of 1848. Although he had left the Point too late to see any action in the Mexican War, he had spent eight years on the Texas prairies, where he had on more than one occasion been engaged in fighting hostile Comanches. In 1858, he had left Texas for the more civilized surroundings of the Hudson Valley and the Military Academy, where he had been an instructor of infantry tactics. When the war came, he had been on garrison duty at Fort Wood in New York, but he had soon been ordered to join his regiment near Washington and was at Bull Run on that disastrous Sunday in July, 1861. For two months after the battle, he had served as commandant of a Camp of Instruction— like Camp Curtin—at Elmira, New York. In the 13 years since he had first left West Point, Dodge had proved himself an intelligent and capable officer, and he would remain a central figure in Harrisburg and Camp Curtin for the better part of four years.[103]

On March 17, 1862, Captain Dodge officially took command of Camp Curtin and replaced William J. Palmer, captain of the Silver Grays, who had been serving as interim commandant since the departure of Colonel Meredith on March 7.[104] The camp was no longer under the jurisdiction of the Commonwealth of Pennsylvania, but was now a United States Army depot for recruits.

While Dodge was technically commandant, he was also still Chief Mustering and Disbursing Officer and Superintendent of the Volunteer Recruiting Service in Harrisburg. He had a great many responsibilities, and adding the menial tasks of commanding the camp, and directing the police and provost operations would only inhibit him. Those duties therefore were handled by another officer designated by Dodge. The first officer so designated was First Lieutenant Frank P. Amsden, Battery H, 1st Pennsylvania Artillery, who was officially post adjutant. Amsden was just 22 years old when Dodge gave him the responsibility of running the camp. Born and raised in Scranton, Amsden was a "stout, hearty, rugged boy," of about average height with brown hair, gray eyes and the fair skin of a college student. He was exceptionally intelligent, having been educated first at Norwich University in Vermont then at a polytechnic institute in Troy, New York. He had emerged from his six years of schooling as a civil engineer, but the times would not allow him to undertake the peaceful industry of building dams and surveying harbors. In June, 1861, when he had finished his studies and left Troy, the war had already begun, so he had hastened home to Scranton and enlisted in Battery H. The battery had been recruited principally in Philadelphia and had gone into Camp Curtin in April. Some vacancies remained in the ranks, though, and Amsden had filled one of them. He had then proceeded to Harrisburg and went into camp, being mustered into United States service as a first lieutenant on August 5, 1861. The battery had departed camp shortly thereafter and had gone directly to Washington, where it went into Camp Barry east of the capitol. Amsden had remained with the battery on Capitol Hill, learning the art of the artilleryman, until January, 1862, when he had been detailed for recruiting duty and ordered back to Harrisburg and Camp Curtin, where he stayed until early April.[105]

Several other officers from various regiments were at the camp on recruiting duty as well, and throughout the war, a small detachment of recruiters would be stationed there while they enlisted men in the Harrisburg area. One such officer was First Lieutenant William M. Carter, Company B, 8th Pennsylvania Reserves. Carter, a Harrisburg resident, had been a machinist in the Harrisburg shops of the Pennsylvania Railroad before the war and had been one of the many brash young men who had come forward to enlist at Lincoln's first call. He had been in Pittsburgh in April, 1861, and had enlisted in a company forming there. Carter and the men of the company found, to their dismay, that Pennsylvania's quota had already been filled and they would not be immediately accepted. The men had stayed together, however, waiting the few weeks until the state legislature passed the Pennsylvania Reserves bill. Carter's company had gone into Camp Wilkins near Pittsburgh and had been made Company B of the 8th. During the excitement of First Bull Run, Carter and the 8th had hurried to Harrisburg on July 21 to be armed and equipped and had been sent on to Washington that same day. The idle autumn and winter months in camp near Washington had been used by regiments to fill up their ranks, and men had been sent home to recruit. Carter had returned to Camp Curtin on such an errand on March 22, 1862. He remained in camp superintending various squads of recruits into May 15, 1862, when he, like many other recruiters away from their regiments, was ordered to rejoin his regiment in the field.[106] It was springtime, and the war was about to begin.

CHAPTER FOUR

"I Have Not Pleasant Memories of Camp Curtin"

MARCH — SEPTEMBER, 1862

Mercifully, spring came early in 1862, relieving the men in Camp Curtin of the bitter cold that had plagued them throughout much of the winter. As usual, the river ran high and freshets upstream brought debris floating down from the mountains. But the people had more on their minds than crops and over-wet soil. The war was entering its second year and although a few blows had fallen, March—the month of Mars, traditionally the time for campaigns to be launched—was at hand. It seemed this year that tradition would be upheld, as the new secretary of war, Edwin M. Stanton, who had replaced Cameron over the winter, busied himself and the army high command in preparing for battle. Regiments and brigades in out-of-the-way places like Baltimore, Annapolis and Harrisburg were moved to where they could be reached more easily, like Washington and Fort Monroe in Virginia. All organized regiments were shipped out of Camp Curtin and unorganized companies were broken up to fill gaps in near full regiments. By mid-March, the camp was virtually emptied of all organized units; only a few hundred or so individual recruits and the old timers of the Silver Grays remained.[1]

The Confederates, too, were preparing for action. Brigadier General Thomas J. "Stonewall" Jackson, Confederate States Army, had spent the winter with his small army in the low hills of northwest Virginia. Jackson's Confederates, like their Northern counterparts, had been drilling through the winter, and had, like the Yankees, spent much energy in trying to keep warm and healthy. They had not had much success, considerably less, probably, than the Northerners since they did not have the advantages of living near large cities with buildings, railroads, plenty of fresh food, and sympathetic women to serve as nurses and deliver morale-boosting dainties. Nevertheless, Jackson had his plans and his orders. He was to protect the Shenandoah Valley, Virginia's prime farm country, where much of the produce that would be needed to feed the Confederate armies in the state was grown. The valley was vital to the Old Dominion's interests, which were those of the Confederacy. Jackson was told to, if possible, keep occupied the Federal forces in the valley, so they could not be used in the expected Federal offensive on the capital of the Confederacy, Richmond.

COLONEL CHARLES F. TAYLOR
13th Pennsylvania Reserves.
(From Thomson and Rauch's "History of the 'Bucktails' ")

The people of south central Pennsylvania did not know all this, of course, and in the early spring, few had probably heard Jackson's name. But after March 23, 1862, when he made his first attack, and during the two and a half months that followed, in which he fought six battles, winning five, defeating three different Federal armies, it looked very much to an anxious Pennsylvania populace that the man could soon be dining in the Jones House on Market Square in Harrisburg. At the very least, throughout May, it seemed likely that the commonwealth was about to be invaded.

To oppose Jackson in the valley were three Federal armies of differing sizes, but despite their advantage in numbers, the Yankees were overmatched. The Confederates were far better led and consequently beat the Northerners on every field except one. Among the troops in the valley trying to catch and defeat Jackson was a battalion of Pennsylvania Bucktails. The regiment had been temporarily divided into two battalions—one of six companies and one of four. The larger of the two was under Major Roy Stone and was with McClellan's army, which was preparing to drive on Richmond. The small battalion was under Lieutenant Colonel Kane, with the second in command Captain Fred Taylor, who at age 22 was the senior captain in the battalion.

On June 6, 1862, the Bucktails tangled with the rearguard of Jackson's Valley Army at Harrisonburg, Virginia. The fight was short, but, as Confederate General Richard S. Ewell described it, "close and bloody."[2]

The Confederate commander on the field was Brigadier General Turner Ashby,

Jackson's chief of cavalry, whom all Virginia had come to love as the dashing ideal of the *beau sabre*. Taylor commanded a portion of the Bucktail line as it advanced into a wood to support other Federal regiments under vigorous attack from Ashby. Kane was wounded in the leg early in the fight, and command of the battalion devolved upon Taylor. Taylor found that he and his men were themselves without supports. Ashby was quick to take advantage of the weakness and flanked the small Bucktail line. Caught in a crossfire, the Bucktails broke and retreated. Taylor later defended his men by saying that the situation had been "hopeless," but he himself had not run. He strode about trying to reform enough riflemen to get off "one good volley" at the onrushing Confederates to buy some time. This he did, and Rebels were slowed long enough for most of the Bucktails to escape and reform farther to the rear. Captain Taylor was not with them, however, for in his efforts to cover the retreat of the battalion, he was overtaken by Rebels and captured. He later learned that Ashby was among the Confederates killed before the Bucktail line of battle. All Virginia mourned his death. Taylor had his own fate to be concerned about, however, as he was sent to Petersburg, Virginia as a prisoner of war.[3]

* * *

The Federal armies in the Shenandoah were operating in a key role in McClellan's offensive plans. They were to defeat Jackson's tiny force of just over 4,000 men, clear the valley of any other Confederate armies, then retreat to the defenses of Washington. With Washington protected and the Shenandoah Valley free of forces that could possibly threaten his own capital, McClellan was free to drive on Richmond. His strategy, however, was complex. Rather than driving straight overland from Washington, where the Federal Army of the Potomac had been gathered, to Richmond, just 100 odd miles away, McClellan opted for a much longer and complicated route. Richmond sat at the head of a peninsula, the tip of which lay in Hampton Roads near where the Chesapeake Bay met the Atlantic Ocean. The peninsula was formed by the York River on the north and the James River on the south. McClellan planned to move his army, all its baggage and equipment, its wagons, mules, horses, artillery and rations, down the Potomac River from Washington, into the Chesapeake Bay,

PANORAMA OF CAMP CURTIN. *(Harper's Weekly, September 13, 1862)*

down the coast of Virginia to the end of the Peninsula, as it would soon be called. There, the army would be disembarked some forty miles from Richmond, and the offensive would begin.

As McClellan's army of approximately 90,000 men landed at the tip of the Peninsula in the last week of March, almost thirty percent of it was composed of Pennsylvanians. The whole army was excited about finally having abandoned the inactivity of life in winter camp, and the men were even more enthusiastic about being in enemy territory. The long-awaited fight would at last be fought. But what happened was not what they expected, and the fight they got was not the one they had hoped for.

The Northern men found that the land of the Peninsula was generally very low. The area was, in fact, part of what was called the Tidewater Region of Virginia, and everywhere were splendid farms and plantations owned by the very cream of the Virginia aristocracy—the Custises, the Carters, the Randolphs, and the Lees. The land was good for growing but was criss-crossed by sluggish creeks and streams that led to swamps and marshes of terrific size and density. These swamps would swell after each spring rain. The climatic situation went from unpleasant to dangerous when the warm weather, much warmer than what the Northern boys were accustomed to that early in the year, aided the stagnant-swamp-dwelling mosquitoes in their breeding. Before very long, malaria and swamp fever had a good portion of the invading army on the sick list.

Health had not been good in any of the winter camps, whether in Washington, Annapolis, Harrisburg or farther north. Many of the men had been ill over the winter and were still recuperating when transported to the Peninsula. In their weakened condition, thousands of men contracted diseases, especially of the intestines, from which they would never completely recover, and hundreds of others died outright, not from the bullets they had expected, but from the bacteria they had not.

One of those who had been ill in the winter was Seneca Simmons of the 5th Reserves. Fifty-three years old and removed from the vigorous life of a soldier since he left frontier duty at Fort Arbuckle, Indian Territory, in 1857, he had spent the two years immediately prior to the war snugly ensconced in a tidy little house on Front Street in Harrisburg with his wife and 19-year-old daughter. The adjustment to life under canvas had not been difficult for him in the summer and fall, but, as it had for many, the continued exposure of unaccustomed lungs to cold, damp winter air took its toll on Simmons. He had been subject to attacks of bronchitis for a number of years, and in late February, labored breathing forced him to seek the treatment of his regimental surgeon, Dr. Samuel Lane. Lane thought the best treatment for Simmons was to get away from his regiment and the miserable weather of Camp Pierpont, outside Washington, where the 5th was encamped. "The dampness of the camp is prejudicial to his recovery," wrote Dr. Lane, "which demands a healthful location and careful treatment." The doctor recommended for the colonel a leave of absence of 14 days, which could be spent under the care of Mrs. Simmons on Front Street. Simmons was granted the leave and went immediately to Harrisburg.[4]

While Colonel Simmons rested, however, others around him moved to action on his behalf. The Pennsylvania delegation in Congress tried to have Simmons promoted to brigadier general. The politicians in Washington and in the various state capitals routinely used what influence they had in championing the advancement of officers from their states, and letters noting the quality and fitness for command of certain officers arrived almost daily at the office of the president. One of Pennsylvania's representatives in the House was Charles J. Biddle, former colonel of the Bucktails who had resigned his commission to assume his seat in Congress. Although Biddle had signed his name to the letter sent Lincoln by the Pennsylvania delegation urging Simmons's promotion, he felt compelled to send along his own personal endorsement as well. Biddle, at least, knew something of Simmons's abilities as a soldier. The two had, with their regiments, left Camp Curtin in June, 1861, on the expedition to Cumberland, Maryland and the relief of General Lew Wallace. "I desire to testify to the zeal, promptitude, and activity of Colonel Simmons," wrote Biddle, "as exibited [sic] on many occasions; his command was always ready at the time appointed, to which his general good discipline and active personal supervision alike contributed...."[5]

The Congressional delegation from Vermont, Simmons's state of birth, added its endorsement in a letter to the president in rhetoric just a tone lower than Biddle's. Finally in early March, just as Simmons returned to duty from his medical leave, Governor Curtin added his voice to the chorus, but he wrote not to the president but the army's commanding general. Whether because of the letters to Lincoln or simply because of Curtin's, General McClellan solicited an opinion of Simmons and his fitness for promotion from the colonel's immediate superior, John Fulton Reynolds.

The 41-year-old Reynolds was a Pennsylvanian, having grown up in Lancaster. He, like Simmons and McClellan, was a professional soldier. He had been graduated from West Point precisely in the middle of the class of 1841 and had served well in Mexico, where he was breveted twice. Reynolds was the model of a quietly-capable soldier. He did his job and usually did it well, but he attracted no attention to himself beyond the sphere of his brother officers. He was respected within the army as an honest and conscientious man, and that respect was growing. Because of this generally-high opinion, what he said about Simmons would count for much more with McClellan than what the politicians had said.[6] On March 8, Reynolds sent his views to McClellan:

> Yours of the 6 inst reached me this evening. I had no personal acquaintance with Col. Simmons prior to my assuming command of this Brigade; when I served with his regt. in Mexico, he was not with it. My opinion is formed entirely from what has occurred under personal observation of, and communication with Colonel S. on duty with his Regt. here.
>
> He has not taken that interest in instructing his officers in the military duties and details pertaining to their company affairs, nor in keeping his regt. in an approach, at least, to that neatness, order and control which

we have a right to expect from an officer whose life has been passed in service.

I ascertained recently, that he has not even kept a file of the printed orders of this Army in his Regt. Office, and could mention other neglects, equally glaring, of his indifference to what should constitute the proper duties of an officer in his position.

I may therefore be permitted to say, that I think Colonel S. would be of more service with his Regt. as Colonel than in any higher position. I can say this much in his favor, he has drilled his regt pretty assiduously tho' he has not a field officer who can do so. They now depend upon him so much, in this particular, that I consider his absense from the Regt. would materially diminish its efficiency at this time.

I am sir,
Very respectfully,
Your Obt. Servt.
John F. Reynolds
Brig. Gen. Vols.[7]

Good soldier that he was, Reynolds did not mince words. Simmons was a hard worker and a good enough colonel, but his failure to teach his junior officers more about handling the regiment, thereby making them better officers, and the general disorderliness in his headquarters indicated, to Reynolds at least, that Simmons did not have the structured, vigorous mind required of a brigadier. Reynolds, however, sought to maintain whatever integrity or stability his brigade had, and he felt that if Simmons were promoted, the 5th Regiment would suffer, at least initially, in efficiency. Furthermore, Simmons was the senior colonel of the brigade, which meant that should anything happen to Reynolds command of the brigade would devolve upon him. Immediately behind Simmons in seniority was Colonel R. Biddle Roberts, the Pittsburgh lawyer who led the 1st Reserve Regiment. Roberts was a politician, not a soldier, and was not truthfully qualified to lead a regiment, let alone a brigade. Eleven months before he had been a lieutenant in the Duquesne Grays and his military experience was restricted to those eleven months. As ineffective as Reynolds thought Simmons would be as a brigadier, Simmons at least was a trained soldier with 33 years of service, and it was far preferable to have him in command of the brigade than Roberts.

Many men were serving as brigadier and even major generals who did not have the qualifications of Simmons. Nor did these men all possess the vigor and orderliness Reynolds thought necessary, or at least desirable, in a general officer. Many of these officers had been politicians, and had received their generalships through political favors. Many of them would make bad officers and worse generals, but others would perform well. Although Simmons was not promoted that spring, it seemed certain that he eventually would be. The fighting had hardly begun and he would have his chance to show what he could do on the battlefield. Regardless of the disorderliness of their regimental offices, fighting colonels with a lifetime of experience were promoted.

Ironically, less than a month after he wrote to McClellan, ending, for the time being, Simmons's chances for promotion, Reynolds was detached from the brigade and assigned to the Military Governorship of Fredericksburg, Virginia. Simmons assumed temporary command of the brigade and remained there throughout Reynold's absence of more than two months. Simmons handled the brigade during its move from Washington to the Peninsula and during the first half of the advance toward Richmond.

Throughout May and June, several battles of varying size and severity were fought by the two armies on the Peninsula. The old Revolutionary War battlefield of Yorktown was the scene of some firing as was the quaint, colonial capital of Williamsburg. Most of the other fields were far more obscure. Perhaps the most notable battle was at Seven Pines, where Confederate Commander Joseph E. Johnston was wounded and temporarily put out of the war. He was replaced by Robert E. Lee.

By the last half of June, the Army of the Potomac was at the very threshold of Richmond. The army had fought and slogged through the mud and swamps all the way up the Peninsula, and some Federal units were just six miles from the city. The spires of Richmond were visible to the Northern boys as they sat smoking pipes and awaiting orders behind their breastworks. They were cheerful and optimistic about bringing an early end to the war, and they had every reason to be since they were in sight of the Confederate capital and had been generally successful in their recent encounters with the enemy. In the last week of June, the Confederate defense had stiffened, but that seemed only natural, since the Rebels had their backs to the wall.

But there might have been another reason for the determined defense. Rumors raced through the ranks that Jackson was moving out of the valley to reinforce the Confederates at Richmond; other rumors had Jackson and his men already on the field. Jackson's victories in the valley had been cloaked in mystery, characterized by long stolen marches and surprise attacks. The Federal generals opposing him literally had no idea at times where he was. All this made Jackson a dark, unfathomable threat, and the mere possibility that he was approaching was enough to rattle some of the generals in blue around Richmond. One of them later wrote, "We did not fear the results of an attack if made by [Lee's] forces from Richmond alone; but, if, in addition, we were to be attacked by Jackson's forces we felt that we should be in peril."[8]

Jackson had indeed left the valley and was on the scene north of Richmond, but all of his men were not yet with him. Lee's men therefore went at it without the help of the veterans of the valley, and attacked on the 26th of June. They struck a very strong Federal position near a small town called Mechanicsville and were convincingly repulsed with heavy casualties. Curiously, despite their victory, the Federal troops at Mechanicsville, which included almost the entire Pennsylvania Reserve Corps, were ordered to withdraw to an even stronger position some six miles to the rear, even farther from Richmond.

The terrain at the new position was dominated by a steep wooded hill, the top of which was a clear plateau used for planting by a farmer named Watt, whose house stood nearby. Not far to the west in a quiet clearing was a five-story brick grist mill with a few small outbuildings clustered around a glassy, oak-fringed pond. Confederate infantry pursued the Federals to the mill pond, which was owned by a Dr. Gaines, and attacked shortly after noon on the 27th. The fight continued for hours with the Pennsylvania Reserves having some success at repelling and driving the attacking Confederates.

Finally, the Rebels launched a swift thrust at the Federal center and caught the Pennsylvanians unprepared. The Reserves had used most of their ammunition and were forced to retire, but not all of them moved fast enough. More than 600 men of the 11th Reserves—virtually the entire regiment—were captured along with almost all of the 4th New Jersey.[9]

The Federals had not been routed at Gaines's Mill, but they had been thrashed soundly enough to necessitate a bit of reorganization. Through the night and into the next morning, the weary, grimy, smoke-stained Yankees were again marched to a new position, this one even more distant from Richmond. Lee's Confederates continued to agressively attack. They fought on the 28th and the 29th. In between was steady marching, and it was obvious by then to every private that the whole army was retreating—why and to where none of them knew. They knew only that they had seen the spires of Richmond, they had looked upon victory and what seemed the end of the war, then had watched as it somehow, inexplicably drifted away from them, receding from view behind the tall scrub pines and brush-covered hills that rose out of the swamps.

The Army of the Potomac had been outflanked as it sat at the threshold of Richmond, and forced to pull back to new lines. McClellan decided to change his base of supply from the York River to the James River; thence, he said, he would start anew his assault on the Confederate capital. But to make his movement, a difficult and dangerous one, he would need time, and that time would have to be bought for him by a stout rear guard defense once his army was in motion. The Pennsylvania Reserves were part of that rear guard.

The Reserves composed the Third Division of the Fifth Corps of the army, and the division commander was Brigadier General George Archibald McCall. McCall was sixty years old, a Philadelphian and a West Pointer, class of 1822. As a member of the 1st U.S. Infantry, he had spent nearly twenty years on duty in Florida, part of the time operating against hostile Seminole Indians. Later, as a captain in the 4th Infantry, he had twice been brevetted for bravery in the Mexican War. After the war, he had been promoted to major and then staff colonel and inspector general. He had resigned in 1853 at age 51 and returned to his comfortable estate, Belair, near West Chester, Pennsylvania. When the war had come, he had offered his services to Governor Curtin and, on May 15, 1861, as part of the legislative bill that created the Pennsylvania Reserve Corps, McCall had been made a major general of Pennsylvania Volunteers and given command of the new corps. Two days later, he had been made a brigadier general of United States Volunteers by President Lincoln. When the Reserves were accepted for U.S. service and went to the main army, McCall was made a division commander.[10]

Before dawn on June 30, 1862, McCall's division was in position near a crossroads called Glendale. The morning was warm. Hints of the delicacy of spring remained on the Peninsula—the air was clear, the trees and shrubs fragrant, the grass and the still young leaves held their vibrant green color—but the air, though fresh, was no longer invigorating. The sharp-edged clarity of the cool damp spring mornings had been dulled, and the air lay warm and thick in the white-skied moistness of early summer. At 7 a.m., the division changed position to allow the immense wagon trains of the army to pass by. The morning was filled with much lounging and tending to the wounded of the fights of the previous days. The rear guard was just to bide its time and cover the retreat of the trains.

McCall's Pennsylvanians had no position of great strength as they had at Mechanicsville or Gaines's Mill. They stood on what McCall called "a beautiful battle ground"—but cover enough for the whole division could not be found. Some of the men were posted in a farm yard and others in the surrounding woods and pastures. The 12th Reserves, under Colonel Taggart, were anchored in the farm yard on the division's extreme left, and the 5th Reserve Regiment was held behind the line in reserve. The 5th was not under direct command of Colonel Simmons that day, but was under Lieutenant Colonel Joseph Fisher. Ironically, after being passed over for promotion to brigadier, Simmons was commanding the brigade. John Reynolds, the regular brigade commander and the man who had killed Simmons's chances for elevation, had been taken prisoner two days before on the night after Gaines's Mill. Exhausted, Reynolds had lain down in the woods during the retreat to get a bit of sleep. When he awoke, he found that his men were not only gone but that they, like good soldiers, had burned the bridges they had used behind them. While Reynolds rode to a Richmond prison, Simmons, as senior colonel, got his chance to command the brigade in combat and prove himself worthy of a brigadier's star.[11]

The attack began about 2 p.m. with picket firing. Slowly Confederate skirmishers appeared at the edge of the woods and the firing picked up until a whole Confederate regiment stepped out of the trees. A breeze lifted the Rebels' blue and red battle flag with the St. Andrew's cross, and the gray line moved forward. From somewhere, Confederate artillery was sending exploding shells toward the Reserves, and the hot metal flew about everywhere as the shots burst among and above the Federals. The Confederate infantrymen moved forward, slowly at first, but they soon broke into a run and began a high, yipping yell that was to become their stomach-knotting bowel-loosening trademark. The assault was full on the front of the 12th Reserves, and Taggart's men opened fire with enthusiasm. Captains and lieutenants strode back and forth behind the firing line, swords in one hand, pistols in the other, shouting encouragements and reminders to aim low and load carefully. The men of the 12th kept firing from that farmyard into the field of smoke and bursting shells until enough of their shots found the mark to convince the Confederates to turn back. Suddenly it was the men in blue who where cheering. The 12th had suffered too, however, and McCall ordered Simmons to shift portions of the 5th and the Bucktails to the left in support of the bloodied 12th. As this was being done, those who were not looking to the wounded or to their weapons were peering anxiously across the smoky field for the next sign of renewed attack. Again on the left Rebels were seen in the woods, moving to the south of some farm buildings around the flank of the 12th, which was itself the division's flank. Simmons was executing McCall's order quickly and went himself with the troops being shifted to the threatened flank. The attack began and firing kept up for well over two hours as lines charged were broken, rallied, reformed, and counterattacked. The fighting was intense and sometimes hand to hand. McCall recalled, rather romantically, that on a part of the field where the 4th Reserve Regiment was engaged, he witnessed "one of the fiercest bayonet fights that perhaps ever occurred on this continent. Bayonet wounds, mortal or slight, were given and received. I saw skulls crushed by butts of muskets, and every effort made by either party in this life-or-death struggle, proving indeed that here Greek had met Greek."[12]

As darkness came, and the firing of the artillery finally ceased, the continuous crackling of musketry slowed to intermittent popping from picket lines. The two armies lay apart in the twilight and looked at one another across the contested field. The cries of the wounded could at last be heard as the firing diminished; both Northerner and Southerner would come to know the sound well. Some of the wounded had been lying helpless on the field since the first assault and had cried themselves hoarse in pleading for help or water. In places where the fighting had been hand to hand, blue and gray clad men lay side by side or on top of one another, their blood mingling as it pooled and was finally absorbed by the Virginia soil.

Both sides had lost heavily, and the casualties were of all descriptions. Colonel George S. Hays of the 8th Reserves was leading his regiment when his horse was hit by a shell and killed instantly. The animal fell on his rider, and the gore-spattered Hays was pinned to the ground, stunned and badly bruised. He escaped, however, when a private of the regiment pulled him free and carried him to the rear. Hays was more seriously hurt than even he expected, and a short time later he resigned

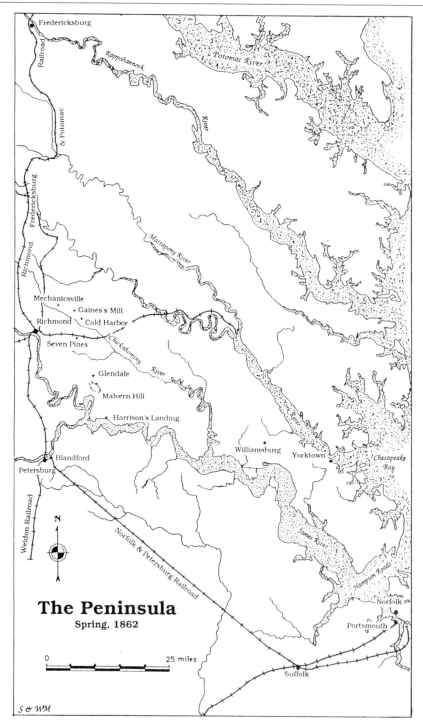

The Peninsula

Spring, 1862

S & WM

and returned to Pennsylvania. He would never completely recover.[13] Colonel Elisha B. Harvey of the 7th was knocked down by stampeding artillery horses wounded when a Confederate volley killed their driver. After being kicked about by the flying hooves, Harvey was even more seriously injured when the cassion the horses were pulling jolted into and rolled over him. The 42-year-old Harvey was also taken to the rear and eventually home to Pennsylvania.[14]

At dusk on the 30th, General McCall, who had been very active throughout the afternoon in rallying troops and finding reinforcements, came upon Lieutenant Colonel William S. Thompson of the 3rd Reserves and a force of about 500 men Thompson had managed to scrape up from broken or disorganized units and stragglers. Anxious to learn what he could of the enemy's position and intentions, the general immediately led the men forward, riding on ahead himself with a few men to reconnoiter. In his report, McCall remembered that, "Having no staff officer with me, I rode forward to ascertain whether some men of the fourth [Reserves] whom I had left a little in advance were still on the ground—they had, as I afterward learned, joined Kearny [Brigadier General Philip S. Kearny, commander of the Third Division of the Third Corps]—and I had not proceeded more than one hundred yards before I rode right into the forty-seventh Virginia Regiment, which, being drawn up under some trees, was not seen by me in the obscurity of the evening until I had ridden in among them...."[15] The Virginians were surprised themselves. Colonel Robert Mayo of the 47th reported that hardly anything could be seen in the murkiness of the woods. "It was then quite dark....Shortly after we ceased firing...the sounds of horses' hoofs [sic] were heard advancing from the direction of the enemy and the regiment was cautioned to be on their guard. They turned out to be four horsemen, who, riding up on our left, inquired who we were. I called out at the top of my voice 'Friends,' but someone on the left having unwittingly called forty seventh Virginia Regiment two of the party turned back and rode off at double quick down the road. They were instantly fired upon....The other two were captured and turned out to be Major General McCall and one of his couriers."[16]

As the shadows crept out of the woods and enveloped the fields of Glendale in darkness, Confederates, who held most of the contested ground, began walking over the open ground to examine the bodies that lay strewn about. They moved through the twilight, hunched over with arms hanging loose, touching each body, speaking to each face looking for friends or simply for life, passing quickly over the ashen faces with the glazed unseeing eyes, and the empty, air-clutching hands. Captain R. L. Lewis of the First South Carolina Rifles was among those grimly hunting through the wreckage. He came to a Federal officer lying in a dust covered uniform. The man was conscious, but had been shot through the side and been bleeding slowly for a long time. Lewis spoke to the man, who quietly told the captain that his name was Colonel Seneca Simmons, and he was badly hurt. Simmons asked his enemy to help him.[17]

Simmons had lain on the field since afternoon. The Rebels, after their quick march to try to flank the stubborn resistance of the 12th Reserves, burst out of the woods and charged across the fields with fixed bayonets into what they thought was the Federal flank. They were surprised to find Simmons's line, composed of the 5th Reserves and a few companies of Bucktails, there to meet them. Unfazed, the men in gray came on, withholding their fire until just 20 or 30 yards from Simmons's line. The companies of the 5th and the Bucktails had all the while been pouring a fire into the advancing line and the Rebels had been dropping, but the gaps in the line were quickly filled and still they came. For more than two hours the fighting here continued, but finally, the Southerners got within point blank range, let loose a well-aimed volley and charged. It was too much to take; the line of the 5th and Bucktails broke and began to crumble back through the farmyard. Simmons was mounted when his line broke, and he began riding to and fro trying to rally a force, shouting for men to stay and fight. Suddenly, a bullet hit him hard in the side, knocking him from his horse. The 53-year-old man fell the five feet or more to the ground and began to bleed. His men retreated past him, leaving him were he lay.[18]

It was there Lewis found him hours later. "I called some of our ambulance corps," remembered the South Carolinian, "and carried him to a vacant house near by. I took off his spurs and sword, which he gave to me, placed him upon a bed and gave him all the help I could. He asked me who was commanding the fight, I told him General Q. U. Anderson. He said, 'I know him. I was with him in the Mexican War.' He then asked me to tell the General that he would like to see him. I conveyed the message to General Anderson, but he said he could not see him."[19]

Dr. O. M. Doyle, a Confederate surgeon, examined Simmons that night. "I was told that Colonel Simmons fell in front of our part of the line, and as our line advanced he was taken up and brought to the field hospital....He was reported by our officers as acting conspicuously brave....That report did much toward stimulating a greater desire on our part to do all that was possible for [him]." The wound was a dangerous one, a ball had pierced both liver and lung and already the Confederates attending to him knew Simmons had little chance. Simmons knew as well. "[He] thanked us sincerely for our attentions," wrote Dr. Doyle some time later. "He gave to some one of our party a gold watch, a picture of his wife, and I think $60 in gold coin with the request [they] be sent to his wife....I treated him in the best manner possible under the circumstances, and had him buried as decently as could be done at such a time."[20]

General McCall, a prisoner in Richmond, heard of Simmons's death and wrote to Mrs. Simmons in Harrisburg.

Richmond, Virginia
Tobacco Warehouse Prison
July 15, 1862.

My dear Madam: It is not to say that I mourn the loss of a friend that I write to you, although twenty years' knowledge of his worth and very many most estimable qualities, had truly endeared your husband to me; nor is it to attempt to offer consolation in your bereavement, which One above alone can give you. I write to inform you that after Colonel Simmons, who, on the 30th of June, commanded the First brigade of my division, was wounded, he was captured by the enemy, carried to their hospital, and laid by the side of Captain [Henry C.] Biddle, of Philadelphia, my assistant adjutant general, who was also severely wounded and a prisoner. During the night of the 1st of July, as I am informed the colonel sank under the effect of his wound and calmly expired at Biddle's side. This I have from Biddle himself, who is here in the hospital.

I have only to add that the Colonel's body has been brought to this city and is interred here, where it may be conveyed to his friends at the proper time.

Believe me, dear madam, very truly and sincerely, your friend and obedient servant,

Geo. A. McCall
Brigadier General, U.S.A.[21]

*   *   *

Just as Harrisburg served, because of its central location and converging railroads, as a point for concentrating companies and regiments on their way to war, so did it serve as a principal station on the route home, especially for the sick and the wounded. Almost daily throughout June and early July, the people of the city watched trainloads of pale and dirty, bloody-bandaged Federal soldiers come streaming into their midst. Some of them went on to the hospitals in Philadelphia or elsewhere, but many remained in Harrisburg and were kept at the hospital at Camp Curtin. Many of those arriving on the trains were not Pennsylvanians. Soldiers from all over the North were given beds in Harrisburg and would be cared for until they could be sent on to their homes. Other large, usually idle buildings, such as churches and schools, were transformed into hospitals, and in the summer heat men rested, bled, and often died in the rooms where children had laughed and learned their letters the winter before.

The war had, until now, used Harrisburg as a stepping-off point. The people of the city had seen nothing but the endless sending away of young men. The war for them had been an action without a reaction. But now the young men were coming home—legless and armless, with chronically loose bowels, labored wheezy breathing and pallid, clammy skin. These young men brought reality with them, and from them Harrisburg learned what the soldiers had already learned: war had little to do with dress parades and sword presentations and salutes fired from Capitol Hill. War did not go away on trains, it came back on them.

Other arrivals in the city, however, created among the people of the city a fascination almost unlike any they had ever known. Since the middle of June, Confederate prisoners had been arriving on trains from the valley. Perhaps the only success the Federals in the valley had had against Stonewall Jackson was the capture of a few hundred of his men. These prisoners were sent north to be confined.

When the citizens of Harrisburg learned the Rebels would be coming through their city, their desire to see the vaunted foe surpassed almost all else. They rushed about like children at a circus. Long before the first trainload was in view, people were lining the tracks all the way across the bridge to Bridgeport on the west bank of the river opposite Harrisburg, hoping to get a glimpse of "Jeff Davis's men."

When the wail of the distant locomotive at last announced the long-awaited arrival, excitement became frenzy. Unfortunately for the gawking citizens, the train's conductor was not going to help them satisfy their curiosity, and, rather than slowing down as the train entered the thickly-populated streets of Bridgeport and Harrisburg, the conductor hurried the train through and on its way out to Camp Curtin. This only charged the crowds further, and everybody began running after the train. Men, women, and children, black and white, ran as if in a panic. Horses were galloped; buggies, sulkies, and wagons were driven in a mad rush. When the train stopped at the siding outside of camp, every bit of space at the fences surrounding the depot was crammed full with anxious onlookers.

After a delay, the prisoners were unloaded. They slowly dropped to the ground and shuffled about as Federal officers and troopers pointed, nudged and guided them into lines. They were marched from the siding around to the front side of camp and to the main gate, on the River Road. The spectators at last got their look at the Rebels, and they were surprised by what they saw. "They looked as if they were half-starved," wrote one. "Their dress was varied—many of them being clothed in a species of homespun with which Southerners generally clothe their slaves. The majority were mere stripplings—while here and there the face of a foreigner made its appearance. There was nothing of the boasted chivalry—but a downcast look and heavy tread—told that the fortunes of war were against them."[22] Another bystander was a bit more observant and a bit less sympathetic. "They were filthy to the extreme. They reminded us more of a party of laborers paraded on the embankment of a railroad or canal then anything we could compare them to. Nearly all of them were in their shirt sleeves, and the variety in the style of hats was marked....We noticed a great many boys—not a few who could not possibly be over sixteen years of age."[23] The Rebels reminded another man of "travel-stained vagabonds. They looked slouchy, listless, torpid,—an ill-conditioned crew, at first sight, made up of fellows as an old woman would drive away from her hen-roost with a broomstick."[24] The "seedy and woe-begone" looking Confederates, numbered about 400, almost all enlisted men.[25] They were assigned to the rear (northern end) of camp where they were to be detained. They would all move on in a few days, most of them to Fort Delaware on Pea Patch Island in the Delaware River just south of Wilmington, Delaware.

The sensation caused by the Rebels did not escape the notice of Captain Dodge. While in Camp Curtin, the prisoners were his responsibility, and he saw the clamor to see his prisoners as nothing more than a threat to security. He immediately issued orders that no person would be allowed into the camp just to see the prisoners. He had no intention of running a sideshow. The order caused some disgruntlement, especially among the hack drivers who had hoped to capitalize on the curiosity of the citizens of Harrisburg, but most of the townspeople realized, as did one articulate observer, that "whatever they may have been guilty of, they are at least human beings, and it would be an outrage to allow the large crowds who are likely to apply for admission...to enter as they would a menagerie, and gratify their curiosity by gazing upon them as they would upon a den of animals, or a party of Hottentots. Capt. Dodge deserves credit for not permitting a show to be made of them."[26] Dodge's refusal to allow visitors did much to quell the excitement in town and the novelty only provided fodder for "three or four days' talk."[27]

*   *   *

By mid-July, President Lincoln was growing concerned about his army on the Peninsula. McClellan was repeatedly requesting reinforcements, claiming that losses in combat had depleted his force, that he was badly outnumbered and that it was impossible to resume offensive operations against Richmond without a greater force at his disposal. Lincoln worried that, if McClellan were as badly outnumbered as he claimed, the Army of the Potomac would seem to be in great danger sitting idly with its back to a large river and no easy line of retreat while in the presence of a powerful enemy. In any event, no more troops were available to send to McClellan, and Lincoln finally directed General-in-Chief Henry W. Halleck to recall McClellan and his army from the Peninsula. Despite McClellan's protests, the army was withdrawn, and the Peninsula campaign came to an unsuccessful close.

If McClellan's constant pleading for men and his ineffectual campaign accomplished nothing else, it made Washington realize that perhaps it had been foolish to close recruiting stations the previous April when more men might be needed after all. Combat and disease had taken a terrible toll on the Northern armies, both in the east and the west, and recruits would be needed merely to maintain their strength. On July 7, therefore, Lincoln issued a call for 300,000 men, assigning a quota of regiments to each state. Pennsylvania was required to furnish 18 regiments to serve for nine months, time enough, it was hoped, to bring the war to a close.

As soon as news of the new regiments spread, applications for colonelcies began arriving at Governor Curtin's desk from all over the commonwealth. The applications for officerships far outnumbered the available positions, but some applicants had the advantage of seeing the governor personally. One of these men was William Wesley Jennings, camp adjutant at Camp Curtin and assistant drillmaster and choirster under Captain Tarbutton. Jennings was a Harrisburg native. His father had operated a foundry

COLONEL WILLIAM WESLEY JENNINGS
127th Pennsylvania Volunteers.
A Harrisburg native. Jennings also led the
26th Pennsylvania Emergency Militia in the
Gettysburg Campaign.
(from the "History of the 127th Pennsylvania")

in the city for more than thirty years and had married into Harrisburg society. Young William had gone to work in his father's foundry at age 15 and learned the skills of a molder. In 1860, at 22, Jennings had started his own iron business and ran it successfully until the war; he had then gone to Camp Curtin with Tarbutton. Even at that young age, he was one of Harrisburg's more solid citizens—a community leader type—active in local business, a member of the volunteer fire company, a singer of repute. He was a very large man, about six feet and 200 pounds, and was well liked by almost all who knew him—a man's man, fair, open-minded, and genial. He also had no military experience. But, because of his outstanding reputation, he had little trouble obtaining permission from the governor to recruit a regiment.[28]

A number of the other familiar faces were among the applicants for colonelcies. Richard A. Oakford, colonel of the 15th Pennsylvania of the three-month volunteers and commandant of Camp Curtin for a few days in May of 1861 was back. Jacob Higgins was back as well. Higgins was a Mexican War veteran and had served for a while as lieutenant colonel of the 1st Pennsylvania Cavalry, of the Reserve Corps. Both he and Oakford would be given colonelcies and permitted to recruit.

But all these would-be colonels found enlisting men difficult. Circumstances in the commonwealth were different than they had been a year earlier when most of the men then in service had begun enlisting. There were still plenty of men available, many of them veterans, but the young men of 1862 seemed less willing to go off to war than had their counterparts of 1861. For one thing, the excitement and enthusiasm of 1861 could not be sustained. The feelings of patriotism that existed for the first three months or so after Fort Sumter were simply too intense, and, after the initial rush of those feelings died down, the people found themselves looking at events more rationally.

Second, the difference of a year had made the young men less naive. Battles had been fought and sick and maimed brothers, cousins and neighbors had come home with horror stories about life in the army, or they had not come home at all and lay beneath a few inches of hurridly tossed soil on the plains above Bull Run, the meadows of the Shenandoah Valley, or the marshy forests of the Yorktown Peninsula. The war was no longer seen purely as an adventure; the risks involved were now very clear and few Northerners still harbored any illusions about the inferiority of Southern soldiers or the myth of the "one-battle war." Perhaps the biggest difference between recruiting in 1861 and 1862 lay in the types of men that could be recruited. Many of those who were still at home in 1862 were married.

The existence of a wife exerted considerable influence on a man trying to decide whether to enlist. War was a colossal gamble in which the stakes were not just the health and even the lives of the participants, but the welfare of those dependent upon them. For the practically-minded women of Pennsylvania—they of the rich Scotch-Irish or German stock—war held no allure as it did for their husbands and sons. The women saw military service clearly as a bad bet against long odds. In that summer of 1862, wives and mothers were urging their husbands and sons not to go, and they were being heard.

These women were no less patriotic than their husbands or other men and women who advocated a continuance of the war against the rebellion; but they were, perhaps, more realistic, and, consequently, more frightened. In an age when few women worked outside the home and even fewer could earn enough by any respectable service to support even a small family, a male wage earner was needed to provide, whether that male be a father, husband or son.

Yet the men that remained had been wrestling with questions of loyalty and responsibility since the very first call for troops. They did not deny their responsibility to their country and wished strongly to protect it, but they recognized a duty as well to those who were dependent upon them and unable to care for themselves. Was a man's duty to his country greater than the more immediate duty he had to his family? The men who had answered the first call and those who had enlisted since had answered "yes"; the men who had not yet gone had answered "no," or had not yet answered.

In August, 1862, Jeremiah Rohrer ran a door and window sash factory at Middletown, Pennsylvania, just a few miles south of Harrisburg. He was a strikingly

MAJOR JEREMIAH ROHRER
127th Pennsylvania Volunteers.
(from the "History of the 127th Pennsylvania")

handsome man in a stern sort of way, being a bit over average height with a florid face, dark hair and brilliant, unsettling, piercing blue eyes. He was described by one who knew him as being "a quiet, self-possessed man, kind and social, temperate in his habits, and decided in his opinions."[29] That August, he was 35 years old and had been married to the former Miss Mary Ann Redsecker of Elizabethtown, Pennsylvania, for nine years. But he also had some little military experience, having been a lieutenant colonel in the state militia before the war. Rohrer waited out the first calls of Lincoln and Curtin, letting the younger, unmarried men go off to fight what might be a short war. But when things began going bad for the Union in the spring and summer of 1862, Rohrer apparently reconsidered. When a company was organized in Middletown early in August, 1862, the men elected Rohrer their captain. Unfortunately, he had also been recently made a father for the third time, and his wife was not at all anxious to have the father of her children, ages eight, five and newborn, march off to a world of disease, explosions and whistling Minie balls. Rohrer felt honor bound to serve, especially since the men had chosen him to lead them. Mrs. Rohrer felt her husband's obligation was to his family. The presence of the baby, their first daughter, whom they had named Mary also, somehow magnified the possibility that the husband might never return. No wife can be blamed for fearing early widowhood or becoming preoccupied by the thought of having to alone raise three young children, one of whom had never known its father. The Rohrer household was an unhappy one in that first week of August, 1862.[30]

Captain Rohrer had hope, however, of if not persuading his wife to agree with him, at least of helping her more gracefully reconcile herself to the reality that he would be leaving her. In this the Rohrers' next door neighbors, the Shotts, were helpful. The Shotts and the Rohrers were good friends; John Shott, in fact, had been a partner with Jeremiah at the door and sash factory. Mrs. Shott, Rohrer recalled, "was very patriotic. She did not cry, but said it was the duty of every able-bodied man to go and fight for the Government. This stimulated her husband to accept the 1st Lieutenancy when it was offered to him. His only child, Frank, also enrolled. This move had a good effect in my family."[31] Mrs. Rohrer, however, remained generally unconvinced that the army's need for her husband was any greater than hers.

At the appointed hour on the appointed day, the men of the Middletown company assembled near the center of town at Union Hall to receive the farewells of their friends and neighbors and to set out for Camp Curtin. Mrs. Rohrer did not come to see her husband off. The captain put his men in line amid cheers and waving handkerchiefs and took up the march to the train station, taking a route that ran directly past his home. When Rohrer reached his house, he saw that all the windows stood wide open in the heat of the August forenoon. The summer curtains floated languidly on warm breezes, and the familiar rooms and hallways within were shrouded in a cool darkness that appeared quite inviting from the captain's place with the company out in the sun. No faces appeared at the windows; no one was in the yard or anywhere to be seen. The house was unusually and unsettlingly silent.

Rohrer could stand it no longer. He immediately called "halt" and bolted into the house, pounding noisily up the stairs. "There my wife sat," he remembered, "crying with the babe in her arms. I thought I would sink through the floor." He almost gave in right then and there, admitting in his diary that if he had done as he felt, he would not have gone. He did go, however, hoping, no doubt, that his fortitude would not be so severely tested on the battlefield.[32]

But the women of Middletown were not yet done with Captain Rohrer's heart. As the march to the depot continued, the company would occasionally be stopped so one or another of the local preachers could deliver a little sermon. During these halts, Rohrer would be besieged by bleary-eyed, wet-cheeked mothers who begged him to look after their boys and to protect them from all harm. "This was more than I could stand," he wrote, and, interrupting the preacher, he barked "Attention" and retreated from the wet cheeks by marching the men away.[33]

When the company arrived at Camp Curtin on August 16, the men were issued tents and rations, but no blankets, so the recruits spent their first night under canvas lying on the cool grass. The weather was good, for which Rohrer was grateful. They awoke the next morning stiff, but invigorated, and, finding the air clear and the sun bright, they were generally pleased with the army so far. "Ugly weather would have worked disasterously," thought Rohrer. "The men had not been sworn in, and if the weather had been rough, they not being accustomed to it, might have walked home and the company been broken up...." This was especially true since many of the men in Rohrer's company were sawmillers, and after they quit their jobs and enlisted the mills in Middletown were almost forced to close for want of workers. A tremendous amount of lumber was required to supply an army with its needs and wants, of course, and the mills had been thriving. The saws were cutting day and night to keep up with contracts, and the millers were making very good pay in working long hours. Leaving the mills at such a time when Lincoln called for volunteers was no small sacrifice for them to make. The company was not mustered in for another two days, but the good weather held and the only thing that seemed to bother the men was the shortage of fresh meat.[34]

During their first week in camp, the Middletown company was designated Company H of the 127th Pennsylvania Volunteers. The regiment was to be composed mostly of companies from towns in Dauphin County, including Harrisburg. Company A was almost wholly from the capital city and had been a militia organization that called itself the "First City Zouaves." The Zouaves were captained by F. Asbury Awl, a clerk at the Harrisburg National Bank. Back on April 18, 1861, just ten days short of his twenty-fourth birthday, Awl had become one of the first volunteers to enter Camp Curtin. He served for three months in the 11th Regiment, but at the close of his term had not reenlisted as much of that remarkable regiment had. Instead, he formed the First City Zouaves with the intention that they would serve as a sort of home guard unit. When he learned the 127th was being formed in Dauphin County, Awl led his company into camp and volunteered. Several weeks would pass before the 127th was organized with their fellow Harrisburg resident, William W. Jennings, as colonel.[35]

Despite the difficulties, volunteer companies came steadily into camp in August and September. To fill their quotas, some cities and counties had induced men to enlist by paying them bounties. This did increase enlistments in many areas, but many of the volunteers knew nothing of the bounties until they were placed in their hands. "Most of us were taken quite by surprize," wrote one drummer boy, "when, a few days after our arrival in camp, we were told that the County Commissioners had come down for the purpose of paying us each the magnificent sum of fifty dollars. At the same time, also, we learned that the United States Government would pay us each one hundred dollars additional, of which, however, only twenty-five were placed in our hands at once. The remaining seventy-five were to be received only by those who might safely pass through all the unknown dangers which awaited us, and live to be mustered out with the regiment three years later." Captain Rohrer was asked one day by a prominent citizen of Harrisburg to march his company into Harrisburg so each private could be given his fifty dollars from the county. "This was unexpected to me and I believe to all the rest of the company. It certainly was a great help to those who left families or parents at home dependent on them."[36]

The payment policy made no difference to most of the volunteers, for they looked upon the money as a windfall, and many had mixed emotions about the matter. "What cared we for bounty?" wrote one, "It seemed a questionable procedure, at all events, this offering of money as a reward for an act which, to be a worthy act at all, asks not and needs not the guerdon of gold. We were all so anxious to enter the service, that, instead of looking for any artificial helps in that direction, our only concern was lest we might be rejected by the examining surgeon and not be admitted to the ranks."[41]

So numerous were the troops arriving in Harrisburg in August, that Camp Curtin was of insufficient size to quarter them all. As early as the middle of the month, the Harrisburg boys of Captain Awl's Company A had moved to the fields north of

Camp Curtin to establish their own camp. As all of the men in the company lived in or near Harrisburg and were allowed to eat, sleep, and spend much of their time at their homes, the establishment of this new camp was not so much for their benefit as for the comfortable accommodation of the many companies and regiments expected in the weeks and months to come.[38] The men of Company A named the new place of encampment "Camp Simmons" in honor of their fellow Harrisburg citizen who had been killed on the Peninsula just weeks before.

A good many of the nine-month regiments spent at least a portion of their time in Harrisburg in Camp Simmons. Captain Tarbutton, who had been steadily performing his duties as drillmaster at Camp Curtin also became a kind of vice commandant in that he would exercise command of the camp during periods of little activity when no field officers were available or willing to do so. Tarbutton was in command when portions of many of the nine-month regiments began arriving.[39] As Camp Simmons was a satellite of the Old Camp, as Camp Curtin was sometimes now being called, Tarbutton exercised command over it as well.[40]

The men who had volunteered were finding life in camp quite pleasant. The weather was not wet or otherwise unbearable, and food was generally plentiful and wholesome. Between 12,000 and 15,000 men crowded into Camp Curtin in August, 1862, but the companionship seemed to put most in good spirits. "As far as I have learned," one soldier wrote home, "all are delighted with camp life. The weather has been fine, though excessively warm during the day—the nights however are moonlit, cool and pleasant. The kind friends at home should not picture to themselves dreary scenes of the camp, and imagine their 'brave soldier boys' are in the least low spirited or discontented, for a more jolly set were never seen. Wit and pleasantry rule the hour and everything goes as 'merry as a marriage bell.'" The same soldier wrote that even the few physical discomforts he and his comrades encountered were not sufficient to depress anyone. While out marching one day, "under a broiling hot sun," the boys began to drag a bit with no relief in sight. "This tried the endurance of the 'delicate young infants' considerably," he wrote. "One of the company, from whom perspiration was rolling profusely, drolly remarked, 'If this continues much longer I am afraid I'll meet a watery grave.' As the remark was considered unpardonable in a veteran, he was politely requested, by a companion in arms, to 'dry up,' which however, he positively refused to do until he reached the shade."[41] Another man wrote to a friend, "Well, I suppose the first question you ask is, How do you like soldiering? And the only answer I can give, so far, is, that I like it very well....I have not been examined and accepted yet, so I am not a regular soldier, and I am allowed to wear my citizen's suit. 'Bully for me.' I am having gay times. I stay in camp as long as I please, go down when I please, eat what I please, drink what I please, and, in fact, I am well pleased....We have a tick to lay on and the air above to cover us;...We get coffee, without cream, twice a day; bread twice a day, soup once and Army crackers once a day....I am in Camp Curtin to-day and will take tea here if nothing more than ordinary takes place. The next Sunday I can not tell where I will take tea, but, I hope in the Shenandoah Valley. The third will find me in Richmond, if nothing happens."[42]

But the longer the men were in camp, the more the novelty of the place and of living there wore off, and once organized into regiments and started to drilling, they saw life a bit differently.

As the month wore on, the men discovered that the constant shuffling of thousands of feet had completely worn away the grass in certain places in camp and pulverized the top soil into a fine white dust, which would hang in the air and cling to uniforms, sweaty faces and almost anything else. One soldier wrote home that the men of his company were so filthy that his lieutenant had taken them down to the river to wash them off. "Let me say," he wrote, "I never saw anything in my life to equal the dust in Camp Curtain [sic] and Harrisburgh [sic]. I think it is at least four to six in. deep and you may know that we *kick up a dust* when a regiment is marching."[43] After hearing a rumor that he and his regiment would soon be leaving, another man wrote, "I will be glad to go, as it is so very dusty here. Clouds of dust are in the atmosphere constantly." One man who came into camp in August said the ground inside the fence looked more than anything else like the "middle of a country road in midsummer."[44] Another newcomer saw the plain in camp, almost entirely unprotected from the sun by trees, as being "as cheerless as a desert," and was shocked to see the condition of the camp, "The barracks were dirty, the water poor, and the police arrangements... defective."[45] Garbage was still improperly disposed of and effluvia sat in an open sink exposed to the hot sun. "Coming as we did from pleasant homes to such a barren, dreary, uninviting spot," summed up one, "it is no wonder that the change was anything but agreeable."[46]

Sickness was, as always, well established with diarrhea being a little more common than usual. The dirt and disease tended to intensify the volunteers' dislike for the new burden of subordination and their impatience over the inactivity. "I have not pleasant memories connected with my stay in Camp Curtin," remembered one man, "and I never heard any soldier who was there speak well of it."[47] When orders to leave finally came, the news "was hailed with universal joy."[48] The historian of the 127th spoke for all the thousands that spent part of the summer of 1862 there when he wrote "there were not expressed regrets at leaving Camp Curtin."[49]

With so many men, discipline and maintaining order again became a problem. Wives, mothers, cousins, brothers and friends of soldiers traveled to Harrisburg to visit the boys before they went off to Virginia. It was a laborious administrative task to admit all these well wishers via the pass system, so exceptions were made. Visitors were allowed to roam freely into and out of the camp until scores of citizens became a part of the mad milieu of frenetic activity. Civilians came and went as they wished, and some took advantage of the opportunity to hawk pies, cakes and muffins to soldiers. Captain Tarbutton lost control of his camp. With all the unauthorized persons coming in and out, trouble could not be far behind. On August 15, an old woman arrived with a few pies to sell. She found buyers, then quickly left. Later that day, seven men died from eating of her pies, which were found to be poisoned. The woman was located and arrested and reportedly revealed herself to be of secessionist sympathies. The tragedy drew attention to the faults in the system, and the free admission policy to the camp was stopped, as was the selling of food to soldiers.[50]

The overcrowding forced a departure from standard procedure, and local recruits were allowed to continue living at their homes. They were required only to report to camp for roll call each morning and night and, of course, to drill with their respective companies.[51] While this freedom was only officially extended to the men from Harrisburg, a great many others from surrounding towns unofficially availed themselves of the chance to sneak out and go home for a few hours. Captain Rohrer requested and received a pass to return to Middletown to settle his affairs. He put his neighbor, First Lieutenant Shott, in command of the company for the night and took a ride to his home by another neighbor, who happened to be in Harrisburg. This was Rohrer's first visit home since he had left with the company for Harrisburg that tearful day, and Mrs. Rohrer was, of course, glad for the visit. The night was not to be a peaceful one, however. Around midnight, recalled the captain, "I heard considerable noise in the street." Running out of his house to investigate, Rohrer found that, "About one-half the company [his company!] were home and having a glorious old time. Scarcely 20 men slept in camp." Few, if any, of the men down from Camp Curtin for the night had passes. The next day, Rohrer settled his accounts, made out his will, and returned to find all of his men back in camp just as if they had never left.[52]

*   *   *

As all through the hot days of summer recruits arrived and added their energy to the bustle of the place, carpenters and teams pulling wagons of lumber became a part of the scene as new storehouses and guardhouses were erected.[53] Squads of men, some in uniform, some without, tramped to and fro in all parts of the camp. For most of the nine-month regiments there, the time for departure came between August 15 and 19, and it came suddenly. What had been a relatively leisurely life of recreation and occasional drill in camp came to an unexpected and abrupt end. It was not perfectly clear to the men of the ranks just why so many men were needed so quickly, but it was not difficult to guess.

Things had been going badly for the Union since the failure on the Peninsula. On July 19, Robert E. Lee began shifting his army. He had waited only long enough to be sure McClellan was no longer the greater threat to Richmond, and then immediately seized the initiative. Within days, Lee's assessment of the situation was proved correct as McClellan, under orders from Washington, began removing his army from the Peninsula. The Confederate commander pulled his army out of the trenches and holes around Richmond and threw portions of it fifty miles to the northwest around Gordonsville, Virginia, determined to take the war away from his own capital and closer to that of the enemy. On August 9, a sharp, costly battle was fought at Cedar Mountain, Virginia and, by the end of that month, Major General John Pope, the new Federal commander in Virginia, had committed the fatal mistake of pushing his army too far south, to the vicinity of Culpeper Court House, nearly 35 miles from his base of supply at Manassas Junction. Lee saw his opportunity, and wasted no time in striking with what was to be his most effective weapon over the next ten months of the war: Jackson.

In two days, Jackson marched his 12,000 men around Pope's flank and into his rear to Manassas Junction, where the supplies for the Federal army were consumed by hungry Confederates or put to the torch. Pope was astounded. He pulled out of his positions near Gordonsville and hustled back toward Manassas, not knowing how large a force was between him and his capital. Lee followed Jackson with the rest of the army, and, on August 30, the two armies clashed on the familiar plains above Bull Run, where the Federals had met with disaster just over a year before. The battle of Second Manassas was a soldier's fight, with charge after charge being repelled. At times, the fighting was hand to hand, with bayonets, clubbed muskets and rocks seeing use. Casualties in the two-day battle were hideous and high; the Federal army was trounced and retreated in disorder the 30 odd miles to Washington. Panic once again gripped the capital city. The triumphant Confederates were just a few short miles away and only the shattered army lay in their path.

Lincoln relieved Pope and again put McClellan in overall command of the army coming into the city. He was to reorganize the army into a force that could repel the expected attack. The circumstances had changed dramatically in two months. The end of June had seen McClellan's army just a few miles from Richmond and the Confederate army under Lee had been on the defensive. By the first of September, it was McClellan's army on the defensive in his own capital and Lee who had the offensive momentum.

But Lee did not attack Washington. He hoped first to relieve the war-ravaged Virginia countryside by taking the war into the North for a time. He hoped to subsist his army on Northern corn and hay and grain in the approaching harvest season. He wished to show to the people of the North, particularly the people of Pennsylvania, war as the people of Virginia had seen it. Finally, he wished to swell the ranks of his army with recruits in central Maryland, an area he believed to be sympathetic to the Southern cause. Lee side-stepped Washington and the disorganized army cowering there and headed up the Potomac River. On September 5, he crossed into Maryland. A few days later during a halt in Frederick, Maryland, he explained to one of his generals, John G. Walker, just what his plans were. The commanding general stood over a large map of Maryland and Pennsylvania and said to Walker, "In ten days from now, if the military situation is then what I confidently expect....I shall concentrate the army at Hagerstown, effectually destroy the Baltimore and Ohio [rail] road, and march to this point." Lee reached out a finger and touched the map at Harrisburg, Pennsylvania. "That is the objective point of the campaign." Lee went on to say that if the Pennsylvania Railroad bridge over the Susquehanna were destroyed, that railroad would be disabled for quite some time. "With the Baltimore and Ohio in our possession, and the Pennsylvania railroad broken up," Lee continued, "there will remain to the enemy but one route of communication with the West, and that very circuitous, by way of the [Great] lakes. After that I can turn my attention to Philadelphia, Baltimore, or Washington, as may seem best for our interests."

Walker expressed some surprise at the boldness of the plan, particularly in that it left McClellan and his entire army alone in the rear of Lee's army. Lee simply asked if Walker were familiar with McClellan, to which Walker replied that he was personally acquainted with him, but was not intimate. Lee replied, "He is an able general, but a very cautious one. His enemies among his own people think him much too. His army is in a very demoralized and chaotic condition, and will not be prepared for offensive operation—or he will not think it so—for three or four weeks. Before that time I hope to be on the Susquehanna."[54]

*   *   *

Those on the Susquehanna already were very much aware of just how close General Lee and his army were. They also knew that the very reasons that made Harrisburg an ideal place to rendezvous troops going to war made it an ideal target for the enemy. During the previous spring, Jackson and his victories in the Shenandoah Valley had created a minor panic in Harrisburg and the southern counties of Pennsylvania.[55] The people of the commonwealth, with the exception of sending men off to war, had been little touched by the conflict and they were not eager for that to change. Harrisburg had been a thriving town even before the war, with houses and public structures being built regularly. In 1856, a beautiful new pumping station had been built on the banks of the river to supply the residents with water, and, throughout the fall of 1861, despite restraints of the war, enough lumber and workmen came down the river and over the rails to enable a minor building boom to occur. More than 50 houses had been built in the city that fall, and, over the winter, proposals were made to construct hundreds more, as well as warehouses and shops. The residents of the city had little trouble imagining what would happen to all these fine new structures, the stately public buildings, the livestock, merchandise and other valuables in the city if the Rebels came. The general belief seemed to be that much of it would be burned, confiscated or stolen.[60]

All of the nine-month regiments had been shipped out, the last to leave, the 137th Pennsylvania, had departed by August 30. By then, Curtin, who was always closely observing events in the field, had begun to worry. After Second Manassas, he seriously began to fear for the safety of the lower counties of his state. By the time Lee crossed into Maryland on September 5, Curtin had already issued a proclamation suggesting that all able-bodied men begin to organize into home guard units and prepare themselves to repel invasion. This was the emergency that the Pennsylvania Reserves had originally been created to face, but the Reserves had been taken from Curtin and had not returned. Pennsylvania was now on its own. The governor sent scouts to Gettysburg and Chambersburg and beyond into Maryland. By the 7th, he was receiving information on the strength, condition and location of the Confederates from his sources and was forwarding it to Washington, or to McClellan or to General John Wool commanding at Baltimore, another threatened point.[57]

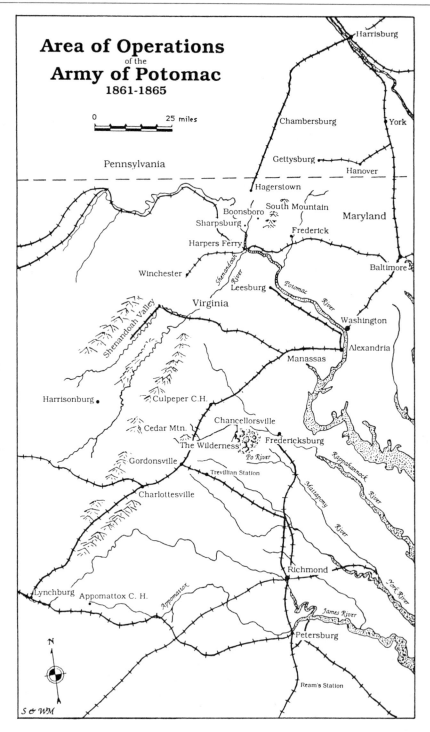

Area of Operations
of the
Army of Potomac
1861-1865

0   25 miles

Pennsylvania

Harrisburg

Chambersburg   York

Gettysburg
Hanover

Hagerstown

Boonsboro   South Mountain   Maryland
Sharpsburg
Frederick

Harpers Ferry

Winchester   Baltimore

Leesburg   Potomac River

Virginia

Washington

Alexandria

Manassas

Harrisonburg   Culpeper C.H.

Cedar Mtn.   Chancellorsville

The Wilderness   Fredericksburg

Gordonsville   Po River

Trevillian Station

Charlottesville

Richmond

Lynchburg   Appomattox C. H.

Petersburg

James River

N

Ream's Station

S & WM

Curtin had engineers survey the heights along the western side of the river in case fortifications would be required. He was not bashful about asking Washington for additional help. He asked the president to send to Harrisburg, "not less than 80,000 disciplined forces, and order from New York and States east all available forces to concentrate here at once. To this we will add all the militia forces possible, and I think that in a few days we can muster 50,000 men. It is our only hope to save the North and crush the Rebel army. Do not suppose for one instant that I am unnecessarily alarmed."[58] On the 10th, Curtin issued a call for 50,000 militiamen to come to the defense of the commonwealth.

To add to Curtin's fears, the Susquehanna was so low it could be forded at almost any point near the city.[59] The state and city authorities immediately began taking action for the security of the city. The state treasurer, Henry D. Moore, had all "bonds and treasure," as well as state and city historical records from both Harrisburg and Philadelphia packed up, and he escorted the lot to New York City for safekeeping.[60] The mayor of Harrisburg instituted a policy that would restrict movement by civilians in and out of the city. Any person wishing to travel from the city over a railroad had to obtain a pass from the mayor's office. This was not only to keep thousands from fleeing northward or westward away from the enemy, but also to hamper spies from moving southward to Lee's army. Most of the applications, however, came from what a local editor called the "craven and blanched cowards" that composed the "Army of exempts." These individuals, the editor wrote, "presented an athletic external appearance, but...represented that they were afflicted with dropsy,...troubled with the rheumatics...or annoyed with a faint spell about five years ago." These persons were, the editor summed up, better left to "the detestation of their friends."[61]

In this time of crisis, the newspapers of the city had, perhaps, their finest hour. Day after day they unabashedly printed recruitment and enlistment propaganda designed to cajole, embarrass, or shame men into enlisting at least for the duration of the emergency. Sometimes they resorted to out and out lies. "The stay at homes," the *Patriot and Union* wrote, "may think soldiering a hard life, but we know to the contrary. There is no place like a camp filled with jolly, good fellows, who make the welkin ring from morn to night with their musical voices. Among a hundred men there is always one...to keep the childish thoughts of home and a well-filled larder from the minds of those who have, perhaps, been tied too long to a woman's apron string. The merry disciples of fun banish dull care to the devil, and days go round unnoticed, so that even the Chaplain often asks on the Sabbath, 'what day is this?' He that calls the life of a soldier a hard one, knows not what he says."[62]

Enough young men were willing to believe that the army could be enjoyable for a while that within five days of Curtin's call almost 24,000 men were organized.[63] Curtin felt that a professional should command the militiamen and requested that Brigadier General John Reynolds, who was again commanding the Pennsylvania Reserves Division in McClellan's army, be detached for the purpose. McClellan protested, claiming Reynolds, who had just recently been exchanged and returned to the army after being taken prisoner, was needed by the army, but Lincoln or Stanton, or both, who wanted Curtin kept satisfied, ordered that Reynolds was to be detached and sent to Harrisburg.[64]

By the time Reynolds arrived in Harrisburg in mid-September, the city was once again overflowing with citizen soldiers. When the militiamen arrived, the barracks and tents in camp filled up first, and then the capitol grounds, as when the three-month volunteers had returned just over a year before. Louis Richards arrived in Harrisburg on the afternoon of September 13 as a member of a company from Reading and was surprised by the "scenes of great excitement and activity." The streets, especially around the capitol, were filled with briskly-walking men in uniform and officers on galloping horses. Bodies of men were being marched about in every direction and shouted commands filled the air. Upon arrival at the capitol itself, Richards saw Curtin and members of his staff were out on the grounds around the building moving among the militiamen and speaking to the company officers. They were personally superintending the organization of the militia companies into regiments.[65]

The volunteers were armed at the Arsenal with muskets and bayonets, which had to be carried fixed to the muskets because of a shortage of scabbards. No ammunition was distributed, which worried the men for, as Richards remembered, "some of [us] had expected to meet the rebels before night." When night came and they realized no Rebels would be confronted at least until morning, the boys relaxed some and concentrated on having some fun. "No military rules were promulgated," wrote Richard of the scene around the capitol "and it was very evident that none were to be observed that night. Chaos reigned supreme. Singing, speechmaking and practical jokes of all kinds filled the hours usually devoted to sleep, while the arrival of new companies, from time to time, appeared to stimulate the orgies as the night advanced."[66]

But the militiamen seemed to be a generally well-behaved lot, and few incidences of drunkenness and brawling were reported, though there were complaints that "little or nothing eatable seemed to be available in this town...."[67] The good behavior of the men, however, did not mean that there were no problems at all associated with their mobilization—10,000 men cannot camp for very long in the middle of a small city and not have a bad effect on things. The odors of thousands of unwashed bodies and clothes mingled with that of roasting meat and the smoke of wood fires and wafted nauseatingly through downtown Harrisburg. This joined with the stench of the effluvia from those same thousands of men, which was simply emptied into the gutter in the streets surrounding Capitol Hill.[68] The September sun was still strong enough to turn the entire place into a most unwholesome bivouac. This was not the same army of "merry disciples of fun" the editor of the *Patriot and Union* had described.[69]

Not all the militia regiments and companies were organized in Harrisburg, but most of the militiamen that responded to Curtin's call that September were probably in the captial city for at least a few days as they were outfitted and armed and moved on to other points. Most of those militia units that were sent someplace were sent to Chambersburg or Hagerstown, Maryland, where they were taught the rudimentary skills of being a soldier, such as loading and firing a gun and moving together in a body. One regiment was sent to Wilmington, Delaware, to guard the Dupont powder mills, whence the Federal armies and navy were supplied with gun powder.

*   *   *

In Maryland, General Lee was finding that the invasion was not to go just as he had expected. McClellan did not take the "three or four weeks" to move his army that the Virginian had expected. The Army of the Potomac had been led out of Washington on September 7. It was tired, frustrated and in disrepair after the recent hard campaigns and defeats in Virginia, but, much to Lee's surprise, the bruised and bloodied army answered the bell for the next round and staggered out of its corner.

The army was bolstered by the arrival of the new nine-month regiments and by a small wave of replacements for old, three-year regiments. One of the latter was 19-year-old George Eminhizer. The new private had left his parents' home on the banks of Marsh Creek in Centre County, Pennsylvania, just days earlier. His brother, Abraham, had enlisted in the 45th Pennsylvania in August, 1861, and this undoubtedly led

PRIVATE GEORGE EMINHIZER AND HIS BROTHER ABRAHAM, both of Company A, 45th Pennsylvania Volunteers.
George survived the war; Abraham was mortally wounded at Cold Harbor.
(from Albert's "History of the Forty-Fifth Pennsylvania")

George to travel to Harrisburg a year later and seek out one of the recruiting officers to enlist in his brother's company.[70] George spent a few days in Camp Curtin until he could be forwarded to the 45th, which lay at Brookes Station, Virginia. He was forwarded completely without training. Soon after he reported to Company A, he found himself drawn up in line with the rest of his new comrades in arms and heard the order to load weapons. "The command embarrassed me very much," he wrote later, "for I did not know how. I turned to my comrade on the right and said: 'Can you tell me which end of the cartridge I must put in first?' He loaded the gun for me."[71]

The Army of the Potomac's march through Maryland was to be remembered fondly ever afterward by the men of the ranks. For many, like Eminhizer, it was the first campaign, and the mild weather coupled with the friendly smiles of the Maryland girls made the rookies think soldiering very fine indeed. The veterans, of course, knew better, but enjoyed the buckets of cool water, the words of encouragement and the girls in their summer dresses as much, if not more, than the recruits. It was indeed good to be among friends again for the army that had spent the better part of a year in enemy country.

By the 14th of September, the Army of the Potomac had pursued the invading Confederates into western Maryland, and the rear guard of Lee's army was finally caught in the passes of low mountains several miles west of Frederick. The South Mountain range represented the eastern slope of the Cumberland Valley, which cut a roughly north-northeast path through Maryland and into Pennsylvania right up to the threshold of Harrisburg. It was up this valley that Lee had intended to march. For the men in the blue ranks, Sunday, the 14th of September began as just another day that promised sweat and dust and steady marching. As an early morning fog lifted from the meadows, the men could see the mountains ahead of them and, perhaps, grumbled about climbing over the steep roads. But good weather, pretty country, and companionship would make any such ordeal bearable, and they set off on the National Road headed west.

Before long, they heard firing ahead of them. Just how serious was none of them knew. The men did not know when or if they would be engaged, but later in the morning they began to get indications. As the men toiled through the wide and especially beautiful meadows approaching South Mountain, they began to see an increase in the activity of their field and staff officers. The veterans in the ranks, having seen such activity before, began to guess what was up, and soon saw other unmistakable signs of what lay ahead. The rookies, like lambs in a slaughterhouse, paid all the excitement around them—the galloping and shouting of the officers—no especial heed, and tramped unnoticingly by the tell-tale debris of playing cards and dice scattered on the road. Some wondered at the sudden change in mood of their experienced friends, and tried to fill the conversational void with news from home. "Do you know what some of the people in Centre County told me when I left home?" offered young George Eminhizer to his comrades in the 45th, "they said the 45th regiment, would see very little fighting, as they are Curtin's pets." One of the veterans, apparently of a nautical bent, simply pointed to the cards on the road and said, "That means breakers ahead."[72] Soldiers in both armies subscribed to the belief of all good God-fearing people that playing cards, and the gambling done with them, were immoral, and the Lord would not look kindly upon any man killed with such evil instruments on his body. The veterans grimly discarded them before battle.

The maritime soldier of the 45th was correct. In less than an hour, the regiment, and much of the rest of the army, hit "breakers" in the passes on South Mountain. The Confederates, about 14,000 of them, had taken strong positions on the crest, in Turner's Gap through which the National Road passed, and in the woods all up the slope.

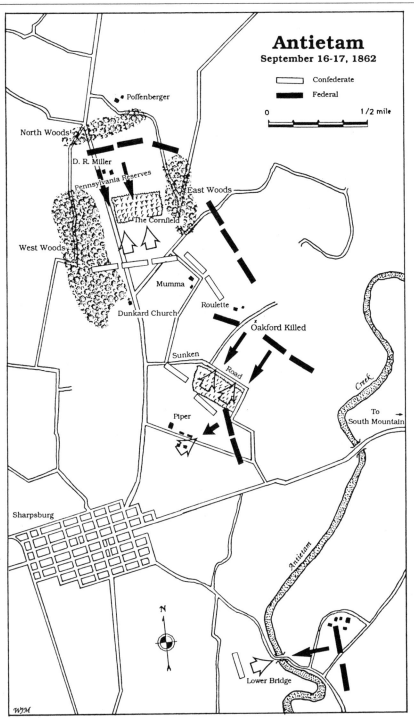

Antietam

September 16-17, 1862

Confederate

Federal

0   1/2 mile

Poffenberger

North Woods

D. R. Miller

Pennsylvania Reserves

East Woods

The Cornfield

West Woods

Mumma

Roulette

Dunkard Church

Oakford Killed

Sunken

Road

Piper

To
South Mountain

Sharpsburg

N

Lower Bridge

Creek

Antietam

WJM

The eastern face of the mountain range was steep and cut everywhere by deep gullies and gorges filled with thicket-covered boulders. A few farms sat in the valley or on the slope near the pass with fields of corn and other crops lying on the less-crazily-tilted parts of the hill and bordered by low stone walls or rail fences. Dense woods covered all else. Brigadier General George Meade, who was leading the Pennsylvania Reserves that day, called the battleground "the most rugged country I almost ever saw."[73] After several hours of firing uphill and clambering up the steep and craggy slopes, the Federals wrested the passes from the Rebel defenders just after dark. Casualties were high, especially in the ranks of the Pennsylvania Reserves.

Among the killed was Lieutenant William Carter of the 8th Reserves, who had spent several months in the spring of 1862 in Camp Curtin as part of the permanent recruiting party. Carter had gone to the Peninsula in June with the 8th and had been wounded in the leg in the battles around Richmond. He had spent much of the rest of the summer at his home in Harrisburg recuperating. His leg had been strong enough on August 18, however, for him to stand in St. Patrick's Church in Harrisburg and take as his wife his longtime sweetheart, 19-year-old Mary Ellen Gross. One story has it that the newlyweds had had one night together before William hastened off to rejoin his company. Less than a month after the wedding Lieutenant Carter was dead, killed instantly by a Confederate bullet as he leapt over a wall on the eastern face of South Mountain.[74]

*   *   *

The Confederate army had needed all the time bought for it by the rear guard at South Mountain. Lee hurriedly brought his army together at a central point, selecting as his battleground the rolling hills and wood lots north and east of the small cross-roads town of Sharpsburg, Maryland, just a few miles west of South Mountain. The deep country roads, cornfields, fences and stands of trees around Sharpsburg allowed plenty of places for companies and regiments to find good defensive cover, and even the open fields were so full of swells and swales that whole regiments could disappear from view in one of the depressions. It was good ground to defend.

On the evening of September 16, Major General Joseph Hooker's First Corps, including the Pennsylvania Reserves, crossed Antietam Creek to the ground Lee had chosen. The Confederates shelled the Federal column as it moved into position on the farm of Joseph Poffenberger. Again, the Bucktails were thrown out as skirmishers through some woods and into the cornfield of Poffenberger's neighbor, D. R. Miller. Preparations were made for a general advance on the Confederate positions, but the day was well advanced, and the two armies merely skirmished briefly before ending the fighting around dark. The Reserves remained on the battle line, ready to resume the fight the next day. Brigade commander Truman Seymour wrote that his men slept "feet to feet with the rebels, and that the battle must begin as soon as it became light enough to distinguish friend from foe."[75]

*   *   *

Dawn in the Maryland farm country around Sharpsburg came gray and damp on the 17th. Both armies lay stretched across the meadows and wood lots with portions of each "close enough to look into each other's eyes." As General Seymour had predicted, the firing began at first light. The Federals, including most of the Pennsylvania Reserves, advanced through Miller's cornfield. Confederate infantry held a shallow rise in the ground at the southern end of the field and Southern artillery controlled the expanse of the field to the north of the rise, so Federal infantry approaching the Rebel lines from the north was subjected to the converging fire of musketry and artillery. Head-high corn was clipped by Minie balls and deep furrows were ploughed in the soft, red earth by solid shot. Men were hit by balls and shrapnel and fell bleeding and writhing onto mats of broken, trampled corn stalks. Blood, brains and green corn pulp was splattered on faces and blue woolen. The air was filled with the sounds of explosions, ripping volleys of musketry and the screams of shells and wounded men.[76] The fighting went on for hours, each advantage met by a counterthrust, and by the end of the morning, the Federals halted their assaults, unable to move the Confederates from the bloody cornfield.

About a mile southeast from the cornfield, still on the other bank of the Antietam, the Second Corps of the Army of the Potomac waited to go into the fight in support of the men in the cornfield. Among the waiting men sat a red-headed, blue-eyed boy of 20 named Elisha Farnum.[77] He had been a mechanic in a small shop in Fallstown, Wyoming County, Pennsylvania, not far from Scranton, when, in the first week of August, 1862, he had gone to war and enlisted as a private in Captain S. W. Ingramm's company of nine-month volunteers. Just two years ago that very week, he had been married to 17-year-old Eliza Ross. Farnum had marked the anniversary by leaving his young, childless wife and going down to Harrisburg, where he was mustered in on the 11th of the month at Camp Curtin. His company had been designated Company B of the 132nd Pennsylvania Volunteers, under Colonel Richard A. Oakford. The regiment had remained in camp a bit over a week, then shipped out to Washington, where it had remained until the first days of September. The men of the 132nd had then joined the army in pursuit of the invading Confederates. Farnum and the men of the 132nd were, for the most part, as green as grass. They had been in the service just a bit over a month. As he sat in the meadow by the Antietam on the morning of the 17th of September, Farnum had been away from his home and wife a mere forty days, and few of his comrades were any more experienced than he.[78] With dry mouths and unsteady stomachs, Farnum and his untested friends sat waiting quietly—perhaps re-reading recent letters from home or anxiously fingering photographs of wives, children or sweethearts—and listened to the fury of the battle raging just a short distance to the north, knowing they would be "going in" before long.

About 6 a.m., the 132nd was ordered forward. Colonel Oakford led the regiment down to the edge of the creek and gave the order for the men to wade across. The order caught many of the rookies by surprise, for this was the first time they had been called upon to cross any water and they were amazed that they were expected

COLONEL RICHARD OAKFORD
132nd Pennsylvania Volunteers.
Oakford served as commandant while his regiment was being formed in Camp Curtin throughout August, 1862. He led his men into the field in early September and was killed just two weeks later at Antietam.
(from Hitchcock's "War From the Inside")

to wade across fully dressed. The gentle waters were about chest deep, and cartridge boxes and muskets had to be held overhead during the crossing. When the men emerged on the far bank, many were excessively bothered by their wet clothes and feet, but the officers chastened them to ignore the discomfort and prepare for the work ahead. Carefully, the ranks were reformed and the regiment set off over some shallow hills toward the fighting.[79] Oakford and his men came onto the property of William Roulette, and a number of the men stopped by a spring to fill their canteens with some of the sweet water. Wounded men streaming back from the firing line were beginning to appear in greater numbers around the 132nd and the rookies were generous in giving their canteens of spring water to the injured.[80] But Confederates were everywhere on the farm, especially in the outbuildings and behind fences, and the Pennsylvanians were quickly formed for battle. The men, maintaining formation, double-quicked through the yard, driving off the Confederate skirmishers and securing the farm. Colonel Oakford and his officers seemed to have the men and the situation well in hand until suddenly a portion of their line disintegrated. Roulette's modest apiary was somehow upset as the men of the 132nd hustled past it, and the air at once became filled with enraged bees. The dressed ranks of the regiment melted into a mob of wildly-screaming, arm-flapping men running in every direction.[81] The officers ran about trying to reform the regiment's broken ranks. Finally, their presence of mind prevailed, and the men were regrouped sufficiently to resume the advance.

The Confederate skirmishers had withdrawn down a narrow farm lane that lay between two knolls. While the 132nd formed for the advance, Colonel Oakford rode among the men offering words of encouragement. When all was ready, the officers dismounted, sent horses to the rear, and the advance began. Almost immediately, the colonel was shot in the left shoulder just below the collarbone. An artery was cut by the bullet, and Oakford, who had been in command of the regiment for just over a month, bled to death in the few minutes before a surgeon could reach him. The advance continued without him.[82]

On the other side of the hills, the unseen Confederates had taken up an extremely strong position in a sunken road about fifty yards over the crest. There they waited, listening to the drums of the approaching Yankees. Soon, the staffs of the Federal flags came bobbing into view over the crest. A Confederate colonel, Alabamian John Brown Gordon, stood in the sunken lane in the early morning sun and was suddenly struck by the beauty of the scene. "The day was clear and beautiful, with scarcely a cloud in the sky," he wrote later. "The men in blue...[were] formed in my front, an assaulting column four lines deep. The front line came to a 'charge bayonets,' and the other lines to a 'right shoulder shift.' The brave Union commander, superbly mounted, placed himself in front, while his band in rear cheered them with martial music. It was a thrilling spectacle. The entire force, I concluded, was composed of fresh troops from Washington or some other camp of instruction. So far as I could see, every soldier wore white gaiters around his ankles. The banners above them had apparently never been discolored by the smoke and dust of battle. Their gleaming bayonets flashed like burnished silver in the sunlight. With a precision of step and perfect alignment of a holiday parade, this magnificent array moved to the charge, every step keeping time to the tap of the deep-sounding drum. As we stood looking upon that brilliant pageant, I thought...'What a pity to spoil with bullets such a scene of martial beauty!' "[90]

Gordon had his men wait until the Federals "were so close that we might have seen the eagles on their buttons," then let them cut loose with a volley in which every bullet seemed to find its mark.[84] Men began screaming and falling instantly, throwing up their arms or dropping to the ground clutching their heads, stomachs, or arms. Almost the entire front rank fell. "We were ordered to lie down just under the top of the hill," remembered Lieutenant Fred Hitchcock, regimental adjutant of the 132nd, "and crawl forward and fire over, each man crawling back, reloading his piece in the prone position, and again crawling forward and firing." No headway was made against the entrenched Confederates, especially once the Pennsylvanians lay down. "The air was full of whizzing, singing, buzzing bullets," recalled Lieutenant Hitchcock. "Once down on the ground under cover of the hill, it required very strong resolution to get up...yet it was the duty of us officers...."[85]

The firing continued on the brow of the hill and in the sunken road for more than an hour. The rookies were struggling to hold their own. "The air was now thick with smoke from the muskets," wrote Hitchcock, "which not only obscured our vision of the enemy, but made breathing difficult and most uncomfortable. The day was excessively hot, and no air stirring, we were forced to breathe this powder smoke, impregnated with saltpetre, which burned the coating of nose, throat, and eyes almost like fire."[86] The Confederates in the road were Alabamians and North Carolinians and they were holding off the Federal attackers well. But they, too, were suffering. Colonel Gordon was hit by five bullets, the last one striking him in the face. He was borne from the field nearly unconscious.[87]

Sometime during the fight, Elisha Farnum was struck by a Minie ball in the middle of his right arm. The ball hit the bones in the elbow joint squarely and cracked the humerus half-way to his shoulder. Private Farnam bled and writhed in the dirt of Roulette's ploughed field, while the stumbling, kicking feet of the men of Company B trampled about him.[88]

While the 132nd was engaged, other portions of the Second Corps were coming up in support. Brigadier General John Caldwell's brigade crossed the creek about 9 a.m. The brigade included the 7th New York, which had been raised principally in New York City and was comprised almost entirely of English-speaking German immigrants, one of whom was Private Henry Gerrish.

Gerrish had come to New York City at age 16 and learned the upholsterer's trade, taking home two and one half dollars a week. At Lincoln's first call in April, 1861, the 21 year old had enlisted in the 7th New York Volunteer Infantry for two years.[89] The 7th had been involved in the fight at Big Bethel on the Peninsula in June, 1861, claimed as the first land battle of the war. The regiment had also been present to watch the battle between the Monitor and the Merrimac in March of 1862 and had then moved on to Richmond in McClellan's fruitless Peninsula campaign. Casualties had greatly reduced the ranks, especially among the officers, and a Captain Charles Brestel, who spoke only broken English, now commanded the regiment.

"The water reached to our armpits," Gerrish remembered later of the crossing of the creek, "[we were carrying] our cartridge boxes around our necks, and at the same time filling our canteens as this was fine fresh clean water..." They emerged dripping on the other bank of the Antietam and reformed for the advance. The Germans, like the 132nd Pennsylvania before them, moved up into the fields and toward the ripping volleys of musketry beyond. They came onto the far left of the Union line facing the Sunken Road, a few hundred yards from where the 132nd was pinned down on the crest of the knoll. The 7th and the rest of the brigade pitched into the struggle and began banging away at the Rebels in the road and in the standing corn beyond. The Confederates there proved not as stubborn as the Alabamians facing the 132nd, and the gray line gave way. The Rebels were pursued into the corn and beyond into an orchard. The 7th moved forward in dressed ranks, colors flying, drums tapping out the cadence, all the while taking a steady fire of grape and solid shot. The New Yorkers came to a farm where Confederates were stongly posted. "There was probably a whole regiment in and around the outbuildings, stationed there with a number of cannons," remembered Gerrish later. "I happened to be the fifth man from our flag in the front rank, and as they began I saw a cannonier [sic] loading a gun, [and] saw it pushed in a position to fire." The gun was rolled up behind a solid board fence and the Rebel gunners stuck the muzzle through a hole created by a missing plank but held their fire as the blue line advanced to within seventy-five feet. The New Yorkers stepped closer, each watching and waiting for the gun to erupt and throw what was undoubtedly grapeshot or cannister into them at near point-blank range. The scene was indelibly impressed on Private Gerrish's memory, for years later he wrote, "I thought I could see half way into the bore of that gun."

Finally the explosion came, and, like a giant shotgun, the Rebel gun spewed hot iron balls at the New Yorkers, knocking a dozen or so men out of the ranks almost instantly. Gerrish was one of them. "The concussion of the shot made me reel about thirty-five feet back from the line before I fell....Of course I had only seconds to think, and when I came to and pulled myself together I found the damage was not as great as it might have been, under the circumstances." A ball or a piece of shrapnel had ripped through his left hand, gashing his wrist and mangling his thumb. He was still dazed, and his wounds were bleeding freely.

It was his great fortune to be carrying in his haversack that day two rolls of bandages. A ladies' charitable society in New York had made a gift to the regiment of hundreds of rolled bandages, and most of the men were carrying two with them as they entered the battle. These bandages possibly saved Henry Gerrish's life. While sitting in the dust, he took one of the rolls from his haversack, and "with my right hand and my...strong teeth I wound it around my wrist to diminish the flow of blood. With the other [bandage] I did up my hand as best I could...."

Gerrish's adventures were far from over, for while he lay flat on the ground, "the bullets from the rebels were whistling over my head in thousands, and small balls from grapeshot the size of pigeon or small hen eggs ploughed up the ground all around me...." Like all wounded men, Gerrish was also in great danger of being trampled by the flailing hooves and pounding wheels of artillery horses and cassions as they thundered in and out of battery. As he lay on the ground beneath the singing Rebel bullets, some Yankee gun crews charged furiously toward him, forcing him to choose which was the lesser of the two dangers, the bullets or the wheels and hooves. He still had his legs in fine working order, so he decided to use them. Springing to his feet amid the shrieking shells and Minie balls he scrambled about and maneuvered between the guns as they were pulled past him at a "wild gallop." He then lost little time in heading back through the corn toward the rear and a hospital.[90]

Another mile or so to the south, an entire corps of the Army of the Potomac was being held off by about three hundred marksmen from Georgia in a very strong position. The creek was a bit deeper at this point, and the Ninth Corps commander, Major General Ambrose Burnside, determined that a stone bridge spanning the stream was the only practical way for his men to cross. The Confederates, though, had dug in on bluffs overlooking the bridge, "ensconced in...rude but substantial breastworks, in quarry holes, behind high ranks of cord-wood, logs, [and] stone piles," and every effort by the Federals to take the bridge had been turned back with severe loss. The Georgians fired too quickly and hit their marks too consistently for the Yanks to make any headway, and hours slipped by as the stalemate remained.[91]

Late in the morning, Burnside decided another attempt had to be made to cross the bridge and secure a foothold on the opposite bank. Brigadier General Edward Ferraro's brigade of four regiments was to make the assault, and Ferraro chose two to head the storming party: The 51st New York and the 51st Pennsylvania.

The 51st Pennsylvania had lost none of its wildness since leaving Camp Curtin. The men still liked to drink and play and steal hogs or whatever else they could find that was edible, but they had tempered their reputation as troublemakers with a reputation for getting things done on the battlefield. The regiment had been engaged at Camden, South Carolina, where it had soundly whipped the small Rebel force against it, and had fought at Second Manassas as well. Colonel Hartranft's men did not always act as ideal soldiers, but they fought well enough, and their officers could not ask for much more. At present, however, the regiment was under a sort of mild punishment for some trifling affair and had been deprived of the whiskey ration often given to troops as a reward for good fighting or marching.

About noon, General Ferraro drew up the two 51sts and gave them what was intended to be a little pep talk. He told them that Burnside himself requested that they make the charge, because he was sure they would take the bridge. One of the Pennsylvanians, however, perhaps recognizing malarkey when he heard it and impatient to know what was in it for him and his buddies, cut the general short by shouting out a proposition: Would the regiment be given back its whiskey ration if it took the bridge? "Yes, by God," shouted the eager Ferraro, "you shall all have as much as you want, if you take that bridge,....if...I have to send to New York to get it, and pay for it out of my own private purse....Will you take it?" The 51sts responded with a resounding "Yes," and the bargain was struck.[92]

The New Yorkers and Pennsylvanians formed their lines within some woods, the nearest available cover from the Confederate sharpshooters. The bridge was a hundred yards or so away, and every inch of it was entirely exposed to the Rebel guns. Finally the order was given, and with a throaty cheer the two regiments swept forward on the dead run. They were met with an accurate fire and many fell before the open ground was passed. A stone wall ran along the bank of the creek on both sides of the bridge, and the two regiments took refuge there to regroup. They opened a hot fire upon the bluffs, now just fifty yards away. The Confederate fire slackened and suddenly Colonel Hartranft was on his feet shouting for the charge. Both regiments immediately got up and onto the bridge, upon which the fire from the bluffs was hotter than ever. The blue wave surged and washed over the narrow, funnel of a bridge, color bearers in the lead. Hartranft stood exposed, hat in one hand, sword in the other, waving both wildly. He had yelled himself hoarse, but managed to rasp out encouragement, "Come on, boys, for I can't holloa anymore."[93]

The bridge had been taken, and the bluffs were evacuated by the Georgians as Ohioans and Bay Staters and Connecticuters and others swarmed across the bridge cheering the work of the New Yorkers and the Pennsylvanians. The whole charge had not taken twelve minutes, but scores of Pennsylvanians and New Yorkers lay strewn over the ground and all across the bridge.[94] Among the wounded was Sergeant Thomas Parker of the 51st. Parker, who had been promoted just two days before the battle, received just a minor wound, so minor it did not even require the services of a doctor. Not so fortunate was First Lieutenant Jacob Gilbert Beaver, younger and only brother of James A. Beaver of the 45th Pennsylvania. Lieutenant Beaver, an officer of promise, fell dead as his company stormed over the bridge.[95]

Burnside's whole corps was soon over the bridge and up on the bluffs and the high ground above the creek, pushing the Confederates back. For the first time that day, the men in the gray and butternut were being driven. They retreated slowly from stone wall to barn to fence line, but they were steadily pushed back toward Sharpsburg and the main road that led to the principal ford across the Potomac, Lee's escape route. Suddenly, in what was one of the more astounding events of the war, Confederate reinforcements unexpectedly arrived from Harpers Ferry. The momentum shifted, and the Rebels began driving the men in blue. Lee's line of retreat, and his army, were saved at the eleventh hour, and finally the long day of fighting came to a close. Neither side would admit defeat, but neither could truthfully claim victory, for neither retreated from the field and both remained prepared to resume the contest. One of the few clear-cut triumphs that day was that the 51st Pennsylvania won back its keg of whiskey.

The armies that lay in the fields around Sharpsburg were through fighting for the time being, but for the armies that lay wounded in the barns, churches, homes and field hospitals, the battle was just beginning. Medical supplies were in distressingly short supply, and surgeons resorted to binding wounds with green corn leaves.[96] In a field hospital to the rear of where the 132nd had fought at the Sunken Road, Lieutenant Fred Hitchcock found a grim scene. "Outside the hospital were piles of amputated arms, legs and feet, thrown out with as little care as so many pieces of wood. Also lying outside were the bodies of many soldiers who had died after reaching the hospital. Inside, on bunches of hay and straw, the men were lying so thickly that there was scant room for the surgeon and attendants to move among them."[97]

Among those lying on the straw was Elisha Farnum. His arm would never be the same, that much was clear to the surgeons who first examined him. Though they had little hope of ever restoring the elbow to working order, surprisingly enough, the surgeons made an attempt to save the arm. The doctors removed the bullet from his arm and found bits of shattered bones embedded in the soft lead. The curiosity was given to Farnum as a souvenir—he would keep it until his death. The surgeons then waited to see if their technique would save the young man's arm, while Farnum endured the nauseating pain of splintered bones and torn flesh. After ten days, the doctors realized the arm could not be saved. The bone was cut about six inches below the shoulder, and Elisha Farnum was sent out of the war, having served for a little more than thirty days and been in one fight.[98]

CHAPTER FIVE

"Cripple Camp"

SEPTEMBER, 1862 — MAY, 1863

More than 23,000 men had been killed or wounded at Antietam, making September 17, 1862 the bloodiest day of the war. Five thousand had been killed outright, but 18,000 others faced the prospect of long stays in hospitals, longer periods of rehabilitation or permanent disability or disfigurement.[1] Some, like Elisha Farnum, faced a grim future. Others, like Henry Gerrish, were fortunate in that their wounds, though painful and temporarily incapacitating, were minor.

In the days following the battle, Harrisburg once again became a concentration point for the wounded and the captured, and the number of arrivals far exceeded the facilities for quartering them. The prisoners were packed into the rear of Camp Curtin and removed to more permanent quarters at Fort Delaware as promptly as possible. In this operation, Company A of the 127th Pennsylvania, which had been kept behind when the rest of the regiment departed, usually served as escort for the prisoners to Delaware. Several hundred Confederates were moved through Harrisburg before the end of September.[2]

The camp's hospital was filled to overflowing, but still the wounded arrived. They took up space in every church, school, hall and willing household in the city. The population of recruits in Camp Curtin was low, so the ambulatory cases, like Private Gerrish, were sent to the barracks there, and they called themselves "The Cripple Brigade."[3] The number of sick and wounded fluctuated as men were shipped farther north to their homes or died of their wounds and were replaced with men from hospitals in Maryland around Sharpsburg.[4] Through the end of September, very nearly 1,000 sick or wounded soldiers lay in the hospitals at camp or around the city. By mid-October, many of the less serious cases had recovered sufficiently to return to their regiments or go home to complete their recovery. A month later, more than 500 remained in Harrisburg hospitals. That number actually grew to more than 700 by the end of November as the cold weather began to have its normally bad effect on the general health of the men in camps. In any event, at no time between mid-September, when the wounded arrived from South Mountain and Antietam, and Christmas was the population of wounded and sick in and around Harrisburg less than 500.[5]

Pennsylvanians throughout the commonwealth were as thoughtful and as generous as ever, and on virtually every train into the capital came boxes and crates and packages of material donated for the comfort of the sick and wounded. The quartermaster's storehouse at Camp Curtin was stocked full with scores of boxes of clean new shirts, socks, trousers and underclothing as well as bandages and lint to help bind up wounds. The supplies came from ladies' and civic groups all over the commonwealth, and the goods unquestionably helped ease the discomfort of the stricken men.

The people of Harrisburg were not to be outdone in kindness or generosity and the hospitals were daily filled with volunteer nurses and friendly visitors bearing cakes and pies and other treats for the soldiers. As time passed, the fatality rate among the wounded steadily dropped; this might have been due to the passage of men through the critical days and weeks after their bodies had received the shock of bullets, shrapnel, loss of blood and surgeons' knives, but it might instead have been due to the cheerful and tireless efforts of the people—particularly the ladies—of Harrisburg. The effect on the health of the wounded of their selfless, spirit-raising goodwill visits cannot be overestimated.

THE CAMP CURTIN HOSPITAL *(Dauphin County Historical Society)*

Also thronging into Harrisburg after the battle were relatives of wounded or killed soldiers from all over the North. They came in search of their soldier or his remains. One such father was Dr. Oliver Wendell Holmes, "The Autocrat of the Breakfast Table." Holmes was a poet and essayist of renown throughout the country, but especially in the North. On the night of September 17, he had been roused from his bed on Beacon Hill in Boston by the bearer of a telegram that told of the wounding of his son, Captain Oliver Wendell Holmes, Jr. of Company A, 20th Massachusetts. Captain Holmes had been shot through the neck during the fighting in the cornfield at Antietam.

Dr. Holmes was on the next train south and traveled to Philadelphia, to Frederick, Maryland, to the battlefield itself, back to Philadelphia and finally to Harrisburg, in search of his son. Captain Holmes was part of the sea of wounded that flooded the barns, churches and schools of Maryland and southern Pennsylvania, and his whereabouts and condition were unknown. The elder Holmes arrived at the Herr House in the center of Harrisburg just days after the battle and found himself among a considerable number of white-haired old gentlemen on errands like his. Looking for clues to the health or whereabouts of his son, the Doctor sought Dr. James P. Wilson, who had charge of all the hospitals in the city.

"A man who has not slept for a fortnight or so is not expected to be, affable," wrote Holmes, but Wilson, with his "thick, dark moustache—chopped off square at the lower edge of the upper lip" greeted Holmes very kindly and good-naturedly. Unfortunately, Wilson had not seen or heard of Captain Holmes, and could only suggest that Dr. Holmes wait in town for a time on the chance that his son would come in on one of the frequently arriving trains from the south.[6] This Holmes did, but he did not sit idly in his hotel room in the meantime. He visited the many hospitals around the city, but did not find his captain. In one hospital set up in a school house, however, he found men from all states and happened upon some Massachusetts boys with whom he was acquainted. They told him of their wounding and of their stay in the hospital. "I learned," wrote Holmes,...that they and their comrades were completely overwhelmed by the attentions of the good people of Harrisburg,—that the ladies brought them fruits and flowers, and smiles, better than either,—and that the little boys of the place were almost fighting for the privilege of doing their errands. I am afraid there will be a good many hearts pierced in this war that have no bullet-mark to show."[7]

Holmes next went with some friends out to Camp Curtin itself and was admitted to the enclosure without difficulty. He found the place "spacious [and] well-kept" but ultimately disappointing, for Captain Holmes was not and had not been at the Camp Hospital.[8]

Not until later that night did Holmes finally receive word of his son. He had been in Hagerstown recovering and would arrive in Harrisburg the next day. After a lengthy delay, which caused the anxious father additional concern lest the train be involved in a wreck, the morning train arrived bringing Captain Holmes, future justice of the Supreme Court of the United States. Father and son were reunited as the train stood at rest by the Harrisburg depot of the Pennsylvania Railroad.[9]

The elder Holmes had good reason to be concerned about train accidents, for they were not uncommon. The high number of trains moving in and out of Harrisburg in the days after Antietam made the risk of mishap even greater, and just nine days after the battle the area's most serious railroad disaster of the war occurred just across the river.

Militia units called out to repel the invasion were gradually returning to Harrisburg to be mustered out of service and sent home. Governor Curtin had issued a proclamation on the 24th of September informing the citizens of the commonwealth that the emergency had passed and the militiamen were no longer needed. The 20th Pennsylvania Militia regiment had been in service at Hagerstown but was on its way home on September 26, returning to Harrisburg via Carlisle over the Cumberland Valley Railroad. The morning was foggy and visibility was poor as the train bearing the regiment approached Bridgeport, on the west bank of the Susquehanna just opposite Harrisburg, about 7 a.m. on the 26th. The locomotive proceeded slowly, not only because of the fog, but because the area was thickly settled. At about the same time, another train left Bridgeport heading south on the same track. No whistles were sounded, and both trains were moving so slowly that neither made much noise. Just outside the town boundary, the two collided head on in the heavy mists at the combined speed of about 14 miles per hour. The force of the collision threw militiamen all about the inside of the cars. A few were thrown completely out of the cars and into the gravel and weeds of the embankment by the tracks.

The sound of the wreck brought people running out of nearby houses. Company A of the 127th Pennsylvania, which had recently returned from one of its trips to Fort Delaware, was encamped on a nearby hill. The men came running down the slope to help the victims. No one knew exactly what had happened, nor did any one know just how many had been hurt and how seriously, but somewhere between four and 11 had been killed and between 30 and 80 had been injured. A number of men from the 118th Pennsylvania had also been on the train and were seriously hurt. The injured men were picked up and carried to nearby homes or put in wagons and taken to one of the hospitals in Harrisburg, but the twisted, smoking mass of metal that lay on the track spouting jets of steam was not so easily taken care of. The important track had to be closed until the engines and damaged cars could be removed. Sometime later, the Cumberland Valley Railroad paid damages to the victims and their families in an effort to atone for their mismanagement that morning, but little could be done for those people whose fathers, sons, or husbands had gone off to war for a few weeks and who were now as dead as if they had been felled by Confederate bullets.[10]

Several times during the war when Camp Curtin was filled to capacity, the grounds of the capitol (cupola visible above the trees) were turned into a campground to handle the overflow. Here militiamen called out during the 1862 Confederate invasion of Maryland drill in their civilian clothes on the grounds and on Third Street (left).

Harper's Weekly, October 4, 1862

Of the thousands wounded at Antietam, comparatively few had the good fortune to be retrieved by a parent. Most could only wait in camp or hospital for their wounds to heal. One of the many required to remain in the care of the surgeon was Henry Gerrish. His torn and bandaged wrist and hand did not heal promptly, and he was kept in Camp Curtin throughout October and November. Gerrish was fortunate in that he had his mobility. He was not confined to a hospital ward where the air was fouled with body odors and the exhalations of scores of diseased men—where men languished in boredom and depression, entirely dependent upon the visits of the kind people of the neighborhood for a lift in spirits. Gerrish could walk about the hospital and the camp. He could sun himself on the banks of the wide, sparkling river and gain strength of spirit by strolling in the open air and taking in the yellow maples, red oaks, and blue sky that became the walls and ceiling of Camp Curtin in the autumn. He found not just the neighborhood agreeable, but the neighbors as well. "The citizens here were very kind and very patriotic," Gerrish wrote later. "This Camp Curtain [sic], or 'Cripple Camp,' was located about one short mile outside the city of Harrisburg, where farming districts began, and alongside the Susquehanna river...we, or those that could walk, had liberty to go beyond the camp and look over the farms and the country in general. On those trips we generally took along our haversacks, and as the farmers were very kind and liberal we were most always well loaded up with apples, pears, tomatoes, sweet potatoes, etc. which we brought to the boys who could not walk, and by them heartily appreciated."[11]

The local people, who had always been generous with the soldiers, did not themselves forget about the men restricted to "Cripple Camp", which Camp Curtin had quite truthfully become. "The farmers," recalled Gerrish, "and other well-to-do people in the vicinity...brought in wagon loads of well cooked provisions at different times for those that happened to be badly wounded or sick. I well remember an old lady in particular who came to our camp about every other day for about six weeks with a wagon load of finely cooked vegetables, soups, chickens, etc. and from her I got a small dish of stewed tomatoes, the first I ever had, and they seemed very fine. We talked with this lady one day, and she told us that her husband was a captain in the cavalry, and that of her five sons, four of them were in the army also. One of them had been killed and two wounded, and if Lincoln would need the fifth she would let him go also...."[12]

The bountiful harvest that allowed the citizens to be so generous heralded the advent of cooler weather. The vigorous outdoor life that had been a benefit to the injured men like Gerrish while the weather was mild could become detrimental to their still weakened bodies as the nights grew cold and the winds from the river began to bite. The army took its cue, and sent many of the wounded to their homes in the North to finish their recuperation. Gerrish, however, was retained, for his wounds were still considered dangerous. He and about 200 of his mates were removed from their rickety shelters at Camp Curtin and were sent to warmer sturdier quarters in the Cotton Mill in downtown Harrisburg. The Cotton Mill had been idle since being shut down for want of cotton a year earlier, but the large, warm rooms were perfect for housing the sick and wounded, and were pressed into service. "Here," remembered Gerrish, "we were very comfortable."

Gerrish and his comrades of "the Cripple Brigade" found life indoors a bit duller than their wanderings over the countryside out at camp, but things were enlivened a bit at the end of November when the ladies of Harrisburg prepared a feast of thanksgiving for the hospitalized soldiers. The hospitals, particularly those at Camp Curtin and the Cotton Mill were decorated with national flags and fragrant boughs of fresh cut evergreen. Roasted meats and fowls were served with vegetables and preserves, breads, cakes, pies, butter, cheese and whatever else could be found to bring delight to the soldiers. Local men of prominence made speeches, bands serenaded and church choirs sang. The soldiers would not soon forget the day, and they repeatedly sent their heartfelt thanks to the thoughful men and women who had made it possible.[13]

As if the generosity of the people of Harrisburg were not enough, Gerrish had even more reason to be grateful when the United States paymaster visited the Cotton Mill to settle accounts. Gerrish had not seen a paymaster for nine months and was given the pay due him, which amounted to the princely sum of $117.[14] He and his friends in the hospital decided to have the best meal Harrisburg had to offer, so they found a restaurant that could obtain and cook for them whatever they wished, and placed orders for their meals a day in advance.

Gerrish and his cronies would remember that meal well into their old age, and years later he would still delight in talking of it. The young German had had "roast stuffed wild pheasant only shot a day ago, the size of a medium sized chicken, many side dishes and a large bottle of fine Rhine wine...to-day it would make more than two meals for me, but during the war our stomachs became like the stomach of a large snake; we could eat if we found it enough to last for three days and trust to luck for quite a while for something to turn up next." His single gargantuan meal cost Gerrish a sinful $3.50, or about eight days pay on his private's salary.[15]

*   *   *

Throughout the autumn and early winter, Gerrish and his wounded comrades were not the only soldiers in Camp Curtin or elsewhere in Harrisburg. New three-year regiments were being formed and recruits and companies were arriving in bunches. One of the first to form was numbered the 148th, which was comprised largely of men from Centre County. Though the ranks were full, the regiment had somehow not been given a colonel, but the men of the regiment had a man in mind to fill the vacant post: James A. Beaver. Beaver was then serving as lieutenant colonel of the 45th Pennsylvania, and, by law, officers in regiments already in service were prohibited from accepting posts in other regiments. This law helped prevent men interested only in personal advancement from switching regiments every time a vacancy opened and helped ensure the integrity of each regiment. But the Centre County men of the 148th had been sincere in their wish to have their neighbor lead them. Beaver himself could not be accused of wishing to satisfy personal motives in accepting the promotion to colonel, for he was already fulfilling the duties of colonel with the 45th, since Colonel Welsh was commanding the brigade, and Beaver knew he would soon be elevated to full colonel when Welsh was made a brigadier general. Governor Curtin, also a Centre Countian and a friend to all involved, had apparently urged Beaver to accept the colonelcy offered to him by the 148th and gave him special dispensation to do so. Beaver accepted.[16]

On September 5, 1862, Beaver was commissioned colonel of the 148th at Camp Curtin. The regiment was ready for the field, and the Confederate army had that same day crossed into Maryland, so without delay, the young colonel had turned around and led his green regiment out of camp, down to the train depot and south to Washington.

Beaver's new regiment was exceptional in that it organized itself rapidly enough to get into the field immediately. Most of the regiments being formed were proceeding slowly, not out of deliberation, but because procuring men enough to fill the ranks was difficult. Recruiters and municipalities had resorted to offering bounties as inducements to enlist. Counties were required by the state government to provide a certain number of recruits so the state could in turn meet the quota of men set for it by the Federal government. The counties, therefore, would offer bounties of $25 or $50 to any man who would enlist. The Federal government would also offer a bounty, often of $100.

COLONEL JAMES A. BEAVER, 148th Pennsylvania Volunteers.
Pictured here as lieutenant colonel of the 45th Pennsylvania (probably at age 24), the "boy colonel" assumed the duties of commandant during the Gettysburg Campaign. He was wounded at Chancellorsville, Cold Harbor, Petersburg and lost a leg at Ream's Station.
(Massachusetts Commandery Military Order of the Loyal Legion Collection, U.S. Army Military History Institute)

In any event, Beaver was not the only man who was returning to Camp Curtin that autumn to form or lead a regiment. A very large number of the officers and men forming the new regiments had been in the three months service and many others had served or, like Beaver, were then serving in active regiments. One such officer was Captain Thomas Chamberlin, Company D, 5th Pennsylvania Reserves, Seneca Simmons's old regiment. Captain Chamberlin had been with his company all through the Peninsula campaign until the 30th of June at Glendale. There, not far from where his colonel had fallen mortally wounded, Chamberlin had been hit in the left calf by a Minie ball—just a few inches below the knee. The ball had passed completely through the leg, and Chamberlin had lain on the field, like Simmons, bleeding while the men of the 5th were forced to pull back. Both colonel and captain had been packed up by Confederates and taken to the rear, where Chamberlin's wound had been treated by a Confederate surgeon. After a brief stay in Libby Prison in Richmond, Chamberlin had been exchanged and sent to Baltimore, where he had spent most of the summer and early autumn in a bed at the Union Protestant Infirmary allowing his leg to heal.[17] In mid-September, he had been approached by members of a regiment then forming in Harrisburg and informed that Secretary of the Commonwealth Eli Slifer had recommended him (Chamberlin) for the majority of the regiment, which was to be designated the 150th Pennsylvania Volunteers. Chamberlin had been nearly well enough to return to the field, but he had declined the position offered him, or had at least postponed accepting it. At the time, Lee and his army were in Maryland, possibly headed for Pennsylvania, and Chamberlin had recognized that a battle was imminent. Therefore, rather than immediately accept his commission in the new regiment, which would be stuck in Harrisburg during the fighting, he had left his hospital bed and hastened across Maryland to join his old regiment and resumed command of Company D. Not until the 18th of September, the day after the battle at Antietam, did he resign his captaincy and accept his majority. Five days later he was mustered into the 150th.[18]

The 24 year old was received well by his new regiment. Of erect bearing and presenting an impeccably neat appearance, Chamberlin's looks alone would inspire confidence. With his dark, curly hair and trimmed goatee, the major looked very much the dashing soldier that could ably lead men into battle. Urbane and extremely intelligent, Chamberlin had been graduated from Bucknell University in 1858 and had spent the next two years in study at the Universities of Heidelberg and Berlin. He returned to Pennsylvania in 1861 and promptly enrolled in the 5th Reserves. The rookies of the 150th looked upon him with something more than admiration. They were rather in awe of this young man, who still walked with a bit of a limp. Not only was he a veteran of combat, but he had fought with the vaunted Pennsylvania Reserves and had been badly wounded in action. He had been a prisoner of war and had seen the inside of a Richmond prison. Perhaps most impressive of all was that he was back for more.[19]

In addition to the three-year infantry regiments being formed in Pennsylvania that autumn, several cavalry regiments were being raised, and Camp Simmons became one of the points of rendezvous for the horsemen. While Camp Curtin was housing the wounded from Antietam, quartering individual recruits for regiments already in the field, and receiving companies for the new three-year regiments about to be organized, the cavalrymen were gathering at Camp Simmons. Because of the different types of soldiers occupying them and the necessarily different supplies and drills required by them, the two camps grew apart and became separate entities. Captain Tarbutton relinquished command of Camp Curtin and concentrated his efforts on running Camp Simmons.[20] The command of Camp Curtin passed to 39-year-old Captain Daniel J. Boynton of Company I, 93rd Pennsylvania.[31]

Boynton was from Middletown, and, like many of the men of that town, he had worked in a lumber mill. In October of 1861, he had left his job as foreman

LIEUTENANT COLONEL THOMAS CHAMBERLIN, 150th Pennsylvania. As a captain in the 5th Reserves, he was wounded at Glendale and as major of the 150th shot through the back and shoulder on the first day at Gettysburg.
(from Chamberlin's "History of the 150th Pennsylvania Volunteers")

at the mill and his wife of 17 years, Diana, and had gone off to a Camp of Rendezvous near Lebanon, Pennsylvania, where the 93rd had been formed. Boynton's experience in handling men at the mill no doubt was part of the reason he had been made captain of his company, despite his dearth of military experience. After leaving Lebanon, the 93rd had gone to the Peninsula with McClellan in the spring of 1862 and had served throughout the campaign to the gates of Richmond. On the afternoon of June 26, 1862, during the fighting at Mechanicsville, however, Boynton's service with the regiment had come very close to an abrupt and premature ending. The captain had experienced the jolt of his life when a Confederate shell had whistled in and exploded just a few feet from him. The concussion had ripped his haversack from his body and blown his sword away. Although his flesh had not been torn, blood vessels burst throughout Boynton's body and he had lain on the field in shock. "[I] was picked up on the field," he later wrote, "and taken to division Hospital by some members of my Company, who thought I was dead." Even as he took command at Camp Curtin, nearly four months after his injury, Boynton still occasionally suffered from internal hemorrhaging from his traumatized veins and arteries.[22]

Within a month of the arrival of the first cavalry company in Camp Simmons, nearly 3,000 cavalrymen were quartered in the camp but few of the companies had been organized into regiments. Little was being done about teaching the men how to be horse soldiers, for they were learning simply to be soldiers first. No horses accompanied these cavalrymen in Camp Simmons, for the camp was already quite crowded and sanitary conditions were poor. Horses required a great deal of space and would only worsen the sanitary problems. On November 10, therefore, a number of companies were brought together, designated the 17th Pennsylvania Cavalry and marched about two miles north from Camps Curtin and Simmons to a newly established camp they called Camp McClellan.[23] By the end of the week two more regiments had entered the camp and all were making preparations for the expected arrival of the more than 3,000 horses that would be needed to mount the regiments.[24] Two of the three regiments were given horses there by the end of the month and Camp McClellan became a true cavalry camp.[25] The men generally had little time to practice with their four-legged partners, though, for within two weeks of being mounted, the three units, the 16th, 17th, and 18th Pennsylvania Cavalry regiment, were forwarded to the front.

As in the previous year, the problem of desertion from the camps had worsened tremendously as the cold weather came on. Men were going over the hill in droves and three of the four provost companies on duty in the city were employed in patrolling the outside of the camps.[26] But perhaps the cold had less to do with the desertions than did the type of men that were coming to camp. The men who arrived throughout October and early November were not volunteers but conscripts; they had been drafted by the Commonwealth of Pennsylvania to serve for nine months and had come to Camp Curtin under protest. They did not wish to serve in the army; they did not wish to go to war. Some of these men had legitimate reasons for wishing to stay home. Invalid parents or spouses, children too young to work who had to be fed or abject poverty were all very good reasons for wage-earning young men not to volunteer. Others, however, had less admirable excuses for remaining part of what were called the "Stay at Home Rangers."[27] Whatever their reasons, the drafted men did not wish to leave their homes, and once the draft had taken them from their hearths, they wished only to get back to them. The result was a good deal of serious trouble in Camp Curtin.

The need to resort to conscription had been recognized by Governor Curtin back in July, 1862, when Pennsylvania was called upon for 18,000 men. It was clear to the governor that volunteers alone would not fill the quota, and he determined that the only way the required men could be enlisted was to draft them. To organize a draft, however, was "a most appalling task," according to the man Curtin asked to do it.[28] Alexander McClure, a state senator, saw his job entailing, "The most careful visitation to every household in the state to ascertain the names of those who were subject to military duty, and to ascertain, also, how many volunteers were then in service from each township or ward. After such enumeration an exhaustive tabulation of the conscripts due from each of the two thousand districts in the State was necessary, and after the draft, each conscript had the right to appeal to a commissioner and surgeon of the county to claim that he had lawful reasons for not accepting military service." McClure also had the politically delicate task of appointing the county draft commissioners and surgeons.[29]

The completion of the census and the making of appointments, took several months, but even then the most difficult part of instituting the draft was not over. Anti-war feeling was strong in certain areas of Pennsylvania and the draft was stiffly—sometimes violently—opposed in these areas. McClure was called upon to use all his political acumen to avoid armed conflict with organized anti-war groups, the most active and infamous of which was the fearsome Molly Maguires, Irish nationalists who operated in the small coal-mining towns of central Pennsylvania, especially in Schuylkill County.[30]

October 16, the day of the actual draft, was met with little trepidation in Harrisburg. All sections of the city were exempt from the draft because the local quota for men had been filled by volunteers. The draft for the other areas of Dauphin County was conducted in the open air on the steps of the courthouse by a blindfolded man.[31] Within two weeks, those unlucky enough to receive one of "Uncle Abe's tickets to Dixie" were called to assemble at points throughout the commonwealth and proceed to Harrisburg.[32] By no means all of those required to report for service did so. Hundreds simply disappeared from their homes and could not be found by the local or state officials sent out to gather them. In Dauphin County alone, 51 men failed to report. The most popular method of disappearing for these draft dodgers seemed to be to simply go hunting. They headed not for Harrisburg, but for the hills where they could not easily be found. While conscripts were congregating at Camp Simmons, scores of others from the rural districts were "scattered about the mountains shooting deer instead of rebels."[33]

But if the conscripts that obeyed the law and reported to Camp Simmons were not clever enough to find an effective dodge, it was not because they were not willing to try. Unfortunately, some resorted to the gruesome, cowardly and idiotic practice of self mutilation in the hope the examining surgeon would reject them. One man cut off the first two fingers of his right hand almost as soon as he had arrived in camp. Some of these men were successful, depending upon how much of themselves they were willing to sacrifice. Those lopping off fingers or toes were often simply transferred to the artillery where those extremities were not as necessary as in the infantry.[34]

The principal means of escaping service was desertion and it proved to be the most successful as well. It was done almost exclusively at night and always at great risk, for the sentries around camp were under orders to shoot at fleeing men. Furthermore, an additional ring of guards was sometimes posted inside the regular camp sentries. Many of the sentries believed their orders to shoot would-be deserters gave them something like a license to kill, and they became trigger happy. Incredibly, some of these guards, members of the provost battalion, professed to be anxious for a shot at a conscript who might be deserting.[35] Virtually everyone, from the citizens of the city, to the newspaper editors, to the officers and men running the camp, looked upon the conscripts with contempt. They were viewed as unpatriotic cowards who would only serve their country when forced to do so. The actions of the no shows who went deer hunting and the self mutilators reflected badly on all of the conscripted men, and no one, perhaps the guards least of all, made any effort to conceal their dislike for the new men. Some guards openly expressed a desire to bring down a deserting draftee and baited the men in camp by saying they "would rather shoot a drafted man than a rebel" and that when they did get a crack at a deserter, they would be "sure to aim at his heart."[36] The conscripts were not the utter cowards everyone thought they were, for they braved such bullying and the bullets that followed and went right on deserting. Squads were sent after those who managed to get away, often trailing the men all the way to their homes, and some were retrieved in this way. A good many others, however, could not be hunted down and never donned the blue.

After the departure of the cavalry regiments, the drafted men went into Camp Simmons, which was now under the command of Colonel Everhard Bierer, a veteran who had seen a war's worth of service in the last six months alone. Bierer was another in a long line of tough, no-nonsense men to exercise command at Camps Simmons or Curtin. Small, thin, wiry with a huge, obtrusive hawk nose, Bierer was an oddly sincere and devout man. He was a biblical scholar and had an intense interest in eastern religions. Just 34, he had already served as captain of Company F, 11th Pennsylvania Reserves and, along with much of that ill-fated regiment, had been taken prisoner at the battle of Gaines's Mill on the Peninsula back in June. He had spent some time at both Belle Island and Libby prisons in Richmond before being exchanged in mid-August, when he returned to his home at Uniontown, Pennsylvania, on a 20-day leave. After spending less than a week at home with his wife Ellen, Bierer had learned of Stonewall Jackson's movements against Pope and the threat posed to Washington. He had been unable to remain in the wings at what might prove to be a crucial act in the drama, and had immediately left Uniontown and set out for center stage. He had rejoined what had been scraped up of his regiment near Washington and had gone with it into battle at Second Manassas. Two weeks later on the slopes of South Mountain, Bierer had taken a Minie ball in the left elbow. The ball lodged in the joint and caused him severe pain, and he was again sent home and out of the war for a while.

By the end of October, though, he was restless. He still carried the Confederate ball in his elbow, but the pain had subsided enough to let him begin thinking about getting back into the war. Curtin thought well enough of him as a soldier to proffer an appointment as colonel of one of the regiments of drafted men. Bierer instantly accepted. He was ordered to Harrisburg where he assumed command of Camp

Simmons and tried to deal with the massive problem of organizing several thousand hostile and disgruntled men into regiments. On November 18, he was commissioned colonel of the 171st Pennsylvania. Seven days later, a surgeon at camp cut the Confederate lead out of his arm, and Bierer began his post-surgical recovery by leading his regiment down to the railroad depot and south to Virginia.

The tenure of the conscripted men in Camp Simmons ended in mid-December. All of the regiments had been formed and dispatched to the front, and the deserted camp was closed down. The cavalry regiments that had been forming at Camp McClellan also departed at about the same time and that camp, after existing just over a month, was abandoned on December 12.[37] Camp Curtin alone remained in service, and it too was almost empty. All of the three-year regiments had departed by the 8th of December, and most of the Antietam wounded had been sent home or to other points and those that lingered, like Gerrish, were in warmer quarters at the Cotton Mill. All that remained in camp were a few recruits waiting to join their regiments and a small number of captured deserters.[38] With the exception of these men, the only troops in the city were the members of the provost guard battalion. Captain Boynton, who had been in command of the camp in the early fall, had left in early November.[39] Captain James F. Andress of Company G, 7th Pennsylvania Cavalry, assumed the duties of commandant after Boynton's departure.

The brown-haired, gray-eyed Andress was a tobacconist originally from West Chester. He was another who had been in the war from the start, having first come to Camp Curtin on April 22, 1861 as captain of Company E of the 9th Pennsylvania Volunteers. After three months of service, he had been mustered out with his company at camp in July and had come back in November with a company for the 7th Cavalry. After a year in the field with the regiment, he was detailed for recruiting duty in August of 1862. He had drummed up enlistments at various points throughout the commonwealth until the first week in November, when he had come to Harrisburg. On November 11, he took command of the camp. He was 28 years old.[40]

With the camps empty, the streets of the city no longer rang with the shouts and laughter of fun-seeking soldiers. The peace was a rarity for the people of Harrisburg, who had endured much hardship in the first year and a half of war. They were grateful for the quiet, and, for a time, the war seemed a little more distant and less a part of their daily lives. At any rate, for the first time in many months, there were not several thousand blue-coated reminders of the conflict walking among them in the streets. A spell of unseasonably pleasant weather and bright sunshine lifted spirits even higher, and thoughts turned from conscription, desertion and other grim matters to more pacific things, such as ice skating on the river and nearby ponds and taking refreshing walks along the beautiful and uncrowded streets of the city. The citizens of Harrisburg rediscovered peace in those mild mid-winter days, and they could not be blamed for wishing to relish it for a time and view the war as did thousands of other cities throughout the North, from the outside as mere spectators.

They looked forward to the prospect eagerly and hopefully. The editor of the *Patriot and Union* spoke for all the beleaguered people of the war-weary city when he wrote on December 11, "We trust our present anticipations of a quiet winter may be fully realized."[41]

Two days later, the Army of the Potomac suffered 15,000 casualties at the battle of Fredericksburg, Virginia, and Harrisburg, like Washington, Baltimore and Philadelphia, was again transformed into a city of hospitals, populated by bloody and horribly mutilated men.

*   *   *

The story of Fredericksburg, which stands as one of the worst disasters of the war for the Union, began in early November. President Lincoln replaced General McClellan as commander of the Army of the Potomac with Major General Ambrose P. Burnside, the man who had ordered the charge of the 51st Pennsylvania on the bridge at Antietam. Burnside, unsure of his own abilities, set about doing the best he could with the army he had been given. He knew indecisiveness and tardiness had done in McClellan, and that the administration in Washington valued action above all else, perhaps even to the point of rashness. Burnside immediately put his army in motion. From northern Virginia, he would make a straightforward, overland thrust at Richmond and force Lee to retreat.

The Federal movement went well, at first, but early gains were mitigated by persistent logistical problems. At Fredericksburg, Virginia, advance elements of the army were delayed in crossing the Rappahannock River, having to wait for the arrival of pontoons upon which could be erected a temporary bridge. By the time the pontoons arrived, the Confederates had caught up, and any advantage Burnside had had disappeared. Still compelled to act, Burnside began forcing his way across the icy river on December 11, and arrayed his army for an assault on the defensive positions the Confederates had occupied. Less than a mile outside of the town of Fredericksburg, a ridge rose abruptly to a long plateau, much of which was owned by the Marye family. Marye's heights became the heart of the Confederate position. While infantry was placed behind a stone wall at the foot of the steep ridge, artillery was lined up hub-to-hub on the plateau above. Burnside, whose army lay in and about the town, planned to assail this position frontally by sending the army across the broad, open land that lay between the heights and the town.

*   *   *

Major General William B. Franklin commanded roughly one third of Burnside's army—the portion given the title of Left Grand Division. Franklin's force was, in fact, positioned on the left of the Federal line, and, as part of the Left Grand Division, the Pennsylvania Reserves crossed the Rappahannock on pontoon bridges about three miles south of Fredericksburg on the 12th of December and bivouacked a mile or more south of the city. They rose early the next morning, those who had gotten any sleep at all in the frigid night, and by 9 a.m. were in a line of battle facing west. From where they stood on a low plateau near the river, the ground to the west and over which they must pass looked deceptively peaceful. The plateau dropped off into a depression several hundred yards in width. Broad cultivated fields covered the bottom of the hollow to the edge of a low railroad embankment at the western end of the hollow. Just beyond the railroad, the ground rose to a ridge, the crest of which was covered with trees. In places, the trees extended down the slope and even across the railroad. On that ridge, in those woods, and behind that railroad embankment lay the Stonewall Jackson's veterans, with whom the Reserves were acquainted.

Standing among the Reserves on the plateau looking out across the broad plain on that foggy morning of December 13 was Sergeant Jacob Heffelfinger, Company H, 7th Pennsylvania Reserves. Heffelfinger was from Mechanicsburg, Pennsylvania, just across the river from Harrisburg, and he had already had a very tough war. He had entered the war as a 20 year old at the very start of hostilities. Leaving his job as a teacher in Mechanicsburg in May, 1861, he had enlisted as a private in a local company raised by Captain Joseph Totten. By that time, however, no more companies were being accepted for three months, and Curtin had been unable to accept any for three years, so Totten's company, like many others, could not have been immediately accepted. But Curtin had been just then trying to form the Reserve Corps, and he had asked that the companies in limbo not disband. Most of the companies had acceded to the request, and many had rented a hall or found a field in which they could encamp or regularly meet and drill. By mid-May, the Reserve Corps had become a reality and all the waiting companies had been accepted for service. Totten's company had spent much of the waiting period in Camp Curtin, and, although the 7th Reserve regiment was being formed at Camp Wayne in West Chester, his company had been designated Company H of that regiment. After spending all of May and the first week of June, 1861, in camp, Private Heffelfinger and the rest of Company H had moved to West Chester to join the regiment.

Heffelfinger had been popular with his comrades and was made a corporal and before long a sergeant. He had gone with the regiment to the Peninsula in the spring of 1862. At just a bit over six feet, the blond, blue-eyed sergeant made a bigger target than most of the men around him and had been shot through the thigh at Gaines Mill. Unable to walk, he had been left on the field by his retreating comrades and taken prisoner. After some weeks in captivity, he had been exchanged, but, his leg was not ready for the life of an infantryman. He had not returned to the ranks of Company H until October, missing altogether the horrors of Second Manassas, South Mountain and Antietam. Fredericksburg would be his first fight in almost six months.[42]

About 1 p.m., skirmishers were thrown out in front of the Reserves and the other divisions in preparation for an advance. Batteries of artillery began firing. Private

S. Dean Canan of Company K of the 136th Pennsylvania lay nearby and would advance with his regiment across the same field the Reserves would cover. Canan remembered the noise from the artillery duel as "almost deafening" as he and his comrades lay on the ground "faces in the mud." About 2 o'clock, the order to move forward was given. Canan remembered moving off on the double-quick as the artillery fire again increased on the plain. "We went midst the bursting of shells and the whistling of bullets; we could feel the wind caused by them, but the boys went on, loading and firing as they went...."[43] Heffelfinger and the rest of the Reserves stepped off from the plateau and into the depression. The long, blue, dressed lines, bristling with glinting rifle barrels and brightly colored flags made for a beautiful sight, but not one to overawe the Confederates on the ridge. Solid shot and grape began falling amid the Reserves as soon as they entered the field. Part way across the field, the Reserves broke into a run and charged toward the railroad and the ridge beyond. The Confederates on the ridge could not withstand the assault and broke and ran. Virtually the whole division of the Pennsylvania Reserves smashed through Stonewall Jackson's line and into its rear. A breach had been made in what had been a strong Confederate position, but the Reserves finally grew tired from their long run and, having broken into the Confederate rear, were forced to halt their advance and wait for reinforcements. Unfortunately, those reinforcements were not on the way, and in the delay, Jackson's broken Confederates were able to rally and received reinforcements from fresh troops. The Reserves received a vicious counter attack and were sent reeling back down the ridge and past the railroad.[44]

Among those who had advanced as skirmishers and who were now retreating were the Pennsylvania Bucktails under Captain Fred Taylor. After his capture at Harrisonburg the previous June, Taylor's tenure as a prisoner of war had been short; he was almost immediately paroled and sent to Camp Parole in Annapolis, Maryland, to await exchange. While at Annapolis, he had missed the summer campaigns and Second Manassas, where many of his men fell. "I am in such a state of restless anxiety that I am half sick and good-for-nothing," he had written to his brother in early September, "The next forty-eight hours will no doubt see either the army of Lee and Jackson broken and routed or Maryland invaded and Washington besieged. And I have to stay here and draw rations for a hundred lazy men!"[45]

Despite his anxiety to get back in the war, Taylor's forced exile had been continued, and he had sat out the Maryland campaign in which the Bucktails had been heavily engaged at both South Mountain and Antietam. After the latter battle he learned that casualties had made him the senior officer in the regiment and he would be in command when he returned to it. "It will be a distinguished honor to command that old regiment," he wrote to his brother from Camp Parole, "and I would rather be its colonel than command half the brigades in the army."[46] The officers and men of the Bucktails returned his affection and had signed a petition to have Taylor promoted and officially made their colonel. The petition was sent up the chain of command and both George G. Meade and John Reynolds endorsed it before it reached

Governor Curtin. The governor knew Taylor and assented to the promotion, but the wheels of politics moved slowly, and several months would pass before Taylor was commissioned colonel.[41]

In November, the long-awaited exchange had come, and Taylor had rejoined his men in Virginia. The 22-year-old captain took to regimental command as though he had been born to it. After reorganizing the badly overfought regiment, he had handled with aplomb the toughest test a commander can face—about 20 frustrated men mutinied because they had not been paid in more than six months. Taylor had quickly taken hold of the situation and meted out punishments. But rather than sending them to the stockade and a court martial, he had merely rebuked them by hurting their pride and shaming them. He had taken from the miscreants their highly-prized Sharps rifles and given them older, clumsier, less efficient weapons.[48] The rest of the regiment applauded his actions and his sense of justice.

At Fredericksburg, Taylor had finally gotten his chance to show what he could do with a regiment in combat. Without the slightest hesitation he had led his small regiment of riflemen across the frozen fields into the very jaws of Jackson's prepared positions. Twice Taylor was wounded and one of his horses was killed beneath him. So active had Taylor been on the firing line that he had drawn the attention of corps commander, General Reynolds, who wrote in his report that Taylor had been among those officers who had been "conspicuous for coolness and judgment."[49] Taylor was earning among his brother officers that high reputation for which he hungered.

The fight at the railroad embankment, over which Taylor had led his regiment, was especially severe. Private Canan of the 136th Pennsylvania had been in the thick of the fight and recorded in his diary what the toll had been in his Company K. "Robert H. Pike, was seen falling, shot in the breast. My friend, James Moore, fell, shot through both legs; Geo. Geddes was shot in the leg; Heiser and Jackson tried to get him off, but we suppose they are all prisoners, if alive. The following named are wounded and in the hospital: George Markle, severely; John M. Barclay, severely; Jacob Hess, flesh wound; Palmer and Hill, slightly; Jacob Ottinger, slightly, and missing. John McCurdy had the letter "K" on his cap shot off; Sawyer, Lowman and Wright had bullet holes in their clothes; Gardner had his gun and cartridge box knocked off with a piece of a shell...."[50]

The entire Pennsylvania Reserves Division had paid a high price for their temporary success. Of the nearly 4,500 men who had started off across the frozen plain and into the woods against Jackson, roughly 2,600 had come back.[51] One of those who did not make the return trip, Sergeant Jacob Heffelfinger, lay somewhere on the frozen fields between the Rappahannock and the Confederate lines on the wooded ridge. A Minie ball had smashed into his left ankle, passed out the other side of his leg, and then entered his right ankle, leaving him completely unable to move himself. For the second time in as many battles, he lay helpless on the battlefield that was

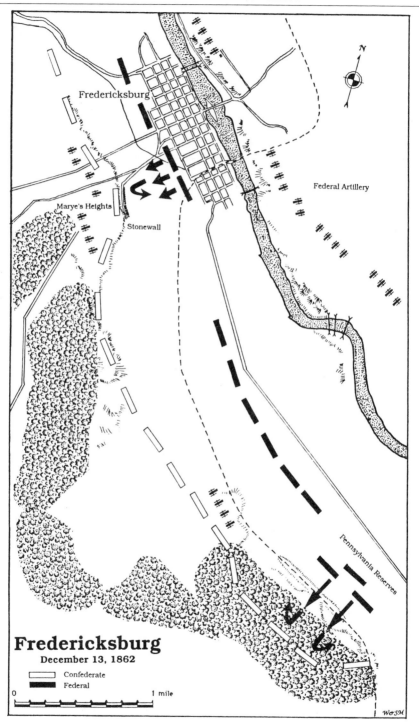

Fredericksburg

December 13, 1862

☐ Confederate
■ Federal

0   1 mile

or would soon be controlled by the enemy. That night, a frigid wind swept merci-lessly across the dark fields, and the thousands of wounded who lay where they had fallen were made to contemplate death by freezing as well as by bleeding. Amid an unearthly chorus of moans and wails of pain, Jacob Heffelfinger was retrieved by Confederates and again made a prisoner of war.[52]

That afternoon, while the Reserves had been gaining a toehold in the Confederate lines, much of the rest of the Army of the Potomac was assailing a stronger Con-federate position a few miles to the north—just outside Fredericksburg proper. One Pennsylvanian remembered rolling out from beneath his frost-covered blanket on the morning of the 13th and getting his first good look at what was to be the battle-ground. "The heights [held by the Confederates] formed a sort of semi-circle around the city, the centre being about a mile distant then gradually sloping toward the river, giving their artillery a splendid chance to play upon an assaulting column. They had built forts and long lines of breast works along the crest of the hill, had entrenched themselves behind stone walls, and taken every possible advantage of the ground. It was, in fact, the most complete slaughter pen into which a gallant army had ever been led."[53]

In the heart of the column to make the assault was the 127th Pennsylvania. The Dauphin County Regiment was still green, not having been under fire in its first three and a half months of service, but as Colonel Jennings had led the regiment across the Rappahannock on a pontoon bridge on the 12th, all that had changed. Confederate artillery had sent an "avalanche of shells" into the river around the bridge and the regimental historian later admitted that the men had been a bit nervous, ducking their heads and watching the skies anxiously every time the scream of an incoming shell was heard. The regimental band had tried to present a cool exterior, strutting across the bridge in the lead blaring a lively version of "Yankee Doodle" to bouy the spirits of the regiment, but the music had been abruptly stopped and band's stiff upper lip quickly softened when a shell scored a direct hit on the band's drum.[54]

The regiment spent the night in the ruins of Fredericksburg. Constant shelling had reduced much of the picturesque and historic old town to rubble, and the 127th found little charm in cold streets strewn with loose bricks, splintered wood and shards of broken glass. About 11 a.m. on the 13th, the regiment was put in line by Colonel Jennings and Major Rohrer and marched to the outskirts of the city where they saw the broad plain leading to Marye's heights. The officers dismounted in accordance with orders and sent their horses to the rear. The plain was broad and broken here and there by fences, which would have to be dismantled or climbed over while the regiment was exposed to the fire of the Southerners. An canal ditch about ten feet wide passed across the plain near the midway point, and it, too, would have to be negotiated. As the men of the Dauphin County Regiment looked at the ridge about 1,000 yards distant, they could see the glint off dozens of polished cannon on the crest and thousands of rifle barrels bristling up from behind the stone wall at the base of the heights.

Just before noon, Jennings received orders that his regiment "was wanted." The men of the 127th unslung their blankets and knapsacks and began the advance on the double quick. The well-dressed blue lines advanced across the frozen pasture with colorful flags flying and bayonets and rifle barrels shining. The wind on the bare plain was sharp, but the thoughts of the men were of other things. It was a time of grim silence. They steadily stepped-off the advance to the tap of the drum with a tight-lipped determination, but with few illusions. Each of them knew well that the chances were very good that he would likely be hit before the day was over. That the men still advanced in this knowledge proved that on that day they became soldiers.

Solid shot began arriving first from the heights and opened gaps in the advancing lines. Musketry from behind the walls and entrenchments and canister from the heights followed as the whole Federal divisions moved across the plain. As anticipated, the advance was slowed by the fences and the canal. A warming sun melted the very top of the deep-frozen earth in places, and men slipped and fell in the still hard turf. All the while, the Confederates poured out a steady fire.[55]

Two of those who fell from the ranks of the advancing 127th were brothers from Harrisburg: John and Charlie Creamer. John Creamer had been 24 years old when he had enlisted as a private back in August. He lived with his mother and father, his brother and his 13-year-old sister, Margaret, in a house at the corner of Market Street and Dewberry Alley in downtown Harrisburg. His father, Alexander, was prone to illness and Mrs. Ester Creamer depended a good deal upon her boys for support. After John had enlisted in Company B of the 127th, Charlie, a 19 year old student and occasional worker on the Pennsylvania Canal with the engineer corps, could likely have been exempted from service because he supported his mother. But Charlie could not bear to be left out of the fighting and had enlisted as well, leaving his mother, sister and ill father to fend as best they could.

John had been having trouble with rheumatic joints throughout the cool autumn, and the severe cold of mid-winter was doing him no good. Nevertheless, he advanced with the company on the 13th, as did Charlie. They had not advanced very far into the assault when John had a finger on his left hand taken cleanly off by a Minie ball or a flying piece of shrapnel. Considering the stomach wounds, shattered arms and legs and other horrors that were knocking down the men around him, John's wound seemed rather minor.[56]

Brother Charlie was not so fortunate; he took two bullets, one in the right shoulder, and another in the right ankle. The bones in the ankle were terribly, hopelessly shattered, and Charlie crashed down into the mud and snow bleeding from two wounds. Unable to walk, Charlie lay helpless until he was taken from the field by some of his comrades.[57]

The 127th never made the stone wall at the base of the heights, nor did any other Federal regiment. Some Federals, though, had come close before being beaten back. Men from Colonel John Brooke's 53rd Pennsylvania got to within about 60 yards, but the regiment paid heavily for the yardage. Brooke took 314 officers and men into action and brought out just 159.[58] The spectacle that lay before the survivors on December 14 was ghastly. Private S. Dean Canan wrote, "I have not the heart to attempt to describe it, and, in fact, did not see any of which I could avoid, but look where we would, we would see the dead and the wounded carried off the field, some of them frightfully wounded, and could hear their agonizing cries...but it is impossible to realize the horrors of a great battle field."[59] Burnside's artless plan of battle on that dreary December day and his stubborn adherence to it had cost 1,300 Northern men their lives. Nearly 10,000 more were maimed or crippled, yet the two armies remained in precisely the same positions they had occupied before the debacle. General Burnside's only accomplishment at Fredericksburg was to ensure a joyless Christmas in thousands of homes throughout the North.[60]

* * *

The Army of the Potomac lay idle for several weeks after the battle until the 20th of January. On that day Burnside put in motion his second effort to dislodge Lee. He began marching his troops out of their camps and upriver to a ford, where they would cross, and attack the Confederate flank. As simple as the plan was, it was foiled by the weather. Sub-freezing temperatures had given way to unseasonably warm weather and steady rain, which had changed the Virginia roads to troughs of red mud. The army wallowed about unproductively in the mire, making scarcely any headway, until Burnside finally turned his men around and sent them back to the camps they had left three days before. The rest of the winter was passed in relative comfort in quarters near Fredericksburg. No moves would be made until spring, when the roads could support the weight of an army.

The excessive exercise and the miserable weather of the "Mud March," as it came to be known, had combined to break the health of a great many men, among them was Captain Frank P. Amsden, 1st Pennsylvania Artillery. Amsden had seen a good amount of service since serving as camp adjutant and unofficial commandant at Camp Curtin in March and April, 1862. He had fought with his battery at the battle at Williamsburg, on the Peninsula and at all the other engagements up to the gates of Richmond. The battery had been engaged at Seven Pines and at Malvern Hill and at all the battles between. When the army had been withdrawn from the Peninsula, Amsden and the battery had remained at Yorktown. In November, Amsden had been promoted to captain of Battery G of the 1st Artillery to rank from August 30. Though he had missed South Mountain and Antietam, he had rejoined the army in October in time to share in the Fredericksburg campaign and had commanded his new battery in the battle. After the battle, the battery had gone into camp until called out at the end of January to participate in the march through the mud.[61]

To that time, army service had seemed to agree with young Captain Amsden. He and his brother, Fred Amsden, a lieutenant in Company B of the 136th Pennsylvania, had seen each other frequently while the army was around Fredericksburg. Fred felt that Frank had actually improved in vigor and robustness during his year and a half in the service. All that changed on January 21 and 22 when Amsden caught a cold while foundering in the mud. When the army had been sent back to its camps, Amsden and Battery G had been intercepted by orders to change the location of their camp. They were, in Amsden's words, to "abandon [the] old camping ground with its log huts and other conveniences, situated on a dry, open knoll, and prepare a new camp in a dense second growth of pines in a swale on an old tobacco field." The cold he had caught on the march settled in his chest and was aggravated first by the hard work involved in changing camps and next by the dark, damp location of the new site. He developed a deep, hacking cough, and, as the weeks and months passed after the "Mud March," Amsden's lungs grew ever weaker as his cough worsened. The cold progressed into bronchitis. He was treated by various surgeons until early March, when he went home on a ten-day furlough, to rest in a warm, dry house in Scranton. At the end of his furlough, he reported directly to a surgeon in Washington for treatment and spent two weeks under the care of a doctor there. On March 29, he reported for duty with his battery, but all the rest and special treatment and care had done little to ease the cough or the pain in his weak, wheezing lungs.

He stayed with Battery G until the end of May, when he again went to see his regimental surgeon, Dr. M. F. Price. His condition was worsening. Surgeon Price detected "evidence of tubercular deposits" in the right lung, and immediately decided that Captain Amsden's military career was over. "A campaign begun in this condition might cause permanent disability," wrote Price, so the captain was told to resign his commission and was given an honorable discharge on a surgeon's certificate. Amsden went home to Scranton.[62]

*   *   *

Throughout December and into January, locomotives belching great heads of white steam and black smoke into the frigid air brought trainloads of men with torn and bleeding bodies to the hospitals, churches, and schoolhouses of Harrisburg. A new building to house and comfort the wounded was opened in Harrisburg that December. The Soldiers' Retreat, sometimes called the Soldiers' Rest, was established in a building beside the Pennsylvania Railroad depot downtown. Two local gentlemen, Eby Byers and John B. Simon, owned and operated the place purely for the benefit of soldiers—wounded or healthy—and their families. Any soldier passing through town, particularly any wounded man enroute home to recuperate, would be put up for the night and fed his meals. Just as welcome at the Retreat were wives, mothers, fathers, sisters and any other member of a soldier's family who was passing through town while in search of a wounded or missing soldier. The people of the city helped support the establishment, making regular donations of money, food staples, linens, and dainties. Byers and Simons often extended their kindness to the point of purchasing at their own expense railroad tickets for soldiers or their family members that they might be able to reach their homes more quickly.[63]

Harrisburg's share of the wounded was smaller than it had been after previous battles, probably due to the location of the battle field in central Virginia.[64] Casualties might not have been sent to the capital of Pennsylvania for another reason. Reports had been circulated that a killer every bit as feared in that era as a Minie ball was present in the city: small pox.

A few isolated cases of the disease had been reported in rural areas around Harrisburg as early as November. In the first week of that month, the four companies composing the provost guard battalion—Company A of the 127th, and Baldwin's, James's, and Jones's independent companies—were vaccinated. Less than a month later, cases were growing more common in rural areas and the presence of the malady in camp was confirmed. Very few men were quartered in either Camp Curtin or Camp Simmons as all organized regiments had shipped out earlier in the month. Most of the men in the camps were recruits, conscripts or apprehended draft dodgers being held until they could be sent to their regiments. If precautions to quarantine these men were taken, they were apparently poorly enforced, for citizens soon began complaining about soldiers with the signs of the disease visibly upon them, moving freely about the city. The physicians of Harrisburg had reported some 30 odd cases among the citizenry by mid-December, hardly an epidemic in a city of more than 16,000, but still enough for concern to be registered about the wisdom of bringing wounded men into the midst of the outbreak. It was a small outbreak, but an outbreak nonetheless.[65]

Around Christmas, an isolated building at Camp Curtin was converted into a hospital for small pox cases, and about thirty men were quartered there by the end of the month. As a precaution, however, all the healthy men at Camp Curtin, only between 50 and 100, were moved out of camp to temporary quarters at the Soldiers' Retreat. The men were all vaccinated, as was each recruit brought into the city enroute to a regiment in the field. This last step was a remarkable show of good sense and foresight on behalf of the authorities in Harrisburg, for disaster could have followed for the army camped on the banks of the Rappahannock if recruits from Pennsylvania had reported for duty carrying a small pox virus picked up on the banks of the Susquehanna.[66]

The U.S. Army took over the Soldiers' Retreat, and, during that winter of sluggish recruiting, the place became a makeshift Camp of Rendezvous, a substitute Camp Curtin. Dr. George A. Bowe, who had been the assistant surgeon in charge of the Walnut Street Hospital in Harrisburg, was detailed by Dr. Wilson to act as examining surgeon at the Retreat to qualify recruits.[67]

Among those who were lying ill out at Camp Curtin was Captain Andress, camp commandant. He was confined to his quarters throughout the month of January with a serious case of the pox, and he apparently sank very low before he began to improve. Captain W. B. Lane, 3rd U.S. Cavalry, who had been mustering officer at camp for some time, assumed the duties of commandant while Andress was ill. Not until mid-February was Andress convalescent, and he soon after returned to his regiment in Tennessee.[68]

Andress was one of the last cases of small pox to be reported and one of the last to heal. By the end of January no new cases had been reported for more than a week and the outbreak was entirely played out by the middle of February. Sometime during that month, Camp Curtin came back into use, and the Camp Hospital was entirely cleaned and refitted by March 19, when it was put back into service.

Even after Camp Curtin came back into use, it remained virtually empty.[69] As no new regiments were being formed, the camp's principal function became that of a way station or a supply depot for recruits. The military inactivity made winter the logical time for recruiting men for regiments already in the field, and regiments with the army sent details home to attempt to enlist men. One such detail came north to Harrisburg from the 47th Pennsylvania, which was then on garrison duty at Forts Taylor and Jefferson in Key West, Florida. The detail consisted of Lieutenant William Wallace Geety, Company H, a Harrisburg resident; Lieutenant W. H. R. Hangen, regimental adjutant, former lieutenant colonel of the 9th Pennsylvania, and first commandant at Camp Curtin; Sergeant William Glace and Private James A. Trexler, both of Company F. The four were ordered north on December 15.[70]

While the others might have been sent to their homes to try to drum up enthusiasm for enlistment, Geety remained in Harrisburg. He was not alone in trying to lure young men of the city and its environs into the service. No fewer than six recruiting offices were open in the capital that winter for the Regular Army alone, and representatives from other Pennsylvania regiments were making the rounds as well.[71] Recruiting men was no easy task at that point of the war, and Geety must have had his problems. In truth, the logic in sending that particular officer on recruiting duty is difficult to understand. Geety had been grievously wounded in battle in the autumn, and tragically, his face had been hideously disfigured. He became a walking illustration of the horrors of war, and his appearance could not have instilled a martial enthusiasm in any young man.[72]

On October 22, 1862, the 47th had been involved in some skirmishing with Confederate infantry and artillery at Pocotaligo, South Carolina. Geety remembered that a Confederate shell burst within five feet of him as he was shouting orders to some of the men of his company. A small cast-iron ball of about a half inch in diameter struck the lieutenant square between the eyes. He was fortunate in that the ball did not penetrate his skull, but glanced downward behind his left jaw and lodged in his neck just short of the carotid artery. The left eye was completely destroyed, and his face and neck badly scarred and mangled. He lay unconscious for three days, only to awake and find his eyesight in the one eye and all the feeling on the left side of his face gone. Only later did he learn that his sense of taste had been destroyed as well. As Geety arrived in Harrisburg, two months after his injury, he still carried the cast-iron shrapnel in his neck, for the surgeons thought the operation too delicate to perform until the young man regained more strength.[73] He had considerable energy, however, and his wounds did not keep him from his duties. On January 5, 1863, he was appointed acting quartermaster at Camp Curtin, relieving Lieutenant Hiram A. Weed of Company E, 52nd Pennsylvania. Geety would hold the post until September, 1864.[74]

The early months of 1863 passed uneventfully at Camp Curtin, the only occurrence of any significance came late on the night of March 31, the eve of April Fool's Day. About midnight, the Reels, the Lobans, and other citizens in proximity to camp were awakened by shouts and alarms of fire. Three unoccupied wooden barracks were blazing out of control, the flames running hungrily along the roofs and leaping high into the black night. According to one observer, the whole made "quite an extensive and brilliant conflageration." The firemen of Harrisburg were called out, but were hindered by muddy roads and were unable to get out to the camp in time to do any good. The buildings burned to the ground.

Private Edwin L. Waterbury, Company G of the 55th Pennsylvania, was accused of arson and was bound over for trial. This was most embarrassing for the private, who was a Harrisburg native and who maintained his innocence, but it was even more embarrassing for his father, Isaac Waterbury, a prominent citizen in Harrisburg and captain of his son's company. Captain Waterbury had acted as a drillmaster in Camp Curtin for some time and was well known by many of the officers in camp. The legal proceedings took place in May at Fort McHenry in Baltimore. Happily, Private Waterbury was absolved and released to rejoin his company, then in South Carolina. Edwin Waterbury survived the war and was honorably mustered out with his company. His father, however, was killed in action in Virginia in 1864.[75]

*   *   *

After the dreary winter, the war actively started again in late April and, by mid-May, another battle had been fought. Burnside had been replaced by Massachusetts-born Major General Joseph Hooker as commander of the Army of the Potomac. Hooker's first plan for assaulting the Confederates bore a resemblance to Burnside's plan that was fouled by the "Mud March." Dry roads enabled Hooker to move the army up the Rappahannock River from Fredericksburg, across the river and into a heavily wooded area locally known as "the Wilderness."

Hooker advanced on the outnumbered Army of Northern Virginia, and clearly held the advantage, but, on May 1, suddenly and inexplicably stopped his advance.

Lee, ever willing to seize an opportunity given to him, sent Stonewall Jackson on his most famous maneuver—a forced march around the flank of the Army of the Potomac. Late in the day on May 2, Jackson and his men fell upon the unentrenched and completely surprised Federals as they sat playing cards and cooking their dinners. The battle swept through the woods around a small crossroads called Chancellorsville, by which name the battle soon became known. Federals reeled back and the Confederates pursued until well after the sun had set and the tangled forest became too black to allow them to continue. Casualties were high, but the single most important in terms of the course of the war was Jackson himself, who fell in the twilight of the 2nd after being accidentally fired upon by his own men. He died days later.

The battle was resumed the next morning. The Rebels retained the offensive momentum and continued pushing the Federals from their position. In action that day for the first time was the 148th Pennsylvania. The rookies under Colonel Beaver were thrown hastily into a threatened point in the Federal line. "I had been directed not to wait to throw out skirmishers," wrote Colonel Beaver later, "[so] we marched by the left flank and entered the thick white oak underbrush which abounds in the Wilderness." The woods were too thick and the tree branches too low to permit Beaver and the other field officers to ride their horses through, so they dismounted and continued on foot. The regiment marched steadily and briskly through the woods, so distracted by the tangled vines and thickets that they walked right over a small group of enemy skirmishers without warning. The Southerners were taken prisoner, and the 148th continued its advance right into a Confederate battle line. The fire from the Confederates was tremendous and accurate. Beaver told his men to lie down and return fire. He then walked along his line to ensure it was strong enough, but found it not quite straight on the enemy. He looked about him for his brigade commander, Brigadier James Caldwell, to signal that his regiment had to be realigned. Just as he and Caldwell saw one another, Beaver was hit. "I fell violently upon my face," he recalled, "my sword flying from my hand and, when I turned upon my back, found a hole in my clothing just beneath the two rows of buttons. Without stopping to consider the matter, I inferred that a ball had entered there and my military service was ended." Two of Beaver's men who had seen him fall ran to him and prepared to carry him to the rear on a blanket. Beaver told them to get back on the firing line as there "would be time enough to bury the dead after the fight." The men ignored their colonel and, abandoning the blanket idea as too slow amid the whizzing Confederate bullets, they simply grabbed Beaver and dragged him to the rear until they met some stretcher bearers. He was taken to a field hospital where Dr. George Potter, surgeon of the 145th Pennsylvania, had a table waiting for him. "Lying on my back," Beaver remembered later, "looking into his face, I could see the deep concern....After opening my clothing and examining the wound, however, and putting his little fingers into the...wound...I noticed, before he said a word, a great change in his face, followed by, 'Ah, Beaver, that's all right.' " The wound was ugly and painful, but not fatal principally because the bullet had been deflected by a pencil in Beaver's coat pocket.

The command of the regiment devolved upon Major George Fairlamb. Beaver stayed in tents and hospitals for a few days until he was sent north, first to Aquia Creek in "a box car with a little hay in the bottom, filled with wounded suffering from all sorts of wounds," then to Washington via steamer, where he was met by friends and attended to until he could endure the long train ride to Bellefonte.[76]

Chancellorsville, despite the bravery and good fighting of individual soldiers and regiments, was yet another defeat for the Army of the Potomac. Another 1,600 Northern men were killed and 9,500 wounded or captured.[77] The trains took the thousands of hurt men north, and Harrisburg received far fewer than after any major battle in the past. In April, all the hospitals in the city had been ordered closed by United States Surgeon General and all the patients had been removed to hospitals in York. Camp Curtin's hospital, still under Dr. Wilson, was the only one allowed to remain open, and fewer than 100 casualties were brought there after Chancellorsville.[83]

The disaster at Chancellorsville was not the only bad news received by the Army of the Potomac that May. That month marked the expiration of the term of enlistment for the nine-month regiments formed the previous August and September. The nine-month volunteers had suffered the ills and discomforts of the campaign, the battlefield, and the encampment and had proved themselves soldiers. They were veterans and were of great value to the army, but now they were going home.

The people in Pennsylvania prepared to offer a hero's welcome. Camp Curtin had not been required to house any significant number of men since shortly after the new three-year men had left there in the late fall and the many idle months had been spent in cleaning and refitting the grounds and the barracks. After the departure of Captain Andress in February, Captain Tarbutton had again assumed command and under his direction the camp was made ready to receive the returning regiments.[79]

The first nine-month regiment to return to Camp Curtin was the 123rd, which arrived on May 10. The next day, the 122nd returned, followed by all the rest between the 12th and the 27th of the month. On the 15th, word was received in Harrisburg that the 127th was enroute home and was even then in York, just an hour or so away. The people began preparations to welcome home their sons. Lookouts were posted along the tracks to watch for the train coming from York, and a relay of messengers were established so word of the approach of the train could be quickly conveyed to the heart of the city. Finally, in the afternoon, the train bearing the regiment appeared at the western end of the railroad bridge over the river. As it began crossing, the citizens who had packed the streets began crying and cheering. A salute of 17 guns was fired from Capitol Hill and all the bells of the city—from the court house to the churches, from the factories to the fire engines and idle locomotives in the train yards—began pealing. Boys and young men pressed forward to run beside the train as it entered the city, crawling along cautiously through the crowded streets. The men of the regiment hung out of the cars and laughed and waved and pointed, slapping the tops of shoulders and squeezing the hands and fingers that were held up to them from the street. When the station was finally reached, thousands packed the depot and cheered. The clanging bells, the cheers, the shouts, the artillery salutes, and the sobs of wives and mothers combined to produce a cacophony few would ever forget.

When the train halted at the depot, the men of the regiment poured out of the cars and into the crowd. Rare was the soldier who was not embraced or kissed or caressed by virtually anyone within reach. Some time was spent in the ecstacy of milling about with parents, siblings, wives, children and friends until Colonel Jennings and his officers mounted their horses and managed to form the regiment for its march to Camp Curtin. "About every house displayed an American flag," remembered one overawed member of the regiment, "and some were profusely and handsomely decorated with bunting and flowers, while in the streets banners and streamers were displayed in lavish extravagance. Some of the banners crossing the streets had brave words of greeting to the gallant boys of the Dauphin County regiment 'Welcome home brave 127th Regiment forever.' 'Our boys are heroes' '...Home, Sweet Home,' and many other suitable and inspiring mottoes were hung across the streets...."[80]

But melancholy mixed with the joy. Though many of the faces were wetted that day by tears of gratitude and relief, not a few sorrowful souls wept out of grief over those who would not be coming back. Even some of those who did return bore permanent scars of their service. Bandaged heads, arms in slings and limps were common in the ranks that passed through the city, and some men, such as Charlie Creamer, could move only on crutches. Those who were still badly wounded and required conveyances were brought along in ambulances at the rear of the procession.[81]

The thin, bronzed and bearded men, hardly recognizable as the clean, fairly well-kempt lot that had left the previous autumn, filed into Camp Curtin and were almost immediately given furloughs while the muster and pay rolls were prepared.[82] For the men of the other regiments in camp who were not fortunate enough to live nearby, the wait for the paperwork to be completed was almost unbearable, especially after the belts and belt plates, guns, cap and cartridge boxes, and various other pieces of equipment had been returned. Desertion and an early return home was not even an option for the bored men, for no one would leave before receiving his pay. But as veterans, the men knew that they were all but beyond punishment by their officers, and took advantage of the situation by devising methods to slip into town for a few hours. Many proved as adept at breaking guard as ever. Others used a new, more sophisticated method of getting out that had been learned in other camps in the field—bogus passes were produced and officers' signatures forged and " 'old soldiers' by the score...were found promenading through the streets of Harrisburg."[83]

These soldiers would need some time to readjust themselves—physically and mentally—to life outside of a tent. Perhaps the easiest transition to make was the return to clean underwear and shirts, or to pants and coats free of the "greybacks" that had been their constant companions since first entering Camp Curtin. One soldier, however, found another aspect of his return to civilization less easy. After accepting an invitation from a friend to spend the night at his home, the soldier slept upon "a feather-bed and beneath the clean, soft, white counterpane; but yet, however, by no means comfortable as [I] slept not a wink during the night, owing to the change being too sudden and different to appreciate."[84]

Perhaps the most difficult change of all was the departure from friends and comrades of the regiment. Enduring the sorrows and privations of war and all the discomforts, disappointments and grief that nature and man could produce in nine months had bound the men together in a way they never had nor ever would again experience. The older men and younger boys alike wept at saying goodbye. And it was not simply the human relationships that were causing the sadness. "I could hardly restrain my tears," wrote Major Fred Hitchcock of the 132nd, "as we finally parted with our torn and tattered colors, the staff of one of which had been shot away in my hands. We had fought under their silken folds on three battlefields, upon which we had left one third of our number killed and wounded, including a colonel and three line officers and upward of seventy-five men killed and two hundred and fifteen wounded. Out of our regiment of one thousand and twenty-four men mustered into service August 14, 1862, we had present at our muster out six hundred and eighteen."[85]

The tears came out of love for each other and for their flag. They came out of remembrance of those who were gone. But although few could or would articulate it, the tears came as well because each man knew that he would never again do anything so noble and momentous and at the same time so exciting. Their part in the drama was over, and they were sorry to see it end.

CHAPTER SIX

"The Entire Lot Would Not Have Amounted to a Row of Pins"

JULY, 1863

In the summer of 1867, a rapidly aging Robert E. Lee, president of Washington College in Virginia, was sojourning in the cool of the West Virginia mountains. The popular resort of White Sulphur Springs had become a personal haven of sorts in the general's efforts to escape the increasingly bothersome heat of the Virginia summers. The large white, pillared hotel in Greenbrier County was surrounded by rich, rolling lawns and shady gardens, and visitors came from all over the reunited country to benefit from the peaceful surroundings and the hot mineral springs.

One summer night in that year, Lee was in attendance at one of the frequent dances held in the hotel's ballroom. The white-haired general with the dark enchanting eyes was surrounded by a bevy of women, most of them young, all of them Southern and each thrilled to be in the handsome hero's presence. Across the ballroom was a party of Northerners. Visitors from the North tended to stay to themselves on the fringe of these social gatherings, and the Southerners in the midst of the social whirl were content to let the outsiders remain where they were. These Northerners, however, attracted rather more attention than usual. They were Pennsylvanians and, after some inquiry, it was learned that the visitors were Andrew Gregg Curtin and his guests.

Curtin was not in good health, and had not been since about the middle of the war. He routinely visited spas on physicians orders, even before the war had ended.

Lee was eager to meet the ex-governor and asked the young ladies around him if any had made the acquaintance of Curtin or any in his party. None of the belles had, and, in fact, none seemed anxious to greet the Yankees or extend any kind of hospitality at all, especially this Yankee. Lee was embarrassed. He had, since the war, become the South's most influential citizen and strongest advocate of accepting defeat and restoring good relations with the North. He reminded his young companions that, as Southerners, the burden of hospitality was upon them and they should do all in their power to welcome the Northerners. The old gentleman rose from where he had been sitting; his carriage still erect, his bearing still that of a man who had been a soldier for almost 40 years. He addressed them coolly and with sadness, "I have tried in vain to find any lady who has made acquaintance with the party, and is able to present me. I shall now introduce myself, and shall be glad to present any of you who will accompany me."

Only one of the girls had regard enough for the general to not let him walk across the ballroom alone. She swallowed enough of her pride to join Lee. As the erect and graceful old man approached the Pennsylvanians, Curtin and his guests rose to meet them. Brief but formal introductions were made, followed by curtsies, slight bows, and grasping of hands, and two of the great figures of the war met for the first time.[1]

There was a time, however, four years earlier, when the two men came rather closer to meeting than Curtin would have liked. The Confederate army had spent the weeks after Chancellorsville reorganizing and refitting and planning to follow up its victory with what it hoped would be the bold, decisive stroke that would end the war. Lee's Confederates set off from the forests of the Wilderness in the first week of June, and headed north, bound on invading Pennsylvania.

A very real threat was posed to the Northern cities and towns that lay before Lee. Pittsburgh and its foundries were vulnerable, as were Philadelphia, Baltimore and even Washington itself. No one outside of the Confederate high command knew Lee's plans or his destination, but two things were certain; by June 1, he had at least a two-day lead on the pursuing Federal army, and he was headed for central Pennsylvania. Beyond that, it took little military acumen to recognize that the biggest plum in the area was Harrisburg. Not only would the capture of the capital of one of the larger and more powerful Northern states be a coup for Lee, but the destruction of the bridges, railroads and canals there, the dispersal of military personnel, including the probable razing of Camp Curtin, the capture of military stores and the disruption of telegraph communications between the west and Washington would immediately benefit Lee and his army militarily. Furthermore, if Lee could get across the Susquehanna, take Harrisburg, destroying the bridges above, at and below the city, the pursuing Army of the Potomac would be forced to ford the river or construct new bridges, giving the Confederates time to move about at will through eastern Pennsylvania, taking Philadelphia, Baltimore and threatening Washington. For Lee, success and possibly ultimate victory lay on the east bank of the Susquehanna.

How this crisis had arisen so suddenly no one in Harrisburg or Washington seemed to know. One moment, the Confederate army was in central Virginia on the south side of the Rappahannock River under the watchful eye of General Hooker and his army, and the next it was around the flank of the Federal army and barrelling down the Shenandoah Valley toward the unprotected borders of Pennsylvania. Governor Curtin was not caught entirely off his guard, but the suddenness with which the feared invasion developed did surprise and eventually embarrass him. Curtin had met in Washington with Lincoln and Stanton at the end of May to discuss what might be done to protect Pennsylvania in the event Lee evaded or once again defeated Hooker. What came out of the meeting was a plan to organize Pennsylvanians into a new kind of militia force.

The force was to be a state militia that was equipped, maintained and controlled by the Federal government, not the state, as were all other militia units. This corps would be called up in times of emergency and disbanded at the end of the crisis. The key was that the men of the corps would remain on call or stand by at all times, but their actual terms of service would be dictated by the president, who would base his decision on the imminence and duration of the emergency. It was a unique approach to the old problem of how a peaceful civilian population should defend their homes from a common enemy. This approach, however, like all previous proposals, was seriously flawed, principally in the ambiguity of the definition of "emergency" and the unspecified term of service.

June 12 found the governor very concerned indeed, as lead elements of the Confederate army were at Winchester, Virginia, in the lower end of the Shenandoah Valley, and no Federal force of any considerable size lay between them and Pennsylvania— or New York, and New England for that matter. After some hurried consultation with Lincoln and Stanton, a groundwork was laid for the defense of the commonwealth. The secretary of war believed Pittsburgh would be the target of any invasion, but Curtin seemed more concerned for Harrisburg and Philadelphia. Lincoln and Stanton therefore created two new military departments in Pennsylvania— The Department of the Monongahela, embracing Pittsburgh and the western portion of the state, and the Department of the Susquehanna, including Harrisburg and everything east. The commanders of the two new departments were to be Major General William T. H. Brooks in the west, and Major General Darius N. Couch in the east. That same day, the 12th, Curtin issued a proclamation to the people of the commonwealth, which gave to Pennsylvanians their first intimation that they might expect trouble in the weeks ahead.

The document revealed that a "rebel force" had been prepared for the purpose of attacking Pennsylvania. The proclamation stated that volunteers were needed and proposed to create a home defense corps that would "give permanent security to our borders," and whose duties would be "mainly the defense of our own homes, firesides, and property from devastation."[2]

Pennsylvanians did not warm to Curtin's appeal that they band together to protect home and hearth. Lincoln followed Curtin's call with one of his own in which he

MAJOR GENERAL DARIUS N. COUCH
Commander of the Second Corps of the Army
of the Potomac at Chancellorsville and later of
the Department of the Susquehanna with headquarters in Harrisburg.
(Library of Congress)

asked for 100,000 volunteers to repel the invasion, 50,000 of which were to come from Pennsylvania and the remaining 50,000 from Ohio, Maryland, and West Virginia. The president's call came on the morning of June 15, and Curtin issued a second proclamation later that day, again calling his people to arms.

In Harrisburg, on that same day, a public meeting was held to introduce Couch as the commander of the new Department of the Susquehanna. Present was former Secretary of War Simon Cameron, who, having recently bought a fine, stone house on Front Street, was now a citizen of Harrisburg. Cameron, Mayor Roumfort, and Couch all appealed to those at the meeting to take the threat to their state and their city seriously and organize for their common defense. Couch went so far as to encourage the construction of earthworks and other defenses across the river on Bridgeport Heights. Few, if any, present paid much attention to the pleas. Couch was more a curiosity than anything else, his name having been in the papers repeatedly since the spring of 1862 when he had led a division on the Peninsula.[3]

Darius Nash Couch was 40 years old when he came to Harrisburg. He had been graduated from West Point a respectable 13th in the vaunted class of 1846, which had included George McClellan and Stonewall Jackson. Couch had served with distinction in Mexico, being breveted for gallantry, but found the peacetime army between the wars boring beyond endurance, as did other young, intelligent officers. In 1855, he resigned and moved to the tiny town of Norton, Massachusetts, where he became an industrialist and a manufacturer. After Fort Sumter, he offered his services to Governor John Andrew of Massachusetts and was made colonel of the 7th Massachusetts Volunteer Infantry. His experience and ability was not to be squandered at the regimental level, however, and he was soon made a brigadier general of volunteers and was eventually given command of a division. He performed efficiently throughout the Peninsula Campaign and through Second Manassas and Antietam as well, after which he was promoted to major general and was given command of the Second Corps of the Army of the Potomac. On the first of May at Chancellorsville, Couch had managed his corps superbly and was in an excellent position to launch an attack whenever Hooker ordered it. It was at that point that Hooker issued his fateful orders to suspend offensive operations and withdraw. Couch was then the senior corps commander, if anything happened to Hooker, Couch would assume command of the largest army on the continent. He was a quiet, capable commander and a dutiful soldier, but he was no admirer of the ostentatious and ambitious Hooker. When the commanding general recalled Couch and his corps just as they were prepared to begin an assault that gave every promise of success, Couch became disgusted. His devotion to his duty and the cause apparently had limits, for he could no longer tolerate Hooker. He asked to be relieved of command in the Army of the Potomac if Hooker were to remain in command of it and requested duty elsewhere. He was assigned to command of the new department in Pennsylvania. On the day he arrived in the state capital, he established his headquarters in a second floor office in the capitol and set to work.[4]

Harrisburg was very quiet in mid-June. The last company of the last regiment of nine-month volunteers had been paid off June 3, and Camp Curtin was again deserted. Captain Baldwin's Independent Company, which had served for many months as part of Harrisburg's provost battalion, had been sent to Washington in the spring to perform similar duty there but had returned on the 2nd of June and was the only military organization in Harrisburg when Couch arrived.[5]

A few days after Couch assumed command, and just a day after Curtin's second proclamation, Harrisburg residents got their first hard evidence that the situation was as serious as they were being told. On the 16th, a train of nearly 500 wagons arrived in Harrisburg. The horses appeared gaunt and exhausted, trudging forward with heads down and with sores on their bodies where the leather harness chafed. The teamsters, too, were fatigued, having been on the road for over 120 miles with little rest. The wagon train had fled from Winchester, Virginia, in the northern end of the Shenandoah Valley, on June 13, just before the Federal garrison there under Major General Robert Milroy was attacked and routed by Major General Jubal Early's Confederates. The attack offered proof that the Rebels were aggressively moving north. The train had fled in panic, and, feeling pursued, had covered the entire distance from Winchester to Harrisburg—100 miles or more—almost without stopping. The tired column entered the city and moved into bivouac on open land north of town not far from Camp Curtin.[6]

A few days later, militia units began to arrive in Harrisburg in response to Lincoln's and Curtin's calls, but few of these militiamen were Pennsylvanians. Only six Pennsylvania organizations had been mustered in for the emergency since the president's call on the 15th, and five of those were companies of fewer than 100 men. The sixth organization, the 20th Pennsylvania Militia, numbered 971 officers and men and was commanded by Colonel William B. Thomas. Most of the first militiamen arriving in response to Curtin's appeals were New Yorkers. Although Lincoln's call for troops to repel the invaders was published broadcast in the newspapers of the threatened area and throughout the North, Curtin took the precaution of writing to the governors of New Jersey and New York asking for assistance. These appeals were followed by one from Stanton at the War Department to the governors of all the Northern states asking that men be sent to Pennsylvania's aid. Governor Horatio Seymour of New York responded immediately by sending fully armed and equipped militia units to Harrisburg. Most of these outfits were "regular militia," ready-organized military groups that met regularly some place in their community and drilled. Although they were uniformed (always smartly, often ostentatiously), armed, equipped and thoroughly drilled, few had even seen battle or hard campaigning. Regardless, they were armed, and were in some measure disciplined, so they had considerably more appeal to Couch and Curtin than the untrained "minutemen" they could expect from Pennsylvania. Besides, these militiamen had a tremendous amount of enthusiasm for what they did, and their spirit was intensified by the thought of their actually being needed to go into the field, to campaign as it were, to assist in a crisis of invasion.

The New Yorkers, a great many from New York City, and the Jerseymen were very excited indeed as they left their homes and moved through cheering crowds into Pennsylvania. The high-spirited young men in their handsome uniforms were off on a great adventure, and took every opportunity to have some fun. A member of the 22nd Regiment of New York State National Guard, remembered the train ride from Philadelphia to Harrisburg. The tracks were often blocked with slow-moving trains full of other troops, guns, supplies or ammunition, and all the traffic over the rails was thus slowed down. "As the train passed along," recalled the New Yorker, "the people of the villages and farm-houses, particularly the women, would throng the track to cheer the troops. Frequently the railroad was completely fringed with girls, very pretty ones too, all wild with enthusiasm." Once when the train was crawling up a steep grade, a group of five country beauties gathered along a fence, waving their handkerchiefs and blowing kisses to the troops. Suddenly, a man of the 22nd leaped from the moving train, rushed over to the girls, "kissed the whole five in a rapid succession before they had a chance to think, and darted back to his train, into which he was hauled by his admiring companions, while the whole brigade burst into applause at his enterprise and grasp of the situation."[7]

Governor Andrew of Massachusetts responded promptly to Curtin's call as well and attempted to persuade some of his nine-month regiments whose terms had expired to remain in service and go to the assistance of Pennslvania. Similar efforts were made by Governor Joel Parker in New Jersey. Colonel E. Burd Grubb had just returned to New Jersey with his regiment, the 23rd New Jersey Volunteers, a nine-month regiment. The 23rd's enlistment had expired on June 13, and the regiment had been shipped to Beverly, New Jersey, where it was to be mustered out. Delays had prevented discharge, however, and Grubb had traveled to Trenton to urge Governor Parker to straighten out the snafu. The regiment had served well during its term, seeing action at Fredericksburg in December and again the following May at Salem Church. New Jersey could take pride in the creditable performance of Grubb and his men, and Parker promised prompt action on sending them home.

As luck would have it, Grubb was lunching with Robert F. Stockton, the adjutant general of New Jersey, on June 17 when Stockton was handed a copy of a wire from Curtin.

"Grubb," said Stockton, "this is terrible news. Lee's whole army is advancing on Harrisburg, and Governor Curtin asks us to send every available man to the assistance of his State." Stockton hesitated. The emergency put a premium on armed, organized troops. If Harrisburg were truly in danger, Grubb's men would be extremely valuable.

"Will your men go?" Stockton finally asked.

"Of course they will," shot back Grubb, and he immediately prepared to return to his regiment. The governor accompanied Stockton and Grubb to Beverly, just a half hour away.

Only about 400 members of the 23rd were waiting in Beverly, the rest of the regiment having been granted furloughs. The 400 were drawn up on a parade ground along with two other regiments, the 24th and 25th New Jersey Volunteers, also returned nine-month veterans. Governor Parker stood, hat in hand, before the assemblage and called upon all his oratorical skills as he loosed an impassioned plea for assistance on behalf of their neighboring state. He read aloud Governor Curtin's dispatch and finally cried, "Now, every man who will go to Harrisburg to-night, step three paces to the front!"

Whatever bragging rights the men of the 23rd had not already won in service they claimed that day, for as Grubb would proudly proclaim in his later years, "Every man of the Twenty-third regiment stepped three paces to the front and not one of the others."

The volunteers were issued twenty rounds apiece for their smoothbore muskets and were put on a train for Philadelphia, 15 miles away. Arriving there late at night, they found that city full of excitement as other volunteers scrambled to organize and entrain for "threatened points." The 23rd took an early train for the state capital and was joined by an emergency light artillery company commanded by Captain E. Spencer Miller of Philadelphia.

When the train finally pulled in at Harrisburg, Grubb, still sleepless except for what he could manage on the bouncing, rocking, whistling night train, immediately sought department commander Couch. The general was glad to see Grubb and his men. He had few troops, though more were arriving all the time, and Grubb's men were the first trained soldiers with any experience to enter the city. Couch said he could give Grubb and his men no additional ammunition, even if they were to need it, for he had none that fit their weapons. Indeed, just the logistical problems of arming, equipping, and feeding the disorganized mobs trickling into town were giving Couch all he could handle.

Grubb remembered Couch's orders to him, "He...said there was a ford near the Cumberland Valley railroad bridge and that if the bridges were burned, he thought the enemy would attempt to cross at that place as the river was very low. He then directed me to take my regiment to Harris Park...on the bank of the Susquehanna, and throw up a demilune rifle pit and to pierce the cellars of all the houses in that vicinity for musketry."

The officers and men of the 23rd worked all that afternoon and into the night in fortifying Harris Park. By dawn on the 19th, they "had a tolerably good rifle pit, extending nearly the whole length of Harris Park and just back of the fence, which was on the river side. The fence was not thrown down so that the rifle pit was masked from the river."

Just three days later, Couch sent the 23rd home when he realized that the emergency, though serious, was not as urgent as the Jerseymen had been initially led to believe. Grubb and his men would have had to remain in Harrisburg for two weeks before any Rebels approached the city, and the men of the 23rd had no desire to do garrison duty behind earthworks for that long a time, especially since their terms had already expired. Their initial willingness to help, however, and their bravery in the face of what they believed to be an emergency was what counted, and Couch and Curtin were grateful.[8]

The men of the 23rd were glad to get out of Harrisburg and go home, and at least part of the reason was disgust with the attitude of the people of Harrisburg. The Jerseymen, along with the New Yorkers arriving in Harrisburg, were disillusioned at having been hurried to the city and then seeing that people of the capital city seemed not to care that their homes and businesses lay in the path of invasion. Beyond the few precautionary arrangements made by some merchants to remove their goods, the citizens seemed to think the tide of invasion would, as it had in September, 1862, crest far to the south of them. Furthermore, they seemed unwilling to help any of the people of the lower counties of their state, who would undoubtedly see Confederates.

The New Yorkers especially remarked on the apathy of the people of Harrisburg. Wrote one New York colonel in his report to his governor, "I did not see but one company of the citizens of Harrisburg organized and on duty for the defense of their own city, and that was a small company of Americans of African descent, drilling under some shade trees in front of the capitol."[9]

Another New Yorker was shocked to see that "hundreds of strong men in the prime of life loitered in the public thoroughfares, and gaped at our passing columns as indifferently as if we had come as conquerers, to take possession of the city, they cravenly submitting to the yoke."[10] Another simply noted that "the people of Harrisburg did not seem prepared or inclined to act on the defensive."[11]

Pennsylvanians, and Harrisburg residents in particular, concerned themselves little with the threats of invasion in mid-June. Most of the men were reluctant to leave their homes to repel the threatened and imminent invasion of Pennsylvania by the enemies of the country. They remembered the call for militia the previous September, and how the then "imminent" invasion never happened. The militiamen who had left their homes and families during the 1862 emergency spent the few weeks of their enlistment fighting only the heat and dust during the day and the wet ground and in leaky tents at night. The people of Pennsylvania objected to being called out to fight for home and hearth and then to be poorly fed, recklessly exposed to the elements and ultimately not used. The Army of the Potomac had stopped the invasion that time and, as far as most Pennsylvanians were concerned, it could do so this time as well.

Still, Curtin continued trying to raise from this apathetic populace a force sufficient to defend the state. He issued General Orders No. 43 outlining the procedures to be followed by the volunteers responding to President Lincoln's call. They were to immediately report to the governor by telegraph from wherever they had rendezvoused so arrangements could be made to muster them into service and transport them to Harrisburg or other threatened points. Other communities in the commonwealth were a bit less lethargic than Harrisburg, and volunteers began arriving in a trickle from towns and villages in central Pennsylvania. They came in ones, twos, tens or more and went into camp. One partial company arrived from Gettysburg under Captain Fredrick Klinefelter and was composed almost wholly of students from Pennsylvania College.

Among the individuals reporting to Harrisburg were some veterans of considerable experience. William Jennings, just recently mustered out as colonel of the 127th, returned to Camp Curtin and went to work organizing the disorganized militiamen into regiments. Jacob Frick, former colonel of the 129th Pennsylvania, also returned and undertook the organization of what would become the 27th Pennsylvania Militia. Brigadier General James Nagle, who had already been colonel of two Pennsylvania regiments and who had commanded a brigade in the Army of the Potomac from Second Manassas to Fredericksburg, also came to the aid of his state and once again entered Camp Curtin.

Stout and handsome with a neatly-trimmed, wooly beard about his mouth, the dark-complexioned Nagle was a veteran of the Mexican War and former sheriff of Schuylkill County. A native of Pottsville, Pennsylvania, he had also served as colonel in the state militia. In the hectic days of April, 1861, just days after his 39th birthday, Nagle went to Harrisburg to assist in organizing volunteers, and he was commissioned colonel of the 6th Pennsylvania. Three months later, he set about organizing a new regiment for three years service. The regiment was eventually organized in Camp Curtin and designated the 48th Pennsylvania; Nagle was named its colonel.

Colonel Nagle had been given command of a brigade of the Ninth Corps at Second Manassas. He had soon afterward been promoted to brigadier general and had served as such throughout the Maryland Campaign. He and his brigade had fought at Fredericksburg, but after Burnside fell from grace and was removed from command of the Army of the Potomac, Burnside's entire Ninth Corps had been sent to the western theatre. Not long after reaching Kentucky, General Nagle had resigned. He was suffering from heart disease, and, though only 41 years old, he had become too unsound to endure life in the field. In May, 1863, he went home to Pottsville.

Nagle had been at home just a month when Lee began to drive north toward Pennsylvania and Curtin called for volunteers to serve in the emergency. The general immediately came forward and helped raise what would become the 39th Pennsylvania Militia. Despite his heart trouble, he was made colonel of the regiment at Camp Curtin, thus becoming the first man to serve as colonel of three Pennsylvania regiments.[12]

One of the founders of Camp Curtin, Joseph Knipe, former colonel of the 46th Pennsylvania, happened to be home in Harrisburg on furlough recuperating from malarial fever. Since leaving camp in September, 1861, with the 46th, Knipe had been wounded four times—in the right shoulder and knee at the battle of Winchester in May, 1862, and twice more in August at Cedar Mountain, Virginia. The latter battle had cost him part of a finger on his left hand and had given him a prominent scar on his forehead where shrapnel had hit him. Despite his wounds, Knipe had led his regiment through the Maryland Campaign and commaded a brigade at Antietam. In May, 1863, just about when he had begun to suffer from malaria, Knipe received word that he had been promoted to brigadier general. He had celebrated by going home to Harrisburg on sick leave and had been home about a month when he, too, came forward and volunteered his services to Couch.[13]

James Beaver, still pained by his abdominal wound from Chancellorsville, had been at his home in sleepy little Bellefonte when Curtin had issued his proclamations calling for men. Away from the army for the first time, he had discovered the disagreeable sensation of helplessness. "I shared...in the uncertainty and anxiety, which must have consumed the people in the rear of the Army during the entire War, to such an extent that I became nervous and excitable and felt as if something must be done...I could not restrain myself."[14] Though his wound had just started to close satisfactorily, he had boarded a train and headed for Harrisburg, where he reported to Couch on June 16. The two were acquainted, for Couch had been Beaver's corps commander at Chancellorsville. Later, Couch would write that Beaver "was among the first who presented themselves for service [during the emergency]. His previous good record and sterling character induced me at once to place him upon my staff."[15] Beaver was still colonel of the 148th, of course, being on leave of absence only until his wound healed. He described himself as "weak and tottery and unfit for active duty of any kind" when he arrived in Harrisburg, so whatever duties he was to be given would have to be physically undemanding.[16] Couch made him an acting aide-de-camp.

But the young colonel was not to remain in that role long. The militia called for by the governor finally began arriving in Harrisburg in larger numbers and was sent out to Camp Curtin. For some unexplained reason, Captain Tarbutton, who was again serving as commandant, chose this tense time to end his long association with the place and "unceremoniously left." None of the other officers in the camp picked up the reins and, as Beaver later wrote, "pandemonium had broken loose among the crowds of disorganized men who were there assembled." The volunteers had no food, no blankets and in many cases no shelter. They were angry and were close to degenerating into a mob. Couch needed someone to take control and straighten out the mess Tarbutton had left. He learned that Beaver had helped run the camp back in the summer and autumn of 1861 as lieutenant colonel of the 45th Pennsylvania, so he did not hesitate to ask him to assume command. Beaver balked, feeling not strong enough yet to bear the taxing burden, but finally relented and took a carriage out to Camp Curtin.[17]

"The scene which met me, as I entered the gate, is indescribable," he recalled. "The entire camp was a mass of unorganized men, without semblance of order." Thousands of men were milling about, and petty squabbles among men and officers of various companies had led to large, loud arguments. "The force [in camp] was immense and untamed," Beaver remembered, "I never saw anything equal to it." Beaver's first act was to establish his headquarters. Camp headquarters had always been upstairs in Floral Hall, but the "tottery" Beaver was unable to climb the stairs. He therefore took control of a small building near the gate and established his office there on the first floor. Next he had the good fortune to encounter Captain Klinefelter's company of well-mannered, intelligent young men from Pennsylvania College of Gettysburg. "I called the boys of this company around me," the new commandant remembered, "instructed them in a very short time how to make out requisitions for camp equipage, wood and provisions, explained the difference between quarter-master and commissary stores, pointed out the location of each of these departments and sent them around with blank requisitions, directing them to call upon the Captains of companies and fill the requisitions for them for what they were entitled to of camp equipage and also commissary stores. In a very short time fires began to be kindled all over the camp and, as the companies became supplied with camp kettles, mess pans, plates, knives and forks and with rations to cook, the scene was entirely changed and, before night, the camp assumed a military aspect...."[18]

It was well that Beaver had gotten control when he did, for in the days after Curtin's second proclamation on the 15th, the camp and the city burst to life. Pennsylvanians awoke from their slumber and began arriving in large numbers. They arrived all day and all night, so fast and thick, in fact, that the *Patriot and Union*, which regularly tried to report the arrival of troops, found it "impossible to give anything like a full account of the various companies and squads."[19] Companies that arrived in daylight were immediately sent to Camp Curtin, those that detrained in the city after dark were generally offered "the hospitalities of the streets and depot," until the morning when they would proceed to the camp.[20]

So many companies arrived so fast that many of them could not be accommodated immediately and had to make due as best they could. On the night of June 22, a semi-organized militia company from Phoenixville, Pennsylvania, arrived at the railroad depot and found that not only had there been no arrangements made for receiving or quartering them but that dozens of other companies already in the city were wandering through the streets entirely without direction. "The streets of Harrisburg were filled with unorganized crowds," one of them wrote, "roaming about aimlessly. Utterly discouraged, many returned home."[21] The officers of the Phoenixville company were obliged to turn their men loose to fend for themselves. One of the privates of the company, a 20-year-old teacher named Samuel Pennypacker, was shocked. Having no food, no money, no place to sleep, and no one willing to lead them or offer guidance through the strange city, Pennypacker and a few buddies, began walking through the dark, unknown streets.

There were hundreds, perhaps thousands, like Pennypacker and his friends in the streets that night. In his wanderings, Pennypacker eventually came to the same conclusion the New Yorkers had, that Harrisburg residents were taking events rather lightly, "for a town which was said to be in great danger of capture, and whose inhabitants had been packing up their effects, and removing them and their persons to other cities for safety, there were entirely too many men in the streets and on the corners who appeared to be taking matters as coolly as if there was no cause for

THE CAPITOL IN HARRISBURG.
This building burned after the war and was replaced by the present capitol on the same site.
(Dauphin County Historical Society)

disturbing themselves." The young private and his mates became depressed, then angry. They "had come a hundred miles from a sense of duty while those in the immediate vicinity of the Capital, who had every incentive to arouse themselves were doing nothing."[22]

The disillusioned young men straggled through the hot night, passing drunken men and shouting policemen, laughing militiamen and indifferent citizens, until they eventually found Capitol Hill. Every foot of space on the lawns and walkways around the capitol was covered with militiamen. Pennypacker and his friends moved up to the capitol itself, hoping they could find shelter for the night there, but the floors and benches of the halls and galleries in the building were all occupied as well. With no where else to go, Private Pennypacker stepped outside the building and "finally pitched upon the stone porch as the most eligible spot, being covered by a roof, more clean, cool and less crowded than inside. Several of the men chose the pavement, but it rained during the night and they were driven within. I spread out my horse blanket, put my bread satchel under my head, and endeavored to go to sleep, but the novelty of the position, the solidity of the bed, and the unpleasant practice...the man above me had of putting his boots on my head, rendered it almost impossible."[23]

In the morning, Pennypacker's company, along with many others, hiked out to Camp Curtin. There they were equipped and given an area on which to encamp. In most, but not all cases, new companies would simply occupy tents that had been left standing by regiment that had recently been organized and shipped out. The tents were so small that occupying one left by other men was much like sleeping in someone else's bed on their soiled linen. This was not the most desireable nor the most sanitary of arrangements, but it was nothing that could not be gotten used to. One regiment, however, a spiffily uniformed "regular" militia unit from Philadelphia found the conditions in Camp Curtin entirely unacceptable; the Philadelphians were "disgusted with its dirt and foul smell,..." so they about faced and walked out of the camp to a nearby field, close by the canal, and pitched their tents there. They named their encampment Camp Russell, and remained there for about a week.[24]

Camp Curtin must not have been a pleasant place in mid-June, 1863, with the heat and ever-present clouds of dust turning everyone and everything filthy. The topsoil from which that dust flew, had been so pulverized by tens of thousands of feet that it could no longer make even a pretense of holding water. Flooding in the lower end, even after a moderate rainfall, became worse than ever. Men of the 74th Regiment of the New York State National Guard were completely flooded out of their tents when the rains came on the night of June 21.[25]

Most of the men seemed to accept such things as the lot of soldiers. Private Pennypacker, with his comrades from Phoenixville, had been designated Company F of the 26th Regiment of Pennsylvania Militia, and the boys were not at all put out by the discomforts of the camp. The company was taken to a corner "very near to the railroad, and by the side of a small tree which stood there. A wheat field was within a few rods, and it answered the same purpose for which an out-house is used generally. On the opposite side of the railroad, and some distance off was a farm house where we got water, went to wash, and sometimes bought milk. It had also attached to it, a fine orchard, the shade of whose trees afforded a pleasant spot to loll and rest upon."[26]

The men of Company F apparently had little opportunity to "loll and rest," for they had among them an irksome lad of 14 who had been given a drum and told to practice with it. Private H. M. M. Richards was a hard-working boy, perhaps too hard working for the temper of the company. He banged upon his instrument incessantly for two days while trying to learn the various calls by which company and regimental movements were ordered. "I cannot recall a single moment that I gave my poor drum a rest during the two days we lay in Camp Curtin,...and I am now sure that my regiment was so promptly ordered to the front in the hope that I might never return with it....I can recall even now how the surgeon at the hospital near us came to me and begged, with tears in his eyes, that I would give his patients what the whole regiment longed for later on, a rest."[27]

Regiments did not lie long in Camp Curtin. Couch put the men to work immediately in fortifying the city. A high, steep hill above the western bank of the river completely commanded Harrisburg on the eastern bank. The eminence was called Bridgeport Heights and offered a magnificent, panoramic view of the capital city. Enemy artillery posted on these heights would force a quick surrender of the city, so Couch ordered fortifications built to defend those heights. Much to the anguish of residents, the hill, and the ridge that ran westward from it for a mile or so, was entirely shorn of the groves of oaks and maples that adorned it. This was necessary not only to lay out the actual entrenchments of the forts themselves, but to create additional obstructions to deter or stop altogether an attacking force. The New York militia units were largely employed with axes in felling trees and obstructing roads over which the enemy might pass, but they did good work in the trenches with picks and shovels as well.[28] Two forts were erected, the larger one was named Fort Washington, and the other, on the ridge about a half mile farther west on what was called Hummel's Heights, was called Fort Couch. Forts Washington and Couch were garrisoned by both New York and Pennsylvania militia, although principally the former.

There came to boil in Fort Washington a dispute that had been simmering since the New Yorkers had arrived in Harrisburg. The people of Harrisburg did not warmly welcome the out-of-state militiamen. The cool reception confused some of the militiamen, but simply disgruntled others and caused the visitors to assume an attitude of aloofness. The behavior of the Harrisburg residents led the New Yorkers to regard them with outright contempt. The militiamen were soon perceiving themselves as vastly superior beings—finer, more pure specimens of manhood—who were condescending to help good-for-nothing wretches that would not even arm themselves in self defense. All residents of the city and its environs and their property were thereafter treated with disrespect. Chickens and eggs were stolen by foraging parties, whole orchards of cherries were pilfered, vacant houses were looted and fences and outbuildings were dismantled for firewood. The New Yorkers claimed innocence and accused the Pennsylvania militia of the depredations. The Pennsylvanians pointed the finger at the New Yorkers, and the residents blamed both.

The Pennsylvania militiamen had their own reasons for disliking the "Yorkers." The nattily-uniformed New Yorkers had been cocky in their attitude from the very start. "Whilst our regiments were forming," wrote a Pennsylvania militiaman, "they came, brave in all their fancy uniforms and bright buttons, with stylish drum corps and still more stylish drum majors, and yet many of us felt at the time that, almost without exception, the entire lot would not have amounted to a row of pins."[29] The Pennsylvanians might have been a bit over sensitive about the matter of uniforms, for they were not immediately given theirs. While they were waiting for their suits of blue, they came under the critical scrutiny of the dapper New Yorkers: "They were mostly men from different parts of the rural and mining districts, without uniforms or officers and destitute of the slightest military training...they seemed...a slovenly and uncouth mob rather than soldiers. Many of them appeared to be already demoralized, and openly stated that they were 'going home'."[30]

Demoralization had nothing to do with it, as far as the Pennsylvanians were concerned. They simply thought the "Yorkers" arrogant bullies and at least one Pennsylvanian, apparently obsessed with the appearance of the visitors, attributed their behavior to the flashy outfits. "Dress a man like a monkey and he will behave like a monkey; put him in a militia uniform and he will feel and act like a militia-man; clothe him as a soldier should be clothed and he will realize that he is a soldier and will do no discredit to his uniform." The writer saw a lesson in all the fuss the New Yorkers made about their appearance, and he claimed he was given ample opportunity to witness "the depressing effect of a fancy uniform on the human mind in a time of hostilities."[31]

If there was anything upon which both the New York and Pennsylvania militiamen could agree, it was their disdain for the behavior of the people of Harrisburg, which seemed to worsen as the crisis grew more acute. The people of the city simply refused to cooperate in defending their state and their homes. Some few did volunteer to work in the trenches during the constuction of Fort Washington—among these were a large portion of the black population—but a good many other citizens agreed to help dig only if they were paid. They were, in effect, asking to be paid to contribute to the public welfare and the protection of their own homes and property. One New Yorker wrote of the citizens as "Panic-stricken poltoons" who "closed their houses and stores,...and were thinking of nothing in their abject fear except how to escape with their worthless lives and their property."[32] Before they escaped, however, they took the opportunity to line their pockets by selling goods to the militiamen at exorbitant prices. Perhaps most mercenary of all were the toll takers on the Camelback

Bridge, the principal route across the river to Fort Washington. Those men repeated-ly demanded payment of tolls from soldiers crossing the bridge to construct and later garrison the fort.[33]

For days, the roads and bridges from the south had been filled with a continuous line of refugees, all telling stories of the gray hordes right behind them. Many of these people had left their homes hurriedly and were tired and hungry by the time they reached Harrisburg. Some were fed at Camp Curtin, but by far the most did not even pause in the capital but continued right on into the Lebanon Valley beyond. Couch had sections of the Camelback Bridge and the Cumberland Valley Railroad Bridge across the river sawn part way through, ready to drop if the Confederates should suddenly appear on the western shore.[34] Despite repeated warnings such as these, the citizens simply shrugged off the reports of invasion as just so many cries of "wolf." On the 27th of June, when a force of Confederate cavalry passed through Carlisle, less than twenty miles away with 12,000 gray-clad infantrymen right behind them and moving closer all the time, the editor of the *Patriot and Union* wrote light-heartedly about the weather and punned about the "reign of terror" that had been afflicting the city for the past week or so. He continued, "the lies and sensation dispatches have been beating about our ears in a more pitiless storm than ever blew out of the thunder and lightning magazines of heaven." He closed by joking that he hoped the recent "reign" would "wet the priming of the rebel guns down in the [Shenandoah] valley, and [give] every mother's son of them the influenza." If the editor had had reports of the nearness of the Confederates, he had ignored them. The enemy was no longer in the Shenandoah, but just a few hours march from the editor's desk and would get closer before very long.[35]

Life went on very much as usual for the heedless civilians. Preparations were made for celebrating Independence Day with the annual picnic of the Liederkranz Singing Association.[36] The commencement ceremony of the Harrisburg Female Seminary was held in late June, complete with singing and piano accompaniment by the young ladies and the reading of personal essays by the members of the graduating class. And, for the edification of those people of Harrisburg devoted to more abstract entertainments, Miss Fanny Wilson was in town during the final days of June appearing at Edward's Gaiety Music Hall on Walnut Street. Miss Wilson endeared herself to her audiences, which were always quite large, with her "persona-tions of Grecian and Roman statuary." One of the many Harrisburg residents charmed by her performance thought that "Her representation of the *Remorse of Cain* and *The Dying Gladiator* [was] life-like and inimitable. With a form thoroughly graceful, and a physical development faultless and symmetrical, she transformed herself into a perfect *fac simile* of those renowned works of art..." The enraptured writer did not hesitate to pronounce Miss Wilson "the best artist of the kind that has ever come under our notice."[37]

For all the foolishness engaged in by Harrisburg residents while the advance of the Confederate army bore down upon them, a few citizens, a very few, were concerned enough to act. Some of the "city" militia was organized on the city ward level and the veterans of the War of 1812, most of them nearing eighty, paraded through the streets trying to stir some patriotic feeling.[38] Among the wealthy citizens, both Simon Cameron and William K. Verbeke stepped forward to lend a hand. Cameron offered to bear the expense of reactivating the recently disbanded Dauphin County Regiment. Only Company A could be reorganized and the company was posted on the river bank near where the 23rd New Jersey had been, virtually in Cameron's front yard. Verbeke organized a company of 36 men and three wagons, and promised to be responsible for their wants and pay as long as the emergency existed. His actions were even more commendable in light of his anti-war political views. He was considered a Copperhead, but realized that if destructive invaders entered Harrisburg, no fine distinctions would be made based upon political leanings, and his property would be taken, broken or burned just as would anyone else's.[39]

With these few exceptions, Harrisburg residents performed dismally in the crisis that confronted them in the last two weeks of June, 1863. It was, perhaps, the most regrettable period in the city's history, and it came as Harrisburg was the focal point of national attention. All the good works and generosity toward the troops by the people of the city, especially the women, through the two prior years of war were overshadowed by those two weeks of public apathy and selfishness.

*   *   *

Despite all the arrivals and activity in Harrisburg, Pennsylvania's response to the threat was still insufficient, or so thought Curtin and Couch. The number of militiamen that came forward from Pennsylvania did not even approach the 50,000 that Lincoln had requested, and the Rebels were now within Pennsylvania and had actually captured and extorted money and supplies from the city of Chambersburg. On the 26th of June, therefore, Curtin appealed to his people a third time. He called for 60,000 men to serve no more than 60 days. "I will not insult you by inflammatory appeals. A people who want the heart to defend their soil, their families, and their firesides are not worthy to be accounted men....You owe your country your prompt and zealous services and efforts. The time has now come when we must all stand or fall together in the defense of our state and in support of our Government. Let us so discharge our duty that posterity shall not blush for us."[40] This proclamation met with a better response than the previous two, but it was then too late. The invasion was in full swing, and any new militiamen could not be organized and transported quickly enough to be of much use.

Just before Curtin's third proclamation, Couch deployed throughout his department what few men he had. Most regiments and independent companies were employed in guarding bridges, railroads, and telegraph lines, but a few actually were pushed forward into the yawning maw of the most aggressive, most successful and most dangerous army on the continent, the Army of Northern Virginia. Colonel Knipe led an expedition of New York Militia to Chambersburg. He had orders from Couch to slow the advance of the Confederates as much as possible without bringing on an engagement. The last part of the order was unnecessary, for the New Yorkers had no intention of fighting anyone born south of the Mason Dixon line. With the exception of some of volunteer cavalrymen, who exchanged a few parting shots with the van of the Rebels, Knipe's entire brigade fled instantly as soon as it was heard that the Confederates were within six miles! They left their guns, blankets, tents, personal possessions—everything—and ran, heading north by whatever conveyance they could find, and Knipe was unable to get them in hand again until they reached Carlisle, some 30 miles away and less than 20 miles from Harrisburg.[41]

The 26th Pennsylvania Militia also moved from Camp Curtin under Colonel Jennings on the 24th of June and headed south to the crossroads town of Gettysburg, Pennsylvania, just 23 miles east of Chambersburg across a range of low mountains. Jennings and his men bivouacked north of town for a day or so awaiting developments. The brief stay was an enjoyable one, especially for the students from Pennsylvania College in Company A. On the morning of the 26th, the little regiment moved through Gettysburg and westward out the Cashtown pike. After a march of about three miles, Colonel Jennings ordered his men into a field by Marsh Creek. The colonel then rode forward to some high ground to survey the land to the west between him and the mountains that rose up several miles away. He saw in the distance riders on the pike. They were followed by a great many men on foot, and to his horror he soon saw that they all wore gray! General Jubal Early's Corps of seasoned Confederates had swung through the mountain passes during the night and descended into the meadows where Jenning's raw little group of civilians in soldier suits were unrolling blankets and pitching tents. Jennings, no coward and no stranger to combat, decided that his 700-odd rookies could do nothing against these veterans and that, under the circumstances, discretion would be the better part of valor. He quickly rode back to his men, had them quickly repack their things, and led them away, using back roads to evade the advancing Rebels.[42]

Despite the extraordinary efforts to raise and organize them, the militiamen—whether from New York or Pennsylvania, whether in fancy uniforms or plain—did not, after all, "amount to a row of pins." Many of them readily admitted that they had no desire to fight or even serve, but showed up at places like Camp Curtin "simply because of the excitement, and because they disliked to remain at home amid so general a movement."[43] Couch, who estimated the total militia force in his department, including Harrisburg, at 16,000, wrote that their quality was so bad that "five thousand regulars will whip them all to pieces in an open field." Confederate General Early, who forced the retirement of first Knipe's force then Jennings's, reported that the militia forces he encountered offered "no resistance at all, but [were] merely a source of amusement to my troops."[44]

Just how helpless the militiamen were might be seen in the example of Henry D. Landis's "Philadelphia Battery." Landis had organized his outfit by combining two companies of an established Pennsylvania National Guard Artillery regiment. The men of the new battery, resplendent in beautiful gray uniforms with many bright buttons, had drilled considerably in Philadelphia in the manual of the piece, that is, going through the motions of loading and firing the gun so every member of the gun crew knew exactly what his role was and was well rehearsed in his particular task. But the problem was that the men had never actually *fired* their guns—they operated wholly on theory. Moreover, the city boys had no experience with the horses they would need to move their heavy cannon. Upon the battery's arrival, it was sent to Fort Washington. After the long climb up the heights to the fort, Captain Landis was ordered to move a section of the battery to another location on the heights. Assembling the horses, harness, cassions, and guns as best they could, the men managed to get the section moved to its new post. They then realized, however, that they did not remember how they had harnessed the horses to the guns and were unable to release them. It was night by this time, and the hot, tired and frustrated Philadelphia boys gave up trying to demystify the complicated harness and turned in for the night, leaving the equally hot and tired horses standing harnessed to one another.

In the morning the men renewed their assault on the problem and appealed to their officers for assistance. The only result was that the officers were embarrassed, for none of them—lawyers, merchants, and professional men that they were—knew how to unharness the animals either. They issued an order born of ignorance and embarrassment: "Try all the buckles and unbuckle those that work easiest." The dilemma was not to be solved that easily, however, for the harness was new and none of the buckles had been worked often enough to unhook easily. For two days the militiamen puzzled over how to free the horses, who were getting more tired by the hour. Finally, some humane soul released the poor animals by unfastening every buckle on the harnesses, reducing the tack to a tangled mass of leather thongs. Someone had the good sense and courage—belated though it was—to ask a professional artilleryman for assistance in reassembling the harnesses. Even then there were mistakes made in the reassembly so the harness did not work as it had been designed to. The result was that some horses had to be led when pulling the guns because they could not be controlled by the driver of the team. When the battery was finally in place, it was found that the gun teams were so short of equipment that not all the guns could be put into action at one time.[45]

It was upon such men that the city would have to depend for protection, and in the last days of June, it looked very much like a stand of some sort would have to be made on the Susquehanna. On the 27th, Brigadier General Albert Jenkins and his brigade of Confederate cavalrymen had moved through Carlisle and encamped north of that town. Jenkins was followed by the full division of Major General Robert Rodes and Edward Johnson. By the next day, Jenkins was in Mechanicsburg, just 10 miles from Harrisburg and it appeared that the men in Forts Couch and Washington would see some Confederates on the morrow. But the Confederate infantry did not follow its cavalry much beyond Carlisle, and Jenkins and his men got no further north than Oyster Point, a little crossroads about two miles from Fort Washington. Some shots were fired and the militiamen, many of whom were the New Yorkers who had fled from Chambersburg while under Knipe, did come out of the defenses to meet the southern cavalrymen, but nothing more serious occurred than an occasional ineffectual volley of musketry or some wasted artillery fire.

On the 30th, Jenkins, under orders, began to pull back. The very advanced units of the Army of Northern Virginia had been recalled by Lee. Harrisburg, for the time being at least, had been removed from the list of Confederate objectives. As Jenkins mounted up his men and headed south, he was harried by the militiamen upon whom he turned his back. There was some more ineffectual skirmishing, but the mounted Rebels outdistanced their footbound pursuers, and the immediate threat to Harrisburg came to an end.

* * *

While Jenkins and his troopers were distressing the citizens of Carlisle, Mechanicsburg and suburban Harrisburg, the Army of the Potomac was pounding the roads of Maryland and Northern Virginia in pursuit of the unrestrained Confederates. The weather was nasty in that last week of June. The heat and humidity contested with one another to make life miserable for the infantrymen, and when rain came to break the heat, the roads turned slippery and heavy with mud, making long marches exhausting affairs. The long columns that wended northward were comprised of silent, spiritless men, who lurched forward not with determination, but with resignation. Their heads hung down, their gaze on the ground or on the heels of the dusty boots of the men in front. Throughout the afternoon, the sun held none of its usual charms and simply burned brazenly, scorching skin and soil alike.

By dusk of the 27th of June, almost all of the Federal army was north of the Potomac. Only Colonel William McCandless's four regiments of the Pennsylvania Reserves remained south of the river. The Reserves had not been with the rest of the main army throughout the winter and spring. They had been detailed for duty in the defenses of Washington in February and had remained there since. On the 25th of June, however, as the seriousness of Lee's threat to Pennsylvania became apparent, the two brigades of Reserves, one under McCandless, colonel of the 2nd Reserves, the other under Colonel Joseph W. Fisher of the 5th Reserves were ordered to rejoin the main army as it marched northward.

The Bucktails, still the brash cocky group that swaggered into Harrisburg two years before in red flannel shirts and lumberman's boots, were part of McCandless's brigade. Fewer of the brash young men marched with the regiment now, many of them having been left on the Peninsula, in the meadows of the Shenandoah Valley, on the slopes of South Mountain, in the cornfield of Antietam, or in hospitals all over Virginia, Maryland and Pennsylvania. Accessions, principally due to the popularity of the regiment back home, had kept the ranks filled to just a bit over one-third of their original strength, but the fragment that remained was largely composed of the veterans—the hardy ones who had withstood the physical rigors of campaigning and the lucky ones who had passed through the maelstrom of battle.

At the head of the Bucktail column rode Colonel Fred Taylor, just 23 and already commanding one of the crack regiments of the army. Taylor had developed into the type of regimental officer every brigade and division commander dreamed about. He was responsible for himself and his men. He was vigorous, thorough, swift and precise in executing orders; he was personally brave—always among or ahead of his men when they advanced into battle. After Fredericksburg, Captain Taylor and his regiment were assigned duty at Fairfax Station on the Orange and Alexandria Railroad near Washington. There he sat and waited and missed another coveted opportunity for glory and recognition, this time at Chancellorsville in May. "As these warm days come on," he wrote home, "I cannot but feel restive and long to be with one of the great armies east or west." It was during this time, though, that he finally was commissioned colonel. The young colonel was ecstatic when the Bucktails were ordered out of their camps and after the invading Confederates. On June 24, he wrote to his sister, "I presume we shall have a stirring campaign. I am very glad of it. We have been here long enough."[46]

On a hill above the north bank of the Potomac, a group of Pennsylvania cavalrymen, Pittsburghers mostly, sat on their mounts, leaned forward in their saddles and watched the already-famed Pennsylvania Bucktails and other regiments of the Pennsylvania Reserves approach the pontoon bridge over which they would cross. "Well do the men of [the] cavalry command remember the evening," wrote Captain William E. Miller of the 3rd Pennsylvania Cavalry. The high spirits of the Reserves as they tramped northward toward their homeland was not only visible from the bluffs, but contagious. "As soon as the band of McCandless's brigade placed foot on the bridge," wrote Miller, "it began to play 'Maryland, My Maryland.' The infantrymen took up the refrain, and it was echoed back by the cavalrymen on the northern hillside. The scene was beautiful and touching beyond description, and formed one of the happy incidents that broke the monotony of the long weary march...."[47]

On the night of June 27, with virtually all of the Union army in Maryland and virtually all of the Confederate army in Pennsylvania, Joe Hooker was relieved of the command of the Army of the Potomac. He was replaced by Major General George Gordon Meade. Though born in Spain, Meade was a Pennsylvanian, a Philadelphian of fine social standing. He was a 48-year-old West Pointer, olive-skinned, hawk-nosed, bearded, and meticulous. As a division commander he had a hand in developing the mettle of some of the best troops in the entire army—the Pennsylvania Reserves, which he had commanded for much of the war. The change was a popular one with a good many in the ranks of the army, especially with the men of the Reserves. "I was proud," wrote one of them, "to think that one of our P.R.C. Generals, one for whom *we* had won the Stars should be placed in the highest and most responsible position....We of the P.R.C. had faith in Gen. Meade as an energetic, cool, determined & brave leader."[48]

Union cavalry was sweeping through northern Maryland and southern Pennsylvania looking for the enemy. Signs of the invaders were plentiful, and scared residents could supply information about when the Confederates had been by, but no real contact with a sizeable force of the enemy had been made for many miles. Finally, on the night of the 30th, Union Cavalry under General John Buford, which had been patrolling broad expanses of territory, located about 2,400 Confederate infantry in the little crossroads town of Gettysburg. The Rebels—a brigade of North Carolinians—withdrew, but Buford believed they would be back. He sent word to the main army and asked for reinforcements from the nearest infantry, the First Corps, at Marsh Run, less than 15 miles south of Gettysburg. With this done, Buford scattered some pickets out on the roads north and west of town in the direction of the retreating Confederates. The remainder of his tired men bedded down for the night. Some of the citizens of Gettysburg, grateful for their deliverance from the foraging Rebels, came out to the camps of the cavalrymen with bread, biscuits, meats, jellies and more good things than the men could possibly eat. After a good meal, the tired troopers went to sleep.[49]

*   *   *

July 1 dawned gray and hazy on the ridges west of Gettysburg. The ground was damp and dew clung in thick, sparkling drops to matted grass and the blue woolen suits of Buford's cavalrymen. It would be another hot day, and humid. The air was already heavy with the sweet, scent of mown hay. Buford's cavalry division was comprised of New Yorkers, Hoosiers, Illinoisans, West Virginians and Pennsylvanians. Among the latter were the men of the 17th Pennsylvania Cavalry who had spent the previous winter organizing at Camps Simmons and McClellan in Harrisburg.

Buford's troopers were spread thinly along the open ridges west of Gettysburg when, just after daylight, the Confederates returned. Firing began on the picket lines, and Buford deployed the rest of his troopers across McPherson's ridge, which took its name from the farmer whose house and barn sat atop it. The Federal pickets began to get the worst of it and slowly pulled back to the ridge. The attacks would continue for more than three hours. The cavalrymen crouched or lay on the ridge loading and firing and beating back one wave after another of Confederate infantrymen, but the pressure from the Rebels became almost too much to bear, and the strain was worsened as ammunition ran low.

About that time lead elements of the Federal infantry from the First Corps began to arrive from the south. As they neared the town, they left the road and ran across country to the ridges west of town, taking the places of the hard-pressed cavalrymen.

The troopers swung into their saddles and headed for the rear, taking their wounded with them.[50]

The First Corps was arguably the best in the army and was superbly led by Major General John F. Reynolds, a former commander of the Pennsylvania Reserves. Unquestionably the best brigade in Reynolds's Corps was a collection of Michiganders, Hoosiers and Wisconsinites dubbed the "Iron Brigade." Included in the brigade were the 5th and the 6th Wisconsin Regiments, both of which had spent some time in Harrisburg back in the early days of the war. Also a part of the First Corps, however, was a brigade of three Pennsylvania regiments—the 143rd, the 149th, and the 150th, Major Thomas Chamberlin's regiment. All three had come from in Camp Curtin and all three had been in service for less than a year, seeing little duty in the field. They had been marching hard in the heat of that first morning in July, the sweat poured off them "in cascades" as one of them remembered, and scores had fallen out of the ranks along the road. The 150th Regiment was led by Colonel Langhorne Wister, Lieutenant Colonel Henry Shippen Huidekoper and Major Thomas Chamberlin. Wister, like Chamberlin, was a veteran. He had been captain of Company B of the Bucktails until September, 1862, when the 150th was formed and he had been offered the commission as colonel. Henry Huidekoper, though Chamberlin's senior in rank, was younger and had less military experience. He was just 23 and fresh out of Harvard, class of 1862.

As the 150th and its two sister regiments hustled forward with the rest of the First Corps, all three were under the command of Colonel Roy Stone of the 149th. Stone was another veteran of the Bucktails. Now, as brigade commander, he led his men through the grounds of a Lutheran seminary, which sat on an elevation between McPherson's farm and the town. A wide, deep swale separated the high ground of the seminary from McPherson's ridge. General Abner Doubleday, commander of the Third Division of the First Corps, met Colonel Stone and his brigade near the seminary. He bore the bad news that Reynolds was dead, having been shot in the head and killed instantly shortly after reaching the field.[51] Doubleday assumed command upon Reynolds's death and immediately directed Stone and his brigade forward.

The raw brigade was going into its first fight, but was remarkably cool. Colonel Wister put his men in line then barked "Forward." A dozen voices called out to remind him that the men had not been ordered to load their weapons yet. Despite the whizzing of Confederate shells everyone let loose and had a good laugh at the overanxious colonel, and the men loaded their pieces. The 397 men of the regiment then dropped knapsacks and moved from the seminary out into the swale and toward their hard-pressed comrades on the ridge beyond.[52]

It was then about 11:30 a.m. The Confederate infantry had temporarily pulled back, but the Southern artillerists were still busy, and the Pennsylvanians moved forward beneath and amid a steady screaming and bursting of shot and shells. The little brigade deployed on the right of the Iron Brigade and sent out skirmishers. Major Chamberlin could see large masses of Confederates forming in his front. They "formed in continuous double lines of battle," he later wrote, "extending southward as far as the accidents of the ground permitted the eye to reach." More Confederate batteries opened on the Federal positions and the long lines of gray and butternut infantry that Chamberlin had seen finally emerged from the trees and started forward. The principal thrust of the assault came not from the west but from the northwest, and Colonel Stone changed the front of the 143rd and 149th to meet the attack. The 150th, forming the wing of the brigade farthest from the attack, was not immediately engaged, but was soon drawn out by the needs of the 143rd and especially the 149th, which had formed its defensive line too far forward and was now paying for the error with heavy casualties. The 150th moved quickly to help repel the charging Confederates and protected the 149th as it returned to a more sensible position, but the effects of the Confederate marksmanship, both with muskets and field guns, began to be felt. Stone was severely wounded twice, and was forced to turn command of the brigade over to Wister, senior colonel of the brigade. Wister, in turn, entrusted the 150th to young Lieutenant Colonel Huidekoper.

Huidekoper found his regiment facing north while a new attack was launched from the west so he immediately began to change front to meet the new attack. Again and again the regiment was required to change front as attacking lines of Confederates appeared first from the west and then from the north. It was not a simple maneuver to realign a regiment so as to meet an assault head on, especially under a heavy crossfire and with no protection, save a bare rail fence that had to be dismantled to allow the changing of face.

The terrain and the continued attacks left the regiment, and the brigade, ripe for sustaining severe casualties, and the men began to fall in great numbers. Colonel Wister was shot in the mouth and, though not grievously wounded, could not give comprehensible orders. Lieutenant Charles Keyser of Company B fell dead, Captain William Dougal of D was wounded, Corporal Charles Reisinger of H was shot in the foot, Sergeant Samuel Phifer of I, of the color guard, was wounded and later died, Lieutenant Colonel Huidekoper received a flesh wound in the leg, then had his right arm shattered by a bullet. Lieutenant Chancellor of Company B was mortally wounded when his thigh bone was fractured by a shell, Lieutenant Gilbert Perkins of C also was wounded in the thigh, Lieutenants Miles Rose of I and Chalkey Sears of F were both wounded, Captain John Sigler of I was hit. Sergeant Elias Weidensaul of D, who had been promoted to lieutenant shortly before the battle but had not yet been commissioned at his new rank, was hit in the stomach and doubled over with his hands over the wound. Adjutant Richard Ashurst saw him and called out "Are you wounded?" and Weidensaul replied, "No, killed" and he fell dead. Moments later Ashurst too fell. Sergeant Thomas Lyons, Company F, had a miraculous brush with death when a Confederate artillery shell that failed to explode whistled toward him and grazed his chest, ripping away his clothing and knocking him to the ground. He was given a terrible shock, and the skin on his chest was badly bruised and later discolored, but it had not been broken and no blood was spilled; the sergeant lived to tell his story.[53]

While the officers and men were dropping all about him, and those wounded that could scurried off to the rear or the shelter of McPherson's house and barn, Major Chamberlin looked through the smoke and beyond the exploding shells to the west where he saw still more Confederate infantry coming up, "regiment upon regiment *en echelon,*" he saw, "followed by supporting columns, extending southward...as far as the eye could reach." The regiment was in trouble, its battle line was growing thinner by the minute and was in terrible disorder. The major had no orders to do anything but hold on and meet the new threat, but if things continued as they were going, nothing would be left of the 150th to meet the new gray wave.[54]

Chamberlin set about gathering up what healthy men were left and began putting them back in line. While hurrying about shouting to the men and directing them in their movements, a Minie ball tore into his upper back and knocked him to the ground. The bullet had entered to the right of his spine near the shoulder blade, glanced upward toward the top of his arm, and finally come to rest just under the very tip of his right clavicle. He lay helpless in the trampled grass until some of his men picked him up and carried him to the McPherson house in what he later described as "a badly disabled condition."[55]

It was nearly 3 p.m., and the little brigade of Pennsylvanians had been withstanding attacks and an almost continuous crossfire of musketry and artillery for more than three hours. The Iron Brigade had been dislodged from the woods on the left and the westerners began to fall back, exposing the flank of Pennsylvanians. Confederate fire came into the 150th from three sides, until finally, mercifully, the order came to fall back. The men needed no urging, and they began to retire from the ridge. The officers, the wounded Adjutant Ashurst in particular, tried to keep some order as the men retreated but had little success. Colonel Wister, despite his mouth wound, was still on the field, but could do nothing but gesture. Lieutenant Colonel Huidekoper returned to the field with a tourniquet on his useless right arm and tried to steady the men, but loss of blood finally forced him again from the field. It made no difference, for an orderly withdrawal was no longer possible. The Confederates were upon the Pennsylvanians, and there was nothing to do but run.

Throughout the day, additional Federal troops had been arriving on the battlefield from the south and an already naturally stong defensive position in and around a cemetery on a hill south of the town had been further fortified with breastworks. Shortly before 5 o'clock, the broken remnants of the First Corps streamed into the defenses on the height and at last rested.

Colonel Stone's brigade of three regiments had entered the fight that morning with just over 1,300 officers and men. As the officers counted heads on Cemetery Hill, they found only a bit more than 400 remained. The 150th had had 17 officers and 380 men present as it went into action; only two officers and 84 men made it to Cemetery Hill, the rest were scattered over the fields west of town, lying in the streets and on the doorsteps of Gettysburg, or marching to the Confederate rear as prisoners.[56] Many lay in McPherson's barn on beds of straw or in stalls or hay ricks. They were learning first hand the horrors of the field hospital, and watched in painful silence as the surgeons who made that place of horrors their own domain moved about quickly in a gruesome race with pounding hearts and severed arteries. Dr. Thomas H. Bache, who was serving as the medical inspector of the First Corps, was one of those Federal surgeons who remained behind to attend to the wounded, and he was working in McPherson's barn when Major Thomas Chamberlin was laid before him with a hole in his back, bleeding freely. Though it was very painful, the wound would probably not be mortal, so Dr. Bache simply arrested the bleeding by stuffing wadding into the hole and passed on to another casualty, leaving the bullet in the shoulder. Chamberlin was later moved to the Lutheran seminary, which was being used by the Confederates as a hospital.[57]

It had been a very bad day for the Army of the Potomac. The Confederates were in possession of Gettysburg, hundreds of Federal prisoners and a confidence that knew no bounds. They had once again whipped the Yanks and, what with reinforcements arriving steadily, felt sure they would finish the job tomorrow. The Federals, who had truly been whipped, held the heights south of town and were considerably less confident than their enemies, but they too were sure of two things, they held a good, strong defensive position and were being reinforced in a continuous stream. If the Rebels were to whip them again tomorrow, they would have their work cut out for them.

* * *

Despite some predawn drizzle, the sun came up on July 2 with the same intensity with which it had burned throughout the day before. All night long, soldiers in blue and in butternut and gray, tramped toward the battleground and all through the morning, the sweaty, dusty men arrived behind the lines of their respective armies. Both commanding generals moved about the field making troop dispositions, Lee with an eye toward making an attack, Meade with an eye toward receiving one.

About noon on the 2nd, Colonel Fred Taylor and the Bucktails came lurching into the Union rear along with the rest of the Reserves and the Fifth Army Corps. They had covered 35 miles in the last day and a half, and marched about 10 miles that morning on three hours of sleep. The weary foot soldiers were finally filed off the road and allowed to rest in the sun on the trampled, weedy grass. Some drank their coffee or ate, others simply lolled in the quiet heat of the day. It was all but certain that they would see combat before the day was out.

The Confederate attack finally came about 4 p.m. on the extreme left of the Union line on the southernmost part of the field. The terrain in that area was varied—heavy woods, cultivated fields, rocky meadows, and sloping ridges. The dominating features were two hills called Round Top and Little Round Top, and the Southerners made them their objective. The ground over which the Confederates advanced was open and rolling pasture with a few wood lots, a field of standing wheat, a number of stone walls, and, just at the front of Little Round Top, a soft boggy valley, through which ran a sluggish creek called Plum Run. The Federal Third Corps was struck by the first Confederate attack and overwhelmed. Wounded and frightened Yankees streamed across the pastures and stone walls back to the safety of the main Union line. The time was about 4:30 p.m.

The Fifth Corps was sent to Little Round Top to defend it against the Confederates assailing and driving the Third Corps. Hordes of Texans, Alabamians and Georgians swarmed past a cluster of huge boulders called Devil's Den and into the Plum Run valley at the western foot of Little Round Top.

The Pennsylvania Reserves had been listening to the fighting from their resting place northwest of Little Round Top. When firing from the Confederate assault grew louder, aides and orderlies appeared galloping madly about with orders to and from the various headquarters. The troops lounging in the sparse shade took in all the rushing about while knowing full well what it meant: they were "going in." The veterans grew pensive then grim when they received the orders to form ranks. The chaplain of the 11th Reserves, remembering a battle that might have been on the minds of many of the Reserves in those minutes, decribed the scene in a letter to his wife. "Hundreds of the men piled their knapsacks together & left them, [and] the peculiar silence in the ranks which I noted on the morning of the 13th of December was equally manifest & impressive...."[58] The Reserve regiments were hurried to the northern crest of Little Round Top by their division commander, Major General Samuel Crawford, and they came immediately under fire. They were principally to serve as supports for the troops engaged, but Colonel McCandless put his brigade in two lines of battle in preparation for receiving an attack. The five regiments quietly shuffled about and into their respective places; Taylor and the Bucktails in the second line on the left. Battery L, First Ohio Artillery was in position on the left of the Bucktails and made preparations to withdraw in the face of the infantry approaching from the smoke-shrouded valley, presuming it to be Southern. Taylor and some of his men shouted to the gunners to keep cool and stay in position, promising to protect them and their guns.

Pine trees near the crest of the hill obscured the brigade of Reserves from anyone on the slope or in the valley. Although the view of the valley from the hill was normally excellent, allowing observation for thousands of yards north and west, smoke made seeing any considerable distance difficult. Colonel Jackson, of the 11th Reserves in the front rank, peered through the pines to see a line of troops very near and still climbing the hill. He was not sure whether the troops were retreating Yankees or advancing Confederates. Two men scrambling up the hill in front of the mysterious line were definitely Federal soldiers. Colonel Jackson called out to them, "How many of our people are down there?" and the two replied, "Not one. Those people you see coming up the hill are johnnies." Colonel Jackson needed to know nothing more. He ordered his men to open fire, which they did and with terrible effect. The surprised Confederates staggered to a halt and became disorganized. Jackson, not wishing to lose the advantage, ordered his men to fix bayonets and charge. The 11th went up and over the trees and rocks and flew down the slope, followed closely by the rest of the brigade. After the Bucktails had opened fire, the Confederates had kept coming, and the fighting became hand to hand. The Southerners finally broke, however, and the Bucktails swept down the hill.[59]

The slope was steep and covered with rocks, boulders and crevasses, so Taylor left his horse behind.[60] The speeding Bucktails captured a good many of the slower Rebels on the way down the hill, but at the loss of Lieutenant Colonel Alanson E. Niles, badly wounded in the hip. With the 1st Pennsylvania Reserves on their right, the Bucktails charged obliquely across the foot of the hill through the boggy valley toward Devil's Den. Major General Crawford himself took the colors of the 1st Reserves and led that regiment in the charge. The Bucktails, however, were following a different leader. Private Richard Beeby of Company H of the Bucktails claimed that though he had earned a reputation as a sprinter, he could not that day keep up with young Colonel Taylor, who was in front of the regiment the entire way from the crest, across the marshy, boulder-strewn valley and to a stone wall on the edge of some woods on the far side of the clearing. Though the woods were infested with Confederates firing at the advancing Pennsylvanians, Beeby saw Taylor, still running and waving his sword to encourage his men, vault over the wall and disappear into the trees. The Bucktails surged after their leader and, swinging or firing their rifles, wrested the wall and the woods from the Rebels. Some of the Confederates surrendered but others withdrew farther into the woods toward a wheat field beyond, which was itself being contested. The Bucktails took cover behind the wall.

The reckless charge had caused the regiment to lose cohesion. Some of the Bucktails were on the left near the very end of the wall while the rest of the Bucktails were well down the wall to the right nearer the wheat field. Taylor had returned to the wall to reform the regiment and was on the right flank with the larger segment of the regiment. As more Bucktails were wounded and others moved to the rear with prisoners, confusion at the wall forced officers to make due with the men they could round up, and men from several different companies would find themselves thrown together under one officer. One such group arrived on the left of the wall under Captain Mack of Company E. Mack took two men, neither from his own company, and entered the woods beyond the end of the wall to see what lay within. The three moved slowly through the thick woods scanning their front for movement. They had gone just a few dozen yards before sighting a large number of Confederates—perhaps a hundred—moving across their front. The trio of Bucktails immediately

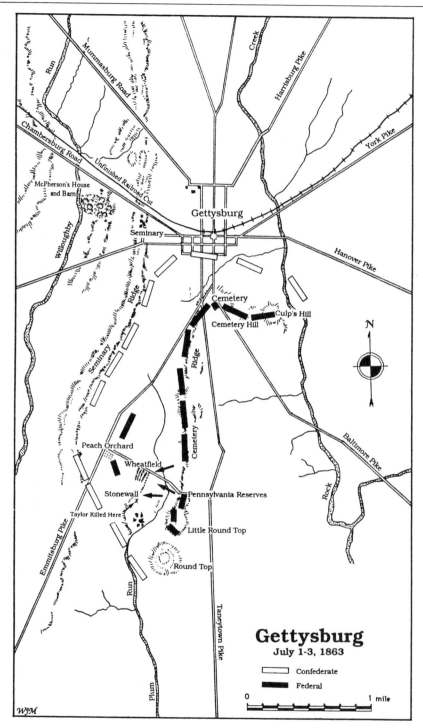

Gettysburg

July 1-3, 1863

☐ Confederate

■ Federal

0 _____ 1 mile

WJM

ducked behind trees and rocks. Just then, they were joined by half a dozen more Bucktails. The reinforcements took cover while the officers began quietly discussing what to do next. The party of Bucktails did not exceed ten men, not nearly enough to attack the large body of Rebels still in the trees to the front and still unaware of the presence of the Pennsylvanians. While the options were being considered, Taylor himself came striding up through the woods from the wall. Seeing the Southerners, Taylor impetuously wished to attack. "Why don't you fire?" he asked reproachfully. Mack replied that he did not think they were strong enough.

Accounts of what followed vary. One version states that Taylor, seeing that the officers were right, said he would order up more men, but was just then seen by the enemy and fired upon. Another account states that Taylor boldly called out to the Confederates to surrender, that some of them, startled, threw down their weapons, but that others, who saw just how few Yankees opposed them, began firing immediately. In any case, Taylor was hit squarely in the chest. Private Aaron Baker, of Taylor's old Company H, was with the colonel when he fell. "He seemed to want to say something," wrote Baker to Taylor's sister, "all I could understand was 'Mum' 'Mum.' I do not think that he lasted over two minutes."[61] The Bucktails carried the body of their boy colonel back to the wall under heavy fire. There, members of Taylor's old Company H, the Wayne Independent Rifles, took charge of him and removed him to the rear. With Taylor dead and Niles out of action, Major William Hartshorne was in command of the regiment. As dark was coming on, Hartshorne thought it prudent to consolidate his scattered regiment and steel the men after their terrible loss. He rounded up as many as he could find and brought them together at the stone wall by the wheat field. There they remained through the dusk and into the night as the Confederate attacks slackened and the Southerners withdrew, leaving the Round Tops in Federal hands.

*   *   *

July 3 was a day of anxiety in Harrisburg. News of the great struggle at Gettysburg, just 35 miles to the south, was arriving steadily, but little of the information was reliable. Rumor and speculation reigned. Past mid-day, a faint thunder was heard in the south. The fair skies gave no indication of rain, however, and the people of the city were puzzled. Perhaps the old veterans in their midst recognized the sound first—the rumble of distant artillery. Slowly, the citizens began to move toward Front Street on the river's bank to better hear the astounding phenomenon. No one knew what the sound meant, but thousands packed Front Street and Harris Park to listen.[62]

The roar came from 140 Confederate cannon. Nearly every field piece in the Army of Northern Virginia was firing on the center of the Union line on and nearby Cemetery Hill. The Federal artillery replied, and the result was the largest artillery duel in the history of the continent. Lee's hope was that his guns would destroy or disable enough of the Union guns and create enough confusion among the Union infantry to make a vigorous attack by Confederate infantry successful. The barrage lasted for more than an hour, and it was promptly followed by a ground attack by 12,000 Confederate infantrymen under Major General George E. Pickett. The attack came at the Union center and over very nearly a mile of open ground. It was reminiscent of Fredericksburg, but with the roles reversed, and the result was to be a little different from the deadly battle in the snow seven months before. The attacking lines were repulsed with tremendously heavy losses. Pickett's men retreated across the long meadow and into the woods on Seminary Ridge. The battle was over, and for the first time the Army of the Potomac had clearly and decisively beaten the Army of Northern Virginia.

The cost to the Federal army, however, had been terrible: more than 3,100 Union soldiers were killed outright; 5,300 were missing or were prisoners and a staggering 14,500 had been wounded.[63] Regiments withered to the strength of a company, companies virtually disappeared. Immediately after the battle, Sergeant John Milton Ray of Company C of the 140th Pennsylvania wrote a brief note on a scrap of paper and sent it home to reassure his sister in West Alexander, Pennsylvania.

> Dear Sister I thank God that my life is still spared but our company suffered severely Our captain is killed Leut Vance had his left hand shot off Frank McNear wounded in the side Ed. Alexander wound in head Jo Lawson is missing Bill Armstrong missing Bob Muldoon wounded in leg Lucas is missing John Blair is missing Ellis J. Cole wounded in left arm & amputated
>
> > I will send this by Leut Vance
> > Your affec Bro
> > Milton[64]

Later, when heads were counted, it was found that Company C retained just 10 men and two sergeants after the fight in the wheat field. "It makes my heart ache," wrote Sergeant Ray, "to look at the little squad left of our large co."[65]

After the Confederates retreated on July 4, the task of finding and trying to save the lives of the wounded still on the field began. Field hospitals had been set up in houses and barns all over the area and injured men were found and brought in to these impromptu surgeries even well after the Army of Northern Virginia had withdrawn. Confederate surgeons remained when their army left and continued operating and amputating in the barns and houses south and west of Gettysburg. One Federal surgeon visited one of these impromptu hospitals and wrote, "Never had we witnessed such sad scenes....The Confederate surgeons were doing what they could for their wounded, but were destitute of medicines and surgical appliances, and even food sufficient to supply those in their charge."[66] Another observer of the surgeons, both Northern and Southern wrote, "I never saw men work harder and complain less of the difficulties that surrounded them."[67]

*   *   *

Throughout July, thousands of sick and wounded men arrived in Harrisburg, and the city assumed its normal post-battle appearance. Churches, schools and private homes became hospitals. Late in June, perhaps in anticipation of a battle nearby, the Cotton Mill had been reopened as a hospital. The walls were whitewashed, more beds added, ventilation improved, and tents were erected outside to house doctors and nurses. Altogether, the place was made more like a genuine hospital and less like a mill.[68] Just a few blocks away, on Walnut Street, a building used as a high school was fitted up with 126 beds and converted into a hospital. Tents were erected outside the building and another 20 beds were installed. The whole was put under the command of Surgeon R. H. Seiler and the Soldiers' Rest at the depot prepared itself for a heavy increase in business as well.[69] Colonel Gabriel DeKorponay, who had commanded the 28th Pennsylvania until March when discharged on a surgeon's certificate, was in general superintendence of operations at the Rest and his efficiency and generosity in feeding or boarding soldiers, militiamen, and their families was exceptional. In the month of July alone, 44,261 rations were issued at Soldiers' Rest.[70]

Limping bandaged men were everywhere. Those who could walk took exercise along the river or on the pleasant avenues in the city. Others sat on porches or under trees and took what pleasure and health they could from the fresh air. The less fortunate lay in the hot rooms of hospitals and houses and waited. They waited for the visits of kind citizens of Harrisburg, who would come by to talk or to read aloud or perhaps write a letter home for one of them. They waited for their wounds to heal, or to worsen, they waited for infection and sometimes for death. It is not exaggeration to say that many lived only to wait for the visits of those kind people who brought cakes or pies, who brought smiles and good nature, and most of all, who brought hope and reminders of home.[71]

Not all the wounded cared for in Harrisburg wore blue. Hundreds of Confederates were quartered in and about the city, and little distinction was made about where they were kept. The East Walnut Street Hospital, the former high school, housed about an equal number of Northerners and Southerners.[72] The hospital on Chestnut Street housed many Rebels as well.[73] This place was run by the Christian Commission, and hundreds of wounded Confederates being sent to points north were fed there during layovers in waiting for rail connections.[74] Some of the Confederates in town were temporarily penned up at Camp Curtin until they were moved to more permanent prisons.[75]

Colonel Beaver was anxious to get away from Camp Curtin and his "position of vexatious toil" as commandant. He wished to get back into the war and had been trying to obtain permission to return to his regiment since late in June. Throughout July, he had been "making almost daily application to be relieved," though he was still far from completely recovered. It had not been until June 27 that his wound had allowed him to mount a horse, but as soon as he had proved to himself that he could climb into a saddle he had asked Couch to relieve him and send him back to the

148th in time for the imminent battle. "A few days will clear our camp entirely," Beaver wrote to his mother on the 27th, "I hope there can then be no excuse for keeping me any longer."[76] But Couch had denied Beaver's request and kept him at camp.

Once the crisis had passed and Beaver had given his bandaged abdomen a few more weeks of rest, Couch was more willing to part with him. The young officer renewed his request to be relieved, and Couch complied, but with regret. The militiamen would be returning soon to be mustered out, and Beaver's experience and abilities would be helpful maintaining order and control in camp until the paperwork could be completed. Nevertheless, on July 15, Couch issued Special Order No. 35 praising Beaver:

> The Major-General commanding tenders his thanks to Colonel Beaver for the important service rendered him in the organization of the troops, which were hurried to the Capitol [sic] and placed under his command at Camp Curtin, notwithstanding he was absent on leave in the Department, on account of wounds received in battle. The zeal and energy he manifested in the cause is worthy of emulation.
>
> By command of Major-General Couch[77]

Beaver hastened off to Virginia.

Beaver's successor as commandant was another combat veteran, Captain William A. Sands of Company L, 1st Pennsylvania Cavalry. Sands had joined his company in July, 1861 as it was being recruited as an independent unit in his hometown of Reading, Pennsylvania. He had gone with the company as a first lieutenant to Harrisburg at the beginning of August and remained there in Camp Curtin as the 1st Cavalry was being formed. He had spent about a month and a half at the camp before going to Washington, where the regiment was finally organized. Early April, 1862, he had been promoted to Captain of Company L and had been detached for recruiting duty a few months later. He had spent almost the entire period since—almost a year—at Camp Curtin performing various duties, including that of vice or interim commandant. Just 5' 5" and about 120 pounds, he was 43 years old when Beaver departed and left him again in command.[78]

While Sands was in command, the role of adjutant, or the overseer of much of the daily functioning of the camp, was filled by Captain John J. Ball. Ball, a Harrisburg native, had been continuously involved in the war effort since its first days. He had raised a company in Harrisburg in the early months of the war and had kept it together and regularly drilled the men until they were incorporated into the 127th in August, 1862, as Company G. He had been wounded in the charge on the stone wall at Fredericksburg, but had been healthy when mustered out with the regiment in May, 1863. His leadership and administrative abilities made him too valuable to be allowed to simply sit about, so he had been put to work at Camp Curtin in July, 1863, to make arrangements for receiving and mustering out the militia.[79]

A portion of the camp was set aside as a holding area for apprehended deserters and stragglers who had been separated from their regiments and were to be sent back to them. The area was called "Strag's Camp," short for straggler's, and was placed under the command of Henry Chritzman, former captain of Company K of the 101st Pennsylvania. Chritzman had been the original captain of Company K when the regiment was formed in December, 1861 and had spent the better part of three months in Camp Curtin that winter. He had been discharged for medical reasons in February, 1863, and was serving purely as a volunteer.[80]

Camp Simmons was reactivated in anticipation of the return of the militia, and Lieutenant Colonel Joseph F. Ramsey was named to command. Ramsey was from Montour County and, like Ball, had been involved in the war almost from the beginning.[81] In October, 1861, he had become captain of Company G of the 93rd Pennsylvania, but had resigned that post a year later. When the emergency arose in June, 1863, he quickly raised a company and led it to Harrisburg. There, the company was made a portion of a battalion of independent infantry raised during the emergency but enlisted to serve six months, and Ramsey was made lieutenant colonel commanding. The outfit, called simply "the First Battalion," remained in Harrisburg and served as provost guard with headquarters at Camp Simmons after Gettysburg.[82]

By the last week of July, about all the stores and equipment that had been removed from the camp during the invasion were returned, and the Pennsylvania militiamen began trickling in. The trickle soon turned to a deluge as 13,000 men descended on the city. Camps Curtin and Simmons were packed, and paperwork was begun immediately.[83] As always, confusion and delay attended the discharging of the men, but during the delay, the militiamen were, to everyone's surprise, on their best behavior. They accepted the "red tapism" stoically and, though anxious to get home, passed the time patiently while waiting to be paid. The docility of the men might have been engendered by a sense of embarrassment. Now that the dark days had passed, they might have been a bit ashamed of their reluctance to wade into the breach and willingly and unconditionally defend their state. They had been asked to do comparatively little and had accomplished less, and while many were thankful for having exchanged a few weeks of boredom for having been spared injury or death on the battlefield, a good many others were wondering if they had acted sooner back in June if they might have had the opportunity to be a part of the greatest battle of the war.

CHAPTER SEVEN

"May You Ever Be Marked As Brave Men"

AUGUST, 1863 — APRIL, 1865

Except for abortive offensives by Lee and Meade that led only to more casualties, the months following Gettysburg were relatively quiet and devoted to healing. The military people in Harrisburg took advantage of the quiet to do some housekeeping. More Regular Army officers were on duty in the capital than had been previously, and the Army and the War Department were taking a greater interest in Harrisburg and its importance to the war effort. For a long time, the pens and corrals at Camp Curtin had been used as a depot for horses enroute to Washington or other points for distribution to the cavalry units. During the summer of 1863, however, the army built a huge storehouse in the city that would allow it to keep all types of supplies and to quickly ship them to almost any point in Maryland, Virginia or Ohio.[1]

Certainly the most significant changes coming during that time were at Camp Curtin itself. A government board of survey appeared there early in August on an inspection tour. The camp and all the buildings were given a thorough going over and, perhaps not surprisingly, the place was adjudged unsatisfactory. The long wooden barracks that had served as animal sheds in the old fairgrounds were, in fact condemned.[2] The camp had been in service for almost two and a half years, in which time more than 200,000 men had been quartered there, considering that the barracks had been dilapidated to begin with, it was probably wise that they be razed and new ones erected.

By mid-August, it had generally emptied of militiamen, and Captain Sands took advantage of the lull by setting the few men present to cleaning up. Tents were struck and relocated and efforts were made toward improving drainage.[3] At the end of that month, the old, original barracks were torn down, leaving the only barracks that had been built in the autumn of 1861, the Headquarters building, Commissary and Quartermaster Departments and the camp hospital as the principle buildings. About that time, Captain Sands began considering the possibility of abandoning Camp Curtin and beginning a new camp elsewhere in the area. The camp's terrain had always been its chief weakness, so now that new barracks were to be built, they might as well be built on more suitable ground. But this meant that the advantages of the Commissary and Quartermaster Departments, hospital, animal pens and railroad siding at Camp Curtin would have to be abandoned. Even if a site could be found near the railroad, facilitating easy movement of troops, erecting new administration buildings and a hospital along with the new barracks would be expensive and time consuming. In any case, Sands went so far as to select a site for the new camp some three miles southeast of the city down the Reading Turnpike on a farm.[4] No action was immediately taken to move the camp once the new site was selected, and the delay, whether caused by poor planning or loss of enthusiasm, became fatal to the project. Camp Curtin clung to life.

In October, there began what would be a winter-long procession of veterans returning to Camp Curtin. In the spring and summer of 1864, the three-year terms of enlistment for the majority of the regiments in the field would run out. These regiments would then be allowed to disband and go home. But since keeping these veteran regiments together and in the service was more desireable than to attempt to replace them with newly raised regiments, efforts were begun early to try to induce them to reenlist. The winter on the front promised to be a fairly quiet one, so the War Department decided to offer veterans who reenlisted a furlough at home as a reward. Almost none of the men in the field had been home in more than two years, and most of them leapt at the chance to visit home, even if it meant returning to the army to finish the fighting in the spring. The War Department also hoped that while home, these veterans could find some recruits to bolster their thin ranks.

The veterans began to arrive in mid-October, the men of the 50th regiment coming first. Camp Curtin was a cheering place for these men, for it was familiar and brought back memories of simpler more innocent times. Furthermore, it was safe; there was not even the remotest chance of a Rebel cavalry raid or a few random shots from Confederate artillery falling in among them. For the first time in nearly three years, the men were entirely safe from the hazards of war.

They did not stay long—a day or so—before moving on to their homes. A month or so later they returned, considerably cleaner, a bit fatter, well-rested and prepared to go back and finish the war. The scenario would be repeated scores of times throughout the winter. Although November and December brought just a trickle of

COLONEL JOHN RUTTER BROOKE
53rd Pennsylvania Volunteers.
Serving as commandant only briefly in
February, 1864, Brooke was a brigade commander for much of the war and rose to the
rank of major general in the Regular Army
by 1897.
(Library of Congress)

furloughed regiments, January, Feb
ruary and March brought a deluge, an
with it came a stream of temporary con
mandants. The colonel or lieutenar
colonel of any of the returning outfit
took a turn at directing the camp opera
tions, temporarily replacing Captai
Sands, who remained, ostensibly still o
recruiting duty.

In late October, George Washingto
Alexander, lieutenant colonel of the 47t
Pennsylvania, came home with some c
his men who had not reenlisted, bu
were going home to recruit.[5] Alexande
assumed command of Camp Curtin, bu
did not hold the position long as his tim
in camp was short. Twenty-five-year-ol
Colonel John Rutter Brooke and his 53r
Regiment arrived later in the winter, an
Brooke, finding himself the senior o
ficer, took command.[6] It was the youn
colonel's fourth visit to Camp Curtin
twice as captain in the 4th Pennsylvani
three-month regiment, and twice as colonel of the 53rd. He had fought with his regi
ment on the Peninsula, at Antietam, where he had commanded a brigade at age 22, an
before the stone wall at Fredericksburg, were he had handled his men so well that he
had been given command of a brigade in the Second Corps, though he had not been
promoted to brigadier general. He had led his brigade at Chancellorsville and a
Gettysburg, where he had been wounded.[7] Brooke had become one of the army'
great assets, but during the idleness of winter, he could be spared from comman
of the brigade while his regiment went home to rest and recover some of its numbers

Between the passage of these officers, Captain Sands would discharge the dutie
of commandant—signing requisitions, completing and approving monthly returns an
the like. In this capacity, Sands was called upon to work with a Regular Army office
who had a reputation for fastidiousness when it came to regulations and official pro
cedures. Lieutenant Colonel James Voty Bomford had been acting assistant provos
marshal general for western Pennsylvania since May, 1863, It was his duty to super
vise conscription efforts and the military police operations that enforced the conscrip
tion laws.

Bomford had been an Army brat, growing up the son of Colonel George Bom
ford, the Army's chief of ordnance. In 1832, he had been graduated 34th in his class a

West Point and assigned to the 2nd United States Infantry. Four years later, he had been transferred to the 8th Infantry, which would be his regiment for the next 22 years. As a captain in Mexico, Bomford had fought in every major battle from Palo Alto to the fall of Mexico City and had been breveted twice for gallantry. He remained in the hot climate after the war, serving at various posts in Texas. In 1849 at San Antonio, he had served with a young second lieutenant fresh out of the Military Academy named Richard I. Dodge. Five years later, the two had been together again at Fort Davis, where they had remained for about two years.

By 1861, Dodge was in New York, and Bomford, at Fort Davis, was a major in the 6th Infantry. In May of that year, he had received orders to evacuate the fort and attempt to escape with the garrison from the Confederate forces that had mobilized in Texas. On May 9, Bomford and the 270 men composing the garrisons of Forts Bliss, Quitman and Davis were crossing the prairies west of San Antonio when they were apprehended by Confederate Colonel Earl Van Dorn and his troopers. Eleven months later, Bomford had been exchanged and had found that he had been promoted to lieutenant colonel of the 16th Infantry. He had joined his new regiment in Major General D. C. Buell's Army of the Ohio, but he had soon been made chief of staff for Major General Alexander McDowell McCook. Bomford had performed with especial gallantry in the battle of Perryville, Kentucky, and was later breveted full colonel in recognition. After Perryville, he had withdrawn from active operations and gone to Indianapolis to become superintendent of the volunteer recruiting services there. He had remained in Indiana until May 30, 1863, when he had come to Harrisburg, again joining Richard I. Dodge, and assumed the duties of provost marshal for Western Pennsylvania.[8]

Through the autumn, most of the wounded from Gettysburg were either sent home from Harrisburg or back to their regiments in the field. By early December, all the hospitals in the city were again closed, except for the Cotton Mill and the camp hospital.[9] A short time later, Major Henry Carey Parry, U.S. Army, a young surgeon who had served in the 8th Pennsylvania as assistant surgeon before entering the Regular Army, assumed command of both hospitals. There were no outbreaks of disease to contend with, like the small pox scare of the previous winter, and the low population in Camp Curtin and the dearth of wounded made the hospitals very quiet. It was the perfect time, from Parry's point of view, at any rate, for an inspection. At the end of March, Dr. Jonathan Letterman, medical director for the Army of the Potomac, came and toured the hospitals in Harrisburg, and apparently found everything to his liking.[10]

As was the story every winter, though, a considerable number of lesser illnesses plagued the men in camp, with respiratory diseases being the chief problem. One soldier, Corporal John F. Woods of Company G, 49th Pennsylvania, was ill so often that he had good reason to wish he had never heard of Camp Curtin or the Army either. Woods was a 23 year old from Spring Mills in Centre County. He had enlisted in August, 1861, and had first come to the camp with his company a month later.

After two weeks, he had gone with the regiment to Washington, where the 49th served until the spring of 1862, and went from there to the Peninsula with McClellan's army. Woods was one of the many thousands who fell ill in the Virginia Tidewater and contracted severe diarrhea. Though he was treated by the regimental surgeon and remained with the regiment, he never fully recovered and, perhaps being rather too incapacitated to resume his place in the ranks, had been detached for duty at Camp Curtin. He was made a clerk at the camp hospital, and, as he had been a clerk in Centre County before the war, he was quite well suited to fulfill his assignment. He discharged his duties well until the winter of 1863-64, when he somehow contracted small pox. There was no serious outbreak of the disease in Harrisburg that winter but it was present in sufficient strength to infect Woods.

As spring came that year, Corporal Woods recovered and was made a disbursing clerk in Major Dodge's recruiting office. There, it became obvious why he had been sent north from his regiment and field duty; his physical constitution was simply not strong enough for army life. He suffered a severe relapse of diarrhea, and, with his body weakened, he became easy prey for other ailments. Finally, bronchitis grabbed him and sent him again to the hospital. Woods was by no means a rarity in the army. The cursory physicals given recruits by examining surgeons could not determine the robustness of the man's physical constitution or his prospensity toward illness. Thousands of seemingly strong, hale young men were accepted for service and only later would be found to be greatly disposed toward illnesses of all kinds.

After that spring of 1864, John Woods devoted a good deal of time to protecting his health. He had spent a fair portion of his service in the hospital or under the care of a surgeon, and he had no desire to continue his visits to either. In the dry heat of the summer of 1864, Woods was already looking ahead with anxiety to the cold weather. "I think it is proper," he wrote in August to his brother at home, "in order to maintain good health, to have our folks make me up a pair of Under-Shirts for fall and winter wear of woolen or flannel goods or anything that will be warm. If you can have the chance to send them down to me why do so...." There is little doubt that, to Woods, the woolen or flannel undershirts from his parents were of the utmost importance. He knew that, given the weakened condition of his lungs, if he so much as caught a cold again, his next trip to the hospital might be his last. A sick bed was not to be taken lightly in those times, and a man who had suffered through small pox, severe diarrhea and bronchitis all in the same year had more to fear than anyone.[11]

*   *   *

With all the recruiting of the winter of 1863-64, perhaps no one was working harder to fill the ranks than newly reelected Andrew Curtin. After sweeping to victory in the election of 1863, Curtin planned a recruiting progam for the Pennsylvania Reserves. The Reserves had been Curtin's brainchild to begin with, and now that they were in need of bolstering, he decided the matter was deserving of his special attention.

It was not the first time Curtin had tried to fill up the ranks of the Reserves. In the autumn of 1862, after Antietam, the ranks had been reduced to about one-quarter of their original strength, and Curtin had made the highly unusual request to have the entire division pulled off the line and returned to Pennsylvania to recruit. The War Department did not share Curtin's especial love for the Reserves and had denied the governor's request. One year later, the Reserves were still badly in need of replacements, and, in December, Curtin had again urged that the corps be allowed to return to Pennsylvania and recruit among the men. So great was the fighting reputation of the corps and so revered had it become in Pennsylvania that it was supposed that men who remained at home would leap at the chance to become members. Curtin's logic made sense, but Washington would not go along with the plan. To begin with, few, if any, of the Reserves themselves had offered to reenlist when their terms ran out in May and June, 1864. Even if the Reserves returned home and substantially increased their number through recruitment, the size of the force would be cut down again in another five months when the original veterans went home, and those remaining would likely still be green. The War Department therefore thought it not worth the trouble to pull the Reserves off the front in Virginia during the winter when a few new recruits could be raised anyway. Curtin was displeased with the decision; he hated to see "his" corps die when fighting remained to be done.[12]

*   *   *

A great majority of the Pennsylvanians who entered the war remained in the eastern theatre, that is Virginia and along the Atlantic coast down to Florida. Some Pennsylvanians were sent to the western theatre, though, to fight beside the men from Iowa, Illinois, Indiana, Minnesota and the other western states whose troops predominated in the western armies. Few of the Pennsylvania regiments sent west early in the war had been formed at Camp Curtin, but a few "Camp Curtin regiments" that had been serving in the east were transferred in 1863 and 1864. Notable among these were the 45th, 48th, 50th and 51st Regiments, all of which had gone west in March, 1863, as part of the Ninth Corps. In February, 1864, the 47th Pennsylvania arrived in New Orleans to be attached to the Federal Nineteenth Corps in Major General Nathaniel P. Banks's army. The 47th had been on duty in forts in the Florida Keys before moving to New Orleans. Throughout the winter, most of the men had reenlisted and the entire regiment had signed on by February, when it was sent west. Colonel Tilghman Good was still in command of the regiment seconded by Lieutenant Colonel George Washington Alexander, back from duty as commandant at Camp Curtin the previous October and from recruiting in Pennsylvania during the winter.

In mid-March, General Banks set off with 17,000 troops on an expedition designed to clear the Red River in western Louisiana. By early April, Banks was moving steadily on Confederate-held Shreveport, Louisiana, but a severe setback on April 8 at a tiny hamlet called Sabine Cross Roads forced him to retreat to a position 15 miles to the rear on a low plateau called Pleasant Hill. The "Hill" was surrounded by steep ravines and was crested by a small settlement of a half dozen or so buildings.

The Confederates had pursued Banks's army vigorously, and about 5 p.m. on the afternoon of April 9, the Rebels fell upon the Yanks at Pleasant Hill. When the attack had come, the 47th had been in a reserve position, but it soon found itself being hustled into the fight. Brigadier General James McMillian wrote in his report that, "I immediately placed myself at the head of the 47th Pennsylvania and was moving at the double-quick when it [the regiment] received a volley from the rebels who had...taken possession of some houses near my position." The suddenness of the volley from an unexpected quarter threw the 47th into confusion, and, according to Captain James Kacy of Company H, "some scared fool flying past ordered [the men] to retire...." The men broke ranks and stampeded to the rear. The regiment had been in the advance of McMillian's brigade and when the Pennsylvanians turned and fled, they ran through the ranks of the 160th New York and the 15th Maine, temporarily throwing those troops into confusion. McMillian rallied the 160th, though it was taking a "withering" fire, and exhorted the New Yorkers to stay put and hold the line. Then he rode off after the 47th, finding the scared Pennsylvanians only a hundred yards or so in the rear of the brigade. The broken regiment's flight had been stopped principally through the bravery of Lieutenant Colonel Alexander. Alexander had been badly wounded in the left shin by a shell fragment while the men were streaming to the rear. His tibia had been fractured, but, not knowing so at the time and seeing his shattered regiment in full retreat, he had staggered to his feet and limped off after them, finally managing to get them under control. About that time, McMillian arrived and helped Alexander get most of the refugees back in line for an advance back into the fray.[13]

After their temporary panic, the men of the 47th regained control of themselves. Perhaps embarrassed that they had behaved like rookies while the stalwart New Yorkers and "Down Easters" had held their ground and picked up the slack, the Pennsylvanians went back into the fight with a vengeance. The whole brigade tore into the Confederate line, "inflicting severe punishment, driving them across the field and for a long distance into the woods."[14] Federal troops in other sectors had similar success and the Confederates were forced from the battlefield.

Pleasant Hill was a solid victory for Banks and his men, thanks in no small degree to the impetuous countercharge of McMillian's brigade, but the day had been no great success for the 47th Pennsylvania. More than the regiment's pride had been lost in the "skedaddle" at Pleasant Hill. On that April afternoon, the career of First Lieutenant Washington H. R. Hangen, regimental adjutant of the 47th and first commandant of Camp Curtin, had come to an abrupt and ignominious end. Hangen had been among the more exuberant runners in the regiment and had not stopped when most of the rest of the men had. He was found far to the rear, as were Major William Gausler and First Lieutenant William Reese of Company C. Hangen had shown no propensity for panic prior to Pleasant Hill and, in fact, not only had been wounded in action in 1862 at Pocotaligo, South Carolina, but also had on other occasions been favorably mentioned in the reports of his superiors as having performed well under fire. All hat was swept away, however, by a few minutes of uncontrollable fear on a plateau n Louisiana. He was placed under arrest on April 11 and four days later was dismissed rom the service for cowardice. Gausler and Reese shared the same fate.[15]

*   *   *

In the east, the spring of 1864 brought a number of changes, both at Camp Curin and with the army in Virginia. In mid-April, something of an era came to an end at the camp as Captain Sands was officially relieved of his duties as commandant and recalled to his regiment. The action was occasioned by a rather angry letter to cavalry division headquarters by Lieutenant Colonel R. Gardner of Sands's regiment, he 1st Pennsylvania Cavalry. Sands, the letter explained, had been absent from the regiment since August 9, 1862, on recruiting duty in Pennsylvania. During those 20 months, Gardner went on, "Sands...has not recruited and forwarded to the Regiment wenty men." It appeared to Gardner that Sands had been living a life of luxury in Harrisburg, enjoying himself while neglecting his duties as a recruiter. This may or may not have been true, but in any event, Gardner was short-handed and needed officers. "His Company now also is much in need of his services," he wrote, "as it numbers One hundred and five (105) enlisted men and has but one Commanding Officer, the 2nd Lieut., present for duty with it." The lieutenant colonel's letter was bumped up the chain of command (being endorsed by David M. Gregg, Philip Sheridan and Meade), and Sands was relieved of duty at Camp Curtin on April 26. He was ordered to return to his regiment "as soon as he has arranged and settled his accounts of Camp & Garrison Equipage, etc." Sands had been a principal figure there for almost two years, first as a member of the permanent recruiting party then, since April, 1863, as a sort of vice commandant. His departure was noteworthy, especially to the men of the camp's staff who had lived and worked with him for most of the war.[16]

In Virginia, the Army of the Potomac prepared to embark on a campaign unlike any it had ever undertaken. It was to be led by Lieutenant General Ulysses S. Grant, who was new to the eastern theatre, but no stranger to success. Grant had started the war as a colonel in 1861 and had risen fast to command the armies of the western theatre by 1863. He was a simple, forthright man, not only in speech and dress, but in his approach to problems. He recognized that the North had a great advantage over the South in manpower. When he arrived in the east and learned first hand the worn condition of Lee's army, he was even more struck by the disparity. It became a principle of his strategy, therefore to capitalize on his advantage in numbers along with his efforts to outmaneuver the opposing army. He did not forego careful planning, but he never forgot his numerical superiority and made it a basic tenet in the formulation of his plans. He had not to consistently beat Lee and his army—he had only to consistently fight him. Both armies would be steadily weakened by continual fighting, but the Confederates would suffer more by steady attrition. They could not replace what they would lose as easily as could the Federals. Grant had only to wear the enemy down until surrender or eventual total defeat on the battlefield were Lee's only options.

The Army of the Potomac and the Army of Northern Virginia opened the spring campaigns of 1864 on familiar ground. Lee was in a position about 20 miles west of Fredericksburg just beyond Chancellorsville in the Wilderness. A great many men in the Army of the Potomac remembered their first foray into the forests of the Wilderness, and those memories were not pleasant. Almost a year had passed since Chancellorsville, but the sting of the humiliating defeat there was still fresh.

Grant began his movement on May 3, 1864, and the army reentered the Wilderness on the 5th. The roads were narrow and unsurfaced, and progress was slow. Grant found, as had Hooker a year earlier, that it was at best extremely difficult to move an army through that forest. When the fighting began, the Federal assaults on the Confederate positions were not conducted smoothly. Commanders had trouble getting their groups to assigned positions at appointed times and the result was an utter lack of coordination in the attacks. The Confederates counter attacked and the battle see-sawed throughout the day. Few or no breezes moved through the trees and underbrush, and the air lay thick and still on the forest floor. The dense sulfurous smoke from the men's guns hung in the air and was steadily intensified by continued firing until it became impossible to see more than a few yards. The infantrymen on both sides continued firing blindly into the haze. The dry leaves and brush that covered the forest floor were ignited by the sparks from powder-fouled muskets and fires sprang up all along both lines. Whole sections of the Wilderness began to blaze and the fight was no longer simply against the enemy infantrymen but the consuming flames as well.

In the chaos of the fighting and the smoke, huge numbers of men were cut off by surging enemy lines and walls of flame. The men of the 7th Pennsylvania Reserves became victims of the confusion. They were in the thick of the fight throughout the day but, unknowingly, continued fighting in the smoke and the gloom even after all supporting units were forced to pull back. While some escaped, 271 officers and men of the 7th, an overwhelming majority of the regiment, were trapped by Confederate infantry and were taken prisoner. Most of these men had less than a month remaining on their three-year terms, but they would spend that month, and many more, in Confederate prisons.[17]

Among the captured was First Lieutenant Jacob Heffelfinger, Company H. After being shot through the ankles and taken prisoner at Fredericksburg, then Sergeant Heffelfinger had been taken to Libby Prison in Richmond, where he was treated for his hurts for about three weeks. Miraculously, very little crippling damage was done to the bones in his ankles. One small bone had been chipped and the achilles tendon had been severed in the left leg, but only muscle had been disturbed in the right leg. Very fortunate, but in great pain, Heffelfinger had again been exchanged and sent to the General Hospital in Annapolis, Maryland, in January. He received a furlough and returned to his friends and family in Mechanicsburg. Two months later, he had been promoted to second lieutenant to date from December 13, 1862. Just before Gettysburg, though still hobbled, he had been elevated to first lieutenant of Company H, and he had passed through that battle unhurt. By January, 1864, the 23-year-old lieutenant was in command of his company, Captain Samuel B. King being in Pennsylvania on recruiting duty. Heffelfinger remained in command into the first week of May when the army plunged into the Wilderness. He was feeling and showing the wear of nearly three years of service by then and was a sick man. Like many of his comrades, he suffered from more or less chronic diarrhea and had that spring developed a severe case of hemorrhoids. So painful was the affliction that, as one of his company sergeants remembered, Heffelfinger could not sit down, and was forced to lie on his stomach on the ground to complete the regimental paperwork.[18] It was in this condition that Heffelfinger was captured in the Wilderness and sent south for the third time in the war.

*   *   *

The fighting in the Wilderness went on for two days and Union casualties mounted to over 15,000. When the two armies finally drew apart, neither could claim victory, but neither would accept defeat. It was at that point on that day, May 7, 1864, that the war took a pivotal turn. Never before had the Army of the Potomac spent two such horribly expensive days and not pulled back to rest or regroup, but neither had it ever fought under Ulysses Grant. No sooner had the two armies disengaged in the forests than Grant ordered a march to the south—toward Richmond. He was not pulling back, he was pushing forward. He was forcing Lee to react to his movements rather than himself waiting to respond to Lee's, as every other Federal commander in the east had done since 1861. So novel was this concept that the men in the ranks did not at first understand what was happening. Once they figured it out, their reaction was very near elation. Despite the losses the army had suffered in the last two days, despite the gruesome scenes of the Wilderness, the resiliency of mind and spirit that the men of the ranks had developed through years of defeat allowed them to disregard their wounds and their sufferings and to pick up their spirits immediately when they discovered they were *advancing* around Lee's flank. They were cheerful at the thought that they finally had a general who would let them fight.

For more than a month, Grant drove relentlessly toward Richmond, and eventually a pattern emerged: terrible fighting, terrible casualties; a flank march and more fighting always farther south. Men were killed and maimed at obscure little crossroads and river banks with names like Spotsylvania Court House, Yellow Tavern, the North Anna, and Cold Harbor. By the end of June, the Army of the Potomac had bludgeoned Lee and his Army of Northern Virginia into a corner. The Confederates had been forced into the defensive works around Richmond and Petersburg, a major rail center just south of the capital city. Casualties had been outrageously heavy on both sides, but that was working to the advantage of the Federals. Lee's army was no longer strong enough to dictate to the Federal army where and on what terms battles would be fought. So severely had the Confederates suffered in the recent battles that they had their hands full merely in defending themselves and their capital.

*   *   *

For many, Grant's campaign, by far the most successful the Army of the Potomac had ever initiated, was their last. But it was not just the killed and wounded who would fight no more. That spring was the third of the war and the men in the regiments that had enlisted for three years in 1861, and who had not reenlisted during the recent winter, were finally at the end of their obligation. They had done their share, and perhaps more, and they were going home. Among those who were to go home were the Pennsylvania Reserves. Not all the Reserves had been mustered in at the same time, so their terms ran out over the course of a few weeks, but for many, their last fight was at Bethesda Church on the 31st of May. That night they were pulled out and shipped north, their fighting done.

The 8th and 9th Reserves had been discharged earlier in May, and the 3rd and 4th Regiments were in western Virginia and would not be discharged for a few weeks yet, but the remaining regiments were sent to the vicinity of Washington where they spent about a week doing nothing in particular but generally being very anxious to get home. They were soon sent to Harrisburg to be mustered out.

THE PENNSYLVANIA RAILROAD STATION IN HARRISBURG, one of the two or three busiest rail depots in the North, probably only those in Baltimore and Washington itself were busier than this station. Although records are elusive, it is likely that more than three-quarters of a million soldiers passed through this station during the war.
(Pennsylvania Historical and Museum Commission. Division of Archives and Manuscripts, Harrisburg.)

On Saturday, June 5, word was received in Harrisburg that the Reserves would be arriving the following morning. Immediately, preparations were begun to welcome the men home. The city began a general sprucing up, citizens cleaned their homes and stocked their pantries, additional animals were slaughtered by restaurant and hotel keepers, and the prominent men wrote speeches and practiced their oratory. It was clear that the capital city intended to mark the occasion with a major celebration. The survivors of the Reserve Corps were unwittingly to be the recipients of perhaps the biggest celebration in the city's history—bigger even than Lincoln's visit in February, 1861, bigger than the return of the 127th Pennsylvania n May, 1862.

At 9 o'clock on the morning of the 6th of June, a solitary bell began ringing over the city. It rang continuously from high in the tower of the County Courthouse on Front Street and soon curious citizens were coming out of their homes milling about in the streets. As the meaning of the tolling became generally known, people began making their way toward the river. The ringing bell was a signal that the train bearing the Reserves was approaching. Residents on Front Street and in Harris Park on the bank of the Susquehanna could see the train moving slowly across the Northern Central Railroad bridge. Already citizens were shouting and cheering and running forward to meet it. Out of the openings of the cars hung the joyful men, waving their hats and cheering in response to the greeting of the excited civilians. The engine entered the city carefully for fear of hitting any of the thousands that lined the tracks and ran beside the cars. At the depot, with complete disregard for order or discipline, the Reserves swarmed out of the cars and into the adoring arms of the huge crowd. Officers had no control whatever and simply let the men and the citizens enjoy themselves.

The riotous welcome was finally halted by some of the more orderly citizens, specifically former mayor Kepner, who was serving as chief marshal of the day's festivities. Kepner invited the Reserves to the Soldiers' Rest where a breakfast feast had been prepared and was awaiting them. With redoubled cheers, the men moved to the Rest and tore into the repast with the energy of men who had been subsisting on hard crackers and heavily-salted beef for three years. For two hours, they gorged themselves on fresh eggs, breads, cakes, bacon, ham and everything else fresh and hot that was placed before them. It was just the first of several impressive meals to which they would be feted during their stay in the capital.

While the veterans were eating and enjoying at the Soldiers' Rest, the people of the city scurried about making last minute preparations for the ceremonies. Everyone who had a national flag displayed it prominently, either by carrying it, wearing it, or hanging it from shops, windows, or roofs. The entire city seemed draped in red, white and blue and many of the people themselves were dressed in the same colors. Businesses were closed for the day and the sidewalks and streets from the depot to the capitol were crowded in expectation of the reappearance of the heroes.

About 11:30, the Reserves, having finished their meal and formed outside the Rest, began the march to the south side of the capitol, near the Arsenal, where they would be officially welcomed. Chief Marshal Kepner led the procession in company with his assistant marshals, General Edward C. Williams and Colonel William Jennings. The band of the 1st Reserves played a quick step as it followed the marshals, and the ranks of the members of civic groups, the city firemen and the veterans of the War of 1812 followed. Finally came the lean, hard, brown-faced men of the Reserves with the practiced stride of soldiers who had been marching from battlefield to battlefield for three years. The bells of every church, schoolhouse and public building in the city were ringing now, and the whistles at the Cotton Mill and on the locomotives in the train yards began blowing as well. Smiles, waves and good-natured cheers were everywhere, and both the white, satin cheeks of the young ladies and the brown, leather faces of the soldiers were wet with tears. Bouquets and single flowers were showered down upon the marchers from the sidewalks and windows, and the men caught them up and symbolically placed the stems down the muzzles of their shouldered rifles, which they would never again fire in anger. The whole parade came to look like a bobbing meadow of flowers.

It was impossible to look upon the scene without being affected by the appearance of the men who had left as boys. They were almost all thin, much too thin. Many wore untidy beards and long hair sprinkled with gray. These young men looked old. Perhaps more saddening was the thought of the thousands who were not there. They were dead or in hospitals or already at home—legless or armless or otherwise mutilated—or they were in Southern prison pens starving. This was especially the case with the 7th Reserves, which had been cut off in the fighting in the Wilderness a month before and now marched down Third Street to the capital with just 53 men of the more than 1,000 who had left in July of 1861.

Finally the soldiers and the civilians were drawn up beside the temporary reception stand by the capitol. Some of the men recognized Governor Curtin as he stood before them. They shouted to him informal greetings and cheers, and Curtin responded with a deep, theatrical bow. Immediately, the entire mass of blue veterans erupted into tumultuous cheering. A battery of artillery in position on the hill commenced firing a deafening salute of 100 rounds.

When everybody eventually quieted down, Mayor Roumfort addressed the crowds and offered the city's official welcome to the Reserves. Then Curtin stepped forward and, remembered one observer, "then ensued a scene of enthusiasm scarce equalled in the history of the old State House...." The volume of the cheering from the 1,400 soldiers' throats rivalled that of the 100 gun salute. If Curtin had ever wondered if his efforts on behalf of the soldiers of Pennsylvania were appreciated, he wondered no more. The roaring continued for several minutes, and Curtin was visibly affected. When he was able to quiet them enough to be heard, he spoke to them with the rhetorical eloquence that had always been his trademark and of which his audiences were so fond. He spoke of the bravery of the Reserves, of how they had fought in virtually every battle of the Army of the Potomac and had emerged with a wholly unsullied record. Finally he spoke sorrowfully of those who did not return. He was sincere in his affection for the men who stood before him, and they in their admiration of him. The Reserves had completed their task and who in the last days of their existence as a unit, Curtin bade them peace and good luck, "May you all find a happy welcome to your homes! May you ever be marked as brave men who served their country faithfully in times of great peril. May you never regret that you belonged to the Pennsylvania Reserve Corps...." An old soldier could ask for very little more.[19]

The ceremonies ended tearfully with the Reserves returning to the governor their grimy, smoke-stained flags. They had borne them bravely and had never disgraced them and it was with sadness that the color bearers relinquished their charges.

When the 13 regiments of Reserve infantry had left Harrisburg in July of 1861, they numbered over 13,000. On June 6, barely 1,400 men returned as part of the nine regiments that enjoyed the massive parade. Those men marched out to Camp Curtin and were given quarters, but a good many did not wish the celebration to end so abruptly and immediately obtained passes or broke guard to go back into the city. Rare was the soldier who bought his own drink that night or paid for his own meal; hundreds were invited by citizens—who were in many cases perfect strangers—into their homes and fed and entertained lavishly. Colonel Fisher of the 5th Reserves and the members of his staff were the guests of Mayor Roumfort. For the sick and wounded and others who could not leave the camp, a feast was prepared and taken to them. The Jones House outdid all others in kindness and loaded up wagons with fresh and prepared foods, hearty staples and fine delicacies, and sent them trundling up the Ridge Road with his compliments. The generosity of the people of the city toward the soldiers in their midst was once again boundless. The veterans, so long away from home and amid enemies could not possibly have been treated any better in Harrisburg, and they responded nobly, for not a single report of disorderliness or any indication of ingratitude was recorded.[20]

The Reserves did not stay long. Some regiments moved on the next day to Pittsburgh or Philadelphia or other points closer to their homes to be mustered out and discharged. The others remained just long enough for the paperwork to be done and until they could be paid, then they took their leave of Camp Curtin and went home. After their departure, the camp was again plunged into one of those lulls that seemed to be coming with greater frequency and lasting longer.

*   *   *

In Virginia, Grant continued his efforts to pierce the Petersburg lines. In mid-June, he undertook a series of frontal attacks on the Confederate entrenchments that had sprung up all around the city. In the middle of the assaults was the 148th Pennsylvania, showing signs of wear. Colonel Beaver in particular had exhibited an uncanny talent for getting in the way of Confederate bullets and shells. His Chancellorsville wound

had healed by the time he had gone into action at Cold Harbor in the first week of
June, where he had been wounded in the hip. He was not out of action long after
that one, though, and had returned to duty in time to participate in the initial assaults
on Petersburg. On June 16, Beaver, as senior colonel, was commanding the brigade
of which the 148th was a part. About 4 p.m., he gathered the field officers of the
brigade around him and informed them that in about two hours they would be ordered
forward in an attack on the Confederate entrenchments that lay before them. "He
explained the plan of attack and its perils," recalled Major William M. Mintzer of
the 53rd Pennsylvania, "[and] designated the officers who were to succeed to the command if he fell." The ground to be charged across was several hundred yards wide,
flat, and completely devoid of cover. Confederate batteries covered every bit of the
plain, but Beaver had his orders and prepared the brigade for the assault. "Knapsacks were piled up," wrote Mintzer, "and everything left that would embarrass the
men in the dash upon the enemy." Beaver supervised the officers in getting the
regiments of the brigade in line for the attack. When all seemed ready, Beaver moved
to the center of the brigade and ordered the advance. He was the first man up and
over the Federal earthworks and out onto the plain. "I shall never forget him as he
looked on that beautiful June afternoon," wrote an admiring Mintzer after the war,
"he turned toward us, removed his sword from its scabbard, and shouted for the charge
in clear ringing tones. He was the picture of a soldier and he had the confidence
of the command as few men had. The men followed him with a shout...." The long
ranks of men behind Beaver broke into a run. "Artillery was kept playing upon us
from the time we started," Beaver remembered, "and musketry commenced when
we were within range." But the veterans were steady, and advanced through the hail
until they "came under the very shadow of the works." The Yanks were so close to
the Rebel earthworks that the Confederate guns had to be severely depressed to fire
upon them. Then, "just as I was about to give the command for a cheer and the double quick," Beaver recalled, the crew of one Confederate gun let loose with a shot
that hurtled straight for the brigade commander and buried itself in the ground right
at his feet. The shell exploded almost directly beneath him, blowing him into the
air feet first and tossing him about like a rag doll. He came down on his shoulders
and lost consciousness. Mintzer saw the shell explode and throw Beaver skyward,
"I and all of us then supposed [him] dead." But the colonel was not yet dead. He regained consciousness a few minutes later and found he was being dragged from the
field by the brigade color bearer. The man had the flag pole under Beaver's arms
and was pulling him rearward off the field. A fragment of the shell had opened a
wide, bloody gash in Beaver's left side and thigh.

The wound "was a very painful one and the issue of it was uncertain for a time."
He went north again to recuperate but returned within a month, unwilling to miss any
of the action. Though he could not yet ride a horse without experiencing great pain,
he reported for duty at Major General Winfield S. Hancock's headquarters in Virginia
in late July. Hancock, though, had developed a respect and a concern for his young

colonel, and, seeing that the man was not healed, refused him permission to resume command until his wounds had closed more thoroughly. Hancock sent Beaver home again.[21]

*   *   *

The whole army was suffering from the ceaseless, daily combat. In the two months between June 15 and August 15, Grant lost very nearly 30,000 men in battle, and it was imperative that some of those men be replaced.[22] New regiments were still being formed throughout the North, but procuring men was more difficult than ever. Accordingly, Federal, state and local bounties had grown to absurd proportions. Hundreds of dollars would be paid a man to enlist, and a regular industry of brokers and bounty businessmen sprang up. These men would procure illiterate, uneducated or unaware men, deliver them to recruiting offices, then collect the bounty due them. Men could no longer be expected to enlist for long periods or for the duration of the war. The regiments being formed in the spring of 1864 would only serve for a year or in some cases much less. In mid-July, for example, General James Nagle of Pottsville was named colonel of a new regiment that had been formed at Camp Curtin to serve for only 100 days. Many of the men in Nagle's regiment, designated the 194th, were veterans of service with other regiments and had reenlisted to take advantage of the large bounties offered them. Nagle himself received no bounty, but accomplished a remarkable feat when he took command of the 194th. He was the first and only man to serve as colonel of four different Pennsylvania regiments. Unfortunately, he was still suffering from the heart condition that had forced him to resign a brigadier generalship earlier in the war. In fact, his discomfort seemed to be increasing, and, perhaps the knowledge that he was dying was what inspired Nagle to again go to Harrisburg in July of 1864 seeking to get back into the war. He had little trouble in getting Curtin to give him command of one of the regiments then being formed.[23]

Grant's intention was to use the reinforcements to isolate Richmond and Petersburg from the rest of the Confederacy. To this end, the Wilmington & Weldon Railroad south of Petersburg was marked for destruction in late August, and among the troops detailed to tear up tracks was the 148th Pennsylvania. Colonel Beaver had spent the better part of two months in Pennsylvania recuperating from his wounds. Rested but still not quite healed, Beaver reported to Hancock's headquarters near Petersburg on August 24 only to find that Hancock and the 148th had both gone forward to destroy the railroad. Beaver was still unable to ride a horse over long distances with any speed, so he commandeered an ambulance and ordered the driver to take him forward to the railroad. There, he borrowed a horse and, after a painful ride, reported to Hancock near a place called Reams's Station.[24]

Hancock seemed happy to see the colonel and said cheerfully, "You are just in time; your Brigade needs you today." Not long after he resumed command of his brigade, which had already begun tearing up the railroad, Beaver was informed that Confederate infantry was massing on his front. A strong line of Confederates advanced as skirmishers and kept up a vigorous fire. Beaver, after getting the brigade into position to withstand the Confederate assault, dismounted and walked down his line to make minor adjustments in the placement of men. Suddenly, just as the attack was beginning, Beaver was hit for the fourth time of the war—it was his third wound in as many months.[25]

Once on the ground, and not immediately feeling pain, Beaver sat up and looked himself over for damage with the calmness and objectivity of a biology student. He saw that his right leg lay in a most unnatural position—at a right angle to his body. He later claimed that he knew right then that it could not be saved. As he sat contorted on the ground, his brigade wavered and finally fell back, leaving the brigade commander on the field. Some Federal cavalry came galloping back from the skirmish lines and Beaver, afraid that they would not see him and trample over him, grabbed his hat and began waving it wildly to attract their attention. A few of the troopers saw him and, with Minie balls whizzing all around them, pulled up their horses, dismounted and carried the crippled man to the rear.

At a field hospital, a surgeon looked at Beaver's leg and came to the same conclusion the colonel had: it could not be saved. The femur had been severed and splintered by a ball, which must have been fired at very long range. The doctor held no hope of the bones being realigned or of their ever knitting properly; they were too badly smashed. Other casualties were arriving at the field station, and the doctors had no time to perform the amputation immediately, so Beaver would have to wait.[26]

On the following morning, 26-year-old James Beaver's right leg was taken off on the upper third of the thigh. After the operation, he was moved to the permanent field hospital of the First Division of the Second Corps where he began the long hard struggle for life. He remained at that hospital for almost six weeks, so dangerously ill that he could not be moved. Dr. W. A. Davis, surgeon of the 148th, stayed with Beaver and attended to him during this time. By the end of September, Beaver had sunk so low that he lost all hope of recovery. He resigned himself to death and scrawled in his pocket diary "Saturday, September 30. Commenced to die."[27]

*   *   *

Throughout the long, hot, quiet summer in Harrisburg, Captain David M. Gilmore, 3rd Pennsylvania Cavalry, had served as commandant at Camp Curtin. Gilmore had been made a member of the permanent recruiting party at camp in January, 1864, and he had been enrolling men for his regiment until spring, when he had become commandant after Captain Sands's departure.

Gilmore had been 21 when he had enlisted for three years in Company H of the 3rd Cavalry at Newville, Pennsylvania. The men of the company had liked the

5'8", fair-skinned, red-haired merchant and had elected him first sergeant. He had served well with the regiment through its campaigns and had regularly been promoted to fill vacancies. He had been made captain of Company D in May 1863, and had come to Harrisburg during the quiet winter of 1864 in search of recruits. He had discharged his routine and unchallenging duties at the camp creditably until being mustered out with his company in August, 1864.[28]

The autumn of 1864 was a season for coming home. The terms of enlistment were running out for many regiments, and those men who had chosen not to reenlist were shipped out from the front, first to camps like Camp Curtin, then to their homes. In September, a number of men from the 47th Pennsylvania returned to Camp Curtin to be mustered out, and among them was Lieutenant Colonel George Alexander. Though he had been wounded in the shin nearly six months earlier at Pleasant Hill, the wound was still open and painful when he arrived in Harrisburg. The bones knitted quickly, if not especially well, but the wound would not close. He had not been to a hospital when he had been wounded simply because, in his own words, "there was not any there to go to." He could not walk well or far because of the swelling and pain, but he had toughened himself to the pain and served out his term. He would no longer be called upon to march and ride and move about quickly on the battle line, however; he was returning to the peace of his home in Reading and the nursing of his wife and two children.[29]

While the regiments began returning to Camp Curtin that autumn and winter, Captain Nicholas Way, Company G, 28th Pennsylvania Volunteers was serving as commandant. Way had enlisted in Company G in early July, 1861. The 19 year old had been elected sergeant and served with the company through much of its hard marching and fighting. After Second Manassas, Antietam, the "Mud March" and Chancellorsville, Way had been promoted to first lieutenant in June, 1863, and commanded the company at Gettysburg the next month. After being promoted to captain, he had gone south with the regiment when it had been transferred to the Army of the Cumberland and had fought at Wauhatchie and Lookout Mountain in Tennessee and, on November 27, 1863, at Ringgold Gap, Georgia, where he was wounded in action. He had stayed with the company until February, 1864, when detailed for recruiting duty in Philadelphia. From there he had been ordered to Harrisburg and Camp Curtin. His tenure as commandant was marked by little of any importance, simply the daily routine of mounting guards, pursuing deserters, feeding and clothing recruits and forwarding men to regiments in the field. When his enlistment expired in November, 1864, Way was discharged with his company at Philadelphia.[30]

After Way's departure, Captain Abraham Cottrell of Company H, 16th Regiment Veteran Reserve Corps, would serve as commandant off and on for several months. Cottrell had been 35 years old when he began his service back in August, 1861, in Lansing, Michigan, when he enlisted for three years in the 8th Michigan Volunteer Infantry. He was made first lieutenant of Company E and served with the company

until he was made an aide de camp to Brigadier General Issac Stevens. On Apr
Fool's Day, 1862, Cottrell broke his right shoulder in a freak accident: his horse bolte
during a dress parade in Beaufort, South Carolina and horse and rider fell into
rifle pit. Cottrell had been treated by the brigade surgeon and returned to duty. H
was still far from well when he went into action on June 16, 1862 at James Islan
South Carolina. There, he took a bullet in the back, the ball lodging in the spin
just above the buttocks. He was left on the field and was taken up by the Confederate
After a stay in the jail of the city of Charleston, he had been sent to Columbia, Sout
Carolina—where the ball was removed from his spine—and thence to Richmond. H
was exchanged and paroled in October, 1862. He was promoted to captain and rejoine
his company in December. He had found his wounds too debilitating, however, an
he had resigned, being honorably discharged for disability on March 19, 1863. H
still felt the urge to serve, however, and had enlisted as a first lieutenant in the Vetera
Reserve Corps in August, 1862. He was later made captain of Company H of the 16t
Regiment and sent to Harrisburg.[31]

The Veteran Reserve Corps was made up entirely of men disabled by diseas
or wounds so they were unfit for active campaigning. These men, however, were sti
healthy enough and willing enough to perform other military functions, such as guar
or clerical duties. They provided a valuable service in that they were able to replac
in rear areas soldiers of sounder health who could be assigned to the armies in th
field. Companies of the 16th Regiment were stationed in Harrisburg for much of 186
and 1865, and Captain Cottrell served much of his time in Camp Curtin.[32]

Autumn wore into winter and veteran regiments continued to arrive at camp t
be mustered out. Everything was dreadfully routine in Harrisburg, except severe col
made life even more uncomfortable. February brought extremely low temperature
throughout Pennsylvania, and, for the first time in the war, the cold at Camp Curti
was almost too much to endure. For much of the first half of the month, a shar
crusty snow almost a foot deep covered the ground and temperatures rarely climbe
above ten degrees Fahrenheit and often fell below zero. Only a few hundred me
were then in camp, but they were suffering greatly. These were the recruits, fres
from the upstairs bedroom at mother's house. They had not yet been inured to th
cold and heat as had the veterans who occasionally arrived from the field to b
mustered out. Major Dodge had the veterans show the new soldiers how to protec
themselves from the cold and how to build comfortable winter quarters, but the
were not much help, for the men were simply not yet constitutionally prepared fo
the intense cold. Finally, a delegation of the freezing recruits went to the capital t
see Curtin. They made their appearance before the governor bundled in overcoat
and with rags and towels tied about their frozen feet. They pleaded for Curtin t
do something for them to keep them from freezing. The soldiers' friend was quic
to sympathize with the recruits and asked Adjutant General A. L. Russell to see wha
specifically could be done to make the recruits more comfortable. As it happened
the Cotton Mill hospital was empty and the beds in the warm rooms were standing

idle. Russell suggested to Dodge that, given the circumstances, it might be better to move the men from Camp Curtin to the Cotton Mill, at least until the weather broke. Dodge was Regular Army with 15 years service on the plains in all kinds of weather, and he did not like this pandering to the weak pleas of undisciplined recruits. He resisted the suggestion at first, but eventually assented. By the middle of February, the recruits were snugly ensconced in the Cotton Mill and Camp Curtin was again nearly deserted.[33]

Dodge's leniency toward the freezing volunteers was almost his last act in Harrisburg. In February, Major Dodge moved on to New York City to become acting assistant provost marshal general for the Southern Division of New York. He was replaced in Harrisburg as acting assistant provost marshal general for the Western Division of Pennsylvania by Brigadier General Edward Winslow Hinks.[34] Hinks, 35 years old, had served as colonel of both the 8th Massachusetts, a three-month regiment, and the 19th Massachusetts. With the 19th, Hinks had seen action at the battles of Balls Bluff, Virginia; Glendale, where he had been wounded; and Antietam, where he had been wounded twice more. On February 27, he had been ordered to Camp Curtin, where he would assume general control.[35]

While Hinks was in command of the post, Camp Curtin itself was, for a short period in January, 1865, under Captain Nathan H. Randlett, Company F, 16th Regiment V.R.C., who had been there for several months. Randlett was from Lebanon, New Hampshire, and had started the war in the 5th New Hampshire Volunteer Infantry. He had served with that later-famous outfit all through its marches and fights on the Peninsula with McClellan. In fact, Randlett had been one of those stout Northerners laid low by the Tidewater climate. He had contracted malaria before the end of the campaign, and was still not over it by the time he and his regiment went into action near the Piper farm at Antietam September 17, 1862. Not far from where Henry Gerrish of the 7th New York was wounded, Randlett was shot through the left thigh. The bone had been grazed, but the worst damage was to the sciatic nerve, which had been almost severed. In constant and extreme pain, Randlett resigned in March, 1863. Six months later, the 25-year-old invalid was feeling somewhat better and enlisted in the 16th. He remained in Harrisburg for many months, exercising occasional control over Camp Curtin and Camp Hinks, the camp for the Veteran Reserve Corps in Harrisburg formed after Hinks's arrival.[36]

The brutally low temperatures in Harrisburg that Hinks and Randlett had to contend with that winter contributed to a minor disaster in and around the city. Almost 15 years had passed since the last time the usually peaceful Susquehanna had gone on a rampage, and, in March, those of short memory were reminded of who was the master of the valley.

An extraordinary amount of precipitation had fallen throughout central and northern Pennsylvania all through February and March led to an overabundance of snow on the ground in the mountains upstate and throughout the Susquehanna Valley. The snowfall was followed by bitter cold air, which froze everything solid from the mountain lakes and streams all the way to the Susquehanna itself. At Marietta a few miles downstream from Harrisburg on the eastern bank, the river was frozen so thick that pedestrians, mounted riders and drawn wagons were able to cross the ice to York County. Such conditions were unheard of by Marietta's oldtimers.[37]

By the end of February, the air started to warm and the ice in the lakes and ponds in the hills began to melt. As the water reached the Susquehanna, it backed up, for the thick ice in the river melted more slowly. A tremendous amount of water backed up in the creeks and ponds, and when the river finally broke up, all the water deluged down the valley at once, swelling the river up over its banks and into, around and through anything in its path. The waters hit Harrisburg on Saturday the 18th of March; the low points of the city were entirely submerged. Front Street and the southern portions of Second and Third Streets were awash in at least two feet of water. Front Street residents were forced to flee their homes or retreat to the upper floors. Portions of the railroad bridge across the river were washed away and there were reports of small children being trapped by rising waters and finally swept away to their deaths. Camp Curtin, though almost empty, sat far enough up the ridge to be out of the reach of the waters and was left untouched.

By Sunday the 19th, the waters had receded into their basin and the ugly task of surveying the damage and planning repairs was begun. Fine, silty mud from two to four inches deep lay everywhere the water had been. Streets, sidewalks, porches, parlors and basements were layered with a heavy brown slime, and logs, lumber and tree branches of all sizes lay almost everywhere in all conceivable positions. Carpets and furniture in front parlors had been destroyed, floor boards had swelled, buckled and warped, and lawns and gardens obliterated. Parts of the Pennsylvania Canal were eroded out of existence, and the Pennsylvania Railroad advertised for 200 extra hands to clear away lumber and debris from sections of track in the area. For the remainder of March and throughout April, the people of Harrisburg had enough to occupy them that they could forget about the war, which was closing its fourth year.[38]

*   *   *

Old soldiers were hardly worth noticing in Harrisburg anymore. The hotels, restaurants, and sidewalks had been filled with them that winter. Even the stories the veterans had to tell were old and passé. They were not treated badly by the people of the city, but a good deal of the novelty of seeing war veterans had worn off since the previous June when the Reserves had come home. So no bands or crowds were at the train depot to meet the gaunt, limping man in uniform who stepped off a train onto the platform in the frigid mid-March air. The veteran was for the first time in more than two years just a few miles from his home. He would that night eat with his family and sleep in his own bed. He was a soldier back from the wars, a hero who had done his duty well and bravely, but he received no hero's welcome.

Jacob Heffelfinger had spent the last ten months in Southern prisons, first at Macon, Georgia, and later at Charleston, South Carolina. He had been quite ill when captured at the Wilderness, and poor diet and unsanitary camps had caused his condition to deteriorate even more. General Grant had halted the practice of exchanging prisoners to make the most of his manpower advantage and because of Southern tinkering with the parole system. So, Heffelfinger had languished in prison, with no hope of being exchanged, long after his term of service had expired. While the rest of the Reserves marched through Harrisburg and enjoyed the feasts given to them by the people of Harrisburg, Heffelfinger and thousands like him, sat in prison, almost despairing, slowly wasting away from diarrhea and malnutrition. Finally, in March, 1865, he was let go and sent home, battered, weak and permanently crippled—a 24 year old with the aches and pains and ills of a 60 year old.[39] He, like thousands of others, had not given his life for the Union, merely his youth.

* * *

While the moody, blustery last days of winter clung to Harrisburg and central Pennsylvania, the rank smell of fresh wet earth and the brilliant verdant green of new shoots and new leaves heralded spring in Virginia. In the last week of March, 1865, the emotions of the hundreds of thousands of men in and around Richmond and Petersburg ran the gamut of possibilities. From the fatigue and frustration of the Confederate soldier to the near despair of their commanding general, to the hope of the Federal soldier and finally to the confidence of General Grant and his lieutenants. It was a season of anxiety and expectation.

The return of warm weather brought fresh assaults from the Federals, and Lee knew that his army could not long endure such assaults. He therefore opted, as he had whenever possible throughout the entire war, to seize the initiative and use boldness and surprise to throw the Federals off balance. He struck in the early dawn of March 25 at Grant's lines at a stretch of entrenchments called Fort Stedman, the Confederates gained initial success, driving the Federals from their positions, but a counter-attack led by Brigadier General John Hartranft, formerly of the 51st Pennsylvania, regained those positions and sent the Confederates reeling back with heavy loss. Lee had landed a solid punch, but that punch no longer packed the wallop it once had.

Grant began in earnest to pound the Confederate positions. Federal forces attacked on the flanks, in the center, in the north of the line and in the south. Terrible battles were fought and thousands were killed, wounded or captured. The Confederates were wearing down to the point where they were no longer strong enough to defend their whole line.

Finally, at dawn on April 2, the Federals launched an attack on the Confederate entrenchments with spectacular results. Like an awl striking a block of ice at precisely the right point, Grant's men, after chipping away for months, cracked Lee's defense wide open with a single, sharp blow. After initially putting up sturdy resistance, the Confederates broke and fell back. Mile after mile they retreated in chaos. The entire defensive line from south of Petersburg to Richmond was abandoned, and Richmond itself was evacuated. The next day, April 3, Federal troops entered Richmond.

Lee's army fled westward from Richmond, but Grant was unwilling to let it go and the Army of the Potomac pursued. With Richmond gone and the Confederate government in flight, the war was as good as over, and the men of the Confederate ranks were not slow to recognize this. The proud Army of Northern Virginia, once perhaps the most powerful fighting machine in the world, began melting away. Thousands deserted, thousands of others were taken prisoner as they left the ranks and fell exhausted by the side of the road. Swift Federal cavalry was everywhere and slipped through the woods and country roads of central Virginia to capture men or supplies, tear up railroads, and cut off routes of escape. Finally, after a week of running, Lee's shrunken army was trapped, surrounded at the small village of Appomattox Court House, the seat of Appomattox County. There was no escape. Fighting seemed hopeless, for the men were worn out and overwhelmingly outnumbered. Lee had no choice but to go see Grant and ask for terms.

At about 4 p.m. on that Sunday, April 9, Lee surrendered the Army of Northern Virginia. The war in Virginia was over.

CHAPTER EIGHT

"Classic Ground"

APRIL — DECEMBER, 1865

As word of Lee's surrender was tapped over the telegraph wires of the North, laughter and tears and wild celebration became epidemic. Impromptu speeches were made and salutes were fired from any kind of gun available. Businesses closed and taverns opened and one day became just like the last with complete disregard for time.

But even before the initial celebrations had ceased, before the wonderful truth and all its ramifications had been comprehended, the joy was abruptly cut short by the news—just five days after Lee's capitulation—that President Lincoln was assassinated. Lincoln was popular throughout the North, even in Democrat strongholds like Harrisburg, which had gone for presidential candidate George B. McClellan in the election of 1864. Throughout the North, the grief was real. The horror of the deed might have had even more realism for Harrisburg residents, for Lincoln had been shot as he watched a performance of "Our American Cousin" with Laura Keene; the same play and the same actress the people of Harrisburg had watched at Brant's Hall just a few weeks earlier.[1]

The slain president was laid in state in Washington and then began the long circuitous train ride to a tomb in Springfield, Illinois. On the 21st of April, the black-draped funeral train arrived in Harrisburg. The coffin was taken to the capitol where it was placed in the House of Representatives chamber. There the people of the city filed by to view the remains of their murdered president. A few military organizations had been sent to Harrisburg to serve as honor guards for the processions between the depot and the capitol and had encamped at Camp Curtin. Two companies of the 201st Pennsylvania, including a good many Harrisburg men, did their best to add dignity and solemnity to the occasion as did a battery of New York Artillery. The ceremonies were sobering after the great news of Lee's surrender.

*　　*　　*

With Lee and his army went the Confederacy's last best hope for winning the war. But there were other Confederate armies still in the field, and there remained hope in the spirits of many bitter Southerners. On April 26, however, General Joseph E. Johnston surrendered the Confederacy's second largest army at Durham Station, North Carolina. On the 26th of May, the last Confederate force of any significant size was surrendered at New Orleans. Federal troops occupied every state of the Confederacy, and even the staunchest secessionist had to admit the war was over.

The surrender of the last Confederate army was anticlimactic in that the North had by then become accustomed to the idea of peace and the return of the boys in blue. The troops would not return immediately, however, for the victorious army could not simply disband overnight. The conquered foe needed time to accept defeat, to understand the futility of again picking up arms and resuming the fight. While Southerners came to these realizations, the victors would remain in their midst as a physical reminder of both the power of the Federal government and its readiness to quickly and violently put down any resurgence of Confederate militarism.

So Union troops remained at garrisons throughout the South, watching, waiting, and enjoying the quiet. In late May, however, large portions of the Federal legions were brought to Washington to participate in the grandest military celebration ever held on the continent. It was called the Grand Review. For two days the veterans of all the Federal armies, east and west, paraded down Pennsylvania Avenue. It was a truly awesome display of the power and spirit that had been raised by the people of the North, and, for those who participated, there were few more memorable experiences in their lives.

After the Review, the veterans returned to the infinitely forgettable camp life around Washington. The men were extremely anxious to get home, not only to be with their families, but, as the tens of thousands of farmers in the ranks knew, seed time was rapidly passing and crops had to be put in before the season became any more advanced. The War Department's plan was to muster regiments out a few at a time, so the army would not evaporate all at once. In June, the War Department began sending the men home.

*　　*　　*

Activity at Camp Curtin had never increased through the end of winter and into the spring. After the bitter cold weather of February and March gave way to the flood waters of March and the rains of April, the men who had been moved into the Cotton Mill were moved back to the camp. It remained sparsely populated through the first five months of 1865. In June, that changed as the veterans began returning.

The officers at Camp Curtin had learned that in times of peak population there simply was not enough room in camp to house all the men that were expected, and it was undesireable to quarter the men on lots in the city or on the capital grounds. For this reason, more land was annexed to Camp Curtin and dubbed Camp Return. While the new camp might have been at first separate from Camp Curtin, the distinction soon faded and the entire "camp complex" on the Ridge Road was being called, even officially, Camp Return.[2] The three mustering officers in the city acquired the forms, clerks, and storage space necessary to mustering out the volunteers and receive from them the government property they had been using during their service.[3]

The final preparation for the onslaught of veterans was the appointment of a new commanding officer. On June 7, 1865, almost as the first regiments began arriving to be mustered out, Lieutenant Colonel William Nicholson Grier, 1st United States Cavalry, replaced General Hinks as acting assistant provost marshal general and chief mustering and disbursing officer for the Western Division of Pennsylvania.[4]

Grier was career Army. He was a Pennsylvanian by birth, and had been graduated from West Point in 1835, standing a lowly 54th in his class. Posted to the 1st United States Dragoons, he had fought in Mexico as a captain, where he had been breveted for gallantry at Santa Cruz. After the war, he had fought Apaches in New Mexico for eight years until 1857, when he had been transferred to Washington territory to fight more hostile Indians. He had been at Fort Walla Walla when Fort Sumter was fired upon and was soon made major of the 2nd Dragoons. In February, 1862, he had been elevated to lieutenant colonel of the 1st Cavalry. At Williamsburg on the Peninsula in May, 1862, he had displayed especial gallantry and been wounded. But in August of 1862, he had left active operations in the field and gone to Columbus, Ohio, to serve as superintendent of the volunteer recruiting service and chief mustering and disbursing officer for the State of Ohio. Later, he had filled the same post for the State of Iowa. He had been posted to Davenport for more than two years before being assigned to the position at Harrisburg.[5]

The returning veterans began arriving slowly at first, a company here, a battalion there, but by the end of the first week in June, nearly 7,000 veterans had come back to Camp Return.[6] They were received with little fanfare, but the men were nonetheless glad to be home. Predictably, there was a run on the saloons of the city, and Provost Marshal Captain W. H. Patterson realized the chaotic possibilities of mixing 7,000 ecstatic veterans with a city full of liquor. All the saloons and taverns in both Harrisburg and Bridgeport were immediately ordered closed until the troops had been mustered out and sent home. It was not a popular order with either soldier or tavern keeper, but it was generally obeyed, though some of the former with severe thirsts usually found a way to get together with those of the latter willing to risk the wrath of the provost marshal.[7]

Despite the absence of artificial stimulants, the joy the veterans felt at being home was almost beyond restraint. Jonathan Kerr of the 200th Pennsylvania, a Harrisburg native, could not even wait for his comrades in arms to reach the city before beginning his celebration. The train bearing the regiments stopped at Bridgeport before crossing the river to Harrisburg. Kerr and some of the non-commissioned officers simply leapt off the idle train and ran headlong across the bridge all the way into Market Square, where they fell in with some friends and spent the rest of the day in town "running and tearing about with old chums."[8] The rest of the regiment marched out to Camp Curtin. Other regiments, the 45th for one, stopped enroute in the city and got a meal at the Soldiers' Rest before going out to camp.

Little attempt was made by officers at preserving order or discipline among the men as they came into the city. The troops simply piled in and out of the boxcars at the depot without regard for seniority or organization. Without delay or ceremony, the carefully constructed and preserved barriers between enlisted men and officer began to decay.[9] Every man—whether private, lieutenant, captain or colonel—now went about as himself and men of all ranks intermixed freely, some men sat on top of the cars and others hung on the sides. Once the men reached Camp Return, they found discipline there lax as well. No guard was mounted, for none was needed. A state of war no longer existed and no man would desert before receiving his pay. While the men were technically supposed to be in the camp, they practically had liberty to go about as they pleased, and they usually pleased to be in the city looking for something to help pass the time.[10]

All through June and July they came, the veterans of the country's battles. The veterans of the 11th Pennsylvania came in June. The 11th, the oldest of all active Pennsylvania volunteer regiments, had originally been formed in April 1861 as a three-month organization but had reenlisted in August of that year for three years and had been allowed to keep its designation. When the three years were up, the veterans reenlisted again. The 11th had lost men in every campaign of the east, and its history was literally that of the war in Virginia, Maryland and Pennsylvania.

The 53rd Pennsylvania returned about the same time as the 11th. Three and a half years earlier, the regiment had left under Colonel Brooke and, like the 11th, had fought in nearly every major battle in the east since. It had had its own day of glory under the steely-gray skies of Fredericksburg, where, through the frigid, knifing winds and over the rutted, frozen turf, the regiment had charged—running, stumbling, lunging over the bodies of their fallen comrades—toward that terrible stone wall. No regiment showed more bravery that day, and none got closer to that invulnerable position of the Confederates, but a good many had fallen who would never be replaced. By the time the 53rd came home in June of 1865, fewer than 100 men were present to be mustered out.

Also among the returning regiments in early June was the 51st. The boisterous, fun-loving men of the 51st, who had spent more than two months in Camp Curtin back in the autumn of 1861, had played a starring role at Antietam on the bloodiest day of the war. The regiment went west after Fredericksburg, leading the prosaic life of a solid, dependable regiment. The 51st returned to the eastern theater in 1864 and participated in the Petersburg Campaign, finally bringing just 170 men home to Camp Return.[11]

Despite the absence of a public outpouring of sentiment by the populace, the return of the volunteers was not without ceremony. Governor Curtin and his staff went out to Camp Return to welcome the veterans and to officially receive from them their battle flags, which, having been entrusted to them by the governor, were the property of the commonwealth. Thousands of men were drawn up on the parade and watched Curtin as he mounted the steps to the reviewing stand. Colonel Alfred B. McCalmont of the 208th Pennsylvania stepped forward on behalf of the men of the regiments returning their colors.

McCalmont had been an excellent lawyer before the war and was an "intelligent and energetic" officer. He had seen action as lieutenant colonel of the 142nd Pennsylvania before going to the 208th and was intimately acquainted with Camp Curtin; he had even served briefly as commandant for a while in August, 1864.[12] Clearly showing his emotions, McCalmont, a noted orator before juries, made a short speech and delivered the torn, smoke-stained banners to the governor. Curtin himself was struggling to keep his emotions in check, but quickly composed himself and addressed the thousands of brown, wrinkled faces below him. He thanked them for their patriotism and their devotion to their duty; he told them of his emotion—of his feeling for them and what they had done. The flags would be a memorial to them and their work, he said, "to be preserved as a part of your history in the archives of the state....I praise God that

COLONEL ALFRED B. McCALMONT
208th Pennsylvania Volunteers.
A veteran of long service in the war, this attorney known for his eloquence served as camp commandant in the spring of 1864.
(Library of Congress)

no tarnish rests upon you, ...and that your flags are returned without dishonor." Finally, he spoke of those of whom all were thinking and who could not join them in rejoicing in victory. "If we could this day dry the tears of the widows and orphans," he concluded, "if we could restore the maimed and call from their graves the heroic dead, our happiness would be complete. But I cannot fail to congratulate you now, before you return to your homes on the part of the great Commonwealth has taken in this bloody drama. We have given our full share of blood and treasure...." Cheers ushered the governor from the rostrum, and he immediately turned and waded into the formation. The men broke ranks and swelled toward him. Curtin willingly met the crowd and began shaking hands and chatting with the veterans. He spent a good while listening to them and their stories, praising them, thanking them and wishing them good luck and Godspeed in the months and years to come. To the cynic, the scene was pure politics, but to Curtin, and the soldiers, it was a sincere exhibition of mutual admiration.[13]

The appearance of these men as they came back from war could not be ignored or passed over by those who had stayed at home. They wore patched and dirty uniforms, caps that had been sweated into until they were a floppy, greasy black, and dusty brogans of thin supple leather, repleat with holes—and lacings so frayed and knotted that they could hardly be untied except with great care. But aside from their clothes, the men themselves had changed physically. They all had the swarthy complexion of men who had lived in the elements, and all walked with an easy, rolling, energy-conserving gait that had been learned through steady practice. They were hairier, having made infrequent acquaintance with razors and shears over the last few years. They were thinner, leaner, harder—some looking trim and fit and quite healthy, others being hunched over at the shoulders and wearing drooping baggy clothes. Most of all, however, they were different in the face. The eyes were squinted and sunken, partly as a natural protective adaptation to constant exposure to the sun and wind, but also due to the effects of poor diet and malnutrition. In many of those eyes was a slight sparkling glaze that, coupled with the sallow cheeks, told of the onset of the initial stages of emaciation. Rare was the soldier who had not been ill at some time during his service, and many had been sick for long periods with sapping diseases like influenza or dysentery.

The manner of the men was, to a great extent, more subdued. The boys who had left at 18 or 19 with high spirits and open, cheering mouths returned as 22 or 23 year olds who had seen too much to keep their hearts perpetually high. To whatever degree it affected them, these veterans bore a sober worldliness—a quiet, manly acceptance of circumstances. They were not morose; there was still plenty of the good nature that had marked them as boys, but it was now tempered by a fuller understanding of life and its value.

The men passed the dull days while waiting to be paid much as they had when first in Camp Curtin more than three years before: they played cards or gambled, played some base ball or went swimming in the river. For the most part, the preparation of the muster and pay rolls and the return of equipment went smoothly. But mysterious delays, the type whose origins are known or understood only by clerks and bureaucrats, sometimes developed with unpleasant results. The men were understandably anxious to get out of the dirt and dust of Camp Curtin and home to their families, and a delay of even just a few days could be very frustrating. John Kerr, who was serving as a clerk for the regimental adjutant of the 200th, remembered that after a few days, "The boys Throughout the Regs. began to spout ugly and be very noisy." Fights broke out, and paymasters, clerks and the officers were all ridiculed and slandered in the most definite terms.[14] No one was upset enough to cause any real trouble, but there was enough displeasure in camp to make things unpleasant for the administrators. The officers and clerks buckled down and the snafus were straightened out.

The day of mustering out finally came for each company of each regiment. Pay rolls would be signed and the men given their pay, which often amounted to quite sizeable sums as some of the men had not been paid in many months. Discharge papers, which the men called "buzzards" because of the large American eagle across the top of them, were issued to each veteran as he was mustered out, and suddenly, it was done—the boys were out, free, their own men once again. Some fled, as fast as their feet would carry them, out of the camp, into the city and over to the depot or to a livery stable or any other place whence they could get transportation home. But a good many others stayed. Some would go home in groups in company with other men from their towns, others would go home alone, but almost all needed to say goodbye, for it was at last time to separate. "I wish it was possible," wrote one soldier, "to express my feelings and make plain our experiences when we started homeward....Sunshine and shadows seemed to play with us....We had hoped and prayed for the end of strife; we were overjoyed that we had won victory and that the end had come; [but] as comrades, we were attached by devoted ties, we loved one another."[15] There was much handshaking and clapping of hands on shoulders as they mingled to say goodbye. There did not seem to be any way to properly depart—none of them had ever had to do anything like what they were being called upon to do. But, in their simple, rough, often silent way, they said goodbye. Tears ran down brown, wrinkled cheeks and slid to the ground or were wiped away with dirty coat sleeves. They all tried to smile and wished one another well, and some spoke about writing or getting together every now and again, but none of them really expected anything to come off. Altogether, it was much more than the parting of friends, for mere friends do not share muddy water, lousy blankets and wormy food for more than three years. Mere friends do not trust one another with their lives or risk their own to save another's. They were much more than friends, and now were splitting up.

And with all this sadness at leaving comrades was mingled the first glimmers of realization that they were ending a portion of their lives that they would never forget. They knew they would never again live a life so thrilling, so dangerous, so boring, so terrible, so wonderful or altogether so intense in all its aspects as they had had for the last three and a half years.

It was a novel experience for those men to walk out of Camp Curtin without regard for passes or the time of day or the hour at which they were expected to return. They no longer had any orders, they could no longer be told what to do and when. One man wrote, "after nearly four years of knuckling down to authority, it seemed a queer and very agreeable sensation to feel that we could go and come when we got ready."[16] No less strange, but perhaps less agreeable, was the experience of paying for train fare home from Harrisburg, "as Uncle Sam had attended to our railroad tickets for almost three and a half years." Even after the arrival home—after the tears and long embraces and the sharing of news and stories—the veterans could not quickly adjust. "It seemed to me," wrote one, "that to be without a musket and with no more camps or campaigns to look forward to, we would be out of an occupation and without a commission. Settling down to routine daily employment in slow shop and store was not favorable to our habits of life; we felt kind of lost."[17]

Nor could the wives and mothers immediately get used to the strange habits of these strange men that came home. One man remembered that three brothers returned from the war to their parents' home in York County. Their mother, happier, perhaps, than she had ever been now that her boys were safely home, looked in on them one night after all three had turned in. She found to her shock that all three beds were empty and the boys were jumbled together on the wooden floor. The clean beds, they explained, were much too soft to provide a comfortable night's sleep.[18]

*　　*　　*

The troops continued to arrive throughout the summer. Toward the end of July a special regiment of veteran volunteers had arrived in Harrisburg and were immediately made the city's provost guard. Earlier in the war, General Hancock had spent an extended period at home in Pennsylvania recuperating from a wound received at Gettysburg. During that time, the idea was hit upon to use Hancock's prestige and popularity to advantage to recruit a special corps of veterans to serve under the general when he should regain his health. Recruiting for the corps was begun, but Hancock grew impatient with the dull routine of life behind the lines and hastened back to the army. Organization of Hancock's Special Veteran Corps—officially designated the United States Veteran Volunteers—was never completed, but there had been some companies and at least one regiment formed: the 6th Regiment U.S.V.V., which came to Camp Curtin in late July, 1865, to serve as provost guard.[19]

When the steady stream of returning veterans slowed to a trickle in August and September, Hancock's 6th often found itself with no one to guard. These keepers of the peace began to get so bored that they would frequently go into town to drink. Almost as frequently they managed to themselves disrupt the peace and quiet Harrisburg residents were again enjoying. It was not unusual for the members of the 6th to retrace their steps out the Ridge Road while nursing "Cracked heads and bloody faces." The men of the 6th were not popular with the people of Harrisburg, and the editor of the *Patriot and Union* thought the withdrawal of the regiment "would be a great relief to our citizens."[20]

The leader of these wildmen was Colonel Charles E. LaMotte. LaMotte was a Delawarean and had begun the war in May, 1861, as a captain in the 1st Delaware Volunteers. By June, 1862, he was first lieutenant and adjutant of the 4th Delaware, and he climbed up through the ranks until he was lieutenant colonel of the regiment in October, 1863. He was breveted twice, to colonel for gallantry and distinguished service during the Petersburg campaign and to brigadier general for gallantry and meritorious service during the war. He was mustered out a lieutenant colonel in June, 1865, and three months later he was made colonel of the 6th Regiment United States Veteran Volunteers—Hancock's Corps.[21]

The good people of the capital had to endure a few more months of drinking and brawling before they could be rid of their protectors, the provost guard. By November, all but a few Pennsylvania regiments had returned from the field, and, except for the members of the provost guard, Camp Curtin was deserted.[22] The only other troops in town were a few companies of the "Invalid Corps" (the Veteran Reserve Corps). The companies were quartered in some large, vacant buildings within the city itself and were under the command of Colonel Joseph B. Kiddoo, who had first come to Camp Curtin in April, 1861, as a private in a company attached to the 12th Pennsylvania. He had since been a sergeant in the 63rd Regiment, lieutenant colonel and colonel of the 137th, major of the 6th United States Colored Regiment and colonel of the 22nd U.S. Colored. He had been wounded twice, the second time severely before Petersburg in October, 1864.[23]

Camp Return, or Camp Curtin, which it was again being called, had seen its last days as a great camp. Most of the mere handful of Pennsylvania regiments still in service would be sent to Philadelphia or some other point nearer their homes than Harrisburg to be mustered out. By autumn, only two or three more regiments were expected to be discharged at Camp Curtin, so the authorities—from the War Department to the local police—began tying up loose ends in the city. The houses of prostitution in Harrisburg, all of which had been doing good business throughout the summer, were shut down.[24] The Soldiers' Rest at the train depot, where tens of thousands of soldiers and members of their families had found hot meals and shelter, was also closed.[25] And finally, plans were made to abandon Camp Curtin.

Occasionally, a remnant of a Pennsylvania regiment arrived and went into camp—about 100 men of the 7th Pennsylvania Cavalry arrived in early September, elements of the 78th Regiment arrived and departed later in the month, and Independent Battery B, Light Artillery, which had been doing service in new Orleans and Texas, arrived in camp on October 30 and departed in the first few days of November—but small arrivals like these were now the rule rather than the exception.[26] Gone forever were the days when thousands of men would pour in and out of camp daily, filling the barracks and tents and kicking up clouds of choking dust that could be seen for miles rising above the trees.

About the time Independent Battery B left camp, the provost guard battalion received orders to abandon Camp Curtin; there was no longer any need for a provost battalion at Harrisburg. On the morning of November 11, 1865, to the relief of the citizenry, Hancock's 6th Regiment marched out of camp, down to the train depot and took the cars out of the city. On that day Camp Curtin ceased to exist as a military post.[27] A few clerks or other such individuals might have remained to complete paperwork, and the hospital remained open for some time, but with no commandant, no staff, no guards and no population, the days of the place as a maintained campground were over. Although the last Pennsylvania unit did not arrive in Harrisburg until May, 1866, and likely bivouacked on the old campground, Camp Curtin had become merely a deserted plot of ground on which to pitch a tent and build a cook fire.[28]

And so the first and greatest Camp of Rendezvous and Instruction of the Civil War faded out of existence. The once grassy sward of the fairgrounds was now a bald expanse of lifeless dust. The snow of the winter of 1865-66 fell on empty corrals and deserted gray wood buildings and lay undisturbed on the frozen rutted ground. The place, once full of life, was now desolate. Never again was it to know the sounds of war—the tramp of thousands of feet, the sharp, ringing shouts of commands, the laughter and cheers of men playing base ball or tossing each other in blankets, the sound of guitars or harmonicas and singing at campfires on cool nights, the cursing of recruits being flooded out of their tents in rainstorms, or the stirring quicksteps played by regimental bands. Now there was only snow, and a haunting, eerie silence broken by the bark crows sitting on the stockade.

Under proper administration, the camp had had a vigorous, healthful atmosphere perfect for learning the skills and duties of a soldier, but more often than not it had been a badly mismanaged place with poor drainage, open and overused latrines, undisposed-of garbage, and disease. Sickness was the camp's only permanent presence, and scores of men—brave, patriotic men who never saw a battlefield—perished in the tents and hospital beds of Camp Curtin. The place had played a significant role, not only in the broad scope of the war, but in the personal lives of the men who had lived there.

As the life of the camp drew to a close, the man for whom it had been named offered an epitaph. In 1865, after the war had ended and while the army was being broken up, Curtin addressed a group of returned veterans at Camp Curtin. He spoke of the camp as one of the great sites of the war. "The field upon which we now stand," he said, "will be known as classic ground, for here has been the great central point of the organization of our military forces. When my administration of public affairs will have been forgotten," he continued, "and the good and evil will be only known to the investigation of the antiquarian, Camp Curtin, with its memories and associations will be immortal."[29]

Epilogue

In April, 1863, President Lincoln was in Falmouth, Virginia, just across the river from Fredericksburg, to attend a review of the Army of the Potomac. He sat on a small, unimpressive horse, which made him appear absurdly large. On one side of him sat Major General Joseph Hooker, then commander of the army, on the other side sat Major General Darius Couch, then senior corps commander in the army. Couch later remembered that Lincoln sat quietly as the thousands of volunteers paraded by, their flags being lifted by wafts of sweet spring air and their bands playing brisk quicksteps. The president exchanged no pleasantries with any of the officers present and seemed to Couch to be distant in his thoughts. Suddenly, Lincoln turned to Couch and abruptly said, "What do you suppose will become of all these men when the war is over?" Couch was surprised and could not answer at first, but later said of the incident, "It struck me as very pleasant that somebody had an idea that the war would sometime end."[1]

*   *   *

Lieutenant Colonel George Washington Alexander, 47th Pennsylvania Volunteers

The former commandant of Camp Curtin returned to Reading, Pennsylvania, after being mustered out in September of 1864. Alexander and his wife added one more child to their family after the war, Nettie Emilia in 1868. The leg wound he received at Pleasant Hill, Louisiana in April, 1864, never healed. The fractured bones mended, but the skin never closed over the wound and an open sore remained for the rest of his life. The wound constantly discharged matter, and the leg frequently swelled so an expandable rubber brace of some sort had to be worn. Even with this brace, Alexander could not walk far unassisted. In later years, the leg was so painful that he was frequently confined to his home. He died May 5, 1903.[2]

Captain Frank P. Amsden, Battery G, 1st Pennsylvania Light Artillery

After being discharged on a surgeon's certificate in late May, 1863, Amsden went home to Scranton. His bronchitis, contracted after the Mud March in January, 1863, did not improve, and for six months he was unable to do any work at all. He remembered that his family physician told him "that in careful nursing, generous diet avoidance of hardships and undue exposure, coupled with such exercise and occupation as I could bear without exhaustion, lay my chances for prolonging my life." In November, he took a job as a civil engineer in New York City and lived in Flushing, Long Island. He remained there for four years then went to work in Dover, New Jersey. In 1872, he moved back to Scranton to practice his profession with his father and brother. The often demanding engineering business left Amsden little chance to rest and improve his health, and he often complained of being broken down and unable to do a "fair day's work." Periods of cold or damp weather would give him chest pains and cause him labored breathing. He steadily lost weight after the war, eventually being some twenty pounds lighter than when he had entered the service. Before his 40th birthday, Amsden's bronchitis had degenerated into tubercular consumption. His date of death is not known.[3]

Captain James F. Andress, Co. G, 7th Pennsylvania Volunteer Cavalry

After relinquishing command of Camp Curtin in February, 1863, Captain Andress returned to his regiment and resumed command of Company G. The regiment was then operating in Tennessee. On the 17th of August, 1863, the 7th was involved in a skirmish at Sparta, Tennessee. Andress took a bullet in his right thigh, which left a very ugly wound and confined him to hospitals for several months. He returned to duty, was promoted to major in March, 1864, and to lieutenant colonel in February, 1865. He was mustered out at Macon, Georgia, in August, 1865 and returned to his home in Pennsylvania. At 31, Andress again established himself as a tobacconist in West Chester, but was never free from the pain and discomfort caused by his leg wound. He felt his eyes had been much weakened by his bout with small pox at Camp Curtin, he still suffered the chronic diarrhea caused by the intestinal disorder developed in the service, and rheumatism had settled in his wounded leg. He moved to Cincinnati, Ohio, and lived there for a time then moved to Greenville, South Carolina. He did not marry. In 1875, his father died, and the duty of supporting his mother fell upon him. Mrs. Andress was forced to sell the family farm in West Chester to pay her husband's debts, after which she was left just $60.

By 1888, Andress was so enfeebled by rheumatism and diarrhea as to be confined to his room for long stretches. He was just 55 when he died of pneumonia on March 15, 1889 at Walhalla, South Carolina. He was buried in Grove Cemetery, West Chester.[4]

Colonel James Addams Beaver, 148th Pennsylvania Volunteers

Beaver did not die in the field hospital near Petersburg as he expected to, but the loss of his right leg at Reams's Station took him out of the war for good. Few soldiers on either side in that war had attacked their duties, and the enemy, with more vigor than Beaver had. He had proved himself a first rate soldier and leader, and officers who knew him, especially his superiors, spoke well of his courage and ability.

After his return to Bellefonte in October, 1864, Beaver's health and spirits improved markedly. In November, 1864, he was breveted brigadier general for his services, but his army days were over. Eventually, he began practicing law again with his partner in the firm of McAllister and Beaver. His association with Mr. McAllister was beneficial to Beaver a number of ways, not the least of which was the introduction to Miss Mary Allison McAllister, his daughter. Mary became wife to the one-legged Beaver on the day after Christmas, 1865. Together they had five sons, Nelson, James, Hugh, Gilbert, and Thomas. Only Gilbert and Thomas lived to adulthood.

Beaver, as might have been predicted, began again working actively for the Republican party in Centre County. He also became prominent in the Presbyterian Church in the commonwealth. He became associated with several public projects, such as the building of a hospital for the insane, and sat on the board of trustees for several colleges and universities. He was commissioned major general in the state national guard and was a delegate to the 1880 National Republican Convention, where his name was mentioned in connection with the vice presidency of the United States. He was subsequently a candidate for United States senator and, in 1882, governor of Pennsylvania, but was defeated for both offices. He retired from public eye and began an iron and nail company in Bellefonte, which he ran successfully. By 1886, however, the spirit of the people of Pennsylvania had changed, and, after Beaver again received the gubernatorial nomination, he was swept to victory by a large majority. It was during his administration the 2,220 people were killed in the infamous Johnstown Flood. Beaver was instrumental in gaining relief for the survivors.

In 1888, he presided over ceremonies at Gettysburg when the monuments there, most commissioned and built by private, regimental organizations, were given to the Commonwealth of Pennsylvania. Though he had been commandant at Camp Curtin in early July, 1863, and had missed the battle because of his Chancellorsville wound, Beaver was a frequent speaker at the many ceremonies and events held at Gettysburg after the war by veterans.

In 1891, Beaver's term of office expired, and he went home to Bellefonte. Four years later, the Pennsylvania legislature created the Superior Court of Pennsylvania, and Beaver was made one of the original seven judges. In a general election the next November, he was confirmed for a term of ten years, and at the end of that ten years, he was reelected. He still held office when he died in Bellefonte at age 76 on January 31, 1914.[5]

Colonel Everard Bierer, 171st Pennsylvania Drafted Militia

Bierer was mustered out of the 171st in August, 1864, but few soldiers were discharged amid as much controversy. Though he was honorably discharged, a movement was afoot to have him dismissed from the service for larceny. While the 171st was serving in the vicinity of Washington, North Carolina, a lieutenant of the 1st North Carolina, a Union regiment serving as the provost guard in the area, accused Colonel Bierer of pillaging a looking glass and recommended that Bierer be dismissed from the service. The charges were forwarded to the War Department before Bierer was given a chance to answer them, in fact, even before he was made aware of them. Bierer was understandably outraged when he learned of them, and immediately protested. Bierer claimed that the lieutenant in question held a personal grudge against him, and that the charges were wholly without foundation. The matter caused Bierer a great deal of trouble when he later applied for a pension, which he badly needed. The wound in his elbow received at South Mountain prevented him from working. He wrote to the pension bureau, claiming that the charges had not been proved, had been attached to him in the first place only through the machinations of "a combination of scoundrels" and that the whole matter had already been cleared up by Judge Advocate General Brigadier General Joseph Holt, who had rendered a decision in Bierer's favor. Bierer finally was vindicated and got a pension of $12 per month.

Bierer and his wife, Ellen, had a total of eight children, including a son born after the war whom they named Andrew Gregg Curtin Bierer. Everard's elbow was a source of constant agony, and rheumatism seated itself there early after the war, making it impossible for Bierer to bend him arm or flex his muscles without great pain. Later in life, Bierer and Ellen moved to Hiawatha, Kansas, where he died the day after Christmas, 1910, at 83.[6]

Colonel James Voty Bomford, 8th United States Infantry

After his service in Harrisburg as provost marshal general of the Western Division of Pennsylvania, Bomford served at other rear area posts in New York, Baltimore and Virginia. He was promoted to colonel of the 8th U.S. Infantry.[7] After the war ended, he served at posts in New York and the Carolinas until 1872, when he was sent out to the plains during the Indian Wars as a Department Inspector in Nebraska and Wyoming. He resigned from the army in 1872 at age 62 and died January 6, 1892.[8]

Captain Daniel Jewett Boynton, Co. I, 93rd Pennsylvania Volunteers

Boynton returned to his regiment after leaving Camp Curtin, but was apparently never the same. The close encounter with the shell at Mechanicsville left him nervous and prone to bursting blood vessels and hemorrhaging. He served to the end of his term and was mustered out in Virginia in October, 1864, when he returned to his wife, Diana, in Middletown. Evidence suggests that Boynton, despite his infirmities, might have reentered the service as a substitute for a drafted man in March, 1865. A Daniel J. Boynton of the same age, occupation and physical description as Captain Boynton enlisted as a private in Company A of the 100th Pennsylvania. If Captain Boynton did reenlist, it is likely he did so to collect a fee paid by the drafted man and would only have served until July, 1865, when the 100th was mustered out. After the war, Boynton got his old job back as foreman at a planing mill and remained in Middletown. He died there at the age of 60 in 1883.[9]

Brigadier General John Rutter Brooke, 53rd Pennsylvania Volunteers

Brooke, who started the war as a captain in the 4th Pennsylvania, eventually rose to brigadier general of volunteers. At Cold Harbor in the spring of 1864 he was adly wounded. He remained in the service until the close of the war, commanding division at the end. He resigned from the volunteer army in 1866, but after, receiving n appointment as lieutenant colonel in the Regular Army, reentered the service just few months later. He rose to become a full major general by the time the U.S. went o war with Spain in 1898. He led troops in that war and then returned to the United States to command a military department for a number of years. He married Louisa Roberts on Christmas Eve, 1863, but she died just four years later. He married again n 1877, to Mary Stearns of New Hampshire. Brooke died at age 88 in Philadelphia, September 5, 1926.[10] He was buried in Arlington National Cemetery, little more than 00 yards from the portico of Robert E. Lee's former home.

Major Thomas Chamberlin, 150th Pennsylvania Volunteers

After being wounded and taken prisoner at Gettysburg, Chamberlin was exchanged and returned to duty August 26, 1863. In March, 1864, the 25 year old was promoted to lieutenant colonel of the 150th, but less than two weeks later, ill health and pain from his wound forced him to resign. Having served with two regiments and been twice wounded, twice captured and twice hospitalized, he was discharged and went home to Lewisburg. The wound he received on McPherson's Ridge was to incapacitate him for life. The bullet had torn through his upper back and wedged between his collar bone and his humerus and, although it was removed, the damage t had done to nerves would cause him intense pain. Even years after the war, he was able to move his arm, his neck, or his head, only slowly, and could use his left arm only slightly for fear the movement would ignite the pain in the other shoulder. He needed help in bathing, dressing, eating, and even sleeping, for it required a great deal of patience to place him in a position he could maintain comfortably throughout the night. He could not so much as move his head without starting bolts of pain that would wake him. Throughout all this, Chamberlin retained his spirit and mental vitality and fell in love with Sarah Frances English of Georgetown, D.C. "Fanny" was a woman of extraordinary energy and compassion, for on October 25th, 1870, she married Chamberlin in Baltimore and undertook the considerable task of caring for him night and day.

Chamberlin and his wife settled in Philadelphia in 1874, and he turned to selling fire insurance, eventually becoming secretary of the Teutonia Fire Insurance Company. They took two years off to travel abroad, and upon their return home Chamberlin began to write. He devoted a great deal of time to writing about the war, publishing a number of articles and a book—an excellent and still much-referred-to history of the 150th. He died on February 22, 1917 at 79.[11]

Private Charles Creamer, Co. B, 127th Pennsylvania Volunteers

After receiving two wounds at Fredericksburg, Creamer spent the next five months in hospitals. When in May, 1863, he appeared in Harrisburg to be mustered out with Company B, he did so on crutches. He remained in his hometown of Harrisburg after the war. But his wounds, especially the fractured right ankle, incapacitated him to varying degrees for the rest of his life; he would never again stand or walk painlessly enough to earn steady wages. He never married and lived with his mother, Esther, in rented houses in the city until his death of a heart disorder at only 45 on August 12, 1888.[12]

Private John Creamer, Co. B, 127th Pennsylvania Volunteers

In mid December, 1862, Esther Creamer was informed that her only two sons had been wounded at Fredericksburg. Soon after, her older boy, John, arrived home on medical leave. He was rheumatic and missing a finger on his left hand. She knew her other son lay in a hospital bed with crippling wounds. Her full share of sorrow was not to be meted until January 1, however, when her husband died at the State Lunatic Asylum at Harrisburg. John's seemingly minor wound proved serious enough to incapacitate him for the next three months. He was nursed by his mother and sister and regularly attended to by a surgeon in Harrisburg. By March, the wound had healed. His rheumatism had worsened, however, and unfitted him for service in the field. John had fought his last battle. After a brief stay in a hospital in Annapolis, he was mustered out at Harrisburg in May.

After the war, he moved to Philadelphia and married Frances Wallace, a New Yorker, in 1876. The couple had two daughters, Mary and Margaret. John's rheumatism worsened and he lost most of his hearing while still fairly young. He lived with his wife in Philadelphia until March 16, 1903, when he died at 65.[13]

Governor Andrew Gregg Curtin

After completing his second term as governor, Curtin was, for a time, a candidate for vice president of the United States on the ticket with General Grant in 1868. He did not secure the nomination, however, and a year later President Grant gave him the post of minister to Russia. He remained there for three years, and, upon his return, estranged some fellow Republicans by splitting with the party and endorsing the Democrat Horace Greely for president over Grant. This falling out eventually led to his declaring as a Democrat, and he ran on that ticket for Congress, albeit unsuccessfully, in 1872. He ran again, however, was sustained, and served three terms in Washington. In 1887, he retired to Bellefonte, where he lived quietly until his illness and death on October 7, 1894. He was 79.[14]

Major Richard I. Dodge, 12th United States Infantry

Dodge left his post as chief mustering and disbursing officer of the Western Division of Pennsylvania in February of 1865. He has served quietly in Harrisburg since October, 1861, and had risen from captain in the 8th U.S. Infantry to major of the

12th, and eventually to brevet lieutenant colonel for "Meritorious and Faithful Services in the Recruitment of the Armies of the United States."[15] He served at various posts in New York after the war, and was sent out to the plains in 1867, serving at Fort Sedgwick, Camp Sargent, Fort Fred. Steele, Fort Sanders, Fort Lyon, Fort Dodge, Fort Whipple, Omaha Barracks, Fort Riley, Fort Leavenworth, Fort Hays, Fort Sill, and Fort Sully. He rose to the rank of full colonel in the 11th Infantry, served as aide-de-camp to General-in-Chief William Tecumseh Sherman, and, in all commanded troops on the western frontier for 20 years after his service in the Civil War. He wrote three books about the west, *Plains of the Great West*, *Black Hills*, and *Our Wild Indians*. Colonel Dodge retired May 19, 1891, and died four years later on June 16, 1895.[16]

Private George Eminhizer, Co. A, 45th Pennsylvania Volunteers

Eminhizer served throughout the war until the whole regiment was discharged in June, 1865. He saw some heavy fighting, from his first battle on the slopes of South Mountain to his last wound in the trenches of Petersburg. He spent some time in the western theatre as well and was wounded in the left hand at Blue Springs, Tennessee in October 10, 1863. After his discharge, he returned home to Marsh Creek in Centre County and again went to farming. In 1866, the 23-year-old veteran married a neighbor's daughter, 16-year-old Elizabeth Long, at the Marsh Creek schoolhouse. Following an introductory period of about two years, George and Elizabeth began building a huge family. Abram H. came in 1868 and William in 1869, then, in an incredible stretch, one child every two years until 1883 (Nathan, Emma, Bertha, Charles, George Cloyd, (Eldy Pearl thrown in in 1880) Lula Jane, and Annie). James Ray (1890) and Blanche (1892) came later. By the time he was 49, George Eminhizer had been married 26 years and had fathered twelve children. About 1875, Eminhizer had given up the plow for the pulpit and became a minister in the United Brethren Church near Bellefonte. He served there for nearly twenty years. The Eminhizers later moved about, settling briefly in Coleville, Pennsylvania and later in Huntingdon County. George died May 10, 1928, a week after his 85th Birthday. His child bride, Elizabeth, died in Ohio four years later.[17]

Private Elisha Farnum, Co. B, 132nd Pennsylvania Volunteers

After leaving the vicinity of Sharpsburg, in September, 1862, Farnum began three months of recuperation in Ascension Hospital in Washington. On January 1, 1863, he signed his discharge by making an "X" with his left hand and went home to Factoryville, near Scranton, to begin his life as a 20-year-old, righthanded mechanic with no right hand.

For a few years, Farnum and his wife, Eliza, quietly collected his pension of $30 per month, the price at which the government had estimated his arm. In 1865, Elisha and Eliza, both 23, had their first child and only child, Maggie. The household was not an altogether happy one, however, for Elisha was frequently ill from his wound and the jagged, still open stump steadily discharged what the family physician called "an offensive pus." It was thought that the trouble was likely caused by the hurried amputation of the shattered arm in a hectic dressing station or field hospital in one of the Maryland pastures around Sharpsburg. Apparently, the surgeon performing the operation did not take time to carefully examine the wound and amputated the arm too far below the shoulder, leaving sections of the fragmented bone intact. Intermittent fever and discharge were the result. Finally, after a long, painful struggle, Farnum died in 1871, only 29 years old. The family doctor was in attendance and wrote "death ended his sufferings on the 15th August. I pronounced it a plain case of Pyemia caused by improper amputation." The bullet that had cost Farnum his arm and that eventually killed him nearly nine years after it hit him had been given to him by the surgeon who had extracted it. Farnum kept the bullet until his death, after which it belonged to his 29-year-old widow and 5-year-old daughter.[18]

Lieutenant William Wallace Geety, Co. H, 47th Pennsylvania Volunteers

Geety remained in Harrisburg on recruiting duty until his discharge in September, 1864, when he was promoted to captain. His lungs were almost constantly congested, having contracted an infirmity around Washington in the autumn of 1861, and his face remained badly disfigured from the wound that had cost him his left eye. He lived in Harrisburg with his wife, Henrietta, and had a son, Wallace, in 1872. His lung condition worsened, and he began hemorrhaging. He died on January 19, 1877 from what was probably tuberculosis. Henrietta lived on her husband's $25 per month pension until her death in 1918.[19]

Private Henry Gerrish, Co. A, 7th New York Volunteers

After leaving the Cotton Mill Hospital in Harrisburg in January of 1863, Henry Gerrish went home to New York City on a 30-day leave. Although his left thumb was still not working properly, he rejoined his regiment in February in their winter quarters around Falmouth, Virginia. Gerrish saw no more fighting. He was mustered out in New York with his company at the expiration of its two year term in early May, 1863, and returned home to Brooklyn. A few months later, just before his 23rd birthday, he moved to Charlestown, Massachusetts, across the harbor from Boston, where he again took up the trade of upholsterer. He married a fellow immigrant named Mary Glanz, who was not only from Germany but from Henry's hometown of Yogenheim. They had four children, Mary, in 1865, Lizzie in 1866, Henry, Jr. in 1868, and Christina in 1870. In that last year, Mary traveled back to Yogenheim, apparently for a visit with friends and family, but she fell ill and died, leaving her husband and children alone in America. With four very young children to attend to, one of them newborn, Gerrish desperately needed a women to help him care for them. To make matters worse, upholstering was a difficult craft for a man with a useless left thumb, and he was struggling in his business. In 1872, however, at age

32, he convinced a courageous 24-year-old girl from Boston named Louisa Wachter to become his second wife and stepmother to his four children. Henry and Louisa added three more children to the brood, Louis in 1873, William two years later, and finally Adeline, "Addie", in 1880. The Gerrishes lived in Charlestown for the next 45 years. Henry developed health problems incident to old age but unrelated to his wound and finally died of what was most likely heart failure on March 10, 1925 at the age of 85. He was buried in Forest Dale Cemetery in nearby Malden, Massachusetts. Louisa followed him a year later.[20]

Brigadier General John Frederic Hartranft, 4th and 51st Pennsylvania Volunteers

The Norristown native, colonel of both the 4th and 51st Pennsylvania, was one of the finer volunteer soldiers to come to prominence during the war. He had served in both theatres and was wounded at Cold Harbor. He had risen to command first a brigade then a division in the final campaigns against Richmond and played an important role in the fall of the Confederate capital. Following the war, Hartranft was involved in guarding the accused assassins of President Lincoln. After that unpleasant business was ended, he was mustered out of the volunteer service. Like many other prominent and successful soldiers, Hartranft turned to politics. He was elected auditor general of the commonwealth in 1865 and governor of Pennsylvania in 1872. He was reelected at the end of his first term, and served until 1879. Under his administration, the leaders of the savage Molly Maguires, who had ruthlessly dominated the coal mining districts for more than a decade, were finally brought to justice and the organization broken up. After leaving the capitol, Hartranft was occupied by other, smaller political posts mostly in Philadelphia. In 1886, the Congress of the United States voted Hartranft the Medal of Honor for his refusal to go to the rear with the rest of the 4th Pennsylvania when its term had expired on the day of the battle of First Bull Run. He died at age 58 on October 17, 1889 and was buried in Montgomery Cemetery in Norristown.[21]

Lieutenant Jacob Heffelfinger, Co. H, 7th Pennsylvania Reserves

The teacher from Mechanicsburg returned to his home in March, 1865. He had been seriously wounded twice, captured thrice (spending about 14 months in Confederate prisons) and still suffered from hemorrhoids contracted in 1864. In 1867, he was breveted captain by general order of the War Department "for gallant conduct at the battle of the Wilderness." He forever after walked with an extreme limp, but otherwise regained some of his robustness after the war and married Miss Louisa Whiting in Baltimore in 1872. They had three children, only one of whom, Louis, survived infancy. Heffelfinger died April 1, 1915 at age 75.[22]

Colonel William Wesley Jennings, 127th Pennsylvania Volunteers, 26th Pennsylvania Emergency Militia

Jennings resumed his position of prominence in Harrisburg after his service, being elected sheriff of Dauphin County twice. He became president of two banks, the

Harrisburg Steam Heating Company and director of the Cumberland Valley Railroad. Jennings died suddenly on February 28, 1895 at age 55, leaving his wife, Emma, and four children, Mary, William, Fanny, and Harry.[23]

Brigadier General Joseph Farmer Knipe, 46th Pennsylvania Volunteers

After the ludicrous performance of the militia under his command in the Gettysburg emergency, Knipe returned to service in Tennessee. In the Atlanta Campaign, he commanded a division in the Twentieth Corps and was wounded at the Battle of Resaca, Georgia, in May, 1864. During the Nashville Campaign, he commanded a division of cavalry, and his troops participated in a decisive victory over General John B. Hood's Confederates. Knipe was discharged in September, 1866, at Harrisburg, where he remained with his wife, Eliza, and his children. He served as postmaster for Harrisburg until 1868, then held a variety of jobs in a number of places, including Fort Leavenworth, Kansas, and Washington, D.C., where he held the position of postmaster for the United States House of Representatives for nine years.

In his old age Knipe suffered from his wounds, especially the two he had received on August 9, 1862 at Cedar Mountain. His left hand was usually numb as a result of the damage done by a piece of shell, and his head constantly ached severely with "neuralgia pains in the right side." His right eye, which was just missed by shrapnel that day at Cedar Mountain, was never quite right and often became inflamed. He died August 18, 1901 at 78 and was buried in Harrisburg Cemetery.[24]

Brigadier General James Nagle, 6th, 48th, 194th Pennsylvania Volunteers, 39th Pennsylvania Emergency Militia

One of the busiest men of the war, having organized and led four Pennsylvania regiments as colonel, Nagle was mustered out for the last time in November, 1864. He went to his home in Pottsville, and died just over a year and a half later of heart disease. He was 44.[25]

Captain Thomas H. Parker, Co. I, 51st Pennsylvania Volunteers

After sustaining a slight wound in taking the bridge at Antietam, Parker remained with Company I and served in all the actions in which the regiment was involved. After Fredericksburg the regiment went west, first to Kentucky then to Mississippi, where it participated in the Vicksburg Campaign, and finally to Tennessee to help in the siege of Knoxville. Parker had risen through the ranks and served through these campaigns and battles as a first sergeant and was fortunate enough to stay out of hospitals altogether. In January, 1864, Parker reenlisted, as did many of the men in the 51st, and that spring he went into and safely out of the Wilderness with the rest of the Army of the Potomac. In August, 1864, Parker was promoted to commissary sergeant and enjoyed a furlough at home with his wife and three children. When he returned to the regiment in the autumn, he suffered his first major bout with illness. He caught a cold that settled in his lungs. He was promoted to captain of

Company I in December but could not rid himself of the severe hacking cough. The spring of 1865 found him still fighting it. The long months of struggling with disease, which had developed into bronchitis, left him pale and visibly weak.

Even the warm weather failed to help Parker regain his vigor, and after his discharge in July, 1865, he still suffered from a "deep, exhaustive cough." The weakness of his lungs never left him, and he was frequently incapacitated with severe fits of bronchitis and would "cough up a great deal of nauseous phlegm." Though friends repeatedly urged him to apply for a pension from the government for having con- tracted the disease while in the service, he never did so. In late December, 1889, he caught a cold that quickly turned into pneumonia. Within three weeks he was dead. Parker's post-war years were not all spent languishing in a sick bed; he published an excellent and witty history of the 51st which for over a hundred years has been helping historians understand what it was like to be a Pennsylvania Volunteer.[26]

Private Samuel Pennypacker, Co. F, 26th Pennsylvania Emergency Militia

Pennypacker survived his service with the 26th Pennsylvania Emergency Militia in the Gettysburg emergency, but he never forgot that sleepless night on the granite steps of the capitol. He became particularly fond of telling and retelling the story of that night, especially after he was elected Governor of Pennsylvania in 1903. He was a lawyer and a judge in the years between and was very active in historical organizations throughout the commonwealth. He died September 2, 1916 at 73.[27]

Major Jeremiah Rohrer, 127th Pennsylvania Volunteers

After being mustered out on his 35th birthday in Harrisburg in May, 1863, Rohrer returned to his wife and children in Middletown. His door factory had survived in his absence, and he wasted no time in going back to work, but just a year later, in the spring of 1864, the Rohrers moved to Lancaster. Jeremiah went into business there as a wholesale liquor dealer. Mary gave birth to three more children in Lancaster, a son, in October of 1864, who was named Grant, another boy, Howard, in 1867, and finally, a girl, Daisy Marguerite, in 1877, by which time Mary was 46 years old. The Rohrers lived quietly in Lancaster until Jeremiah's death on October 23, 1910 at the age of 83. He was buried in Greenwood cemetery in Lancaster. Mary followed him a year and a half later at 81.[28]

Captain William Sands, Co. L, 1st Pennsylvania Cavalry

After returning to the field and resuming command of his company, Sands and a large number of his men were taken prisoner on June 21, 1864, near Trevilian Sta- tion, Virginia. Like so many before him, he was taken to Libby Prison in Richmond, where he was kept in those large, bare, stinking, overcrowded rooms throughout the heat of the summer. In December, 1864, he was paroled and sent home to Reading, Pennsylvania, the war was over for him. Although his stay in Libby had not been especially lengthy, it was destructive. On his poor diet there, Sands developed scurvy and a bladder disorder that would enfeeble him prematurely. The scurvy cost him all his teeth. By 1892, the scurvy, rheumatism, kidney disease, and senility left him almost helpless, and entirely dependent upon the $12 a month he collected in pension from the government. In May of 1897, Sands collected his check from the government for the last time. There is no record of his death—he simply disappeared—and the pension bureau was unable to learn what had happened to him. Senile and crippled as he was, it is probable that the 77-year-old Sands died that month or soon thereafter. He had never married.[29]

Mrs. Elmira Simmons

Shortly before he was killed, Colonel Simmons came under the observation of a poet named N. P. Willis during a rain storm. "I had never before thought that water could embellish a soldier," wrote Willis upon seeing Simmons. "Of a most warlike cast of feature, his profuse and...grizzly beard was impearled with glistening drops, and, with his horse and accoutrements all dripping with water, he rode calmly through the heavy rain like a Triton taking his leisure in his native element. It was the finest of countenances and the best of figures for a horseman. He looked indomitable in spirit...as handsome and brave when tired and wet, as he would be when happy and dry! I was quite captivated by the picture...." After her husband's death, Mrs. Simmons and her 19-year-old daughter, Elmira Adelaide, continued to live in Harrisburg in the house on the corner of Front and South Streets. Mrs. Simmons had difficulty wading through the morass of government forms enroute to receiving the widow's pension due her, but she eventually was awarded $30 a month for having sacrificed her husband. Elmira Adelaide remained unmarried until she was 44; she became wife to a miller two days before Christmas, 1886. Mrs. Simmons did not live to see the wedding, however, for she had died the previous February at age 78. She was buried in Pottsville with an honor escort provided by the Grand Army of the Republic. The veterans, many of whom had served under or been mustered in by her husband, read a burial service in addition to that performed by an Episcopal minister and, even in the dead of winter, left the grave piled high with flowers.[30]

Captain William A. Tarbutton

Tarbutton stayed active in the Locust Street Methodist Church choir after his duty as drillmaster at Camp Curtin. He died in Baltimore about 1875.[31]

Colonel Charles Frederick Taylor, Pennsylvania Bucktails

Funerals were common in Pennsylvania the second week of July, 1863, but the mourners who stood in a warm, torrential rain in a cemetery in the tiny village of Kennett Square took no solace from the knowledge that their sorrow was commonplace. The old men and women who clustered in the puddles and muddy, matted grass beneath a cypress tree to bury their neighbor, Fred Taylor, could only lament their loss as the casket was lowered into the wet grave.[32]

Fred Taylor had been brought home a hero, and, like Lafayette, was laid beneath a tree in the Brandywine Valley to rest. He had been in three battles in his career and had been a casualty in all three. An intelligent, cultured, dedicated and extraordinarily brave young farmer, Taylor had, as a soldier, won not only the affection of his men but the notice and respect of his superiors. Surviving Bucktails helped erect two monuments to his memory, one at Gettysburg on the spot where he fell, and the other over his grave in Longwood Cemetery. Another friend, a neighbor in Kennett Square, had his romantic soul stirred by the combination of Taylor's courage and great promise and paid homage in verse.

> He fell as many a hero falls,
>   Untimely, in the fearful fray.
> Who only asks where duty calls,
>   Then bravely leads the ordered way.
>
> Undaunted by the battle storm,
>   "Come on, come on, boys!" he cried;
> Dismayed they saw his reeling form,
>   But conquered where their leader died.
>
> And now he sleeps the endless sleep;
>   Naught shall disturb that blest repose.
> Though friends may sigh and kindred weep,
>   His heart no pain nor sorrow knows.
>
> Young hero, rest! Thy strife is o'er,
>   And thou hast gained a sweet release;
> The bugle's blast, the cannon's roar,
>   No more shall break thy spirit's peace.

Westdale, Delaware County, Pa.   D.B.S.[33]

Brigadier General Thomas Welsh, 45th Pennsylvania Volunteers

Welsh did not survive the war, and became the first of Camp Curtin's principal figures to die. He had been, perhaps, Camp Curtin's best commandant and had an outstanding record throughout his brief war career. After leading the 45th Pennsylvania through the Fredericksburg Campaign, he was promoted to brigadier general in March, 1863. He went west and led troops in Grant's army. Suddenly, however, he took ill and died within days of pneumonia. So swiftly had illness been followed by death that friends and family in Columbia were scarcely informed of the former before the latter. It was a great shock to the men who knew him in the army, with whom he was popular. He died August 14, 1863 in Cincinnati at age 39. He left his wife, Annis, one son, Blanton, who eventually was graduated from West Point, and four daughters, Alice, Mary, Effie, and Lillian. Welsh was buried in Mount Bethel Cemetery in Columbia, Pennsylvania.[34]

Colonel Edward C. Williams, 9th Pennsylvania Cavalry

Williams resigned his colonelcy of the 9th Pennsylvania in October, 1862 over "a question of rank." He returned to Harrisburg and his trade, but did not reenter the war in any capacity. In May, 1865, while most of Harrisburg was rejoicing over the end of the war, Williams was grieving over the death of his wife, Salima. Six years later, at 52, he remarried. He and his new wife, Anna, later moved to Chapman, Pennsylvania, where Williams died six days after his 81st birthday.[35]

Dr. James P. Woods

Dr. Woods had served as surgeon in charge at Camp Curtin for more than 2 years when he decided to leave Harrisburg. He became surgeon of the 187th Pennsylvania in April, 1864, but saw little action. While the regiment served in Grant's spring campaign to the gates of Richmond and Petersburg, Woods was back in Harrisburg on his death bed. He died there of undetermined causes on July 5, 1864.[36]

John Woods, Co. G, 49th Pennsylvania Volunteers

Woods, who had served so long as a clerk for Major Dodge in Harrisburg and who had frequently been on the sick list, was finally discharged in October of 1864. In August, 1864, he had written to his brother about two young ladies, sisters, from their hometown of Spring Mills, Pennsylvania, who had been rivalling for John's attention through the mails. "I have a letter from Bell this morning. She is full of fun—she + Alice are as jealous of each other, as two fair damsels are of a lover, tending both. I wrote to Alice the other day—the first in a long while, won't that make Bell cross? I like to make them jealous of each other. Bell though has shown considerable *affection* toward me lately—and I have been writing to her very frequently (no love as yet)...."

Two years later, in September, 1866, John married 20-year-old Belle, whose true name was Mary Arabella. John continued working as a clerk and suffering from intestinal problems and bronchitis. After some time, he went to school to study medicine and although it is unclear whether he ever formally became a physician, he did work as a sort of intern or associate and regularly prescribed medication for himself. He died on Christmas eve, 1894 at 53. Belle survived him by almost 42 years.[37]

"It is but little, at the most, that the State can do to honor rightly the memory of the fallen, or repay the services of the living. Monuments should rise through all the valleys of State, rehearsing the names and deeds of the dead....Nor should the living heroes be allowed to pass from a grateful remembrance. Patriotism should meet its public rewards, and thus be enshrined as a virtue in the hearts of the people."

A. L. Russell
adjutant general of
Pennsylvania, 1866

Appendix I

THE SIZE OF CAMP CURTIN IN RELATION
TO OTHER NORTHERN CAMPS

Camp Curtin was the largest camp in the Northern states. It was not necessarily the largest in the area or in capacity, but it was the largest accommodator of troops. More troops passed through Camp Curtin than passed through any other camp in the North—and probably the South as well.

A number of attempts have been made at estimating the number of men who passed through Camp Curtin throughout the war. In 1922, the Reverend Alvin Williams, historian for the committee to erect the statue of Governor Curtin on the site of the camp, estimated that 300,000 men passed through its gates. That figure appears on the memorial, but the actual number is surely considerably higher.

But accurately calculating the number of men who spent any time there is impossible simply because there is no way to know how many men passed through more than once as members of different companies or regiments. While numbers dealing with *men* are slippery, the number of *regiments* and *companies* that were in camp can be determined with more assurance of accuracy. More regiments, battalions, batteries and independent companies were formed in Camp Curtin than were formed in the entire *cities* of New York City, Chicago, Boston, Philadelphia, Pittsburgh, Indianapolis, Cincinnati, Columbus, or Springfield, Illinois.

In the regimental histories section of his monumental *Compendium of the War of the Rebellion,* Frederick Dyer gave, wherever possible, the city and specific camp in which every Federal regiment was organized. A close examination of this section reveals that more Federal organizations, excluding militia, were activated in Harrisburg than in any other city in the North. Were militia companies and regiments counted, Harrisburg's advantage might even be greater, as dozens of such organizations were formed there in September, 1862, and in June and July, 1863. The scores of regiments from Pennsylvania, Ohio, Wisconsin, New York, New Jersey and other states that were formed elsewhere but that were quartered or passed through Harrisburg and Camp Curtin on their way to the war are likewise not counted. Harrisburg's location at the junction of several railroads just hours from Washington, D.C. and Harpers Ferry meant that perhaps more Federal troops passed through it than any other city in any other Northern state. Harrisburg was certainly one of the two or three busiest cities in the North during the war, excluding Washington.

In the course of the war, 106 regiments and 28 independent companies were formed in the Pennsylvania capital. These figures include units organized at Camps

237

Simmons, Cameron and McClellan as well as Camp Curtin, but fewer than 10 regiments were organized at these other three camps combined, and most of those that were had been quartered in Camp Curtin before "overflowing" to any of the auxiliary camps. By contrast, at the several camps in New York City, which was far larger than Harrisburg and contained many more encampments, 92 regiments and 12 independent companies were formed. In Indianapolis, Indiana, where Camp Morton was the principal depot, 67 regiments and 40 companies were organized. In Philadelphia, the second largest rendezvous point in Pennsylvania, 65 regiments and 39 companies were formed, but more than two dozen camps were operated within the city of brotherly love during the course of the war. Columbus, Ohio, where Camp Chase was the main camp, was the starting place for 61 regiments and 14 independent companies. Camp Butler was the principal camp in Springfield, Illinois, and 49 regiments and 8 independent companies were formed in that city. Another 48 regiments and 33 independent companies began in Cincinnati, site of Camp Dennison, and in Pittsburgh, where at least three camps were operated, 24 regiments and 18 companies independent companies started their service.

Many of the regiments formed in Pittsburgh or Philadelphia came home through Harrisburg, where many of them spent time in Camp Curtin, several of them being mustered out there.

While Camp Chase or some of the other big camps might have quartered more men at any one given time than did Camp Curtin, some of these camps were used as permanent or semi-permanent prisoner of war camps and were therefore not purely Camps of Rendezvous or Instruction. Camp Curtin's sole purpose was to produce Federal soldiers, and it did that until the end of the war.

Appendix II

THE CAMP CURTIN MEMORIAL

Camp Curtin retained a prominent place in the memories of the Pennsylvania veterans who had served there. Veterans groups, especially Post 58 of the Grand Army of the Republic (GAR) made several attempts to have the site of the camp marked, but little came of these efforts. Not until just before World War I was enough interest stirred in the Pennsylvania legislature that actual steps were taken toward commemorating the camp's importance to the Union.

At 2:30 p.m., on October 19, 1922, a 100-square foot park and a monument was dedicated in Harrisburg on the site of Camp Curtin. The park was established by the legislature and remains the smallest state park in the nation.

The dedication was attended by both Governor William Cameron Sproul and Lieutenant Governor Edward E. Beidleman as well as Judge J. W. Willet, commander in chief of the Grand Army of the Republic. Amid the pomp of speeches and band music, the monument was unveiled by William W. Curtin, the governor's son, and Laura and Helen Gastrock, great granddaughters of General Joseph Knipe. A bronze statue of the governor stood upon a granite base, onto which four bronze tablets were affixed. One of the tablets read:

In memory of the more than 300,000 soldiers of the Civil War, the flower of the Nation's youth and the maturity of her manhood, who passed into and out of this camp to the field of battle; A United Nation enjoys the fruit of their victory for Liberty and Union.

Here, printed in its entirety, is the story of how the Camp Curtin Memorial was finally established as related by the Rev. Alvin S. Williams in the program for the *Ceremonies at the Dedication of the Statue of Andrew Gregg Curtin, War Governor of Pennsylvania on the Site of Camp Curtin. Erected by the Commonwealth of Pennsylvania on a part of the Camp Curtin Site at Sixth and Woodbine Streets, City of Harrisburg October 22, 1922.*

The Memorial Park and Statue

The fact that Camp Curtin has not been adequately marked or remembered until this time does not express deliberate neglect or disinterest on the part of the citizens of Harrisburg or the State of Pennsylvania. For again and again there has been effort to realize what at this time has been achieved. For years the citizens of Harrisburg and especially the members of the Grand Army of

The Republic desired to appropriately mark and commemorate the old Camp. A Memorial Arch to be placed at the intersection of Sixth and Maclay Streets, the point of the old gateway to the Camp, was at one time seriously considered. But nothing practical was accomplished. The sentiment was kept alive but action tarried. The city at last spread over the old Camp Area and great schools and churches were erected on these grounds for the educational and religious protection of the people. The daughters of the American Revolution realizing the historic importance of this great civil war rendevous for soldiers placed a bronze tablet on the Camp Curtin School Building located on the South East Corner of Sixth and Woodbine streets. The Methodist Episcopal Congregation of this section of the city memorialized the camp by building a handsome stone church on the East Side of Sixth street and Warton Avenue calling the church, "The Camp Curtin Memorial." This edifice is one hundred and fifty feet distant from the Camp Curtin School Building and on the same side of Sixth street. Certain Memorials relating the history of Camp Curtin may be found within this Church edifice. It was after this recognition of Camp Curtin that petitions were circulated, principally among the citizens of the tenth ward, asking the State of Pennsylvania through the constituted authorities to erect a suitable and fitting Memorial. An organization was formed to take charge of these petitions and enlist the interest of patriotic citizens throughout the city and state in this project. This society soon received encouragement from Governor Martin G. Brumbaugh and Senator E. E. Beidelman. The Governor favorably mentioned "The Memorial" in his message to the Legislature (1917) and Senator Beidelman prepared and sponsored the following Bill which passed both houses of the Assembly, July 25th 1917:

An Act

Authorizing the governor to appoint a commission to purchase for public park purposes the site occupied by Camp Curtin during the Civil War providing for the purchase and erection of a suitable monument or memorial conferring certain powers on the commission and making an appropriation.

Whereas During the Civil War our Pennsylvania troops were trained and mustered into the national service at Camp Curtin a site now within the limits of the city of Harrisburg and which site is now rapidly developing into an important residential district and

Whereas A small area of the original site yet remains unim-
proved and may be purchased by the Commonwealth therefore

Section I *Be it enacted by the Senate and House of Representatives of the Commonwealth of Pennsylvania in General
Assembly met and it is hereby enacted by the authority of the
same* That the sum of twenty-five thousand dollars ($25,000.00)
is hereby appropriated for the establishment of a park in the city
of Harrisburg to be known as Camp Curtin Park and which is
to be located on the site occupied during the Civil War by Camp
Curtin where the Pennsylvania troops were trained and mustered
into the service of the United States The sum hereinbefore appropriated shall be used for and applied to the following purposes

For the purchase of the ground for said park the sum of eight
thousand dollars ($8,000.00) or so much thereof as may be necessary

For the erection of a suitable monument or memorial commemorative of the use of said camp during the Civil War the sum
of ten thousand dollars ($10,000.00) or so much thereof as may be
necessary.

For the purpose of placing said grounds in suitable condition
for park purposes for the erection of necessary fences for building
roads for incidental expenses of the commission and for the
dedication of said park and monument the sum of seven thousand dollars (7,000.00) or so much thereof as may be necessary

Section 2 For the purposes of carrying out the provisions of this
act the Governor is authorized to appoint a commission of seven
members to be known as the Camp Curtin Commission The commission shall organize by the election of a chairman and secretary
The commission is authorized to enter into negotiations and to
purchase in the name of the Commonwealth of Pennsylvania the
site of Camp Curtin for use as a public park The commission
shall have power to enter into contracts for the purchase and erection of a suitable monument or memorial to place said site in proper condition for a public park to arrange suitable devices for
dedication of said park and said monument and to have all such
other powers as may be necessary to carry out the provisions of
this act

Section 3 The members of the commission shall serve without
pay but shall be allowed all actual and necessary expenses

Section 4   The moneys herein appropriated shall be paid by warrant of the Auditor General upon the State Treasurer upon the filing of proper vouchers signed by the chairman and secretary of the commission

Governor Brumbaugh although greatly interested in this Memorial found it necessary to cut the amount of money to be appropriated by this bill to $13,000.00. He appointed the following persons to be members of the Camp Curtin Commission: Robert A. Enders, William E. Bailey, William H. Bricker, John A. Herman, Thomas M. Jones, Noah Walmer, and Alvin S. Williams. The Commission organized by making Robert A. Enders, President, and Thomas M. Jones, Secretary, and immediately sought an appropriate site for the Memorial. On January the 31st, 1917 an agreement was signed for the purchase of a plot one hundred feet square located on the North East Corner of Sixth and Woodbine Streets between the Camp Curtin School Building and The Camp Curtin Memorial Church. After a thorough consideration it was decided to accept the proposition of The Van Amriuge Granite Company of Boston, Mass. and erect a monument consisting of a bronze statue of Governor Curtin, by Clark Noble, elevated on a granite base. The monument is over sixteen feet high and its granite base is embellished on four sides with bronze tablets two of these in relief commemorating incidents in life of Camp Curtin. The settings for the monument and the development of the plot were secured from the Bureau of Municipalities of the Pennsylvania Department of Internal Affairs; Mr. Carl B. Lohmann, Designer. Messrs S. W. Shoemaker and Son received the contract for levelling the plot and for concrete walks and curbs etc., while Berryhill Nursery Company planted grass and arranged and planted trees and shrubbery. The completed work as it stands to-day speaks for itself.

It was necessary for the Commission to apply to the Legislature of the State for additional funds. Two bills other than the original were prepared and favorably enacted; one sponsored by Senator Frank A. Smith during the session of 1919 for eight thousand dollars; the final sponsored by Hon. David I. Miller for two thousand five hundred dollars passed in the 1921 session. Governor Sproul has shown deep interest in the project, reappointing the original commission to complete the work and gladly signing bills for additional appropriations of money needed to complete the memorial.

To fill the vacancies on the board caused by the deaths of Thomas M. Jones and William H. Bricker, Governor Sproul appointed Lloyd C. Clemson and Francis H. Hoy. John A. Herman, on the death of Thomas M. Jones, was chosen Secretary of the Commission.

The statue to Governor Curtin still stands in that tiny state park at Sixth and Woodbine in Harrisburg. The Camp Curtin Memorial is situated between the Camp Curtin Memorial United Methodist Church and the Camp Curtin YMCA. The Camp Curtin Junior High School stood for many years on ground that had once been part of the camp. Today that section of the city is still referred to as Camp Curtin.

Mural in sanctuary of Camp Curtin Memorial United Methodist Church showing Christ appearing to a dying Civil War soldier. The soldier is symbolically clad in blue and gray.
(Courtesy Camp Curtin Memorial United Methodist Church)

Appendix III

NAMES AND DESIGNATIONS OF COMPANIES, BATTALIONS, AND REGIMENTS THAT ENCAMPED IN CAMP CURTIN, CAMP RETURN, CAMP SIMMONS OR ANY OF THE OTHER CAMPS OR FORTS IN THE HARRISBURG AREA, INCLUDING CAPITOL HILL AND OTHER SITES WITHIN THE CITY PROPER, 1861-1866

As a major rail center, Harrisburg was at least an intermediate destination for hundreds, perhaps thousands of companies, battalions, and regiments from all over the North. Many of these organizations simply passed through the city without even detraining, others merely changed trains at the depot and still others were in Harrisburg just long enough to be uniformed, armed or equipped at the State Arsenal. A great many of the troops that came to Harrisburg, however, did enter Camp Curtin or establish a new camp for themselves somewhere nearby. Unfortunately, the movement of troops through the city was often so rapid and so voluminous that no official records could be kept. This was especially the case in the confusing early months of the war. After the United States Army took over the camp in March of 1862, monthly returns showing the troops and officers present in camp were kept and forwarded to the War Department, but dates of arrival and departure were not always noted on these returns and only a few of the documents are extant. When troops began returning to Harrisburg after the close of the war, reports and receipts of arrivals, musterings out, payments and departures were kept at Camp Return, but there is no way of knowing if the extant reports constitute all of the records kept. Therefore, no one knows, nor ever knew, the name or designations of all the organizations that spent any time in Camp Curtin much less Harrisburg.

The following is a list of some of the organizations that encamped in Camp Curtin or elsewhere in the Harrisburg area. All organizations that simply passed through the city or were there only briefly have been excluded. Only organizations that entered Camp Curtin or some other campground and remained at least one night have been included. This is by no means an inclusive list, as such a thing is impossible, but it is the most extensive and accurate list that could be compiled given the dearth of official records.

Sole sources used for compiling this list, in descending order of reliance and authority, are monthly returns for Camp Curtin, reports of arrivals and departures at Camp Return, muster rolls, receipts and authorization slips from the Quartermaster's Department at Camp Curtin, personal letters and diaries of soldiers, regimental histories, accounts in Harrisburg newspapers of troop movements, *The Official Records of the War of the Rebellion*, Bates's *History of the Pennsylvania Volunteers*, and Dyer's *A Compendium of the War of the Rebellion.*

The name or designation and term of enlistment is given for each regiment, battalion and independent company. When a unit was definitely or probably formed, organized, or mustered in at Camp Curtin or elsewhere in Harrisburg, the names of the two principal field officers are given, as is all available information regarding the dates of arrival and departure, the duration of the unit's stay, and the specific location of its campsite. Campsites referred to simply as "camp" were within Camp Curtin. Each organization is given in numerical (and therefore roughly chronological) order, except for those from other states, which are listed alphabetically.

Pennsylvania Regiments

1st Pennsylvania Volunteer Infantry   3 months

Colonel Samuel Yohe, Lt. Colonel Thomas H. Good

Companies C, D, E, F, and I arrived in Harrisburg 18 April 1861 and went into camp that day. The Regiment was organized 20 April and departed camp the same day.

Returned 25 July 1861 and remained in camp until it departed for home 26 July.

2nd Pennsylvania Volunteer Infantry   3 months

Colonel Frederick S. Stumbaugh, Lt. Colonel Thomas Welsh

Companies A, C, D, F, H, and I arrived in Harrisburg 19 April 1861 and went into camp that day. The Regiment was organized 21 April and departed camp that same day.

Returned to Harrisburg 22 July 1861, but because of crowded conditions at Camp Curtin, the Regiment was not given admittance until the next day. The men were mustered out 26 July and departed for home.

3rd Pennsylvania Volunteer Infantry   3 months

Colonel Francis P. Minier, Lt. Colonel John M. Power

Company G (Captain T. H. Lapsley's Johnstown Infantry) and Company K (Captain J. M. Power's Johnstown Zouave Cadets) both entered Camp 18 April 1861 and were the first two companies to bivouac on the ground that had not yet named Camp Curtin. Company H arrived later that day, and Companies A, D, E, F, and I arrived 19 April. The Regiment was organized 20 April and departed camp that same day.

Returned 24 July 1861, was mustered out 29 July, and departed for home.

4th Pennsylvania Volunteer Infantry   3 months

Colonel John C. Hartranft, Lt. Colonel Edward Schall

Company F arrived 19 April 1861, and other companies arrived the following day. The Regiment was organized and departed camp 20 April.

After returning to camp, Regiment was mustered out 27 July 1861 and departed for home.

5th Pennsylvania Volunteer Infantry
3 months

Colonel R. P. McDowell, Lt. Colonel Benjamin C. Christ

Company K was among the first organizations to enter camp on 18 April 1861. Company B arrived in camp on the 19th and all other companies arrived later that day or on the 20th. The Regiment was organized 21 April and departed the same day.

Returned 22 July 1861, was mustered out 25 July and departed for home.

6th Pennsylvania Volunteer Infantry
3 months

Colonel James Nagle, Lt. Colonel James J. Seibert

Companies arrived at Camp Curtin 21 April 1861. The Regiment was organized on the 21st and was mustered in by Captain Simmons on 22 April and departed camp that same day.

Returned 24 July 1861, and encamped not at Camp Curtin, but at a neighborhood Baptist Church. Company H encamped at the South Ward School House and remained there until 31 July 1861. Regiment mustered out 27 July.

7th Pennsylvania Volunteer Infantry
3 months

Colonel William H. Irwin, Lt. Colonel Oliver H. Rippey

Companies arrived in camp throughout the first few days of rendezvous and the Regiment was organized 22 April 1861. The 7th was mustered into service by Captain Simmons on 23 April and departed camp that same day.

Returned 25 July 1861, was mustered out 29 July and departed for home.

8th Pennsylvania Volunteer Infantry
3 months

Colonel A. H. Emley, Lt. Colonel Samuel Bowman

Company F arrived in camp 19 April 1861. Companies were mustered in by Captain Simmons as they arrived on 21 April and 22 April, and the Regiment was organized 22 April. Departed camp that same day.

The Regiment finally returned to Harrisburg 24 July 1861 and encamped behind the capitol.

The 8th was mustered out 29 July and departed for home.

9th Pennsylvania Volunteer Infantry
3 months

Colonel Henry C. Longnecker, Lt. Colonel Washington H. R. Hangen

Company F arrived in camp 19 April 1861 and all other companies had arrived by 24 April.

Companies were mustered in by Captain Simmons as they arrived from 22 April to 24 April.

The Regiment was organized 22 April. Lt. Col. Hangen served as commandant of camp from 22 April until his departure with the Regiment on 4 May.

Returned to camp 24 July 1861 and was mustered out 29 July.

10th Pennsylvania Volunteer Infantry   3 months

Colonel Sullivan A. Meredith, Lt. Colonel Oliver J. Dickey

Companies began arriving at camp 22 April 1861 and were mustered in by Captain Simmons as they arrived from 22 April to 29 April. The Regiment was organized 26 April and departed camp 1 May.

Returned 25 July 1861, was mustered out 31 July and departed for home.

11th Pennsylvania Volunteer Infantry   3 months

Colonel Phaon Jarret, Lt. Colonel Richard Coulter

Companies F, H, and I arrived at camp 25 April 1861. The Regiment was organized 26 April and departed camp 4 May. The Regiment volunteered for reenlistment upon the expiration of its first term of service, but was sent back to Harrisburg to be mustered out with the other three-month volunteers.

Returned 28 July 1861 and was mustered out 31 July. Many of the men remained in camp while recruiting squads travelled to home counties to fill up the ranks.

11th Pennsylvania Volunteer Infantry   3 years

Colonel Richard Coulter, Lt. Colonel Thomas S. Martin

In early August, the Regiment was reorganized in camp for 3 years service, maintaining its original numerical designation (the only Pennsylvania Regiment to do so). There was widespread sickness and 11 deaths in the Regiment during its lengthy stay in camp. Departed camp 27 November 1861.

After reenlisting yet again in February, 1864, elements of Returned enroute home on furlough and recruiting duty on the 11th of that month. On 29 March 1864, these elements rendezvoused once more at camp before returning to the field.

101 men and 1 officer arrived at Camp Return 2 June 1865 and were paid off and disbanded there 7 June. Remainder of Regiment mustered out 1 July 1865 in Washington. 309 men and 21 officers arrived at Camp Return 3 July 1865 and were paid off and disbanded there 7 July.

12th Pennsylvania Volunteer Infantry   3 months

Colonel David Campbell, Lt. Colonel Norton McGiffin

The Regiment was organized 22 April 1861 at Pittsburgh and moved to Harrisburg 24 April, where it was mustered in by Captain Simmons 25 April. Departed camp the same day.

Returned to Harrisburg late in July, 1861, and was mustered out 5 August.

13th Pennsylvania Volunteer Infantry   3 months

Colonel Thomas Rowley, Lt. Colonel John Purviance

Regiment arrived in camp 25 April 1861, except for Company H, which did not arrive until the next day. Companies were mustered into service by Captain Simmons on the 25th and the 26th.

The Regiment was organized 25 April and departed camp 27 April.

Returned 25 July 1861, encamped on the capitol grounds, was mustered out 6 August, and departed for home.

14th Pennsylvania Volunteer Infantry   3 months

Colonel John W. Johnston, Lt. Colonel Richard McMichael

Companies began arriving in camp as early as 19 April 1861, and they were mustered in as they arrived between 22 April and 27 April. The Regiment was organized 30 April and departed Camp 9 May along with the 15th Regiment.

Mustered out 7 August 1861 by Captain Hastings at Carlisle, Pa. and stopped at Camp Curtin 8 August while enroute home.

15th Pennsylvania Volunteer Infantry   3 months

Colonel Richard A. Oakford, Lt. Colonel Thomas Biddle

The Regiment was organized 26 April at Camp Curtin and was mustered in by Captain Simmons the next day. Col. Oakford served as commandant of camp for a short time before departing with the Regiment on 9 May together with the 14th Regiment.

Mustered out at Carlisle, Pa. 8 August 1861.

16th Pennsylvania Volunteer Infantry   3 months

Colonel Thomas A. Ziegle, Lt. Colonel George J. Higgins

Company C arrived in camp 20 April 1861 and was mustered in for 3 years—the first Pennsylvania company to so volunteer. All companies had been mustered in by Captains Simmons and Hastings by 30 April. The Regiment was organized 3 May and departed camp that same day. Returned 23 and 24 July 1861, was mustered out 30 July, and departed for home.

25th Pennsylvania Volunteer Infantry   3 months

Colonel Henry L. Cake, Lt. Colonel John B. Selheimer

Only individual companies were in camp at any one time as the Regiment was organized and disbanded in Washington. Regiment was composed of unattached companies that remained after the formation of most of the other Pennsylvania Regiments. Among the companies that formed the Regiment were some of the First Defender Companies. Company F, the Lochiel Grays, was in Camp Curtin 2 May 1861. Company K, the Carbondale Guards, was also in camp about that time.

oth companies departed for Washington 16 May.

egiment returned to camp 25 July 1861 and was mustered out 1 August.

8th Pennsylvania Volunteer Infantry   3 years

1 men arrived at Camp Return 9 June 1865

9th Pennsylvania Volunteer Infantry   3 years

4 men arrived at Camp Return 9 June 1865

0th Pennsylvania Volunteer Infantry (1st Pennsylvania Reserves)   3 years

olonel R. Biddle Roberts, Lt. Colonel Henry M. McIntire

he Regiment was organized at Camp Wayne in West Chester, Pa. on 9 June 1861.
Moved to Camp Curtin on 20 July 1861 and departed the next day.

he Regiment finally returned to Harrisburg 6 June 1864, was mustered out 13 June
nd departed for home.

1st Pennsylvania Volunteer Infantry (2nd Pennsylvania Reserves)   3 years

olonel William B. Mann, Lt. Colonel Albert L. Magilton

The Regiment was raised in Philadelphia, moved to Camp Washington, Easton, Pa.
n 21 June 1861 and was organized there 29 June. Arrived at Harrisburg 21 July and
ncamped near the Roundhouse of the Pennsylvania Railroad in the city. The Regi-
nent moved to Washington the next day.

The Regiment finally returned 8 June 1864, was mustered out 16 June, and departed
or home.

2nd Pennsylvania Volunteer Infantry (3rd Pennsylvania Reserves)   3 years

olonel Horatio G. Sickle, Lt. Colonel William S. Thompson

The Regiment was organized at Camp Washington, Easton, Pa. on 21 June 1861. Ar-
ived at Camp Curtin 22 July and departed the next day.

Mustered out 17 June 1864 at Pittsburgh.

3rd Pennsylvania Volunteer Infantry (4th Pennsylvania Reserves)   3 years

olonel Robert G. March, Lt. Colonel John F. Gaul

The Regiment was organized at Camp Washington in Easton, Pa. 21 June 1861. Ar-
ived at Camp Curtin 16 July and was mustered in the next day. Departed for
Washington, via Baltimore, on the 18th.

250 men, all that remained of the Regiment, finally returned 8 June 1864 (Company
E arrived on 6 June), and were mustered out 17 June.

34th Pennsylvania Volunteer Infantry (5th Pennsylvania Reserves)   3 years

Colonel Seneca G. Simmons, Lt. Colonel Joseph W. Fisher

Company F arrived in camp 6 May 1861, Company A arrived 10 May, Company H arrived 5 June, and Company E arrived in camp 7 June. The Regiment was organized 20 June and departed camp the next day in company with the 13th Reserves and Battery A 1st Pennsylvania Artillery for Cumberland, Maryland and the relief of Federal troops in that area. Returned to Harrisburg from the Cumberland Expedition 31 July 1861 and encamped in a field just outside Camp Curtin. Departed 9 August 1861.

Returned to Harrisburg June, 1864, and was mustered out 13 June.

35th Pennsylvania Volunteer Infantry (6th Pennsylvania Reserves)   3 years

Colonel W. W. Ricketts, Lt. Colonel William Penrose

Company C, the Honesdale Guards, 70 men, arrived in camp 20 April 1861. Company H arrived 30 April; Companies F and I arrived on 2 May and would not be accepted for 3 months service, so they enlisted for 3 years. Company D arrived 6 May; Company A arrived 8 May; Company B arrived in Harrisburg by canal boat 14 May and entered camp 16 May. The Regiment was organized 22 June from companies remaining in camp after the departure of the 5th and 13th Reserves and the 1st Artillery for Cumberland, Md. Departed 12 July 1861.

Returned to Harrisburg June, 1864, and was mustered out 11 June.

36th Pennsylvania Volunteer Infantry (7th Pennsylvania Reserves)   3 years

Colonel Elisha B. Harvey, Lt. Colonel Joseph Totten

The Regiment was organized 26 June 1861 in Camp Wayne, West Chester, Pa. Company H, from Cumberland County, was in Camp Curtin as early as 4 May and remained until 5 June, when it moved to West Chester to join the rest of the Regiment. Company I was also in Camp Curtin, arriving 10 May 1861. The entire Regiment moved to Harrisburg 21 July 1861 and departed 23 July.

Returned to Harrisburg June, 1864, and was mustered out 16 June.

37th Pennsylvania Volunteer Infantry (8th Pennsylvania Reserves)   3 years

Colonel (Dr.) George S. Hays, Lt. Colonel S. Duncan Oliphant

The Regiment was organized 28 June 1861 at Camp Wilkins, near Pittsburgh. Arrived at Harrisburg 21 July and departed later that same day.

The Regiment finally returned 21 May 1864, directly from the battle of Spotsylvania Court House. Mustered out 24 May and departed for home.

38th Pennsylvania Volunteer Infantry (9th Pennsylvania Reserves)   3 years

Colonel Conrad F. Jackson, Lt. Colonel Robert Anderson

The Regiment was organized 28 June 1861 at Camp Wilkins, near Pittsburgh. Arrived at Harrisburg 24 July and encamped in the vicinity of the "Seventh Street road" (Bates , p. 784).

Mustered in 28 July and departed 5 August.

Returned to Harrisburg May, 1864, and was mustered out 12 May.

39th Pennsylvania Volunteer Infantry (10th Pennsylvania Reserves)   3 years
Colonel John S. McCalmont, Lt. Colonel James T. Kirk

The Regiment was organized 29 June 1861 at Camp Wright, up the Allegheny River from Pittsburgh. Mustered in at Camp Curtin 21 July and departed for Washington, via Baltimore, the next day.

Returned to Harrisburg June, 1864, and was mustered out 11 June.

40th Pennsylvania Volunteer Infantry (11th Pennsylvania Reserves)   3 years
Colonel Thomas F. Gallagher, Lt. Colonel James R. Porter

The Regiment was organized at Camp Wright near Pittsburgh 1 July 1861. Arrived at Camp Curtin 24 July and departed camp later that same day.

Returned to Harrisburg June, 1864, and was mustered out 13 June.

41st Pennsylvania Volunteer Infantry (12th Pennsylvania Reserves)   3 years
Colonel John H. Taggart, Lt. Colonel Samuel N. Bailey

Company A, the Wayne Guards, of Philadelphia, arrived 7 June 1861. Company D arrived 10 June; Company K arrived 13 June; Company F arrived 21 July. Many companies arrived in May or June, but would not be accepted for three months service. They stayed in camp and were mustered in for three years individually. The Regiment was organized 25 June but remained in camp until 10 August.

Returned to Harrisburg June, 1864, and was mustered out 11 June.

42nd Pennsylvania Volunteer Infantry (13th Pennsylvania Reserves)
1st Pennsylvania Rifles, Pennsylvania Bucktails   3 years
Colonel Charles J. Biddle, Lt. Colonel Thomas L. Kane

Companies A and E arrived in camp 30 April; Company I arrived 2 May 1861; Company F arrived 4 May; Company G arrived about 6 May and Company H arrived 16 May. The Regiment was organized 12 June and departed camp 21 June with the 5th Reserves and Battery A 1st Pennsylvania Artillery for Cumberland, Maryland, and the relief of Federal troops in that area.

Returned to Harrisburg 31 July 1861 and encamped with the 5th in a field just outside of Camp Curtin. The Regiment departed for Sandy Hook, Maryland, 8 August 1861.

Returned to Harrisburg June, 1864, and was mustered out 11 June.

43rd Pennsylvania Volunteers (1st Artillery)   3 year

Colonel Charles T. Campbell, Lt. Colonel H. T. Danforth

The Regiment was organized all through July and into August, 1861 at various point throughout the commonwealth. Battery H, Brady's Artillery, arrived at Camp Curti 23 April. Most of the Regiment arrived at camp 24 May 1861, when they were to b mustered into service for 3 years. About half of the Regiment balked at being mustere for 3 years, and departed for Pittsburgh a few days later. Battery D arrived 23 Jun in camp and Battery B arrived 24 July. Battery A left camp 21 June with the 5th an 13th Reserves for Cumberland, Maryland, and relief of Federal troops in that area The Battery returned to Harrisburg 2 July. Guns were drawn from Camp Curtin t the railroad depot 6 August preparatory to the Regiment's departure.

The Batteries were mustered out individually at various points. 160 men (probabl Battery B) were mustered out at Camp Curtin 1 June 1865. Battery M at Camp Curti 9 June 1865; Battery F at Camp Curtin 5-10 June; 49 men of Battery C paid and dis banded 24 June 1865, 63 men and 2 officers of Battery C and 49 men and 2 officer of Battery D arrived at Camp Return 27 June; Battery A at Camp Curtin 25 July

44th Pennsylvania Volunteers (1st Cavalry)   3 year

Colonel George D. Bayard, Lt. Colonel Jacob Higgins

Companies A, K, and I were organized at Camp Wilkins near Pittsburgh and late moved to Camp Curtin. Company B arrived in camp in the very last days of July 1861. Five unorganized companies moved to Washington at the end of July. Othe Companies, meanwhile, continued to rendezvous at Camp Curtin. Company L wa mustered in at Reading 30 July and arrived at Camp Curtin 3 August; Company C arrived 8 August; Company D arrived 9 August; Company F arrived 17 August; Com pany G arrived 21 August. Command of the Regiment was offered to Captain Danie Hastings, U.S.A., but was declined. The companies at Camp Curtin moved t Washington and there the Regiment was organized mid-September.

Consolidated with the 6th and 17th Pennsylvania Cavalry to form 2nd Pennsylvani Provisional Cavalry in June, 1865. Mustered out 7 August 1865.

45th Pennsylvania Volunteer Infantry   3 year

Colonel Thomas Welsh, Lt. Colonel James A. Beaver

Companies arrived in camp between 3 September 1861 and 1 October. The Regimen was organized 21 October and departed camp in the very early hours of the 22nd

After reenlisting, elements of Regiment returned enroute home on furlough. Rendez voused once more at camp before returning to the field 19 March 1864.

34 men arrived at Camp Return 13 June 1865. Bulk of Regiment mustered out 1 July 1865 at Alexandria, Virginia. 550 men and 38 officers arrived at Camp Retur 18 July 1865 and were paid off and disbanded there 22 July.

46th Pennsylvania Volunteer Infantry   3 years

Colonel Joseph F. Knipe, Lt. Colonel James L. Selfridge

Companies arrived in camp through August, 1861. The Regiment was organized 1 September and departed camp 16 September.

37 men arrived at Camp Return 9 June 1865. Bulk of Regiment mustered out 16 July 1865 in Alexandria Virginia and 502 men and 25 officers arrived at Camp Return 18 July 1865 and were paid off and disbanded there 22 July.

47th Pennsylvania Volunteer Infantry   3 years

Colonel Tilghman H. Good, Lt. Colonel George Washington Alexander

Companies arrived in camp all through August and into September, 1861. The Regiment was organized September and departed camp 20 September.

Mustered out 9 January 1865 in Philadelphia.

48th Pennsylvania Volunteer Infantry   3 years

Colonel James Nagle, Lt. Colonel Joshua K. Siegfried

Companies arrived in camp early in September, 1861. The Regiment was organized in camp and departed camp 24 September. After reenlisting, elements of Regiment returned enroute home on furlough and rendezvoused once more at camp before returning to the field 15 March 1864.

The Regiment was mustered out 15 July 1865 at Alexandria, Virginia and finally returned to Camp Return 17 July 1865. 647 men and 37 officers were paid off and disbanded at camp 19 July.

49th Pennsylvania Volunteer Infantry   3 years

Colonel William H. Irwin, Lt. Colonel William Brisbane

Companies began arriving in camp before 6 September 1861. The Regiment was organized in camp and departed 21 September.

The 439 men and 25 officers that remained of the Regiment finally returned 15 July 1865 and were paid and disbanded 21 July.

50th Pennsylvania Volunteer Infantry   3 years

Colonel Benjamin C. Christ, Lt. Colonel Thomas S. Brenholtz

Companies began arriving in camp about 20 September 1861. The Regiment was organized 28 September and departed camp 1 October.

Elements of the Regiment were in camp 1 October 1863, probably enroute home on furlough or recruiting duty. Elements again in camp 20 March 1864.

131 men and 1 officer arrived at Camp Return 3 June 1865 and were paid 7 June. Bulk of Regiment mustered out 31 July 1865 at Georgetown, D.C. and returned to Camp Return the same day. 600 men and 33 officers paid off and disbanded at camp 1 August.

51st Pennsylvania Volunteer Infantry   3 years

Colonel John C. Hartranft, Lt. Colonel Thomas Bell

Companies arrived in camp as early as 10 September 1861. The Regiment was organ
ized 16 November and departed camp that same day.

After reenlisting, elements of Regiment returned 9 February 1864 enroute home on
furlough and rendezvoused once more at camp before returning to the field 20 March.

186 men and 1 officer arrived at Camp Return 3 June 1865 and were paid off and
disbanded that day. 688 men and 37 officers arrived at Camp Return 29 July and were
paid off and disbanded there 2 August.

52nd Pennsylvania Volunteer Infantry   3 years

Colonel John C. Dodge, Lt. Colonel Henry M. Hoyt

All 10 companies arrived in camp 1 October 1861. The Regiment was organized 7
October and departed camp the night of 7-8 November.

110 men and 1 officer arrived at Camp Return 1 July 1865 and were mustered out
12 July.

568 men and 19 officers paid off and disbanded at camp 22 July.

53rd Pennsylvania Volunteer Infantry   3 years

Colonel John R. Brooke, Lt. Colonel Richard McMichael

Companies arrived in camp in early September, 1861. The Regiment was organized
28 September and departed camp 7 November. The Regiment served as Provost Guard
for Harrisburg while in camp.

180 men returned to camp 30 December 1863 enroute home on furlough. Colonel
Brooke temporarily served as commandant of Camp Curtin during this time.

90 men and 1 officer arrived at Camp Return 2 July 1865 and were paid 7 July. 562
men and 27 officers were paid off and disbanded 8 July.

54th Pennsylvania Volunteer Infantry   3 years

Colonel Jacob Campbell, Lt. Colonel Barnabas McDermit

Companies arrived in camp all through late August and into September, 1861. The
Regiment was organized in camp in September, but was detained in camp until 28
February 1862.

A new company was formed in camp in October, 1862, and departed on the 9th of
that month to join the Regiment in the field.

The Regiment finally returned 10 July 1865, was mustered out 15 July and departed
for home.

55th Pennsylvania Volunteer Infantry   3 years

Colonel Richard White, Lt. Colonel Frank T. Bennett

Companies began arriving in Harrisburg in early November, 1861, and by the 11th of that month, most of the companies had been formed. Companies B, E, and G were formed in Camp Cameron. The Regiment was organized in camp and departed 20 November.

After reenlisting, elements of the Regiment returned 26 January 1864 enroute home on furlough and rendezvoused once more at camp before returning to the field 13 March. Mustered out 30 August 1865 at Petersburg, Va. and finally returned to camp 31 August.

56th Pennsylvania Volunteer Infantry   3 years

Colonel Sullivan A. Meredith, Lt. Colonel J. William Hoffman

Companies arrived in camp through the autumn of 1861. Eight companies were organized 7 March 1862 and departed camp the next day.

69 men and 1 officer arrived at Camp Return 1 June 1865 and were paid off and disbanded 3 June. Bulk of Regiment mustered out at Philadelphia 1 July.

57th Pennsylvania Volunteer Infantry   3 years

Colonel William Maxwell, Lt. Colonel Elhannan W. Woods

Companies arrived in camp from September to December, 1861. The long stay in camp might have been due in part to the widespread illness within the Regiment. The Regiment was organized 14 December and departed camp that same day.

After reenlisting, elements of the Regiment returned enroute home on furlough and rendezvoused once more at camp before returning to the field 21 February 1864.

169 men and 1 officer arrived at Camp Return 3 June 1865. 555 men and 34 officers arrived at Camp Return 2 July and were paid off and disbanded there 6 July.

58th Pennsylvania Volunteer Infantry   3 years

Colonel J. Richter Jones, Lt. Colonel Carlton B. Curtis

Companies E, F, G, H, and I rendezvoused at camp around 20 September 1861. These companies were originally intended to form part of the 114th Pennsylvania Volunteers, but organizational problems prevented that Regiment from ever forming, and the 5 companies departed camp 9 March 1862 and merged with companies from Philadelphia to form the 58th.

Mustered out 24 January 1866 at City Point, Va.

59th Pennsylvania Volunteers (2nd Pennsylvania Cavalry)   3 years

Colonel Joseph P. Brinton, Lt. Colonel Charles F. Taggart

Some companies arrived in camp in early September, 1861, until 8 companies were present on 11 September. Other companies rendezvoused at Camp Patterson near Philadelphia. The Regiment could not be filled and organized and remained in camp until April, 1862, when it moved to Baltimore and merged with companies from Philadelphia.

61st Pennsylvania Volunteer Infantry   3 years

Colonel Oliver H. Rippey, Lt. Colonel George C. Spear

Regiment was organized in Pittsburgh August, 1861, and moved en mass to Camp Curtin 2 September, where the men were uniformed. The Regiment departed the next day.

Mustered out 28 July 1865 at Washington.

62nd Pennsylvania Volunteer Infantry   3 years

Colonel Samuel W. Black, Lt. Colonel T. Frederick Lehman

Organized in Pittsburgh and moved en mass to Camp Cameron in Harrisburg 24 July 1861, and remained there until at least 13 August.

250 survivors of the Regiment returned 4 July 1864 and were mustered out 13 July.

64th Pennsylvania Volunteers (4th Cavalry)   3 years

Colonel David Campbell, Lt. Colonel James H. Childs

Companies gathered in Harrisburg, Philadelphia and Pittsburgh from August through October, 1861. The Regiment rendezvoused at Camp Curtin in October, where it was organized and mustered into service.

After reenlisting, elements of the Regiment returned enroute home on furlough and rendezvoused once more at camp before returning to the field 30 March 1864.

Mustered out 1 July 1865 at Lynchburg, Va.

67th Pennsylvania Volunteer Infantry   3 years

110 men arrived at Camp Return under Captain J. Hoganback enroute home 23 June 1865.

68th Pennsylvania Volunteer Infantry   3 years

Elements in camp 14 January 1862.

73rd Pennsylvania Volunteer Infantry   3 years

14 men arrived at Camp Return 9 June 1865

74th Pennsylvania Volunteer Infantry   3 years

Portion of the Regiment arrived 31 August 1865 after being mustered out 29 August in the field. 228 men and 11 officers arrived 11 September.

75th Pennsylvania Volunteer Infantry   3 years

The Regiment arrived late August, 1865. Mustered out 1 September but not paid until 13 September.

76th Pennsylvania Volunteer Infantry   3 years

Colonel John M. Power, Lt. Colonel D. H. Wallace

Companies arrived in Camp Cameron throughout early autumn, 1861. Regiment was organized 18 October but did not depart Camp Cameron until 17 November.

Six companies of the Regiment, 345 men and 17 officers, finally returned to Harrisburg 23 July 1865. Other companies followed on 25 July after surviving the wreck of the steamer *Quinnebaugh* off the South Carolina coast. 540 men and 24 officers paid off and disbanded 28 July.

78th Pennsylvania Volunteer Infantry   3 years

Regiment arrived 17 September 1865 after being mustered out 11 September.

79th Pennsylvania Volunteer Infantry   3 years

Colonel Henry A. Hambright, Lt. Colonel John H. Duchman

After reenlisting, elements of the Regiment arrived in Harrisburg from the western theatre 14 March 1864 enroute home on furlough. Departed for home, Lancaster, 16 March.

80th Pennsylvania Volunteers (7th Cavalry)   3 years

Colonel George C. Wynkoop, Lt. Colonel William B. Sipes

Companies arrived in Camp Cameron September through December, 1861. The Regiment departed Camp Cameron 19 December 1861.

After reenlisting, elements of the Regiment returned to Camp Curtin 26 January 1864 enroute home on furlough and rendezvoused once more at camp before returning to the field 3 March 1864. Company A was still in camp 21 March.

A remnant of the Regiment (100 men) finally returned 1 September 1865 after having been mustered out 13 August.

81st Pennsylvania Volunteer Infantry   3 years

Company I, under Lt. Sydney Hawk, in camp 24 March 1864, probably enroute from furlough.

83rd Pennsylvania Volunteer Infantry   3 years

Elements of the Regiment arrived at Camp Curtin 12 September, 1864 enroute home on furlough.

48 men arrived at Camp Return 1 June 1865. Remainder of the Regiment, 551 men

and 28 officers arrived at Camp Return 30 June 1865 after being mustered out at Washington 28 June.

Men paid and disbanded 3 July.

84th Pennsylvania Volunteer Infantry   3 years

Colonel William G. Murray, Lt. Colonel Thomas C. McDowell

Companies rendezvoused at Huntingdon and Harrisburg and arrived in Camp Curtin from August through October, 1861. Huntingdon companies were brought to Harrisburg 27 November and went into camp 28 November. The Regiment was organized 23 December and departed camp 31 December 1861.

Consolidated with 57th Pennsylvania Volunteers 13 January 1865 (see)

87th Pennsylvania Volunteer Infantry   3 years

533 men and 20 officers of the Regiment arrived 1 July 1865, after having been mustered out 29 June at Alexandria, Virginia, and were paid and disbanded 3 July.

89th Pennsylvania Volunteers (8th Cavalry)   3 years

Portion of Regiment departed Camp Return 20 August 1865.

92nd Pennsylvania Volunteers (9th Cavalry)   3 years

Colonel Edward C. Williams, Lt. Colonel Thomas C. James

Company G arrived in Camp Curtin 2 May 1861. Regiment formed in Camp Cameron October through November, 1861. The Regiment was organized around 18 November and departed Camp Cameron 20 November.

Elements of the Regiment (300 men) returned 25 April 1864 enroute home on furlough.

555 men and 33 officers arrived at Camp Return 23 July 1865 after having been mustered out 18 July at Lexington, Kentucky, and were paid off and disbanded 27 July.

93rd Pennsylvania Volunteer Infantry   3 years

After reenlisting 7 February 1864, elements of the Regiment arrived at Camp Curtin 9 February enroute home on furlough.

166 men and 3 officers arrived at Camp Return 22 June 1865. 575 men and 27 officers arrived at Camp Return 29 June and were paid off and disbanded there 1 July.

100th Pennsylvania Volunteer Infantry   3 years

25 men arrived at Camp Return 3 June 1865. 696 men and 35 officers were paid off and disbanded at Camp Return 28 July.

101st Pennsylvania Volunteer Infantry   3 years

Colonel Joseph H. Wilson, Lt. Colonel David B. Morris

Companies B, D, and K arrived in camp throughout the autumn of 1861. 7 other companies arrived from Camp Fremont in Pittsburgh about 1 November. The Regiment was organized 21 November but remained in camp until 27 February 1862.

995 men and 35 officers arrived at Camp Return 20 July 1865 and were paid off and disbanded the same day.

102nd Pennsylvania Volunteer Infantry   3 years

Colonel Thomas A. Rowley, Lt. Colonel Joseph M. Kinkead

Elements of the Regiment were in Harrisburg in early September, 1864. Mustered out at Washington 28 July 1865 and 720 men returned to Harrisburg 1 July 1865 enroute home.

103rd Pennsylvania Volunteer Infantry   3 years

Colonel Theodore F. Lehmann, Lt. Colonel Wilson C. Maxwell

Companies began forming in Camp Orr, Kittanning, Pennsylvania, on 7 September 1861. They arrived in Camp Curtin 16 February 1862 and remained in camp until 2 March 1862.

Mustered out 25 June 1865. 801 men and 30 officers arrived at Camp Return 9 July 1865. 946 men and 30 officers were paid off and disbanded there 14 July.

105th Pennsylvania Volunteer Infantry   3 years

250 men in Harrisburg 15 February 1864.

12 men arrived at Camp Return 2 June 1865.

106th Pennsylvania Volunteer Infantry   3 years

A remnant of the Regiment was in Harrisburg early September, 1864.

107th Pennsylvania Volunteer Infantry   3 years

Colonel Thomas A. Zeigle, Lt. Colonel Robert W. McAllen

The first companies arrived in Harrisburg 22 August 1861 and went into Camp Cameron that day. As other companies arrived, they were divided between Camps Cameron and Curtin until the entire regiment was brought together in Camp Curtin on 15 September 1861. The Regiment was organized 5 March 1862 and departed camp 9 March.

After reenlisting, elements of the Regiment returned 3 April 1864 on furlough and departed 5 April. 138 men and 1 officer arrived at Camp Return 9 June 1865. Bulk of regiment mustered out at Washington and Petersburg, Virginia 13 July 1865. 245 men and 21 officers were paid off and disbanded there 17 July.

108th Pennsylvania Volunteer Infantry   3 years

Elements in camp 14 January 1862.

110th Pennsylvania Volunteer Infantry   3 years

Colonel William D. Lewis, Jr., Lt. Colonel James Crowther

Companies formed in Huntingdon, Harrisburg and Philadelphia. Huntingdon companies rendezvoused with Harrisburg companies in Camp Curtin 1 December 1861 and that portion of the regiment, by far the larger portion, remained in camp until 2 January 1862.

66 men and 2 officers arrived at Camp Return 2 June and were paid off 7 June. 313 men and 17 officers arrived at camp 30 June 1865, after being mustered out at Washington 28 June, and were paid off and disbanded there 3 July.

111th Pennsylvania Volunteer Infantry   3 years

Colonel M. Schlaudecker, Lt. Colonel George A. Cobham, Jr.

The Regiment was organized in Erie 24 January 1862, arrived in Harrisburg 27 February, and went into camp that day. The Regiment departed camp 1 March.

32 men arrived at Camp Return 9 June 1865.

114th Pennsylvania Volunteer Infantry   3 years

Elements in camp 14 January 1862.

115th Pennsylvania Volunteer Infantry   3 years

Colonel Robert E. Patterson, Lt. Colonel Robert Thompson

Companies were organized in Harrisburg and Philadelphia 28 January 1862. The entire Regiment was brought together at Harrisburg 31 May 1862 and remained in Camp Curtin until 27 June with the men serving as guards over Confederate Prisoners.

72 men in camp 5 June 1865.

116th Pennsylvania Volunteer Infantry   3 years

162 men and 10 officers paid and disbanded at Camp Return 19 July 1865.

122nd Pennsylvania Volunteer Infantry   9 months

Colonel Emlen Franklin, Lt. Colonel Edward McGovern

The Regiment was organized 12 August 1862 in Lancaster, moved to Camp Curtin 14 August and departed the next day.

The Regiment returned to camp at the end of its term on 11 May 1863 and remained until 16 May, when the men were mustered out and began departing for home.

123rd Pennsylvania Volunteer Infantry   9 months

Colonel John B. Clark, Lt. Colonel Frederick Gast

The Regiment was organized at Allegheny City, near Pittsburgh, in August, 1862.

It arrived in Harrisburg on the morning of 21 August and departed that night after being armed at the Arsenal.

The Regiment returned to camp at the end of its term on 10 May 1863, was mustered out 13 May and departed for Pittsburgh en masse.

124th Pennsylvania Volunteer Infantry   9 months

Colonel Joseph W. Hawley, Lt. Colonel Simon Litzenberg

Companies began arriving at camp 8 August 1862. Preliminary organization effected mid-August, and Regiment departed 15 August. Organization was not completed until 17 August at Washington.

The Regiment returned to camp at the end of its term on 12 May 1863, was mustered out 16 May and departed 18 May.

125th Pennsylvania Volunteer Infantry   9 months

Colonel Jacob Higgins, Lt. Colonel Jacob Szink

Companies arrived in camp as early as 10 August 1862. Organization was effected 16 August and the Regiment departed camp that same day.

The Regiment returned to camp at the end of its term on 12 May 1863 and was mustered out 18 May.

126th Pennsylvania Volunteer Infantry   9 months

Colonel James G. Elder, Lt. Colonel D. Watson Rowe

Companies began arriving in camp 6 August 1862. The Regiment was organized 10 August and departed camp 15 August.

The Regiment returned to camp at the end of its term on 15 May 1863 and was mustered out 20 May.

127th Pennsylvania Volunteer Infantry   9 months

Colonel William W. Jennings, Lt. Colonel Henry C. Alleman

Company A, the First City Zouaves of Harrisburg, was in Camp Curtin 26 July 1862. Company B arrived 9 August. Other companies continued to arrive until the Regiment was organized 16 August. Prior to the organization, since many of the men in the regiment were from Harrisburg or the surrounding country, and virtually all of the volunteers were from Dauphin County, the men of the Regiment were not strictly confined to camp and many were given furloughs and allowed to sleep and eat at their homes until they were called. Nine companies departed camp 17 August while Company A remained. Soon after, Co. A moved from camp to the heights overlooking the Susquehanna from the west and established a bivouac there.

The Regiment returned to camp at the end of its term on 15 May 1863 and the furlough system was again put into effect. Company H was the last to be discharged, on 29 May.

128th Pennsylvania Volunteer Infantry   9 months

Colonel Samuel Croasdale, Lt. Colonel W. W. Hamersley

Companies arrived in camp throughout early August, 1862, until the Regiment was organized 15 August and departed 17 August.

The Regiment returned to camp at the end of its term on 14 May 1863 and was mustered out 19 May.

129th Pennsylvania Volunteer Infantry   9 months

Colonel Jacob G. Frick, Lt. Colonel William H. Armstrong

Companies arrived in camp throughout early August, 1862, the Regiment was organized 15 August and departed camp the next day.

The Regiment returned to camp at the end of its term on 13 May 1863 and was mustered out 18 May.

130th Pennsylvania Volunteer Infantry   9 months

Colonel Henry I. Zinn, Lt. Colonel Levy Maish

Companies arrived in camp as early as 10 August 1862. The Regiment was organized 17 August and departed camp on the 18th.

The Regiment returned to camp at the end of its term on 12 May 1863, was mustered out 21 May, and departed for home 22 May.

131st Pennsylvania Volunteer Infantry   9 months

Colonel Peter Allabach, Lt. Colonel William B. Shaut

Companies began arriving in camp late in July, 1862. The Regiment was organized 6 August and departed camp 18 August.

Returned to camp at the end of its term on 16 May 1863 and was mustered out 23 May.

132nd Pennsylvania Volunteer Infantry   9 months

Colonel Richard A. Oakford, Lt. Colonel Vincent M. Wilcox

Companies began arriving in camp at least as early as 11 August, 1862. The Regiment was organized 15 August and departed camp 19 August.

Returned to camp at the end of its term on 16 May 1863, was mustered out 24 May and departed for home that same day.

133rd Pennsylvania Volunteer Infantry   9 months

Colonel Franklin B. Speakman, Lt. Colonel Abraham Kopelin

Companies arrived in camp on the 1st through the 10th of August, 1862 and were organized as they arrived. The Regiment departed camp 19 August.

Returned to camp at the end of its term on 19 May 1863, was mustered out 19-28 May and departed for home.

134th Pennsylvania Volunteer Infantry 9 months

Colonel Matthew S. Quay, Lt. Colonel Edward O'Brien

Companies arrived in camp throughout August, 1862. After being organized, Regiment departed camp 20 August.

Returned to camp at the end of its term on 18 May 1863, was mustered out 26 May and departed for home 28 May.

135th Pennsylvania Volunteer Infantry 9 months

Colonel James R. Porter, Lt. Colonel David L. McCullough

Companies arrived in camp throughout August, 1862. Regiment was organized 19 August, and departed that same day.

Returned to camp at the end of its term and was mustered out on 24 May 1863.

136th Pennsylvania Volunteer Infantry 9 months

Colonel Thomas M. Bayne, Lt. Colonel Isaac Wright

Companies arrived in camp throughout August, 1862. Regiment was organized 20 August, and departed 29 August.

Returned to camp at the end of its term on 21 May 1863 and was mustered out on 29 May.

137th Pennsylvania Volunteer Infantry 9 months

Colonel Henry M. Bassert, Lt. Colonel Joseph B. Kiddoo

Companies arrived in camp throughout early August, 1862. Regiment was organized 25 August, and departed soon after.

Returned to camp at the end of its term on 27 May 1863, was mustered out on 1 June, and the last company departed for home on 3 June.

138th Pennsylvania Volunteer Infantry 3 years

Colonel Charles L. K. Sumwalt, Lt. Colonel M. R. McClennan

Companies arrived in camp 16-26 August 1862 and were organized as they arrived. The Regiment departed 30 August.

514 men and 26 officers arrived at Camp Return 26 June 1865 and were paid and disbanded 30 June.

140th Pennsylvania Volunteer Infantry 3 years

Colonel Richard P. Roberts, Lt. Colonel John Fraser

Companies arrived at camp from Pittsburgh in the first week in September, 1862. The Regiment was organized and mustered in 8 September and departed camp 10 September. 232 men and 23 officers arrived at Camp Return 2 June 1865 and were paid and disbanded at Pittsburgh 3 June.

141st Pennsylvania Volunteer Infantry   3 years

Colonel Henry J. Madhill, Lt. Colonel Guy H. Watkins

Companies B, C, D, E, and I arrived on 19 August. Companies F and H came in on the 23rd, Company G on the 24th, and Company K on the 26th. Companies were organized into the 141st Regiment 28 August, although Company A did not arrive until 15 September. Regiment departed camp soon after.

245 men and 22 officers arrived at Camp Return 31 May 1865 and were paid and disbanded 3 June.

142nd Pennsylvania Volunteer Infantry   3 years

Colonel Robert P. Cummins, Lt. Colonel Alfred B. McCalmont

Companies arrived in camp in late August, 1862. The Regiment was organized 1 September 1862 and departed camp that same day.

Mustered out 29 May 1865 at Washington and 288 men arrived at Camp Return 1 June 1865 and were paid and disbanded 3 June.

143rd Pennsylvania Volunteer Infantry   3 years

Colonel Edmund L. Dana, Lt. Colonel George E. Hoyt

Companies organized 18 October 1862 in Wilkes-Barre. Arrived in Camp Curtin 7 November 1862 and departed 8 November.

552 men and 33 officers arrived at Camp Return 17 June 1865 and were paid and disbanded 20 June.

145th Pennsylvania Volunteer Infantry   3 years

185 men and 8 officers arrived at Camp Return 2 June 1865 and were paid and disbanded 3 June at Pittsburgh.

147th Pennsylvania Volunteer Infantry   3 years

Colonel Ario Pardee, Jr., Lt. Colonel John Craig

Companies F, G, and H enlisted in Harrisburg and went into camp in early September, 1862. The Regiment was organized 10 October on Loudon Heights, Va. The three companies in Harrisburg having left camp prior to that time.

188 men arrived at Camp Return 9 June 1865.

148th Pennsylvania Volunteer Infantry   3 years

Colonel James A. Beaver, Lt. Colonel Robert McFarlane

Companies arrived in camp 14-27 August 1862. Col. Beaver arrived from the field, where he had been serving as lt. col. of the 45th PVI, on 6 September and took command. The Regiment was organized 8 September and departed camp that same day.

228 men and 31 officers arrived at Camp Return 4 June 1865 and were paid and disbanded 7 June.

149th Pennsylvania Volunteer Infantry   3 years

Colonel Roy Stone, Lt. Colonel Walton Dwight

Company D arrived in Camp Curtin from Pittsburgh 23 August 1862, although most companies had arrived in camp prior to that date. Departed camp 30 August.

Mustered out 24 June. 523 men and 33 officers arrived at Camp Return 26 June 1865 and were paid and disbanded 30 June.

150th Pennsylvania Volunteer Infantry   3 years

Colonel Langhorne Wister, Lt. Colonel Henry S. Huidekoper

Companies A and B arrived in camp 1 September 1862. After all companies had arrived, the Regiment was organized 4 September and departed camp the next day.

Company K served as the Presidential Guard at the Soldiers' Retreat in Washington, and 84 men and 3 officers of the company arrived at Camp Return 15 June and were paid and disbanded 17 June. 238 men and 17 officers of the Regiment arrived at Camp Return 26 June 1865 and were paid and disbanded 28 June.

151st Pennsylvania Volunteer Infantry   9 months

Colonel Harrison Allen, Lt. Colonel George F. McFarland

Companies began arriving in Camp Simmons in September, 1862. The Regiment was organized in Camp Curtin 18 October-24 November 1862 and departed camp 26 November.

Returned to camp upon the expiration of its term 21 July 1863 and was mustered out 27 July.

153rd Pennsylvania Volunteer Infantry   9 months

Colonel Charles Glanz, Lt. Colonel Jacob Dachrodt

Companies arrived in Camp Curtin 6 October 1862 from Easton, where the Regiment had been organized. Departed camp 12 October.

813 men of the Regiment returned to camp 16 July 1863 upon the expiration of their term, were mustered out 24 July and departed for home 25 July.

155th Pennsylvania Volunteer Infantry   3 years

Colonel Edward J. Allen, Lt. Colonel James Collard

Companies arrived in Camp Curtin from Pittsburgh 3 September 1862. The Regiment was armed and equipped and rushed forward to Washington the next day.

Mustered out at Washington 2 June 1865. 350 men arrived at Camp Return 3 June.

161st Pennsylvania Volunteers (16th Cavalry)   3 years

Colonel John Irvin Gregg, Lt. Colonel Lorenzo D. Rogers

Companies began arriving in Camp Simmons October, 1862. Moved from Camp Simmons to Camp McClellan early in November. The Regiment was organized 18 November, was mounted and equipped 23 November, and departed 30 November.

Mustered out 7 August 1865 in Richmond. 1,108 men and 47 officers arrived at Camp Return 15 August, 1865 and were paid and disbanded 20 August.

162nd Pennsylvania Volunteers (17th Cavalry)   3 years

Colonel Josiah H. Kellogg, Lt. Colonel John B. McAllister

Companies arrived in Camp Simmons in October, 1862. The Regiment was organized 18 October, moved from Camp Simmons and founded Camp McClellan 10 November and departed that camp 25 November.

Consolidated with 1st and 6th Pennsylvania Cavalry to form 2nd Pennsylvania Provisional Cavalry 17 June 1865.

163rd Pennsylvania Volunteers (18th Cavalry)   3 years

Colonel Timothy M. Bryan, Jr., Lt. Colonel James Gowan

Companies B, C, D, E, I and K were all in Camp Simmons in early November, 1862. Other companies formed in Pittsburgh. The companies in Harrisburg moved from Camp Simmons to Camp McClellan 13 November and remained there until 8 December when they departed.

Mustered out 31 October 1865 at Clarksburg, West Virginia.

166th Pennsylvania Infantry (Drafted Militia)   9 months

Colonel Andrew J. Fulton, Lt. Colonel George W. Reisinger

The Regiment was organized in Camp Franklin, York, Pennsylvania.

Arrived in camp 21 July 1863 at the expiration of its term and was mustered out 28 July.

167th Pennsylvania Infantry (Drafted Militia)   9 months

Colonel Charles A. Knoderer, Lt. Colonel Joseph De Puy Davis

The Regiment arrived in Harrisburg upon the expiration of its term 8 August 1863 enroute home. It departed for Reading 10 August, where it was mustered out 12 August.

168th Pennsylvania Infantry (Drafted Militia)   9 months

Colonel Joseph Jack, Lt. Colonel John Murphy

The Regiment was organized at Camp Howe, Pittsburgh.

Upon expiration of its term, the Regiment arrived in Harrisburg 21 July 1863 and was mustered out 25 July.

169th Pennsylvania Infantry (Drafted Militia)   9 months

Colonel Lewis W. Smith, Lt. Colonel Samuel M. Wickersham

The Regiment was organized at Camp Howe in Pittsburgh. Arrived at Harrisburg upon the expiration of its term and was mustered out 27 July 1863.

171st Pennsylvania Infantry (Drafted Militia)   9 months

Colonel Everard Bierer, Lt. Colonel Theophilus Humphrey

Companies arrived in camp in late October, 1862, and the Regiment was organized late November. Departed camp 27 November.

Upon the expiration of its term, returned to Harrisburg 4 August 1863 and was mustered out 6 through 8 August.

172nd Pennsylvania Infantry (Drafted Militia)   9 months

Colonel Charles Kleckner, Lt. Colonel Thadeus G. Bogle

Companies began arriving in camp 27 Ocober 1862. The Regiment was organized 29 November and departed camp 2 December.

Upon the expiration of its term, the Regiment returned to Harrisburg 28 July 1863, was mustered out 1 August, and departed for home 4 August.

173rd Pennsylvania Infantry (Drafted Militia)   9 months

Colonel Daniel Nagle, Lt. Colonel Zaccur P. Boyer

Companies began arriving in camp in late November, 1862. The Regiment was organized 27 November and departed camp 30 November.

Upon the expiration of its term, the Regiment returned to Harrisburg 14-15 August 1863 and was mustered out 18 August.

176th Pennsylvania Infantry (Drafted Militia)   9 months

Colonel Ambrose A. Lechler, Lt. Colonel George Pilkington

The Regiment was organized at Philadelphia.

Upon the expiration of its term, the Regiment arrived in Harrisburg 15 August 1863 and was mustered out on the 19th and departed for Philadelphia that day.

177th Pennsylvania Infantry (Drafted Militia)   9 months

Colonel George B. Wiestling, Lt Colonel Hugh J. Brady

Companies began arriving in camp October, 1862. The Regiment was organized 20 November and departed 3 December.

Upon the expiration of its term, the Regiment returned to Harrisburg 2 August 1863 and departed 7 August.

178th Pennsylvania Infantry (Drafted Militia) 9 months

Colonel James Johnson, Lt. Colonel John Wimer

Companies began arriving in camp 20-25 October 1862. The Regiment was organized as the companies arrived through 27 November and departed camp 5 December.

Upon the expiration of its term, the Regiment returned to Harrisburg 21 July 1863 was mustered out 27 July and departed that same day.

179th Pennsylvania Infantry (Drafted Militia) 9 months

Colonel William H. Blair, Lt. Colonel Daniel M. Yost

The Regiment was organized at Philadelphia.

Upon the expiration of its term, the Regiment arrived at Harrisburg 8 July 1863, was mustered out 27 July and departed that same day.

181st Pennsylvania Volunteers (20th Cavalry) 6 months/3 years

Colonel John E. Wynkoop, Lt. Colonel William Rotch

Companies arrived in camp throughout June and July, 1863. The Regiment was organized in Camp Couch on the west bank of the Susquehanna in early July for 6 months service, and departed that camp 7 July.

Upon expiration of its term, the Regiment returned to Harrisburg 26 December 1863 was mustered out, and departed 8 January 1864. Some of the companies did not disband, however, and returned to Harrisburg to be reorganized and remustered for three years of the war. Reorganization began in February, 1864, in both Philadelphia and on the west bank at Harrisburg. The Harrisburg companies picketed roads and fords in the area during reorganization and departed 22 February 1864.

182nd Pennsylvania Volunteers (21st Cavalry) 6 months

Colonel William H. Boyd, Lt. Colonel Richard F. Moson

Companies arrived in Camp Couch on the west bank of the Susquehanna 28 June 1863. The Regiment was mounted and equipped at Camp Couch before being hastened to Chambersburg, where organization was completed.

Portion of the Regiment passed through to Harrisburg 23 August 1863.

Upon expiration of its term, Regiment was mustered out 24 February 1864. Some of the companies desired to reenlist, and were reorganized and remustered around 25 February 1864 at Chambersburg.

1,073 men and 31 officers paid and disbanded at Camp Return 18 July 1865.

184th Pennsylvania Volunteer Infantry 3 years

Major Charles Kleckner

7 companies only arrived in camp before 12 April 1864 under command of Major Kleckner.

Organized early in May and remained in camp until 14 May.
217 men and 8 officers arrived at Camp Return 5 June 1865 and were paid and disbanded 18 July.

185th Pennsylvania Volunteers (22nd Cavalry)   6 months/3 years

Colonel Jacob Higgins, Lt. Colonel Andrew J. Greenfield, Major Mortimer Morrow

The Battalion, commanded by Major Morrow, was organized in Harrisburg June, 1863, and picketed roads and fords until after Gettysburg when it joined in the pursuit of the retreating Confederate army. The Battalion was mustered out upon the expiration of its term 5 February 1864. Companies were reorganized under Col. Higgins in Chambersburg for 3 years service 22 February 1864. Company A was in Camp Couch in May, 1864.

187th Pennsylvania Volunteer Infantry   3 years

Colonel John E. Parsons, Lt. Colonel Joseph F. Ramsey

Companies A-F arrived in camp throughout February, 1864. Other companies rendezvoused in Philadelphia. The Regiment was organized 3-4 March and the companies dispersed to areas all around the commonwealth to serve as provost guards. Companies C and E, which had been originally part of a battalion organized and led by Lt. Col. Ramsey during Emergency of 1863, remained in camp as part of Harrisburg provost guard.

The companies reassembled at Camp Curtin 18 May 1864 and departed 19 May.
723 men and 31 officers arrived at Camp Return late July, 1865 and were paid and disbanded 5 August.

190th Pennsylvania Volunteer Infantry   3 years

55 men and 1 officer arrived at Camp Return 5 June 1865 and were paid and disbanded 7 June.
547 men and 20 officers arrived at Camp Return 1 July 1865 and were paid and disbanded 3 July.

191st Pennsylvania Volunteer Infantry   3 years

45 men and 1 officer arrived at Camp Return 5 June 1865. 631 men and 24 officers arrived at Camp Return 30 June 1865 and were paid and disbanded 3 July.

192nd Pennsylvania Volunteer Infantry   100 days/1 year

Colonel William B. Thomas, Lt. Colonel Benjamin L. Taylor

Nucleus of the Regiment was the disbanded 20th Pennsylvania Militia of 1862. Companies for the 192nd arrived in camp throughout July, 1864, and departed camp on the 24th of that month. Upon expiration of its term, Regiment returned in early

November, 1864, and was mustered out on the 11th.

Reorganized February, 1865, for 1 year.

768 men and 35 officers arrived at Camp Return late August, 1865, and were paid and disbanded 29 August.

194th Pennsylvania Volunteer Infantry   100 days

Colonel James Nagle, Lt. Colonel Richard McMichael

Both Captain John Bell's company from Harrisburg and part of Company E, the Curtin Fencibles, arrived in camp 15 July 1864. Company D and the rest of Company E arrived on the 19th and Company G on the 20th. The Regiment was organized 22 July 1864 and departed camp that same day.

Returned 3 November 1864, was mustered out 6 November and departed that same day

195th Pennsylvania Volunteer Infantry   100 days/1 year

Colonel Joseph Fisher, Lt. Colonel William L. Bear

The Regiment was organized at Camp Curtin 24 July 1864 and departed the same day. Upon the expiration of its term, the Regiment returned to camp and was mustered out 4 November 1864. In February, 1865, Colonel Fisher received permission to recruit new companies to fill and reactivate the Regiment for 1 year. Portions of what had been Company H reenlisted and arrived at Camp Curtin 7 February 1865. The Regiment was reorganized 16 March 1865 in Martinsburg, West Virginia.

Mustered out 31 January 1866.

200th Pennsylvania Volunteer Infantry   1 year

Colonel Charles W. Diven, Lt. Colonel William H. H. McCall

Company K arrived in camp 29 August, 1864. Regiment was organized 3 September and departed camp 9 September.

The Regiment was mustered out in the field 30 May 1865. 850 men and 35 officers arrived at Camp Return 31 May 1865, and were paid off and disbanded 3 June.

201st Pennsylvania Volunteer Infantry   1 year

Colonel F. Asbury Awl, Lt. Colonel J. Wesley Awl

Companies E and F arrived in camp 29 August 1864. The Regiment was organized 29 August and departed camp the next day (Company H remained in Harrisburg until 28 October).

Two companies returned to Harrisburg 21 April 1865 to serve in Lincoln's funeral procession. Remainder of Regiment, 775 men and 31 officers arrived at Camp Return 19 June 1865, and were paid off and disbanded 24 June.

202nd Pennsylvania Volunteer Infantry   1 year

Colonel Charles Albright, Lt. Colonel John A. Maus

Companies arrived in camp throughout August, 1864. The Regiment was organized 3 September and departed camp 9 September for Camp Couch, Chambersburg. The Regiment returned to Harrisburg 31 July 1865, was mustered out 3 August, and 1,002 men and 39 officers were paid off and disbanded 7 August.

205th Pennsylvania Volunteer Infantry   1 year

Colonel Joseph A. Mathews, Lt. Colonel William F. Walter

Companies arrived in camp throughout August, 1864. The Regiment was organized 2 September and departed camp the next day.

821 men and 24 officers arrived at Camp Return 3 June 1865, and were paid off and disbanded 7 June.

207th Pennsylvania Volunteer Infantry   1 year

Colonel Robert C. Cox, Lt. Colonel W. W. S. Snoddy

Companies arrived in camp throughout July and August, 1864. The Regiment was organized 8 September and departed camp 12 September.

869 men and 35 officers arrived at Camp Return 1 June 1865, and were paid off and disbanded 5 June.

208th Pennsylvania Volunteer Infantry   1 year

Colonel Alfred B. McCalmont, Lt. Colonel M. T. Heintzelman

Companies arrived in camp early in September, 1864. The Regiment was organized 12 September and departed camp 13 September.

773 men and 36 officers arrived at Camp Return 2 June 1865, and were paid off and disbanded 6 June.

209th Pennsylvania Volunteer Infantry   1 year

Colonel Tobias B. Kauffman, Lt. Colonel George W. Frederick

Companies arrived in camp early September, 1864. The Regiment was organized 16 September and departed camp the next day.

Mustered out 31 May 1865 at Alexandria, Virginia. 712 men and 30 officers arrived at Camp Return 1 June 1865, and were paid off and disbanded 6 June.

210th Pennsylvania Volunteer Infantry   1 year

Colonel William Sergeant, Lt. Colonel Edward L. Witman

Companies arrived in camp early September, 1864. The Regiment was organized 24 September and departed camp soon thereafter.

Mustered out at Washington 30 May 1865. 525 men arrived at Camp Return 1 June 1865, and were paid off and disbanded 6 June.

211th Pennsylvania Volunteer Infantry   1 year
Colonel James H. Trimble, Lt. Colonel Levi A. Donald

The Regiment rendezvoused and was organized at Camp Reynolds, Pittsburgh.

652 men and 31 officers arrived at Camp Return 3 June 1865, and were paid off and disbanded 3 June at Pittsburgh.

Pennsylvania Militia

1st Regiment Pennsylvania Militia   Emergency
Colonel Henry McCormick, Lt. Colonel Robert Lamberton

The Regiment was organized 11 September 1862 and departed that same day. After service, the Regiment arrived in Harrisburg on or before 19 September and was mustered out 23-25 September.

2nd Regiment Pennsylvania Militia   Emergency
Colonel John Wright, Lt. Colonel David Smith

The Regiment was organized 6-13 September 1862. After service, the Regiment arrived in Harrisburg on or before 19 September and was mustered out 23-25 September.

7th Regiment Pennsylvania Militia   Emergency
Colonel Napoleon Kneas, Lt. Colonel Charles Graeff

The Regiment was organized 12 September 1862 and moved to Chambersburg 16 September.

Discharged 24 September.

15th Regiment Pennsylvania Militia   Emergency
Colonel Robert Galway, Lt. Colonel James Cooper

Companies arrived in Harrisburg 17 September 1862, Regiment organized that same day, and departed 21 September.

Returned 25 September and departed for home the next day.

20th Regiment Pennsylvania Militia   Emergency
Colonel William Thomas, Lt. Colonel Ben Lloyd James

The Regiment was organized 18 September 1862 and was disbanded 26-30 September.

1st Independent Battalion Emergency Militia Infantry

Lt. Colonel Robert Litzinger

Five companies composing the Battalion organized in Harrisburg and Philadelphia 23-25 June 1863. Discharged 8 August at Chambersburg.

1st Independent Battalion Emergency Militia Cavalry

Lt. Colonel Richard Moson

Four companies composing the Battalion organized in Harrisburg and Mustered in 2-10 July 1863. Mustered out 21 August.

20th Regiment Pennsylvania Emergency Militia

Colonel William Thomas, Lt. Colonel William Sickles

In the Emergency of 1863 the Regiment was organized 17 June and departed 21 June. The Regiment was mustered out 10 August and departed for home.

26th Regiment Pennsylvania Emergency Militia

Colonel William Jennings, Lt. Colonel Joseph Jenkins

Portion of Company A from Gettysburg in camp 15 June 1863. Other companies arrived in Harrisburg 22 June 1863 and bivouacked on the capitol grounds and later in Camp Curtin. The Regiment departed camp 24 June, returned 28 July after seeing service around Gettysburg, and was discharged 31 July.

27th Regiment Pennsylvania Emergency Militia

Colonel Jacob Frick, Lt. Colonel David Green

Organized in Harrisburg 22 June 1863. Mustered out 31 July.

28th Regiment Pennsylvania Emergency Militia

Colonel James Chamberlin, Lt. Colonel John McCleery

The Regiment was organized 19-24 June 1863 in Harrisburg and departed Camp Curtin 25 June. The Regiment returned 27 July and was discharged the next day.

29th Regiment Pennsylvania Emergency Militia

Colonel Joseph Hawley, Lt. Colonel Norris Yarnall

Organized in Harrisburg 23 June 1863. Mustered out 29 July.

30th Regiment Pennsylvania Emergency Militia

Colonel William Monies, Lt. Colonel David Mathewson

The Regiment was organized 20-25 June 1863, departed Harrisburg shortly thereafter, returned 22 July, and was discharged 1 August.

31st Regiment Pennsylvania Emergency Militia

Colonel John Newkumet, Lt. Colonel David Griffith

Organized in Harrisburg 30 June 1863. Mustered out 8 August.

32nd Regiment Pennsylvania Emergency Militia

Colonel Charles Smith, Lt. Colonel Isaac Starr, Jr.

The Regiment was organized 26 June 1863 in Camp Russell, Harrisburg, and departed camp 28 June.

Discharged 1 August at Philadelphia.

33rd Regiment Pennsylvania Emergency Militia

Colonel William Taylor, Lt. Colonel N. Hicks Graham

Regiment of approximately 800 men organized in Camp Curtin 26 June 1863 and departed that day. Mustered out 4 August.

35th Regiment Pennsylvania Emergency Militia

Colonel Henry McKean, Lt. Colonel Edward Scheiffelin

Organized in Harrisburg 4 July 1863. Mustered out 7 August.

36th Regiment Pennsylvania Emergency Militia

Colonel H. C. Alleman, Lt. Colonel Ralph McClay

Regiment arrived in Harrisburg 4 July 1863, was organized that same day and departed camp soon thereafter.

Returned 8 August and was discharged 11 August.

37th Regiment Pennsylvania Emergency Militia

Colonel John Trout, Lt. Colonel Benjamin Keefer

Organized in Harrisburg 4 July 1863. Mustered out 3 August.

39th Regiment Pennsylvania Emergency Militia

Colonel James Nagle, Lt. Colonel James Campbell

The Regiment was organized 1-7 July 1863 at Reading and was discharged 2 August at Harrisburg.

40th Regiment Pennsylvania Emergency Militia

Colonel Alfred Day, Lt. Colonel Ralph Alton

Organized in Harrisburg 2 July 1863. Mustered out 16 August.

43rd Regiment Pennsylvania Emergency Militia

Colonel William Stott, Lt. Colonel George Arnold

The Regiment was organized 6 July 1863 at Reading and was discharged 13 August at Harrisburg.

44th Regiment Pennsylvania Emergency Militia

Colonel Enos Woodward, Lt. Colonel Charles Knight

The Regiment was organized 1-9 July 1863 at Philadelphia, although at least some of the men were mustered in at Camp Curtin 10 July.

Discharged 27 August at Philadelphia.

45th Regiment Pennsylvania Emergency Militia

Colonel James Clancy, Lt. Colonel Theodore Loockerman

The Regiment was organized 1-6 July 1863 at Philadelphia, although at least some of the men were mustered in at Harrisburg.

Discharged 29 August at Philadelphia.

46th Regiment Pennsylvania Emergency Militia

Colonel John Lawrence, Lt. Colonel C. F. Huston

The Regiment was organized 1-8 July 1863 at Huntingdon and was discharged 18-19 August at Camp Curtin.

47th Regiment Pennsylvania Emergency Militia

Colonel James Wickersham, Lt. Colonel Charles McDougal

The Regiment was organized 9 July 1863 at Harrisburg.

Discharged 14 August at Reading.

49th Regiment Pennsylvania Emergency Militia

Colonel Alexander Murphy, Lt. Colonel James Perot

The Regiment was organized 2-14 July 1863 at Philadelphia, although at least some of the men were mustered in at Harrisburg.

Discharged 2-3 September at Philadelphia.

50th Regiment Pennsylvania Emergency Militia

Colonel Emlen Franklin, Lt. Colonel Thaddeus Stevens, Jr.

The Regiment was organized 1-11 July 1863 at Lancaster, although at least some of the men were mustered in at Harrisburg.

Discharged 15 August at Lancaster.

1st Pennsylvania Provisional Cavalry

Organized Cloud's Mills, Virginia, 17 June 1865. Mustered out 13 July 1865. Companies arrived in Harrisburg 15 August 1865.

2nd Pennsylvania Provisional Cavalry

1,050 men and 49 officers were paid and disbanded at Camp Return 16 August 1865.

6th Pennsylvania Provisional Cavalry

Companies arrived in Harrisburg 15 August 1865.

17th Pennsylvania Provisional Cavalry

Companies arrived in Harrisburg 15 August 1865.

Independent Companies and Battalions

McMullen's Independent Company Rangers   3 months

Captain William McMullen

Company organized in Camp Curtin 31 May 1861.

Patterson's Cavalry Company (1st Regiment Virginia Union Volunteers)

Captain Robert H. Patterson

Company organized 25 August 1861. Later became Company G, 1st Maryland Cavalry.

Palmer's Independent Company Cavalry (Anderson Troop)

Captain William J. Palmer

Organized in Harrisburg September, 1861, and mustered out 30 April 1862.

The Silver Grays

Captain William Palmer

Company arrived in Harrisburg 4 December 1861 and bivouacked in Camp Curtin. The company was not mustered into U.S. service, but remained in camp performing various duties until 6 May 1862.

Ulman's Independent Battery

Captain Joseph E. Ulman

Battery organized at Camp Curtin and mustered in 14 February 1862. The battery was to be converted into infantry, but the men refused, so the unit was disbanded 7 March.

Mitchel's Independent Guard Company Militia Infantry   90 days

Captain David Mitchel

Company organized in Harrisburg 18 July 1862 and was discharged 2 September 1863.

Baldwin's Unattached Company

Captain Charles E. Baldwin

Organized at Garland, Pennsylvania, 9 August 1862 and mustered in 28 August. Served in Philadelphia 12 September to 22 September 1862. Served as portion of provost guard in Harrisburg until 11 December 1862. Company returned from provost duty in Washington 3 June 1863 and mustered out in Harrisburg 5 June.

Independent Battery "G", Pennsylvania Light Artillery

Captain John Jay Young

Battery organized in Harrisburg 22 August 1862. Mustered out 18 June 1865.

Independent Company C   3 years

Captain DeWitt C. James

Company organized in Warren County as "Warren County Rifles." Arrived in Harrisburg 4 September 1862. On picket duty in southern Pennsylvania from about 5 September to about 27 September 1862, when it returned to Harrisburg. Remained in the city as portion of the provost guard until February, 1863. Departed 20 March for Washington.

A detachment of 54 men was paid and disbanded at Camp Return 12 June 1865. Remainder of company mustered out 20 July 1865 in Harrisburg.

Dougherty's Artillery Company   Emergency

Captain James Dougherty

Organized in Harrisburg 11 September 1862 and departed 16 September. Returned to Harrisburg 27 September and was discharged that same day.

Young's Middletown Cavalry Company

Captain Samuel Young

Company arrived in Harrisburg 15 September 1862.

Jones's Independent Infantry Company

Captain Wellington Jones

Company organized in Harrisburg 2 October 1862. Served as part of provost guard in Harrisburg until 11 December 1862. Later attached to the 97th Pennsylvania Volunteer Infantry. Discharged 9 July 1863.

Roberts's Independent Battalion Pennsylvania Heavy Artillery (four companies, A-D)

Captain Joseph Roberts

Battalion organized in Harrisburg and Philadelphia 8 October - 14 November 1862. The four companies composing the battalion were later made Companies C, D, & F of the 3rd Pennsylvania Heavy Artillery.

Luther's Independent Company Drafted Militia Infantry   9 months

Captain Edward Y. Luther

Company organized in Harrisburg and mustered in 16 October 1862. Discharged 23 July 1863.

Murray's Independent Company Emergency Militia Cavalry

Captain Frank S. Murray

Company organized in Harrisburg and mustered in 17 June 1863. Departed with Myer's Company for duty in the field 26 June 1863. Discharged in Harrisburg 11 August 1863.

Comly's Independent Company Emergency Militia Cavalry

Captain Samuel W. Comly

Company organized in Harrisburg and mustered in 17 June 1863 and was discharged 30 July 1863.

Miller's Independent Militia Battery   Emergency

Captain E. Spencer Miller

Company organized in Harrisburg and mustered in 19 June 1863. Discharged 25 July 1863.

Brown's Independent Company Emergency Militia Cavalry (Luzerne Rangers)

Captain Henry H. Brown

Company organized in Harrisburg and mustered in 19 June 1863. Discharged 1 August 1863.

Myers's Independent Company Emergency Militia Cavalry

Captain Alban H. Myers

Company organized in Harrisburg and mustered in 20 June 1863. Departed 26 June. Company discharged 31 July.

Jones's Independent Company Emergency Militia Cavalry (Curtin Horse Guards)

Captain John W. Jones

Company organized in Harrisburg and mustered in 24 June 1863. Discharged 12 August 1863.

Hastings's Independent Keystone Battery

Captain Matthew Hastings

Having seen prior service, Company A arrived in Harrisburg 26 June 1863 to be reorganized for the Emergency.

Landis's Independent Emergency Militia Battery

Captain Henry D. Landis

A "regular" militia company of the city of Philadelphia. Mobilized 27 June 1863 for the Emergency. Moved to Harrisburg and was posted in Fort Washington on Bridgeport Heights.

Discharged 30 July.

Nevin's Independent Battery   6 months

Captain Robert J. Nevin

Battery organized June-July 1863 in Harrisburg and was discharged 7 January 1864. Majority of discharged men remained in camp and reenlisted in Independent Battery I.

Independent Battery "I", Pennsylvania Light Artillery   6 months

Captain Robert J. Nevin

Battery organized in Harrisburg in December, 1863, and departed around 7 January 1864. Later were remustered and sent to Philadelphia where the ranks were filled up. Finally mustered out 23 June 1865.

2nd National Guards (of Philadelphia)

Captain Gray

Company arrived in Harrisburg 10 July 1863.

Sanno's Independent Company Cavalry   100 days

Captain Edward B. Sanno

Company was organized in Harrisburg, was mustered in 15 July 1864, and departed 23 July.

Mustered out 29 October 1864.

Stroud's Independent Cavalry Company

Captain George Stroud

Company arrived in Harrisburg from Philadelphia 20 July 1864 and departed 22 July.

Murray's Cavalry Troop   Emergency

Captain Frank A. Murray

In Harrisburg 23 July 1864.

Lambert's Independent Cavalry Company   100 days

Captain Bruce Lambert

Company organized in Harrisburg and mustered in 12 August 1864. Mustered out 25 November 1864.

Warrens's Independent Company Cavalry

Captain Edward M. Warren

Company organized in Harrisburg and mustered in 17 August 1864. Discharged 30 November 1864.

2nd Independent Company

Company organized in Harrisburg 15 December 1865 by the consolidation of enlisted men from the 12th, 14th, 20th, and 21st Regiments of the Veteran Reserve Corps. Mustered out by detachment 5 March to 30 August 1866.

Independent Battery "B", Pennsylvania Light Artillery

150 men arrived 30 October 1865 from duty in New Orleans and Texas and went into Camp Curtin.

Troops From Other States

6th Regiment, United States Veteran Volunteers (Hancock's Corps)

Portion of the Regiment arrived in Camp Curtin 22 July 1865 and remained in camp as part of the provost guard battalion. Departed 11 November 1865.

3rd Regiment Maryland Potomac Home Brigade Infantry, Company B

Captain William F. Cardiff

Company was organized in Harrisburg 2 December 1861.

1st Michigan Volunteer Infantry

This Regiment was quartered at Camp Curtin for an undetermined period prior to the 1st day of July, 1861.

2nd Michigan Volunteer Infantry

Arrived in Harrisburg 8 June 1861 and departed the next day.

4th Michigan Volunteer Infantry

Arrived in Harrisburg 27 June 1861 and bivouacked on the lot near the Roundhouse of the Pennsylvania Railroad. The Regiment already had a number of sick and these men were attended to by the people of Harrisburg. The Michiganders departed 1 July 1861.

26th Michigan Volunteer Infantry

305 men arrived in Harrisburg 5 June 1865 after having been mustered out the day before at Washington.

1st Minnesota Volunteer Infantry

Arrived in Harrisburg 25 June 1861 and bivouacked on the Roundhouse lot. The Regiment departed the next day.

1st New Jersey Militia

2 companies totalling 100 men arrived in Harrisburg 2 July 1863.

23rd New Jersey Volunteer Infantry

Arrived in Harrisburg 18 June 1863 and bivouacked in Harris Park in "Fort Yahoo." The Regiment departed 20 June.

1st New York Light Artillery, Battery A

Battery was in Harrisburg as a part of the post garrison May-August, 1864. Participated in the parade and celebration to welcome home the Pennsylvania Reserves 6 June 1864.

2nd Fire Zouaves of New York

Arrived in Harrisburg 31 August 1861.

4th Regiment New York State National Guard Heavy Artillery

750 men arrived in Harrisburg 21 June 1863 and went into Fort Washington. Company E, the "New York Herald Guards," in Camp Curtin 25 June.

5th Regiment New York State National Guard

Arrived in Harrisburg 20 June 1863.

8th Regiment New York State National Guard

Arrived in Harrisburg 19 June 1863 and departed 15 July.

11th Regiment New York State National Guard

Arrived in Harrisburg 19 June 1863 and did duty in Fort Washington.

11th Regiment New York Heavy Artillery

Four companies arrived in Harrisburg 25 June 1863. Moved to Carlisle July 1 but returned to Harrisburg soon thereafter and remained until July 10.

12th Regiment New York State National Guard

Arrived in Harrisburg about 19 June 1863 and departed for duty in Fenwick, Pennsylvania.

13th Regiment New York State National Guard

Arrived in Harrisburg 21 June 1863 and did duty in Fort Washington.

22nd Regiment New York State National Guard

Arrived in Harrisburg 20 June 1863 and did duty in Fort Washington. Departed 17 July.

23rd Regiment New York State National Guard

Portion arrived in Harrisburg 19 June 1863. Additional companies arrived 26 June and did duty in Fort Washington.

28th Regiment New York State National Guard

Arrived in Harrisburg 21 June 1863.

37th Regiment New York State National Guard

Arrived in Harrisburg 20 June 1863 and did duty in Fort Washington.

56th Regiment New York State National Guard

Arrived in Harrisburg 19 June 1863 and departed 17 July.

65th Regiment New York State National Guard

Arrived in Harrisburg about 20 June 1863 and did duty at Mount Union, Pennsylvania. Departed Harrisburg to return to New York 15 July.

68th Regiment New York State National Guard

Arrived in Harrisburg about 25 June 1863.

71st Regiment New York State National Guard

Arrived in Harrisburg 24 June 1863 and departed 15 July.

74th Regiment New York State National Guard

Arrived in Harrisburg about 19 June 1863 and did duty at Mount Union, Pennsylvania.

176th New York Volunteer Infantry

Arrived in Harrisburg 18 June 1863.

1st Ohio Volunteer Infantry

Arrived in Harrisburg on the morning of 20 April 1861 and bivouacked on the grounds of the capitol. The Regiment departed the night of 22 April.

2nd Ohio Volunteer Infantry

Arrived in Harrisburg with the 1st Ohio Regiment on the morning of 20 April 1861 and bivouacked on the grounds of the capitol. The Regiment departed the night of 22 April.

2nd United States Cavalry, Company E

Arrived in Harrisburg 26 April 1861 from Carlisle. After being mounted and equipped, the company departed 28 April.

5th United States Artillery, Battery I

The battery was encamped in Camp Greble in Harrisburg until it departed 3 March 1862.

50th Company, 2nd Battalion, United States Veteran Reserve Corps (formerly Company I, 20th U.S.V.R.C.)

Organized at Harrisburg August, 1863. Designation changed 25 May, 1864. The Regiment was mustered out by detachment 5 September 1865 to February 1866.

95th Company, 2nd Battalion, United States Veteran Reserve Corps (formerly Company I, 22nd U.S.V.R.C.)

Organized at Harrisburg Spetember, 1863. Designation changed March, 1864. The Regiment was mustered out by detachment 14 August to 20 November 1864.

16th Regiment United States Veteran Reserve Corps

Organized at Harrisburg 10 October 1863. The Regiment was mustered out by detachment 15 July to 26 November 1865.

2nd Wisconsin Volunteer Infantry

Arrived in Harrisburg 22 June 1861 and bivouacked on the lot near the Pennsylvania Railroad Roundhouse in downtown Harrisburg. The Regiment had not departed as of 25 June.

4th Wisconsin Volunteer Infantry

Arrived in Harrisburg 18 July 1861 and bivouacked on the lot near the Pennsylvania Railroad Roundhouse. The Regiment departed 22 July.

5th Wisconsin Volunteer Infantry

Arrived in Harrisburg on the night of 26-27 July 1861 and bivouacked on the lot near the Roundhouse. The Regiment moved to a field near Camp Curtin on 30 July, and departed hurriedly 31 July.

6th Wisconsin Volunteer Infantry

Arrived in Harrisburg on the night of 30-31 July 1861 and bivouacked on the lot near the Roundhouse, recently vacated by their fellow Wisconsinites. The Regiment was wanting arms and was not supplied therewith for a few days. The 6th departed 3 August.

19th Wisconsin Volunteer Infantry

Arrived in Harrisburg 4 June 1862 and departed the next day.

Chapter Notes

PROLOGUE

1. *Harrisburg Patriot & Union* 16 January, 1861. (hereafter *PU*)

2. William H. Egle, *Life and Times of Andrew Gregg Curtin* (Philadelphia: The Thompson Publishing Co., 1896) 24-25.

3. *Ibid.*, 26-27.

4. *Ibid.*, 28-29.

5. Dumes Malone, ed., *Dictionary of American Biography*, (New York: Charles Scribner's Sons, 1946) 2:606-608. (hereafter *DAB*).

6. Curtin's inaugural address in George E. Reed, ed., *Pennsylvania Archives*, (Harrisburg: State Printer 1902), Series IV, *Papers of the Governors*, 8:337 (hereafter *Pennsylvania Archives*).

7. Egle, *Life and Times*, 211.

8. *Ibid.*, 211.

CHAPTER ONE *"Reveille at the Dawn of Day"*

1. Alexander McClure, *Abraham Lincoln and the Men of War Times*, (Philadelphia: Times Publishing Co., 1892), see account of meeting, 58-61.

2. Egle, *Life and Times*, 213-14.

3. *Ibid.*, 213; On April 16, the day after Lincoln's call for 75,000 volunteers, the following bogus advertisement appeared in the Mobile Alabama *Advertiser.* "75,000 BLACK COFFINS WANTED — Proposals will be received to supply the Southern Confederacy with 75,000 black coffins. No proposals will be entertained coming from north of Mason and Dixon line. Direct to JEFF DAVIS, Montgomery Alabama." Allen D. Albert, *History of the Forty-fifth Regiment Pennsylvania Veteran Volunteer Infantry 1861-1865*, (Williamsport, Pa.: Grit Publishing Co., 1912) 391 (hereafter Albert).

4. John Rowell, *Yankee Cavalrymen*, (Knoxville: University of Tennessee Press, 1971), 19. Rowell incorrectly cites source of story as Egle's *Commemorative Biographical Encyclopedia of Dauphin County* 244.

5. William Egle, *Commemorative Biographical Encyclopedia of Dauphin County*, 244 (hereafter Egle *Dauphin County*).; John Trussell, *Brig. Gen. Joseph F. Knipe, U.S.V.*, 4.

6. Egle, *Dauphin County*, 1195; Trussell, 1-3. Though only 19, Knipe misrepresented his age as 21, possibly because he had not his parents' consent. Trussell gives Knipe's rank as captain, but orders issued by Major General William H. Keim, commanding the 5th Division of Pennsylvania Militia gives Knipe's rank as of 15 January 1861 as major; see *PU* 16 January 1861.

7. Samuel P. Bates, *History of the Pennsylvania Volunteers 1861-1865*, 5 vols., (Harrisburg: State Printer 1869) 1:4-5.

8. Ezra Warner, *Generals in Gray*, (Baton Rouge: Louisiana State University Press, 1959), 232-233 (hereafter Warner, *Gray*).; Francis Heitman, *Historical Register and Dictionary of the United States Army*, 1789-1903, (Washington, D.C.: Government Printing Office, 1903), 1:781. The two sources disagree as to the date of Pemberton's resignation. The date given by Warner is given here; As a Confederate, Pemberton would lose his cloak of anonymity. Just over two years later, as a lieutenant general in the Confederate States Army, he would surrender his command of twenty thousand men at Vicksburg to Major General Ulysses S. Grant. His surrender of the Vicksburg garrison marked the beginning of the final phase in the history of the Confederacy.

9. Muster rolls in the Pennsylvania State Archives.

10. Bates, 1:5.

11. Bates, 1:32.

12. *PU* 19 April 1861, Eleven companies arrived in Harrisburg on the 18th.

13. Alvin Williams, *Ceremonies at the Dedication of the Statue of Andrew Gregg Curtin...On the Site of Camp Curtin...October 19th, 1922*, (Harrisburg: Telegraph Printing Co., 1922), 8.

14. Marian Underwood, *Then and Now in Harrisburg*, (Harrisburg, 1925), 90; Philip German map of Camp Curtin, Dauphin County Historical Society.

15. "Camp Curtin at one time occupied the entire space of what is now Fifth Street to Seventh Street, and from Maclay Street to within a very few yards of Reel's Lane...." Francis Hoy, Sr., "Harrisburg in the Days of the Civil War," *Harrisburg Telegraph*, 3 October 1905 (hereafter Hoy, "Harrisburg.").

16. Harry H. Hain, *History of Perry County, Pennsylvania*, (Harrisburg: Hain-Moore Company, 1922), 656.

17. *A Biographical Album of Prominent Pennsylvanians*, Second Series, (Philadelphia: The American Biographical Publishing Co., 1889), 7-8 (hereafter *Prominent Pennsylvanians*).

18. Story of the founding of Camp Curtin comes from Knipe's daughter (later Teresa Hogentreler) and is contained in an unidentified newspaper clipping in the Philip German Notebook at the Dauphin County Historical Society. Col. Trussell identifies the clipping as being from the *Harrisburg Evening News* of 18 October 1922, the eve of the dedication of the Camp Curtin Memorial.

19. John D. Billings, *Hard Tack and Coffee*, (reprint, Williamstown, Mass.: Corner House Publishers, 1984), 47.

20. William W. H. Davis, *History of the Doylestown Guards*, (Doylestown, Pa.: 1887), 104.

21. Men awakened "by the beat of the drum for a half hour drill before breakfast" after their first night in Camp Curtin. George D. Harmon "The Military Experiences of James A. Peifer," *North Carolina Historical Review*, 32 (1955): 387.

22. Edward G. Everett, "Pennsylvania Raises an Army," *Western Pennsylvania Historical Magazine*, 39 (1956), No. 2:90.

23. *PU* 6 May 1861.

24. Everett, 89.

25. Diary of an unidentified member of the 1st Pennsylvania, Pennsylvania State Archives.

26. *PU* 20 April 1861.

27. Josiah R. Sypher, *History of the Pennsylvania Reserve Corps*, (Lancaster, Pa.: Elias Barr & Co., 1865), 65-6 (hereafter Sypher).

CHAPTER TWO: *"The Madness That Rules the Hour"*

1. *PU* 25 April 1861; Williams returned to Harrisburg just four days later having successfully complete⸱ his assignment and formed Camp Scott in York.

2. Both Reverend Williams, in the program for the *Dedication of the Monument to Governor Curtin* and Sarah Mae Book, in *Northern Rendezvous*, (Harrisburg: Telegraph Press, 1959), state that Colo⸱ nel George A. C. Seiler, assistant adjutant general of Pennsylvania and a native of Harrisburg, wa⸱ the first commandant of Camp Curtin, but this is incorrect. In the Pennsylvania State Archives ar⸱ requisition slips from the Quartermaster Department at Camp Curtin. These slips are all dated an⸱ signed by an officer capable of authorizing the requisition. Quite a number of these slips are fron⸱ the first few days of the camp's operation and several are clearly signed, "Washington H. R. Hangen⸱ Commandant Camp Curtin." Colonel Seiler did serve as commandant, but later. He was not the firs⸱ man or even the second to exercise command at Camp Curtin. There is some confusion about Hangen'⸱ name. On camp documents, he signed his name "Washington H. R. Hangen," and the alphabetica⸱ rolls of the 9th Regiment clearly show his name as such. Later in the war, he served in the 47th⸱ Pennsylvania and his name was listed on the regimental rolls as "Washington H. R. Hangen," bu⸱ Bates and other historians have contorted the name into "W. H. H. Hangen," "William H. H. Hangen,⸱ and other erroneous minor variations. That the lieutenant colonel of the 9th Regiment and the adju⸱ tant of the 47th were the same man is indisputable, however, for in the military record of the Lt⸱ Hangen that served in the 47th it is noted that he had served previously as lieutenant colonel of the 9th⸱

3. see Sypher, 50.

4. Everett, 88-9; *PU* 27 April 1861.

5. *PU* 1 May 1861; during busy or moderately busy periods throughout the war, 5,000 men would routinel⸱ be housed in camp, and, at times of crisis, as many as 8,000 or 10,000 would be kept there with man⸱ more encamped in fields outside the camp, on the grounds of the capitol, and in vacant lots in th⸱ city. The Camp Commissary was responsible for issuing sustinance to all the soldiers encamped i⸱ the city and sometimes had to provide for upwards of 15,000 men.

6. *The War of the Rebellion, A Compilation of the Official Records of the Union and Confederat⸱ Armies*, (Washington, D.C., 1880-1901), Series I, 3:550 (hereafter *OR*).; George Washington Cullun⸱ *Biographical Register of Officers and Graduates of the U.S. Military Academy*, (New York; 1869), 2:166-⸱

7. *PU* 1 May 1861.

8. *PU* 20 June 1861; Charles Roumfort and Harry Kosure, brother of Alex Kosure, meat contractor, ha⸱ the contract for furnishing the bread. They gave out subcontracts to other bakers, among whom wer⸱ Thomas Findley (Findley's bakery on Market where Patriot and Union was in 1905) and Williar⸱ Miller. They continued to furnish the bread until the government established a bakery opposite th⸱ site of the old Roumfort bakery...at Fourth and Chestnut. Hoy, "Harrisburg."

9. *PU* 6 August 1861.

10. Francis Hoy, just a boy in 1861, remembered that "For the first couple of weeks the meat was delivere⸱ to camp cooked. Alex Kosure had the contract for furnishing it and I was employed by him to hel⸱ cut it up and hand it to the soldiers." Hoy, "Harrisburg."

11. *PU* 23 April 1861.

12. *PU* 6 August 1861.

13. Anonymous letter signed "Smith" and addressed to "friend Black" dated 27 August 1862 in Manuscri⸱ Group 6, Pennsylvania State Archives.

14. *PDT* 22 May 1861.

15. Davis, *Doylestown Guards*, 109. These offenses were sited as having occurred at Camp Scott in York, but such probably happened at Camp Curtin as well.

16. *PU* 27 May 1861.

17. Mr. Robert L. Martin, Esq., of Delaware County, was appointed by Curtin to work with Captain George Gibson, of the United States Army in manufacturing uniforms for Pennsylvania's first volunteers.

18. *PU* 23 April 1861.

19. *PU* 25 July 1861; Davis, *Doylestown Guards*, 109.

20. *PU* 6 May 1861.

21. *Ibid.*

22. John Donaghy, *Army Experience*, (Deland, Fla.: E. O. Painter Printing Co., 1926), 4-5.

23. *PU* 4 May 1861.

24. *PU* 1 May 1861.

25. B. N. Miller, ed., *Diary of Jacob Heffelfinger*, unpublished typescript, U.S. Army Military History Institute, entry of 18 May 1861 (hereafter Miller, Heffelfinger Diary).

26. *PU* 1 May 1861.

27. *PU* 11 December 1862; *PU* 22 January 1863.

28. *PDT* 30 May 1861; another popular refreshment spot for the volunteers was the State Capital Brewery, which was owned by a Mr. Frisch, who also operated a saloon at the corner of Fifth and Market Streets. *PU* 26 October 1861.

29. *PU* 1 August 1861.

30. *PU* 11 June 1861, Ritter belonged to the "Iron Artillery" *PU* 12 June 1861.

31. *PU* 15 June 1861.

32. Maurice R. Donovan, ed., *Kane Pennsylvania Centennial Program 1864-1964*, Hooper productions, 1964, unpaginated; Warner, *Blue*, 256-57.

33. O. R. Howard Thomson and William H. Rauch, *A History of the "Bucktails,"* (Philadelphia: 1906), 11.

34. Edwin A. Glover, *Bucktailed Wildcats*, (New York: Thomas Yoseloff, 1860), 26.

35. *Ibid.*, 34; also see *PU* 25 May 1861 for a general description of the Bucktails and their leader, Colonel Kane; Nile's and Sherwood's companies went in wagons 32 miles to Troy, trained to Williamsport and then to Harrisburg, where they were the first Bucktail companies to arrive between April 20-24 1861; Glover, 23.

36. *PU* 6 May 1861.

37. *PU* 8 May 1861.

38. Glover, 34.

39. Glover, 35, sites Tioga County *Agitator* 19 June 1861.

40. *PU* 30 July 1861.

41. Letter of C. F. Taylor to brother, Bayard Taylor, dated 31 January 1861 in Charles F. Hobson and Arnold Shankman, "Colonel of the Bucktails: Civil War Letters of Charles Frederick Taylor," *The Pennsylvania Magazine of History and Biography*, vol 9, 3:335 (hereafter Hobson & Shankman).

42. Letter from C. F. Taylor to sister, Annie Taylor, dated 1 April 1863 in Hobson & Shankman, 35(

43. Sypher, 54-55.

44. *PU* 22 April 1861.

45. *PU* 29 April 1861; the disbursement of funds was performed by the Military Relief Committee i the Exchange building on Walnut Street *PU* 17 May 1861.

46. *PU* 20 April 1861.

47. William H. Locke of the 11th Pennsylvania, in his regimental history, *The Story of the Regimen* (Philadelphia: J. B. Lippincott & Co., 1868), wrote of the "...band of noble women of Harrisburg, prin cipal among whom were Mrs. George H. Small, Mrs. James Denning, and Mrs. Lile Cornyn. Th constant care of these ladies for the sick of the regiment in the camp hospital, and when the diseas became serious removing the patient to their own homes....Locke, 41; *Pennsylvania Daily Telegraph* 12 May 1861 (hereafter *PDT*), In this newspaper account is mentioned the Camp Hospital, which ha been under construction for some time. It can be assumed that the building was completed and ope for business by this date. A Dr. Charles Bower was put in charge of the Hospital at Camp Curti in late June (see *PU* 2 July 1861, also *PU* 8 July 1861). Other women formed massive sewing circle and produced such necessities as haversacks (of which not fewer than 5,000 were made by the en of May), socks, and lint, which was pulled from old pieces of linen and would later be used to dres wounds. See *PU* 24 April 1861, and *PU* 27 May 1861.

48. *PU* 10 May 1861.

49. *PU* 30 July 1861.

50. *PU* 20 April 1861.

51. *PU* 24 April 1861.

52. *PU* 23 April 1861.

53. *Ibid.,* 23 April 1861.

54. *PU* 4 July 1861; *PU* 3 July 1861.

55. William Lochren, "Narrative of the First Regiment," in *Minnesota in the Civil and Indian Wars,* (St Paul: The Pioneer Press, 1890-93). 1:6.

56. *PU* 11 June 1861: A Mr. D. O. Gehr of Chambersburg was awarded a contract for funishing the army with 100 mules from four to nine years old, fourteen hands high, at $124.50 each; *PU* 7 August 1861 A Mr. William Colder was given a contract to build 30 new wagons per week for the army; *PU* 1C May 1861 for gunpowder and casket advertisements.

57. *PU* 25 October 1861.

58. Route taken by hacks to camp was up Third Street to North Street to Elder Street, to Forster Street to the Ridge Road, thence to camp. Hoy, "Harrisburg"; See also *PU* 8 May 1861.

59. *PU* 23 April 1861.

60. Hoy, "Harrisburg."

61. *PU* 7 November 1861.

62. *PU* 17 July 1861.

63. Sypher, 52.

64. *Pennsylvania Archives, IV,* 8:337-78.

65. *Ibid; Biographical Encyclopedia of Pennsylvania in the Nineteenth Century,* (Philadelphia: Galaxy Publishing Co., 1874), 128-9.

66. William Henry Darlington letter September, 1861, by permission of the Houghton Library, Harvard University.

67. *Ibid.*

68. Egle, *Dauphin County,* 294.

69. Cullum 1:579; Egle, *Dauphin County,* 294.

70. Cullum 1:579; Egle, *Dauphin County,* 292; Samuel P. Bates, *Martial Deeds of Pennsylvania,* (Philadelphia: T. H. Davis & Co., 1875), 408.

71. *PU* 18 June 1861; *PU* 24 July 1861; William H. Egle, ed., *Notes & Queries, Historical, Biographical and Genealogical,* (Harrisburg: Harrisburg Publishing Co., 1893), series 4, 1:88; Eva Draegert Schory, *Everyname Index to Egle's Notes & Queries Chiefly Relating to Interior Pennsylvania* (Decatur, Ill.: Decatur Genealogical Society, 1982), 457.

72. Glover, 36; *PU* 18 June 1861; Glover, 37.

73. *PU* 20 June 1861.

74. *PU* 1 July 1861.

75. Glover, 36.

76. *PU* 24 April 1861.

77. *Ibid.,* 24 April 1861.

78. W. R. Kiefer, *History of the 153rd Regiment Pennsylvania Volunteer Infantry,* (Easton, PA.: The Chemical Publishing Co., 1909), 15.

79. William Simmers and Paul Bachschmid, *The Volunteer's Manual or Ten Months with the 153rd Pennsylvania Volunteers,* (Easton, PA: D. H. Neiman, 1863), 6.

80. *PU* 22 May 1861.

81. *PU* 1 May 1861.

82. *PU* 3 July 1861.

83. Bates lists the private in question as "Henry Welch" 1:984.

84. *PU* 10 August 1861, the report states Welsh was from Pittsburgh, but according to Bates the battery was recruited in Philadelphia. The report in the *P & U* also states that the vent tender was named Knight. Bates lists no Knight in Battery C, it is assumed McKnight was the man in question; *Annual Report of the Adjutant General of Pennsylvania for the year 1861.*

85. *PU* 17 May 1861; See *PU* 10 July 1861 for more about the shutting down of the Cotton Mill, and *PU* 17 July 1861 for wheat crop; The legislature had been in recess since May 16, contributing to the general dullness.

86. *PU* 13 July 1861.

87. Charles E. Davis, *Three Years in the Army: The Story of the Thirteenth Massachusetts Volunteers,* (Boston: Estes and Lauriat, 1894), 2.

88. *OR,* I, 2:166.

89. Locke, 38.

90. OR, I, 2:749.

91. Darlington letter of 23 July 1861.

92. The "Archy Dicks" was the name the men of what eventually became Company F had given themselves when they first formed at Rockdale, Delaware County, whence most of the men came.

93. Darlington letter of 23 July 1861.

94. Evan M. Woodward, *Our Campaigns; or the Marches, Bivouacs, Battles, Incidents of Camp Life and History of Our Regiment During Its Three Years Term of Service, Together with a Sketch of the Army of the Potomac, Under Generals McClellan, Burnside, Hooker, Meade and Grant*, (Philadelphia, John E. Potter and Co., 1865), 45.

95. *PU* 31 July 1861.

96. *PU* 24 July 1861.

97. *PU* 7 August 1861.

98. *PU* 31 July 1861.

99. As the volunteers came home, the Committee of the Volunteer Relief Fund of Dauphin County removed the names of the men from the rolls of the families entitled to disbursement. As others from the county enlisted, their names were added to the files. *PU* 25 July 1861.

100. *PU* 1 August 1861.

101. *PU* 24 July 1861; 25 July 1861.

102. *Ibid.*, 24 July 1861.

103. *PU* 1 July 1861.

104. *PU* 31 July 1861.

105. *PU* 29 July 1861.

106. *PU* 1 August 1861.

107. Glover, 33.

108. *PU* 7 August 1861.

109. *PU* 20 July 1861.

110. *PU* 13 July 1861.

111. *PU* 30 July 1861.

112. *Ibid.*, 30 July 1861.

113. *PU* 26 July 1861.

114. *PDT* 19 July 1861; Martin Hardin, *History of the Twelfth Regiment Pennsylvania Reserve Volunteer Corps.* (New York: Martine D. Hardin, 1890). 196-97 (hereafter Hardin, *Twelfth Reserves*).

115. Hardin, *Twelfth Reserves*, 5.

116. *PU* 29 July and 30 July 1861.

117. *PU* 1 August 1861.

CHAPTER THREE: *"The Colonel Seems to be Boss"*

1. Albert, 14-15.

2. *PU* 14 August 1861, William B. Edwards, *Civil War Guns*, (Secaucus, NJ: Castle Books, 1978), 210-12.

3. Black founded his camp on the road to the county poor house in "Cameron's Woods." The place was described as a good place for a camp: the ground was high, there was a spring of good fresh water located nearby and a grove of trees provided shade. Another camp had been established in the Harrisburg area, although precise details of its founding are not known. The site was christened Camp Greble, and although its exact location is not known, it apparently was situated in fields east of the city in the Paxton Creek valley. Camp Greble became home at various times to batteries of the 5th U.S. Artillery. Battery I is the only battery definitely known to have occupied the camp, but Batteries B and E possibly were based in the camp while they were attached to the Department of the Susquehanna (B in June and July, 1863, and E from May, 1862 to April 1864). Battery I, much of which was reportedly recruited in Harrisburg, departed Camp Greble 3 March 1862 after having spent "many months" drilling in the camp. After the departure of the battery, the *Patriot and Union* reported that the camp was "broken up," but the report is unconfirmed. See *PU* 3 December 1861 and 4 March 1862.

4. See *PU* 7 August 1861 for movement of Black's regiment to Camp Cameron. The camp was founded 6 August 1861.

5. *PU* 3 September 1861. A number of other small, regimental camps were founded in the area in late July early August, but most of these were closer to Camp Curtin than was Black's camp. When space became available in Camp Curtin, these other camps were broken up and the men moved into Curtin. Camp Cameron was the exception and was maintained for a while.

6. Albert, 16; see *PU* 12 September 1861.

7. Ezra Warner, *Generals in Blue*, (Baton Rouge: Louisiana State University Press), 550-51.

8. *PU* 12 September & 18 September 1861; *PU* 12 October 1861.

9. Albert, 15-16.

10. Warner *Blue*, 211-12.

11. Ellwood Roberts, ed., *Biographical Annals of Montgomery County Pennsylvania*, (New York: T. S. Benham & Co. and the Lewis Publishing Co., 1904), 1:517-18.

12. *PU* 31 August 1861, quoted from Philadelphia *Evening Bulletin*.

13. *PU* 26 September 1861.

14. Descriptions of departures from home abound in regimental histories, among the best are those in Albert's *History of the 45th Pennsylvania Volunteers*.

15. T. F. Dornblazer, *Sabre Strokes of the Pennsylvania Dragoons in the War of 1861-1865*. (Philadelphia: Lutheran Publication Society, 1884), 13.

16. Diary of Stryker A. Wallace, 153rd PVI.; Pennsylvania State Archives.

17. Albert, 264.

18. Albert, 272.

19. Dornblazer, 15. Dornblazer mistakenly gives Camp Cameron's location as "three miles south of the depot." The camp was actually between 1.5 and 2 miles east of the city on the old "poor house road."

20. Letter of Private Samuel North, Company C, 126th Pennsylvania to his brother in Ted Alexander, ed., *History of the 126th Pennsylvania*. (Shippensburg, PA: Beidel Printing House), 109.

21. Albert, 264; see also Joseph R. Orwig, *History of the 131st Penn'a Volunteers*, (Williamsport, Pa. Sun Book and Job Printing House, 1902), 9.

22. J. D. Bloodgood, *Personal Reminiscences of the War*, (New York: Hint & Eaton, 1893), 3.

23. *PU* 6 August 1861.

24. Oliver C. Bosbyshell, *The 48th in the War*, (Philadelphia: Anvil Printing Co., 1895), 19-20; the 48th was at Camp Hamilton in late September, 1861.

25. *PU* 19 October 1861 & 22 October 1861.

26. *PU* 11 September and 14 September 1861.

27. Mayne enlisted on 9 August 1862, see Bates 4:127.

28. Bates 4:127-128, 139; see David W. Rowe, *A Sketch of the 126th Regiment Pennsylvania Volunteers*, (Chambersburg, Pa.: Cook & Hays, 1869).

29. See Thomas H. Parker, *History of the 51st Regiment of P. V. and V. V.*, (Philadelphia: King and Baird, Printers, 1869), 24-25.

30. *Ibid.*, 12-13.

31. Parker Pension File and Service Record, National Archives.

32. Parker, 13.

33. The killed man's name was reported as John Donough of Captain [Lieutenant] John Cotterell's company, of the 110th Pennsylvania, the "McClellan Regiment." Bates does not list Donough, but see 3:1004; *PU* 16 December 1861; see *PU* 7 November 1862 for more reports of desertions.

34. Robert S. Westbrook, *History of the 49th Pennsylvania Volunteers*, (Altoona, Pa.: Altoona Times Print, 1898), 89.

35. Dornblazer, 18-19.

36. *Ibid.*

37. *PDT* 5 September 1861.

38. Parker, 20-22.

39. See McClure *Old Time Notes of Pennsylvania*, 2:489-99, for details of Tenallytown.

40. Not all the Reserves were present at Tenallytown. Four companies of the 1st Regiment were on detached duty in Annapolis under Colonel Roberts, and both the 2nd Regiment and the Bucktails were serving in the Shenandoah Valley.

41. See Sypher, 114-118 for more about the reviews at Tennallytown.

42. *PU* 16 October 1861; *PU* 2 October 1861; *PU* 26 October 1861.

43. *PU* 26 October 1861.

44. Parker, 17-18.

45. *PU* 30 September 1861.

46. *PU* 20 October 1861.

47. *PU* 30 September 1861; *PDT* 30 September 1861.

48. *PU* 14 October 1861.

49. The Harrisburg newspapers in the fall of 1861 were filled with evidence of the goodness and generosity of the hearts of Pennsylvanian women. Donors were usually thanked publicly, and long lists of names and goods appeared frequently—too frequently to list all the dates here, but donations began about October 1st.

50. *PU* 10 December 1861.

51. *PU* 7 October 1861; see *PU* 5 March 1862 for a fairly typical acknowledgement of goods received and a listing of the donors and an illustration of the tremendous variety of things donated.

52. Parker, 19-20.

53. Albert, 264.

54. *Ibid.*

55. Albert, 465.

56. Egle, *Notes & Queries*, 1:320.

57. Pennsylvania Daily Telegraph, 30 August 1861 (hereafter *PDT*); Egle *Notes & Queries*, 1:320.

58. Parker, 18.

59. Kieffer, Harry M. *The Recollections of a Drummer Boy*, (Boston: Houghton, Mifflin and Co., 1890), 41.

60. Parker, 19.

61. *Ibid.*

62. Darlington letter of 10 September 1861.

63. Albert, 224.

64. Albert, 204; *PU* 30 October 1861.

65. Locke, 41.

66. Parker, 19.

67. Miller, *Heffelfinger Diary*, 19 May 1861.

68. The Rev. John Davis is quoted in *PU* 25 October 1861.

69. Kiefer, 15.

70. Miller, *Hefflefinger Diary*, 12 May 1861.

71. See *PU* 7 September 1861.

72. *PU* 31 October 1861; the Rev. Junkin was the father of Jackson's first wife, Elinor, who had died in childbirth in 1854.

73. *PU* 11 October 1861.

74. *PU* 12 October 1861.

75. Parker, 22.

76. Parker, 23.

77. Bloodgood, 17.

78. Orwig, 10.

79. *Ibid.*

80. A. G. White, *History of Company F of the 140th Pennsylvania Volunteers*, (Greenville, Pa.: The Beaver Printery, 1908), 7-8.

81. Kieffer, 40-41.

82. Albert, 265.

83. The presentation of colors was an important event in the history of a regiment and truly meant a great deal to most of the individual soldiers themselves. Accounts of the ceremonies at the presentations are included in almost every regimental history with emphasis placed upon the words of the governor.

84. Parker, 27; James M. Martin, et al, *History of the Fifty-Seventh Regiment P. V. V. I.*, (Meadville, Pa.: McCoy & Calvin), 14.

85. *PU* 12 October 1861.

86. Bates 1:1269.

87. Letter of John Woods to his mother dated 23 September 1861; Woods family papers, Pennsylvania State Archives; Westbrook, also of the 49th, relates his version of the story, which is very similar to Woods's, in his regimental history, 90; Bates 1:1269; see also Donaghy of 103rd for another incident of a soldier's injury.

88. *PDT* 22 October 1861; *PU* 22 October 1861.

89. Warner *Blue*, 320-21; Somewhere, a story began that credited Sullivan Meredith with having a hand in organizing 30,000 volunteers in the early days of the war. This would have been difficult for him to do, having no military experience and only being in Harrisburg for three weeks between mid-April and May 1st, when he shipped out of Camp Curtin with his regiment, the 10th. These volunteers came from all over the state and were organized at Pittsburgh, Harrisburg and Philadelphia. It would have been impossible for him to have been at all three places. If he assisted his brother clerically in organizing volunteers, he still would not have been able to have had a hand in organizing 30,000 men, for that figure represents many more than the total number of Pennsylvania men who were formed into regiments before May, assuming that Meredith was busy enough with his own regiment thereafter.

90. Martin, 14; The Bucktails were particularly hard hit by measles. There were almost 20 cases in the Camp Hospital in mid May and that number stayed fairly constant until near the end of June. The number of troops in camp at this time was estimated at 2,000; *PU* 22 May 1861; see also *PU* 18 May 1861.

91. *PU* 2 December 1861.

92. *Ibid.*

93. *PDT* 25 October 1861; see also Mr. Reel's public note of thanks in *PU* 26 October 1861.

94. *PU* 20 September 1861; This stampede was not an isolated incident; *PU* 26 October 1861, another stampede noted in *PU* 12 March 1862.

95. *PU* 30 October 1861; Muster Rolls Pennsylvania State Archives.

96. See *PU* 27 December 1861; 2 May and 6 May 1862 for other items about Silver Grays.

97. *PU* 10 December 1861.

98. This included the 11th and 23rd three-month regiments, which reenlisted for 3 years.

99. *Report of the Commissary General of Pennsylvania for 1861.*

100. *PU* 26 November 1861; The new barracks would not be completed until well into the winter; *PU* 14 January 1862.

101. *PU* 12 October 1861; *PU* 30 October 1861.

102. *PU* 29 October 1861; Dodge set up his principal recruiting office in Market Square in downtown Harrisburg.

103. Cullum, 2:356-57.

104. *PU* 20 March 1862; Post returns for Camp Curtin, March-May, 1862, National Archives; *List of Persons and Articles Hired at Camp Curtin,* in the National Archives, shows that a contract signed 1 March 1862 required the government to pay Pennsylvania $80 per month for the use of the campground as a principal recruiting depot.

105. Amsden Pension File and Service Record, National Archives; Bates, 1:1000, 1006; *Returns of Camp Curtin;* See also *PU* 28 April 1862.

106. *PU* 17 September 1862; Carter Pension File, National Archives.

CHAPTER FOUR: *"I Have Not Pleasant Memories of Camp Curtin"*

1. *PU* 20 March 1862; The number of recruits in camp reached about 600 by the end of March. *PU* 28 March 1862.

2. OR, I, 12, pt. 1, 782.

3. Hobson & Shankman, 347-51.

4. Simmons Service Record with 5th Reserves, National Archives; Simmons had been home to Harrisburg for Christmas before the attack of bronchitis in February.

5. Letter dated 8 February 1862 from House of Representatives; Simmons Service Record, National Archives.

6. Warner *Blue,* 396-97; Mark Mayo Boatner, *The Civil War Dictionary,* (New York: David McKay Company, Inc.), 694, Reynolds was in command of the 1st Brigade as of 3 October 1861, and was military governor of Fredericksburg 4 April - 12 June 1862.

7. Simmons Service Record, 5th Pennsylvania Reserves, National Archives.

8. Major General Fitz John Porter in Robert Underwood Johnson and Clarence Clough Buel, eds., *Battles and Leaders of the Civil War,* 4 vols., (New York: Century, 1887, reprint, Castle Books, 1982), 2:325 (hereafter *B & L*).

9. Sypher, 228-29.

10. Warner, *Blue,* 289-90. The Pennsylvania Reserves were first assigned to the First Corps in the Army of the Potomac, but were later made a part of the Fifth Corps, in which most of the regiments remained throughout their service. See Boatner, 634-35.

11. See *B & L,* 2:360-61 for details of the reunion between D. H. Hill and Reynolds.

12. OR, I, 11, pt. 2:391-392.

13. Sypher, 279-319.

14. *Ibid.,* 279-318.

15. OR, I, 11, pt. 2:391-392.

16. *Ibid.*, 844-846.

17. Egle, *Dauphin County*, 293.

18. See report of Lt. Col. Fisher, OR, I, 51, pt. 1:112-13.

19. Egle, *Dauphin County*, 293; None of the Andersons who served as Confederate generals had the initials "Q. U." The general referred to here might have been Richard Heron Anderson, George Burgwyn Anderson or Joseph Reid Anderson, for all three were on the field at Glendale.

20. *Ibid.*, 293-94.

21. *Ibid.*, 293.

22. *PU* 16 June 1862; Virtually all the prisoners that came to Camp Curtin arrived over the Cumberland Valley Railroad through Bridgeport, present day Lemoyne.

23. *PU* 23 June 1862.

24. Oliver Wendell Holmes, "My Hunt After 'The Captain.' " *The Atlantic*, December, 1862, 756 (hereafter Holmes, "My Hunt.").

25. *PU* 23 June 1862.

26. *PU* 17 June 1862.

27. *PU* 20 June 1862.

28. Egle, *Dauphin County*, 418-419.

29. J. Chandler Gregg, *Life in the Army, in the Departments of Virginia, and the Gulf*, (Philadelphia: Perkinpine & Higgins, 1866), 103.

30. Rohrer Pension File, National Archives.

31. Jeremiah Rohrer Diary, Manuscript Group 243, Division of Archives and Manuscripts, Pennsylvania Historical and Museum Commission.

32. *Ibid.*

33. *Ibid.*

34. *Ibid.*

35. *History of the 127th Regiment Pennsylvania Volunteers*, (Lebanon: Press of Report Publishing Co., 1902). 23-5.

36. Rohrer Diary, Pennsylvania State Archives.

37. Kieffer, 35.

38. *History of the 127th Pennsylvania*, 25.

39. Thomas Chamberlin, *History of the One Hundred and Fiftieth Regiment Pennsylvania Volunteers*, (Philadelphia: F. McManus, Jr. & Co., 1905), 28.

40. *PU* 16 August 1862; At this time, Camp Simmons was really just an extension of Camp Curtin and did not really have an identity of its own, this would change later in the war. Upon the departure of the nine-month regiments, yet another camp was established in the vicinity. Company A of the 127th, was retained in Harrisburg as the other nine companies of the regiment headed south. The company was to act as the provost guard for the city, and consequently established its own camp

away from the others. The company proceeded across the river to the heights above Bridgeport and overlooking the river. There was established Camp Dodge named after Captain Richard I. Dodge. Morning Reports of Company A, 127th PVI, Pennsylvania State Archives.

41. Letter signed "K" dated 9 August 1862 printed in Ted Alexander, ed., *History of the 126th Pennsylvania*, (Shippensburg, Pa.: Beidel Printing House, Inc., 1984), 107 (hereafter Alexander). Alexander states the letter appeared in *Chambersburg Valley Spirit* 13 August 1862.

42. Anonymous letter from "Smith" to "friend Black" and dated 27 August 1862 in Pennsylvania State Archives; Dr. Vicot Miller of Greencastle, Pennsylvania, later surgeon 78th Pennsylvania might have been examining surgeon at Camp Curtin at this time, see Alexander, 107.

43. Letters of J. M. Ray, Co. C, 140th Pennsylvania to his sister, Lizzie, dated September 7 and 10, 1862, Allegheny County Soldiers and Sailors Memorial.

44. Bloodgood, 15.

45. David Craft, *History of the One-Hundred Forty-First Regiment Pennsylvania Volunteers*, (Towanda, Pa.: David Craft, 1885), 1st page of ch. 2.

46. Bloodgood, 15.

47. *Ibid.*

48. Craft, 1st page, chapter 2.

49. *History of the 127th Pennsylvania*, 148.

50. This incident mentioned in letter from "Smith" to "friend Black" and dated 27 August 1862 in Pennsylvania State Archives.

51. John F. Koerper diaries, Manuscript Group 6, Pennsylvania State Archives.

52. Rohrer Diary, Pennsylvania State Archives.

53. *PU* 18 July 1862.

54. *B & L*, 2:605.

55. *History of the 127th Pennsylvania*, 24.

56. *PU* 12 October 1861; 25 October 1861; 4 March 1862; 20 March 1862; 16 June 1862.

57. OR, I, 19, pt. 2:203-204.

58. *Ibid.*, 268.

59. *PU* 17 September 1862.

60. *PU* 16 September 1862.

61. *Ibid.*

62. *PU* 17 September 1862.

63. Bates 5:1147-1221.

64. OR, I, 19, pt. 2:252.

65. Louis Richards, *Eleven Days in the Militia During the War of the Rebellion*, (Philadelphia: Collins, Printer, 1883), 18.

66. Richards, *Eleven Days*, 19.

67. *Ibid.*

68. *PU* 17 September 1862.

69. *PU* 16 September 1862.

70. Eminhizer Pension File, National Archives.

71. Albert, 195.

72. Albert, 195, Much of the 45th had been recruited in Curtin's home county of Centre.

73. OR, I, 19, pt. 1:268.

74. *PU* 19 September 1862; Carter Pension File, National Archives; Bates, 1:761.

75. Sypher, 379-80.

76. Sypher, 382-84; Meade's report OR, I, 19, pt. 1:268-71.

77. Farnum's name is spelled a variety of ways on various documents, depositions and rolls. Variations include "Farnam" and "Farnham".

78. See Frederick H. Dyer, *A Compendium of the War of the Rebellion*, (Des Moines: 1908), 3:1615.

79. Frederick L. Hitchcock, *War From the Inside*, (Philadelphia: J. B. Lippincott Co., 1904), 56.

80. Hitchcock, 58.

81. Oliver Christian Bosbyshell, ed., *Pennsylvania at Antietam*, (Harrisburg: Antietam Battlefield Memorial Commission, 1906), 190-91. It is interesting to note that in their relation of the beehive incident, both James V. Murfin in *The Gleam of Bayonets*, (Baton Rouge: Louisiana State University Press, 1965), 249, and Stephen W. Sears in *Landscape Turned Red*, (New Haven, Conn.: Ticknor & Fields, 1983), 239, state that a Confederate shot upset the hives. The original account, cited here and by both Murfin and Sears, states only that the men were under fire while running through the yard when the hives were tipped over. No Confederate shell is specifically mentioned as overturning the apiary.

82. Hitchcock, 58, 66.

83. John B. Gordon, *Reminiscences of the Civil War*, (New York: Charles Scribner's Sons, 1903, Reprint. Time Life Books, 1981), 84-85.

84. *Ibid.*, 87.

85. Hitchcock, 59.

86. *Ibid.*, 61.

87. See Gordon, 88-91. Gordon lived to fight again, eventually attaining the rank of major general and becoming one of the key leaders in the Army of Northern Virginia after recuperating from his wounds (see Boatner, 348-49); Lt. Col. Wilcox of the 132nd stated in his report that each man of the regiment entered the fight with 60 rounds of ammunition, yet most of them expended all of that and were forced to scramble about taking additional rounds from the killed and wounded who lay all about them. See OR, I, 19, pt. 1:330-31.

88. Farnum Pension File, National Archives.

89. Henry Gerrish papers, Civil War Times Illustrated Collection, USAMHI.

90. Gerrish papers, USAMHI; The farm Gerrish mentions is the Piper's farm. Most of the officers who filed reports emphasized the fighting at the sunken road or the cornfield and orchard beyond. Hancock,

however, speaks of an advance upon the Piper house "by the brigade of Caldwell [which included the 7th New York] and the two regiments under Colonel Brooke, under a heavy fire of musketry and artillery, the enemy having a section of brass pieces in the front firing grape and battery to the right throwing shell. This advance drove the enemy from the field and gave us possession of the house and its surroundings—the citadel of the enemy at this position of the line, it being a defensible building several hundred yards to the rear of the sunken road...." OR, I, 19, pt. 1:278.

91. Parker, 233.

92. Parker, 232; Jerome M. Loving, ed., *Civil War Letters of George Washington Whitman*, (Durham, NC: Duke University Press, 1975), 67.

93. Parker, 232.

94. *Ibid.*, 235.

95. *Ibid.*, 235-36; Parker Pension File, National Archives; for Beaver see Hain, *Perry County*; Bates, 2:35.

96. Ishbel Ross, *Angel of the Battlefield*, (New York: Harper & Brothers, 1956), 44-45.

97. Hitchcock, 73.

98. Farnum Pension File, National Archives; The 132nd had 728 officers and men present at roll call on the morning of the 17th and lost 2 officers killed, 4 wounded, and 28 men killed, 110 wounded, although 30 of these later died, see Hitchcock.

CHAPTER FIVE: *"Cripple Camp"*

1. Livermore, Thomas, *Numbers and Losses of the Civil War*, (Reprint, Dayton, Oh.: Morningside Books, 1986), 92-3.

2. *PU* 17, 19, 25, 30, September 1862.

3. Gerrish papers, USAMHI; "We had about five thousand cripples," wrote Gerrish, "and therefore named it 'The Cripple Brigade.' " While Gerrish's estimate is probably high, the Cripple Brigade was of considerable size.

4. Many of those who died throughout the war in Harrisburg of wounds or illness, both Union and Confederate, were simply buried in Harrisburg Cemetery, where their graves were marked and can still be seen. Frances Terry Ingmire has published an extremely helpful and much needed book entitled *Confederate P.O.W.'s: Soldiers and Sailors Who Died in Federal Prisons and Military Hospitals in the North*, (St. Louis: Ingmire Publications, 1984). Ms. Ingmire, whose work becomes ever more precious as the government issue grave markers in cemeteries across the North weather into illegibility, lists on page 175 the Confederates buried in Harrisburg Cemetery:

	rank	company	regiment	date died	grave no. & location
Moore, William	—	—	C.S.A.	12/19/63	58 Soldiers' Lot
Norman, W. Y.	—	G	3rd Ala.	7/21/63	74 Soldiers' Lot
Hicks, Derry	—	—	C.S.A.	7/24/63	78 Soldiers' Lot
Grady, Preston F.	—	—	C.S.A.	—	107 Soldiers' Lot
Brice, William	—	—	C.S.A.	10/4/63	108 Soldiers' Lot
Rice, B. F.	—	—	C.S.A.	10/22/63	110 Soldiers' Lot
Jackson, Boker	—	—	3rd Ala.	7/27/63	131 Soldiers' Lot
Page, Solomon S.	Color Cpl.	D	59 Ga.	8/7/63	132 Soldiers' Lot

	rank	company	regiment	date died	grave no. & location
Simms, E. B.	Cpl.	E	10 Ala.	9/19/63	133 Soldiers' Lot
Bowman, J. T.	Pvt.	I	16th NC	9/22/63	134 Soldiers' Lot
Coates, John H.	—	—	C.S.A.	10/10/63	135 Soldiers' Lot
Witherington, M.	Pvt.	D	50 Ga.	10/17/63	136 Soldiers' Lot
Williams, James M.	Sgt.	B	22 Ga.	10/22/63	137 Soldiers' Lot

As can be seen, all of the Confederate fatalities came in the months after Gettysburg.

5. *PU* 10 October, 10 November, 13 November, 22 November, 13 December 1862.

6. Holmes, "My Hunt," 754.

7. *Ibid.*, 755.

8. Holmes wrote that "The camp was on a fair plain, girdled with hills, spacious, well-kept apparently, but did not present any peculiar attraction for us. The visit would have been a dull one, had we not happened to get sight of a singular-looking set of human beings on the distance. Yet these were the estrays from the fiery army which [had given] our generals so much trouble,—"secesh prisoners.... There was a wild-haired, unsoaped boy, with pretty foolish features enough, who looked as if he might be about seventeen, as he said he was.
"What State do you come from?" asked Holmes.
"Georgy."
"What part of Georgia?"
"Midway."
[Holmes found this remarkable, for his father had been a pastor at a church in Midway, Georgia several decades before.] "Where did you go to church, when you were at home?"
"Never went inside 'f a church b't once in m' life."
"What did you do before you became a soldier?"
"Nothin'."
Holmes moved away shaking his head in pity of the "...poor ...dwarfed and etiolated soul, doomed by neglect to an existance but one degree above that of an idiot." Holmes, "My Hunt," 756-57.

9. *Ibid.*, 759-60.

10. *PU* 27 September 1862; *PU* 22 January 1863.

11. Gerrish papers, USAMHI.

12. *Ibid.*

13. *PU* 29 November; 2 December, 1862.

14. Gerrish had not been paid in nine months.

15. Gerrish papers, USAMHI.

16. Welsh commanded the 2nd Brigade, 1st Division of the Ninth Corps from April to September, 1862. In November of that year, he was promoted to Brigadier General, USV. Beaver then would have been senior officer in the 45th.

17. Chamberlin Pension File, National Archives.

18. Chamberlin, 29; William H. Powell, *Officers in the Army and Navy*, (Philadelphia: L. R. Hamersly & Co., 1893), 260; Bates, 4:649.

19. Lewis R. Hamersly, *Who's Who in Pennsylvania*, (New York: L. R. Hamersly, 1904), 118; Powell, 260.

20. *PU* 10 October 1862.

21. *PU* 16 October 1862.

22. Boynton Pension File, National Archives.

23. Camp McClellan was located "about two miles from the city near the Jonestown road" *PU* 12 November 1862; It was reported that Governor Curtin selected the name for the camp in honor of General McClellan who had just a few days before been relieved of this command; *PU* 12 November 1862.

24. *PU* 17 November 1862.

25. *PU* 25 November 1862.

26. *PU* 29 November 1862.

27. *PU* early November 1862 (date illegible); Oliver Wendell Holmes, "The Sweet Little Man" in The Poetical Works of Oliver Wendell Holmes, 2, Boston: Houghton Mifflin Company, the Riverside edition, 1908) 252-38; disgusted at the thousands of healthy, able-bodied young men he saw promenading on the sidewalks of Boston while thousands of others, including his son, Oliver Wendell, Jr., were off suffering on the front, Holmes wrote the following piece of propaganda, quoted only in part:

DEDICATED TO THE STAY-AT-HOME-RANGERS

Now, while our soldiers are fighting our battles,
Each at his post to do all that he can,
Down among rebels and contraband chattels,
What are you doing, my sweet little man?

All the Brave boys under canvas are sleeping,
All of them pressing to march with the van,
Far from home where their sweethearts are weeping;
What are you waiting for, sweet little man?

You with the terrible warlike mustaches,
fit for a colonel or chief of a clan,
You with the waist for sword-belts and sashes,
Where are your shoulder-straps, sweet little man?

Bring him the buttonless garment of woman!
Cover his face lest it freckle and tan;
Muster the Apron-String Guards on the Common,
That is the corps for the sweet little man!

Give him for escort a file of young misses,
Each of them armed with a deadly rattan;
They shall defend him from laughter and hisses,
Aimed by the low boys at the sweet little man....

28. McClure, *Old Time Notes of Pennsylvania*, 1, 540.

29. *Ibid.*

30. For a fascinating and detailed relation of the political difficulties of instituting the draft in Pennsylvania, see McClure, *Old Time Notes*, 1:540-51.

31. *PU* 16 October 1862.

32. *PU* 30 October 1862.

33. *PU* 13 November 1862.

34. *PU* 28 October 1862.

35. The provost guard was composed of 4 companies: Company A of the 127th, which was encamped at Camp Dodge across the river until Camp Curtin began thinning out in mid December, when they took up quarters there, and three independent companies—Captain Charles E. Baldwin's, which had been part of the battalion since September, Captain DeWitt C. James's, and Captain Wellington Jones's. Baldwin's Company encamped on the grounds of the capitol before the Arsenal, which it was the company's duty to guard, until December, when cold weather forced it into more comfortable quarters outside the Cotton Mill. Wooden shanties were erected there especially to house the companies of the provost battalion, and from mid December on, Baldwin's, James's and Jones's men were quartered there by the river; *PU* 11 December 1862; *PU* 15 December 1862.

36. *PU* 2 December 1862.

37. *PU* 15 December 1862.

38. *PU* 19 December 1862.

39. *PU* 13 November 1862.

40. *Ibid.*; Andress Pension File, National Archives; Andress was on duty in Unionville, Pennsylvania, immediately before coming to Camp Curtin in November, 1862.

41. *PU* 6 December 1862; *PU* 11 December 1862.

42. Heffelfinger Pension File, National Archives.

43. Henry Wilson Storey, *History of Cambria County Pennsylvania*, (New York: The Lewis Publishing Co., 1907), 2:249.

44. Report of Meade, OR, 1, 21:512.

45. Letter from C. F. Taylor to brother dated 1 September 1862, Hobson and Shankman, 351.

46. Letter from C. F. Taylor to brother dated 25 October 1862, Hobson and Shankman, 335.

47. Hobson and Shankman, 337.

48. *Ibid.*

49. OR, I, 21, 455.

50. Storey, 2:249-50.

51. OR, I, 21:140, 512.

52. Heffelfinger Pension File, National Archives.

53. Amos M. Judson, *History of the Eighty-Third Regiment Pennsylvania Volunteers*, (Erie, Pa.: B. F. H. Lynn, Publisher, Reprint, Alexandria, Va.: Stonewall House, 1985), 57.

54. *History of the 127th Pennsylvania*, 120.

55. *Ibid.*, 122-133.

56. John and Charles Creamer Pension Files, National Archives.

57. Charles Creamer Pension File, National Archives.

58. OR, I, 21:226, 261 (reports of Hancock and Colonel Brooke).

59. Storey, 2:250.

60. Livermore, 96.

61. Dyer, 3:1573-74; Amsden Pension File, National Archives.

62. Amsden Pension File, National Archives.

63. *Harrisburg Daily Telegraph*, 8 January 1863 (hereafter *HDT*), *PU* 17 January 1863. Establishments similar to the Soldiers' Retreat were operated in some other cities, one of the first and probably the greatest was the Refreshment Saloon in Philadelphia.

64. 360 men occupied hospital beds in Harrisburg three weeks after Fredericksburg, compared to well over 600 at the same interval after Antietam. Sharpsburg was geographically closer to Harrisburg than to Washington or Baltimore and a railroad ran from Hagerstown, not 15 miles from the battlefield, directly up the Cumberland Valley to the Keystone State's capital, so men were shipped north to the banks of the Susquehanna.

65. *PU* 8 November 1862, *PU* 11 December and 15 December 1862. The severity of the outbreak of small pox in Harrisburg was greatly exaggerated in story and rumor, especially in other cities in the commonwealth. The actual extent and course of the outbreak can be fairly well gauged and followed through a series of small pieces in the *Patriot & Union* between 8 November and 19 March.

66. A number of drafted men, mostly deserters and men who had never reported in the first place but had eventually been rounded up, continued to arrive in Harrisburg throughout December, even after the drafted regiments had departed. As Camp Curtin was under restriction, and the Soldiers' Retreat was occupied by recruits, there was no place to quarter these men. In mid January, then, a camp was formed right on the river bank, above the city proper and below Camp Curtin, and was named Camp Sands, after former commandant of Camp Curtin Captain William Sands. The *Daily Telegraph* of 16 January 1863 gives the location of the camp as "near the river bank, above Hardscrabble," which was a neighborhood of Harrisburg. There were then only about one hundred fifty men in the Camp Sands, and the population never grew much over 200. In the first week in March, after the small pox had run its course, the camp was abandoned and the 200 or so men were moved to Camp Curtin. *PU* 17 January, 21 January 1863, *PU* 6 March 1863; *PU* 29 December 1862, 3 January and 6 January 1863; *HDT* 5 January 1863.

67. *HDT* 15 January and 16 January 1863 *PU* January 1863. As of 26 February (see *PU* of that date), Dr. S. S. Schultz was in charge of the Cotton Mill Hospital, J. J. Seiler of the Walnut Street Hospital, and J. M. Kelker of the German Reformed Church Hospital.

68. *PU* 13 January 1863; 18 February 1863.

69. *HDT* 16 January 1863.

70. See Dyer, 1:1589; William Wallace Geety papers, Harrisburg Civil War Round Table Collection, USAMHI, S.O. #386 of the Department of the South.

71. *HDT* 16 January 1863.

72. *PU* 26 December 1862.

73. *PU* 12 June 1863, Dr. Wilson removed the ball on June 5, 1863 at Camp Curtin.

74. Geety papers. Order appointing Geety to the quartermaster post at Camp Curtin was signed by Captain W. B. Lane, 3rd U.S. Cavalry, acting commandant. Lieutenant G. M. Brayton of the 15th U.S. Infantry was post adjutant.

75. *PU* 2 April 1863, *PU* 21 May 1863, Bates 2:201, 204; Williams, *Ceremonies at the Dedication at Camp Curtin*, 14.

76. Joseph W. Muffly, *The Story of Our Regiment, A History of the 148th Pennsylvania Volunteers*, (Harrisburg: Meyers Print House, 1889), 84-5. *Biographical album of Prominent Pennsylvanians*, 9, Frank A. Burr, *Life and Achievements of James Addams Beaver*, (Philadelphia: Furguson Bros. & Co., 1882), 60-61.

77. Livermore, 98.

78. *PU* 13 May 1863, *PU* 18 April 1863, *PU* 25 May 1863.

79. *PU* 5 May 1863.

80. *History of the 127th Pennsylvania*, 198-200.

81. *Ibid.*

82. *Ibid.*, 202.

83. George F. Sprenger, *Camp and Field Life of the 122nd Penn's Volunteers*, (Lancaster, Pa.: New Era Steam Book, 1885), 322-323.

84. Sprenger, 322.

85. Hitchcock, 243.

CHAPTER SIX: *"The Entire Lot Would Not Have Amounted to a Row of Pins"*

1. Charles Bracelen Flood, *Lee: The Last Years*, (Boston: The Houghton Mifflin Company, 1981), 165-66.

2. OR, I, 27, pt. 3:79.

3. *PU* 16 June 1863.

4. Cullum, 2:266-67, Warner *Blue*, 95-6, Boatner, 204-05; *PU* 16 June 1863.

5. *PU* 4 June 1863. Later in the month, another new camp was founded in the area, this one on the property of a Mr. A. Boyd Hamilton east of town. It was to serve as a depot for cavalry horses that had been purchased and were being shipped by the army. The new camp, like Camp Curtin, was to be under the control of the Army. Captain J. F. Brisbin, U.S.A. was said to have been responsible for establishing the camp. *PU* 25 June 1863.

6. *PU* 19 June 1863; Milroy's wagon train was camped "on the flats the other side of the canal," until 18 June when it moved to a new site "about three miles out on the Jonestown Road...." OR, I, 27, pt. 3:162 Couch reported the arrival and size of Milroy's train on 16 June.

7. George W. Wingate, *History of the Twenty Second Regiment of the National Guard of the State of New York From Its Organization to 1895*, (New York: Edwin W. Dayton, Publisher and Bookseller, 1896), 156-57.

8. From an article by E. Burd Grubb that appeared in the Burlington, NJ, *Gazette* and reprinted in a Harrisburg paper. Unidentified clipping from Harrisburg newspaper in possession of Dauphin County Historical Society, Philip German Notebook 1; The fence on river bank in Harris Park is no longer standing, but a photograph shows that a plain, white picket fence did stand in Harris Park just on the edge of the bluff that dropped to meet the water.

9. OR, I, 27, pt. 2:256-57 report of Colonel Chauncy Abbott, 67th NYSNG.

10. John Lockwood, *Our Campaign Around Gettysburg*, (Brooklyn: A. H. Rome & Brothers, Stationers & Printers, 1864), 23.

11. OR, I, 27, pt. 2:241 report of Brigadier General Philip S. Crooke, NYSNG.

12. Henry Weldmar Ruoff, ed., *Biographical and Portrait Cyclopedia of Schuylkill County, Pennsylvania*, (Philadelphia: Rush, West and Co., 1893), 299-300.

13. Knipe Pension File, National Archives.

14. Muffly, 91.

15. Burr, 63-64, letter of Couch dated Norwalk, Connecticut, 1882.

16. Muffly, 92.

17. Burr, 60-62; Muffly, 92.

18. Hain, 661; Muffly, 92.

19. *PU* 17 June 1863.

20. OR, I, 27, pt. 2:256, report of Colonel Chauncey Abbott.

21. H. M. M. Richards, *Pennsylvania's Emergency Men at Gettysburg: A Touch of Bushwhacking*, (Reading, Pa.: H. M. M. Richards, 1895), 5.

22. Samuel W. Pennypacker, "Six Weeks in Uniform: Being a Record of a Term in the Military Service of the United States in the Gettysburg Campaign of 1863," in his *Historical and Biographical Sketches*, (Philadelphia: Robert A. Tripple, 1883), 312.

23. Pennypacker, 313.

24. James W. Latta, *History of the First Regiment, National Guard of Pennsylvania*, (Philadelphia: J. B. Lippincott, 1912), 80.

25. OR, I, 27, pt. 2:271, report of Colonel Watson Fox, 74th NYSNG.

26. Pennypacker, 315.

27. H. M. M. Richards, 7.

28. OR, I, 27, pt. 2:257.

29. H. M. M. Richards, 6.

30. Wingate, 158.

31. H. M. M. Richards, 6.

32. Lockwood, 23.

33. *PU* 22 June 1863.

34. Muffly, 94; One span of the old Mulberry Street Bridge was also partially cut. Hoy, "Harrisburg."

35. *PU* 27 June 1863.

36. *PU* 22 June 1863.

37. *PU* 27 June 1863.

38. *Ibid.*; *PU* 25 June 1863.

39. Hoy, "Harrisburg."; *Harrisburg Evening Telegraph* 15 June 1863; *PU* 22 June 1862.

40. *Pennsylvania Archives*, IV, 8:502-04; See also OR, I, 27, pt. 3:347-8.

41. Jacob Hoke, *The Great Invasion of 1863*, (New York: Thomas Yoseloff, 1959), 128-29.

42. See H. M. M. Richards, 8-10; Nye, 272-73.

43. Pennypacker, 315.

44. Edwin B. Coddington, *The Gettysburg Campaign: A Study in Command*, (New York: Charles Scribner's Sons, 1984), 144; OR, I, 27, pt. 3:407.

45. Wingate 160-162.

46. Letter from C. F. Taylor to Annie Taylor dated 24 June 1863 in Hobson and Shankman, 360.

47. *B & L*, 3:397.

48. Letter from Sgt. Major A. P. Morrison, 9th Pennsylvania Reserves, to brother Will dated 21 July 1863. Adam Torrance Papers, Division of History, Pennsylvania Historical and Museum Commission (viewed in Pennsylvania Reserves file at Gettysburg National Military Park library).

49. Storey, 2:334, recollections by Colonel Jackson, 11th Reserves.

50. Bates, 4:1003; see *Pennsylvania at Gettysburg: Ceremonies at the Dedication of the Monuments Erected by the Commonwealth of Pennsylvania to Major General George G. Meade, Major General Winfield S. Hancock, Major General John F. Reynolds and to Mark the Positions of the Pennsylvania Commands Engaged in the Battle*, (Harrisburg: Board of Commissioners for the erection of monuments to mark the position of the Pennsylvania commands engaged in the battle of Gettysburg, 1904), 2:875.

51. It is ironic that Reynolds died on July 1st. Exactly one year earlier Seneca Simmons, then a colonel in Reynold's brigade, died after being wounded the evening before at the battle of Glendale. Simmons was then in temporary command of Reynolds's brigade, but it had been Reynolds who had ended Simmons's chances for promotion to brigadier general.

52. *Pennsylvania at Gettysburg*, 2:745.

53. *Ibid.*, 746.

54. *Ibid.*, 749.

55. Chamberlin, *150th*, 128.

56. Chamberlin Pension File, National Archives.

57. *Pennsylvania at Gettysburg*, 2:754.

58. Chamberlin Pension File, National Archives.

59. Letter of Chaplain Adam Torrance, 11th Pennsylvania Reserves, to wife dated 6 July 1863, Adam Torrance Papers, Division of History, Pennsylvania Historical and Museum Commission (viewed in Pennsylvania Reserves file at Gettysburg National Military Park library); Thomson, 266-67; OR, I, 27, pt. 1:653, 657.

60. Thomson, n266.

61. *Pennsylvania at Gettysburg*, 1:301-02; Thomson, 268-70; Letter from Aaron Baker to Annie Taylor dated 11 July 1863 in Hobson and Shankman, 360-61.

62. "Cannonading was very plainly audible in Harrisburg. Front Street was packed during the early days of July to hear the battle. Some say it could be heard in Wilkes-Barre." Hoy "Harrisburg."

63. Livermore, 102.

64. Letter of J. M. Ray dated 5 July 1863, Allegheny County Soldiers and Sailors Memorial, see Bates 4:418-420 for names of wounded and company roster.

65. Letters of J. M. Ray dated 6 and 10 July 1863, Allegheny County Soldiers and Sailors Memorial.

66. George T. Stevens, *Three Years in the Sixth Corps*, (Albany: S. R. Gray, Publisher, 1866, Reprint. Time Life Books, 1984), 254.

67. OR, I, 27, pt. 1:25, report of John M. Cuyler, Medical Inspector United States Army.

68. *PU* 25 June 1863.

69. *PU* 31 August 1863.

70. *PU* 29 July 1863.

71. See *PU* 27 July and August, 1863 for notes on arrival of wounded. At an undetermined point in the city, an "invalid camp" was established for the throngs of ambulatory cases that were too sound to be in hospitals and too weak to be with their regiments.

72. *PU* 31 August 1863.

73. *PU* 19 August 1863.

74. See *PU* 23 July 1863; other hospitals in the city housing Confederates were the "German Reformed Church and the school house on the corner of Cherry and Raspberry alleys." On July 22nd, a huge shipment of over 1,000 wounded Confederates passed through Harrisburg. Some were retained in the city, but by far the most continued on to New York City, where they would be kept on or about Staten Island. *PU* 23 July 1863.

75. See *PU* 23 July 1863 and 19 August 1863 for notes on number and descriptions of some of the Confederate prisoners after Gettysburg.

76. Muffly, 93, Burr, 63; see also Hain, 661.

77. Burr, 63-64; see also Muffly, 94.

78. Sands Pension File and Service Record, National Archives; Bates, 1:1049.

79. *PU* 23 July 1863.

80. *PU* 23 July 1863; Bates, 3:629.

81. *PU* 23 July 1863, says Camp Simmons was "Immediately in the rear of Camp Curtin."

82. Bates 5:222; Ramsey later became lieutenant colonel of the 187th Pennsylvania, organized in March, 1864.

83. *PU* 23 July 1863.

CHAPTER SEVEN: *"May You Ever Be Marked As Brave Men"*

1. *PU* 1 September 1863; The new commissary building at Harrisburg completed about the end of August was located "opposite the foot of Mulberry St." and measured 57' x 160'. The odd shape was due to the structure sitting on a piece of land between the Pennsylvania Canal and the railroad tracks. The establishment was under the charge of a Captain Gilman, U.S.A.; Francis T. Miller *Photographic History of the Civil War*, (New York: The Review of Reviews Co., 1912), 4:328, for mention of the cavalry depot in Harrisburg.

2. *PU* 8 August 1863.

3. *PU* 27 August 1863.

4. *PU* 12 September 1863, The *Patriot and Union* reported that Captains Sands and Critzman "were charged with selecting a new site [for the camp]." Just who charged them with the task in not known. The farmland on the Reading Pike that the captains selected belonged to a Mr. Rutherford.

5. Alexander Pension File, National Archives.

6. *PU* 2 February 1864; Brooke arrived with his men on the last day of January, 1864, and took command of the camp.

7. *DAB*, 1:71.

8. Cullum 1:524-25; OR, I, 1:567-68; OR, III, 5:888-89; see also George D. Ruggles's revealing observations of Bomford recorded in OR, III, 4:519-23.

9. *PU* 9 December 1863.

10. Henry C. Parry diary, The Parry Family Collection, USAMHI.

11. Letter of John Woods, Woods Family Collection, Pennsylvania State Archives; Woods Pension File, National Archives.

12. OR, I, 33:636-38, 773.

13. OR, I, 34, pt. 1:416-18; report of General McMillian; Alexander Pension File, National Archives; Letter of James Kacy to W. W. Geety dated 29 May 1864 in Geety Papers, Harrisburg Civil War Round Table Collection, USAMHI.

14. OR, I, 34, pt. 1:416-18; report of General McMillian.

15. Letter of James Kacy to W. W. Geety dated 29 May 1864 in Geety Papers, Harrisburg Civil War Round Table Collection, USAMHI; Hangen Service Record, National Archives; Hangen left virtually no record of his post war life. He did have a daughter who married in Allentown but nothing more is known about Hangen himself; see Bates 1:1157, 1165.

16. Sands Service Record, National Archives. Sand's commanding officer, Colonel John Taylor, was also commander of the cavalry brigade to which the regiment belonged, and he shared Lt. Col. Gardner's displeasure over Sands's long absence. In endorsing Gardner's letter, he wrote that it had been suggested to Sands a number of times that he return to the regiment, but that the captain had ignored all such suggestions and requests. Taylor therefore recommended that Sands be "dismissed that the position may be filled by one more deserving."

17. Bates 1:730.

18. Deposition of Sergeant John McLane, Co. H., Heffelfinger Pension File; Heffelfinger Service Record, National Archives.

19. *PU* 7 June 1864.

20. For accounts of the return of the Pennsylvania Reserves to Harrisburg, see Sypher 547-553; *PU* 7 and 9 June 1864; Glover 265-66; letter dated 8 June 1864 from John Woods, Woods family Collection, Pennsylvania State Archives.

21. Hain, 662-63 for Mintzer's recollections; Muffly, 136 for Beaver's remembrances.

22. *B & L*, 4:593.

23. Ruoff, 298-300.

24. Muffly, 136-37.

25. *Ibid.*, 137.

26. *Ibid.*, 137-38.

27. *Ibid.*, 138-39; see also Burr.

28. Gilmore Service Record, National Archives.

29. Alexander Pension File, National Archives.

30. Way Service Record, National Archives.

31. Cottrell Service Record, National Archives.

32. Cottrell was far from being a well man, when he came to Camp Curtin, and his lengthy stay there would do him no good. Toward the end of his time in Harrisburg, an examining surgeon at Camp Return in March, 1865 found him suffering from "functional disorder of the liver and general debility," which Cottrell always believed he had acquired at Camp Return. He was severely affected by the disease and by late summer he could no longer perform the duties of commandant. He took a leave of absence and returned to Lansing, but he could not regain his health and on September 15 he was discharged. Except for the leave of absence in August, 1865, Cottrell appears to have been in command of Camp Return for most of the summer of 1865. He died January 16, 1901. Cottrell Service Record and Pension File, National Archives.

33. *PU* 15 February 1865; The Camp Hospital remained open and functioning throughout the winter, and in January, 1865, was under the charge of Assistant Surgeon Thomas Sherwood. RG 617, *Returns of Military Posts, Harrisburg*, 1862-1866, National Archives.

34. Cullum, 2:356-57; OR, III, 5:888-89.

35. Warner *Blue*, 229-30.

36. Randlett Pension File, National Archives. Camp Hinks was home to three companies of the 16th Regiment V.R.C. during its stay in Harrisburg after March, 1865, and while its location is unknown, two of its commanders are. Randlett was definitely in command in June, 1865, and Captain Henry C. Herr, Company A, 16th Regiment V.R.C. was in command in November, 1865 (see RG 617, *Returns of Military Posts, Harrisburg*, 1862-1866, National Archives.) Maps and newspaper accounts indicate that a camp was located just outside the main gate of Camp Curtin between the Ridge Road and the Pennsylvania Canal. This camp might have been Camp Hinks. The 16th Regiment was also billeted in some buildings on Second Street near the capitol for a time, and it is possible that they may have referred to the "barracks" and the surrounding area as "Camp Hinks."

37. *PU* 27 February 1865.

38. *PU* 8, 14, 15, and 19 February 1865 for weather preceding flood, *PU* 20, 21, and 30 March 1865 for flood and aftermath.

39. Bates 1:730; Heffelfinger Pension File, National Archives.

CHAPTER EIGHT: *"Classic Ground"*

1. *PU* 25 February, 28 February 1865, Miss Keene starred in two productions in Harrisburg during the week of February 25, 1865: "She Stoops to Conquer" and "Our American Cousin." The house was packed for the shows and all who attended went away raving about the talent and ability of Miss Keene.

2. The precise location of Camp Return is not known, but it is likely that it was on the ground that was once Camp Simmons. A member of the 57th Regiment states, that the regiment was "marched out to what was called 'Camp Return,' adjoining 'Old Camp Curtin,' " Martin, 161.

3. *PU* 30 May 1865; the principal mustering officer was Major William Hyde Clark, who was assisted by a Lieutenant Doebler and a Lieutenant Catlin.

4. See OR, III, 5:888-89.

5. Cullum, 1:491-92.

6. *PU* 7 June 1865.

7. *PU* 5 June 1865.

8. Jonathan W. Kerr diary, Manuscript Group 6, Pennsylvania State Archives.

9. Albert, 303.

10. *Ibid.*, 303; Westbrook, 253.

11. *PU* 5 June 1865.

12. *History of Venango County, Pennsylvania,* (Philadelphia: Brown, Runk, & Co., 1890), 182-3.

13. *PU* 8 June 1865; Harrisburg residents were not entirely uninterested in seeing the returned veterans and the ceremonies at camp, and the hacks again did a good business, so good, in fact, that they created a traffic problem in the heart of the city. To reduce the severity of the problem, the city council and the mayor were forced to designate hack stands from which the carriages could operate. There was competition to the hackmen, however. Street car or trolley tracks had been laid from a point downtown out to camp, and in July, a solitary passenger car began making regular runs out to camp. The newfangled thing was fraught with problems, however, and continually jumped its track, leaving passengers stranded in the heat and dust of the no man's land between Camp Curtin and the city. The hackmen survived the competition of invention. *PU* 8 July 1865; *PU* 2 August 1865.

14. Kerr Diary, Pennsylvania State Archives.

15. Albert, 302.

16. *Ibid.*, 187.

17. *Ibid.*, 303.

18. *Ibid.*, 302-303.

19. See Curtin's Annual Message of 1865, *Pennsylvania Archives*, IV, 8:659-62.

20. *PU* 8 August 1865.

21. Because his men were the only troops in Camp Return in the autumn of 1865, LaMotte was nominally in command of the camp until November. He was honorably discharged March 22, 1866 and died May 24, 1887; Heitman, 2:613.

22. *PU* 5 August 1865; *PU* 10 August 1865.

23. *PU* 14 August 1865; *PU* 21 August 1865; The members of the Veteran Reserve Corps still in the city in August, 1865, were quartered in what was called a barracks on Second Street; see Bates 4:337; 5:992; and Boatner, 458-59 for Kiddoo. Colonel Kiddoo apparently acted as commandant of Camp Curtin from time to time, especially in May and June, 1864. RG 617, *Returns of Military Posts, Harrisburg,* 1862-1866, National Archives.

24. *PU* 5 October 1865.

25. *PU* 26 September 1865.

26. *PU* 2 September 1865 for 7th Cavalry; *PU* 21 September 1865 for 78th PVI; Janet Mae Book incorrectly states in her *Northern Rendezvous,* that Camp Curtin was abandoned in September of 1865. The root of the error might lie in this report in the *Patriot & Union* of 21 September, which states that Camp Curtin was deserted. Examination of later issues of the same paper indicate that the camp existed officially into November, 1865, and was probably used as a resting place by a few late returning regiments perhaps as late as May, 1866. There is no way of determining precisely when the last tent was struck from Camp Curtin, but it was most certainly after September, 1865; *PU* 31 October 1865 for Battery B, see also Dyer, 3:1574.

27. *PU* 11 November 1865.

28. The Camp Curtin Hospital remained open well into 1866 to care for sick and wounded veterans. Assistant Surgeon H. B. Silliman was in charge. RG 617, *Returns of Military Posts, Harrisburg,* 1862-1866, National Archives.

29. *PU* 5 June 1865.

EPILOGUE

1. Shelby Foote *The Civil War: A Narrative* (New York: Random House, 1963), 2:250.

2. Alexander Pension File, National Archives.

3. Amsden Pension File, National Archives.

4. Andress Pension File, National Archives.

5. *Biographical Album of Prominent Pennsylvanians,* 1889, 11-12; Donehoo, 3:1509; Hain, 665-66; Beaver Pension File, National Archives.

6. Bierer Pension File, National Archives.

7. Cullum 1:524-25.

8. Heitman 1:229; Heitman gives Bomford's retirement date as 8 June 1874.

9. Boynton Pension File, National Archives.

10. *DAB,* 2:70-71.

11. Chamberlin, *History of the 150th,* 170, 203; Powell, 260; Hamersly, *Who's Who,* 118; Chamberlin Pension File, National Archives.

12. Charles Creamer Pension File, National Archives.

13. John Creamer Pension File, National Archives.

14. *DAB,* 2:606-08.

15. Heitman 1:377.

16. Cullum 2:356-57.

17. Eminhizer Pension File, National Archives.

18. Farnum Pension File, National Archives.

19. Geety Pension File, National Archives.

20. Gerrish Pension File, National Archives.

21. Roberts, *Montgomery County,* 1:517; George P. Donehoo, ed., *Pennsylvania: A History,* (New York: Lewis Historical Publishing Co., Inc., 1926), 3:1479-88; Warner, *Blue,* 212.

22. Heffelfinger Pension File, National Archives.

23. Egle, *Dauphin County,* 418-19.

24. Knipe Pension File, National Archives.

25. *Biographical and Portrait Cyclopedia of Schuylkill County Pennsylvania,* 298-300.

26. Parker Pension File, National Archives.

27. Donehoo, 3:1532.

28. Rohrer Pension File, National Archives; It is unclear just when Rohrer went into the liquor business in Lancaster, but it is known that he was engaged in that occupation as of 1907.

29. Sands Pension File, National Archives.

30. Bates, *Martial Deeds*, 409; Simmons Pension File, National Archives; Egle, *Dauphin County*, 294.

31. Egle, *Notes and Queries*, Series 4, 1:320.

32. Hobson and Shankman, 339.

33. Frank Moore, *Rebellion Record; A Diary of American Events*, 7:52.

34. *Biographical Annals of Lancaster County*, Beers, 11; Bates, *Martial Deeds*, 582-83.

35. Egle, *Dauphin County*, 244; Williams Pension File, National Archives.

36. Bates, 5:232.

37. Woods Pension File, National Archives.

Acknowledgements

In 1985, I moved from Harrisburg, Pennsylvania to Brookline, Massachusetts. The logistical problems alone of writing about Harrisburg from a distance of over four hundred miles were tremendous. I am therefore greatly indebted to the following people who helped shorten the distance between Massachusetts, where most of the writing was done, and Harrisburg, where most of the history was enacted. It is not the slightest exaggeration to say that this book would not exist without their help.

Any researcher or writer is fortunate to have in his acquaintance a knowledgeable librarian; I am blessed with the friendship of two. The expertise, the selflessness, the willingness to help me and the good common sense of Ms. Donna Ferullo of the Social Work Library at Boston College and Mr. Tom Duszak, librarian for the Senate of Pennsylvania, enabled me to complete this book. They have my gratitude and respect—as friends and professionals.

A number of people gave me the benefit of their knowledge through extended conversation, correspondence or cooperation. I am grateful for the generosity of Rosine Bucher, librarian and genealogist at the Soldiers and Sailors Memorial Hall of Allegheny County in Pittsburgh, of Karen E. Atwood, then executive director at the Dauphin County Historical Society, and of Colonel John Trussell of the Pennsylvania Historical and Museum Commission (retired) for the loan of his manuscript biography of General Joseph F. Knipe. Tom Schaefer, formerly of the Dauphin County Historical Society, was a source of both encouragement and material assistance, as was Betty Smith, curator at the Susquehanna County Historical Society and Free Library Association in Montrose, Pennsylvania. Ms. Resta M. Tressler, president of the Historical Society of Perry County in Newport, Pennsylvania, provided me with difficult to find and much needed information about Governor James Beaver. Michael Musick, Military Records Branch of the National Archives, afforded invaluable assistance in tapping the resources in Washington. John Shelly of the Pennsylvania State Archives and both Bob Mason and Bill Carlson of the Newspaper Library at the State Library of Pennsylvania endured what must have seemed an interminable number of requests for assistance during innumerable visits to their respective offices. Mr. Gary Bechtel of Gettysburg National Military Park, and Mr. Larry James, Mr. A. Wilson Greene and Ms. Janice Frye of Fredericksburg National Battlefield all provided courteous assistance during my visits to their respective facilities, and I am grateful to them. I thank Dr. Richard Sommers, archivist at the U.S. Army Military History Institute at Carlisle Barracks, Pennsylvania, for his help in discovering important manuscript sources at his institution, and Mr. Randy Hackenburg for his genial and professional assistance in locating and reproducing photographs from the MOLLUS collections at the USAMHI.

Thanks also to all the many people who answered my letters and questions or helped me in other ways, including Mr. Kenneth Rapp of the archives of West Point, Mrs. J. F. Parsons, librarian at the Vermont Historical Society in Montpelier, Rodney G. Dennis, curator of Manuscripts at the Houghton Library at Harvard University; Phebe R. Jackson of the Maryland State Archives Hall of Records, Annapolis; Betty Ammons of the Baltimore Conference United Methodist Historical Society; Ruth S. Reid, archivist at the Historical Society of Western Pennsylvania, Pittsburgh; Theresa Snyder of the Pennsylvania Historical Society in Philadelphia; the Reference and Interlibrary Loan staff at the Brookline, Massachusetts, Public Library; Mrs. Wanda Dowell and staff at Fort Ward Museum in Alexandria, Virginia: and Gloria Anderson of the City of Harrisburg's Engineering Division.

I thank Mr. and Mrs. Winfield Loban of Harrisburg, who have had a life-long interest in Camp Curtin. Mr. and Mrs. Loban were present at the dedication of the Camp Curtin Memorial in 1922 and shared with me their considerable knowledge about the memorial and the movement to erect it. The Lobans also related family anecdotes about Camp Curtin—Mr. Loban's grandfather, John Loban, lived not far from Camp Curtin and is mentioned in this history. His wife baked pies at this farm and sent them by her son, Winfield Loban's father, to Camp Curtin to be sold to the soldiers. Mrs. Loban neglected to tell the boy that he was to sell the pies, for he took them to camp and stood by as the soldiers helped themselves. Both mother and son were surprised when the lad returned home penniless. I am grateful also to Pastor James Bishop of the Camp Curtin Memorial Methodist Church for his patience in allowing me to photograph the mural in his beautiful church.

Thanks go to my friends Ken Fody, who helped me solve the logistical problems of obtaining hard-to-find books, and Jeff Cox, who was exceedingly generous of his time and energy in providing an exceptionally critical reading of the manuscript. Author-historian Kevin Ruffner, a friend and neighbor, also gave me the benefits of his insights after a thorough reading, and he has my thanks. For his interest, encouragement and friendship I am grateful to Canon Charles Martin of Washington Cathedral, headmaster emeritus of St. Albans School. The unexpectedly difficult task of obtaining the photographs in this book was eased considerably by the generosity of Chuck and Valerie Norville of Alexandria, Virginia, and to them I am much indebted. Jay and Janet McClatchey and their son, Sean, offered me the hospitality of their home during research visits to Washington, and Dick and Nancy Lou Jenkins were equally gracious on my visits to Pittsburgh, and I thank them all. Many thanks are due to Dr. Martin Gordon and the staff at White Mane for their patience and guidance. I am also grateful to Mr. Joseph Casino of Villanova University, who helped me understand what writing history is all about, and, also to Dr. Oliver G. Ludwig of Villanova, who had much to do with the writing of this book and whatever quality might be perceived in it.

Finally, I thank my wife, Susan, who not only helped me materially, but was a constant source of inspiration. But for her, it would not have been done.

Bibliography

GENERAL REFERENCE AND OTHER WORKS

Amann, William Frayne, ed. *Personnel of the Civil War*. vol. 2. *The Union Armies*. New York: Thomas Yoseloff, 1961.

Boatner, Mark Mayo III. *The Civil War Dictionary*. New York: David McKay Company, Inc., 1959.

Coddington, Edwin B. *The Gettysburg Campaign: A Study in Command*. New York: Charles Scribner's Sons, 1984.

Commager, Henry Steele, ed. *The Blue and the Gray*. 2 vols. Indianapolis: Bobbs-Merrill, 1950; Reprint. New York: The Fairfax Press, 1982.

Cullum, George Washington. *Biographical Register of Officers and Graduates of the U.S. Military Academy*. New York: 1869.

Dyer, Frederick H. *A Compendium of the War of the Rebellion*. 3 vols. Des Moines, Iowa, 1908.

Egle, William H., ed. *Notes & Queries: Historical, Biographical and Genealogical*. 4th series, vol. 1. Harrisburg Publishing Company, 1893.

Heitman, Francis B. *Historical Register and Dictionary of the United States Army, 1789-1903*. 2 vols. Washington, D.C.: Government Printing Office, 1903.

Hoke, Jacob. *The Great Invasion of 1863*. New Edition. New York: Thomas Yoseloff, 1959.

Holmes, Oliver Wendell. *The Poetical Works of Oliver Wendell Holmes*, vol. 2. Boston: Houghton Mifflin Company, The Riverside Edition, 1908.

Ingmire, Frances Terry. *Confederate P.O.W.s: Soldiers and Sailors Who Died in Federal Prisons and Military Hospitals in the North*. St. Louis: Ingmire Publications, 1984.

Johnson, Robert Underwood and Clarence Clough Buel, eds. *Battles and Leaders of the Civil War*, 4 vols. New York: Century, 1887, Reprint. Castle Books, 1982.

Leech, Margaret. *Reveille in Washington, 1860-1865*, New York: Harper & Bros., 1941.

Livermore, Thomas L. *Numbers and Losses in the Civil War in America. 1861-65*. Reprint. Dayton, Ohio: Morningside Books, 1986.

Long, E. B. *The Civil War Day by Day*. Garden City, New York: Doubleday & Company, Inc., 1971.

Malone, Dumas, ed. *Dictionary of American Biography*. 11 vols. New York: Charles Scribner's Sons, 1946.

Miller, Francis Trevelyan, ed. *The Photographic History of the Civil War*. vol 4. New York: The Review of Reviews Co., 1912.

Moore, Frank. *Rebellion Record: A Diary of American Events*, vol. 7. New York, 1861, 1868.

Mulholland, St. Clair. *Medal of Honor Legion of the United States*. Philadelphia: Town Printing, 1905.

Murdock, Eugene C. *One Million Men: The Civil War Draft in the North*. Madison, Wisconsin: The State Historical Society of Wisconsin, 1971.

Nye, Wilbur S. *Here Come the Rebels!* Baton Rouge: Louisiana State University Press, 1965. rpt. Morningside Bookshop, Dayton, Ohio, 1984.

Scott, Robert Garth. *Into the Wilderness with the Army of the Potomac*. Bloomington, Indiana: University of Indiana Press, 1985.

Sears, Stephen W. *Landscape Turned Red*. New Haven, CT: Ticknor & Fields, 1983.

Townsend, Thomas S. *The Honors of the Empire State in the War of the Rebellion*. New York: A. Lovell & Co., 1884.

United States Government. *The Medal of Honor of the United States Army*. Washington, D.C.: U.S. Government Printing Office, 1948.

Warner, Ezra J. *Generals in Gray*. Baton Rouge: Louisiana State University Press, 1959.

_____. *Generals in Blue*. Baton Rouge: Louisiana State University Press, 1964.

War of the Rebellion, A Compilation of the Official Records of the Union and Confederate Armies. 70 vols. in 128 parts, Washington, D.C., 1880-1901.

Whipkey, Harry E. *Guide to the Manuscript Groups in the Pennsylvania State Archives*. Harrisburg: Pennsylvania Historical and Museum Commission, 1976.

Whitman, Walt. *Specimen Days*.

BIOGRAPHY AND GENERAL PENNSYLVANIA HISTORY

A Biographical Album of Prominent Pennsylvanians. Second Series. Philadelphia: The American Biographical Publishing Co., 1889.

Barton, Michael. *Life by the Moving Road, An Illustrated History of Greater Harrisburg*. Woodland Hills, Ca.: Windsor Publications, 1983.

Bates, Samuel P. *History of the Pennsylvania Volunteers 1861-65*. 5 vols. Harrisburg: B. Singerly, State Printer, 1869.

_____. *Martial Deeds of Pennsylvania*. Philadelphia: T. H. Davis & Co., 1875.

Biographical Annals of Lancaster County. J. H. Beers & Co., Publishers, 1903.

Biographical Encyclopedia of Pennsylvania of the Nineteenth Century. Philadelphia: Galaxy Publishing Co., 1874.

Book, Janet Mae. *Northern Rendezvous*. Harrisburg: Telegraph Press, 1959.

Burr, Frank A. *Life and Achievements of James Addams Beaver*. Philadelphia: Furguson Bros. & Co., 1882.

Carmer, Carl. *The Susquehanna*. New York: Rinehart & Co., 1955.

Crist, Robert Grant. *Confederate Invasion of the West Shore—1863.* Lemoyne, Pa.: Lemoyne Trust Co., 1963.

Donehoo, George P., ed. *Pennsylvania: A History.* vol. 3. New York: Lewis Historical Publishing Co., Inc., 1926.

Donovan, Maurice R., ed. *Kane, Pennsylvania Centennial Program.* Kane, Pa.: Hooper Productions, 1964.

Egle, William H. *An Illustrated History of the Commonwealth of Pennsylvania.* Philadelphia: E. M. Gardner, 1880.

_____. *Notes and Queries: Historical, Biographical and Genealogical,* 4th series, vol. 1. Harrisburg: Harrisburg Publishing Company, 1893.

_____. *Commemorative Biographical Encyclopedia of Dauphin County, Pennsylvania.* Chambersburg, Pa.: J. M. Runk & Company, Publishers, 1896.

_____. *Life and Times of Andrew Gregg Curtin.* Philadelphia: The Thompson Publishing Co., 1896.

Everett, Edward G. "Pennsylvania Raises an Army." *Western Pennsylvania Historical Magazine,* 39, No. 2 (1956): 83-108.

Flood, Charles Bracelen. *Lee: The Last Years.* Boston: The Houghton Mifflin Company, 1981.

Gresham, John M. and Samuel T. Wiley. *Biographical and Portrait Cyclopedia of Fayette County Pennsylvania.* Chicago: John M. Gresham & Co., 1889.

Guide to the Historical Markers of Pennsylvania. Harrisburg: Pennsylvania Museum and Historical Commission, 1975.

Hain, Harry H. *History of Perry County, Pennsylvania.* Harrisburg: Hain-Moore Company, 1922.

Hamersly, Lewis R. *Who's Who in Pennsylvania.* New York: L. R. Hamersly, 1904.

History of Franklin County, Pennsylvania. Chicago: Warner, Beers & Co., 1887.

History of Venango County, Pennsylvania. Philadelphia: Brown, Runk & Co., 1890.

Hobson, Charles F. and Arnold Shankman. "Colonel of the Bucktails: Civil War Letters of Charles Frederick Taylor." *The Pennsylvania Magazine of History and Biography,* 97 (1973), 3:333-60.

Inglewood, Marian.] *Then and Now in Harrisburg.* Harrisburg: 1925.

Laverty, George Lauman. *History of Medicine in Dauphin County Pennsylvania.* Harrisburg: Telegraph Press, 1967.

Morgan, George H. *Annals of Harrisburg.* Harrisburg: Publishing House of the United Evangelical Church, 1906.

Powell, William H. *Officers of the Army and Navy.* Philadelphia: L. R. Hamersly & Co., 1893.

Reed, George E., ed. *Pennsylvania Archives.* Series 4, *Papers of the Governors.* vol. 8. Harrisburg: State Printer, 1902.

Roberts, Elwood, ed. *Biographical Annals of Montgomery County, Pennsylvania*. New York: T. S. Benham and Co., and the Lewis Publishing Co., 1904.

Ross, Ishbel. *Angel of the Battlefield*. New York: Harper & Brothers, 1956.

Ruoff, Henry Woldmar, ed. *Biographical and Portrait Cyclopedia of Schuylkill County, Pennsylvania*. Philadelphia: Rush West and Co., 1893.

Schory, Eva Draegert. *Everyname Index to Egle's Notes and Queries Chiefly Relating to Interior Pennsylvania*. Decatur, IL: Decatur Genealogical Society, 1892.

Stocker, Rhamanthus M. *Centennial History of Susquehanna County, Pennsylvania*. Philadelphia: R. T. Peck & Co., 1887.

Storey, Henry Wilson. *History of Cambria County Pennsylvania*, vol. 2. New York: The Lewis Publishing Co., 1907.

Trussell, John B. *Brig. Gen. Joseph F. Knipe, U. S. V.* unpublished manuscript, Pennsylvania Historical and Museum Commission, 1980.

Westhaeffer, Paul J. *History of the Cumberland Valley Railroad 1835-1919*. Washington, D.C.: Washington, D.C. Chapter, National Railway Historical Society, 1979.

Williams, Alvin S. *Ceremonies at the Dedication of the Statue of Andrew Gregg Curtin...On the Site of Camp Curtin...October 19th, 1922*. Harrisburg: Telegraph Press, 1922.

MANUSCRIPTS

Awl, F. Asbury, Company A, 127th Pennsylvania Volunteers. Papers, Morning Reports, Co. A, 127th PVI. Manuscript Group 16, Division of Archives and Manuscripts, Pennsylvania Historical and Museum Commission.

Baldwin, George H., Company H, 151st Pennsylvania Volunteers. Letters. Susquehanna County Historical Society.

Brown, Richard C. *Theodore Gregg An American*. unpublished typescript. Manuscript Group 233, Division of Archives and Manuscripts, Pennsylvania Historical and Museum Commission.

Borland, M. H., Company G, 123rd Pennsylvania Volunteers. Diary, typescript. Historical Society of Western Pennsylvania.

Darlington, William H., Company A, 1st Pennsylvania Reserves. Letters. Houghton Library, Harvard University.

Delamarter, Jacob, Company H, 151st Pennsylvania Volunteers. Letters. Susquehanna County Historical Society.

Geety, William Wallace, Company H, 47th Pennsylvania Volunteers. Papers. Harrisburg Civil War Round Table Collection, U.S. Army Military History Institute.

Gerrish, Henry, Company A, 7th New York Infantry. Papers. Civil War Times Illustrated Collection, U.S. Army Military History Institute.

Hopkins, Daniel S., Company A, 140th Pennsylvania Volunteers. Papers. "Reminiscense" of Service. Manuscript Group 6, Division of Archives and Manuscripts, Pennsylvania Historical and Museum Commission.

Kerr, Jonathan W., Adjutant's Office, 200th Pennsylvania Volunteers. Papers, Diary. Manuscript Group 6, Division of Archives and Manuscripts, Pennsylvania Historical and Museum Commission.

Koerper, John F., 47th Pennsylvania Volunteers. Papers, Diary. Manuscript Group 6, Division of Archives and Manuscripts, Pennsylvania Historical and Museum Commission.

Miller, B. N., ed. *Diary of Jacob Heffelfinger*, Company H, 7th Pennsylvania Reserves. typescript, unpublished manuscript. U.S. Army Military History Institute.

Parry, Edward Owen. *A Life Relived (1838-1870) The Young Manhood of Brevet Major Henry C. Parry.* Copyrighted 13 February 1984. The Parry Family Collection, U.S. Army Military History Institute.

Parry, Henry C., 47th Pennsylvania Volunteers. Papers, Diary. The Parry Family Collection, U.S. Army Military History Institute.

Ray, J. Milton, Company C, 140th Pennsylvania Volunteers. Letters, typescript. Allegheny County Soldiers and Sailors Memorial.

Rice, Harvey S., Company B, 17th Pennsylvania Cavalry. Letters. Susquehanna County Historical Society.

Rohrer, Jeremiah, 127th Pennsylvania Volunteers. Papers, Diary. Manuscript Group 243, Division of Archives and Manuscripts, Pennsylvania Historical and Museum Commission.

Letter from "Smith" to "Friend Black". Manuscript Group 6, Division of Archives and Manuscripts, Pennsylvania Historical and Museum Commission.

Torrance, Adam. 11th Pennsylvania Reserves. Papers. Division of History, Pennsylvania Historical and Museum Commission.

Unidentified member of 1st Pennsylvania Volunteers. Papers, Diary. Manuscripts Group 6, Division of Archives and Manuscripts, Pennsylvania Historical and Museum Commission.

Wallace, Stryker A. (a.k.a. Stephen), Company G, 153rd Pennsylvania Volunteers. Papers, Diary. Manuscript Group 6, Division of Archives and Manuscripts, Pennsylvania Historical and Museum Commission.

Williams, Henry G., Company B, 17th Pennsylvania Cavalry. Letter. Susquehanna County Historical Society.

Woods, John F., Company G, 49th Pennsylvania Volunteers. Papers. Woods Family Collection, Manuscript Group 188, Division of Archives and Manuscripts, Pennsylvania Historical and Museum Commission.

OFFICIAL DOCUMENTS AND REPORTS

Annual Report of the Quartermaster General of the Commonwealth of Pennsylvania, 1864.

Annual Report of the Commissary General of the Commonwealth of Pennsylvania, 1861.

Annual Report of the Surgeon General of the Commonwealth of Pennsylvania, 1863.

List of Commissioned Officers of the General Hospital at Camp Curtin, PA. August. 1862. Record Group 393, Series. 3237, vol. 59. National Archives.

List of Deserters Imprisoned at Camp Curtin. May 1863-Aug. 1864. Record Group 393, No. 324. National Archives.

List of Officers and Enlisted Men on Recruiting Duty at Camp Curtin, PA. Oct. 1863-Jan. 1864. Record Group 393, Series. 3216, vol. 54. National Archives.

List of Stragglers, Convalescents, and Furloughed men at Camp Curtin May 1863-Feb. 1865. Record Group 393, Series. 323. National Archives.

Post Returns for Camp Curtin, PA. Mar. 1862-May 1862. National Archives.

Post Returns for Harrisburg, PA, 1862-1866. Record Group 617, *Returns of Military Posts.* National Archives.

Quartermaster Receipts from Camp Curtin, Record Group 19, Division of Archives and Manuscripts, Pennsylvania Historical and Museum Commission.

Reports of the Arrival and Payment of Troops at Various Places [Camp Return]. *1865.* Record Group 393, Series. 3215. National Archives.

Reports of Persons Employed and Articles Hired at Harrisburg, PA. Aug. 1864-Mar. 1866. Record Group 393, Series. 3213. National Archives.

United States Adjutant General's Office. Pennsylvania Volunteers and Militia Called into Service During the Gettysburg Campaign. in Rosters of Union Troops in Principal Battles May, 1863 to April, 1865.

PERSONAL RECOLLECTIONS AND UNIT HISTORIES

Albert, Allen D. *History of the Forty-fifth Regiment Pennsylvania Veteran Volunteer Infantry 1861-1865.* Williamsport, Pa.: Grit Publishing Co., 1912.

Alexander, Ted, ed. *The 126th Pennsylvania.* Shippensburg, Pa. Beidel Printing House, Inc., 1984.

Beck, Harry R., ed. "Some Leaves From a Civil War Diary." *Western Pennsylvania Historical Magazine,* 42 (1959); 363-382.

Benson, Edwin N., R. Dale Benson, and Theo. E. Wiedersheim. *History of the First Regiment Infantry, National Guard of Pennsylvania.* Philadelphia: William H. Dole & Company's Printing House, 1880.

Billings, John D. *Hard Tack and Coffee.* Reprint, Williamstown, Mass. Corner House Publishers, 1984.

Bloodgood, J. D. *Personal Reminiscences of the War.* New York: Hint & Eaton, 1893.

Bosbyshell, Oliver Christian. *The 48th in the War.* Philadelphia: Anvil Printing Co., 1895.

——————. *Pennsylvania at Antietam.* Harrisburg: Antietam Battlefield Memorial Commission, 1906.

Boyle, John Richards. *Soldiers True, The Story of the One Hundred and Eleventh Regiment Pennsylvania Veteran Volunteers.* New York: Eaton & Mains, 1903.

Chamberlin, Thomas. *History of the One Hundred and Fiftieth Regiment Pennsylvania Volunteers.* Philadelphia: F. McManus, Jr. & Co., 1905.

Craft, David. *History of the One-Hundred Forty-first Regiment Pennsylvania Volunteers.* Towanda, Pa.: David Craft, 1885.

Crater, Lewis. *History of the Fiftieth Regiment, Pennsylvania Veteran Volunteers, 1861-65.* Reading, Pa.: Coleman Print House. 1884.

Davis, Charles E. *Three Years in the Army: The story of the Thirteenth Massachusetts Volunteers.* Boston: Estes and Lauriat, 1894.

Davis, William W. H. *History of the Doylestown Guards.* Doylestown, Pa., 1887.

Donaghy, John. *Army Experience.* Deland, Fla.: E. O. Painter Printng Co., 1926.

Dornblazer, T. F. *Sabre Strokes of the Pennsylvania Dragoons in the War of 1861-1865. Interspersed With Personal Reminiscences.* Philadelphia: Lutheran Publication Society, 1884.

First Annual Re-Union Association of the Bucktail, or First Rifle Regiment P.R.V.C. Williamsport, Pa.: Printed by the Association, 1888.

Gibbs, James M. *History of the First Battalion Six Months Volunteers and 187th Regiment Pennsylvania Volunteer Infantry.* Harrisburg: Survivor's Association One Hundred and Eighty-seventh Regiment Pennsylvania Volunteer Infantry, 1905.

Glover, Edwin A. *Bucktailed Wildcats.* New York: Thomas Yoseloff, 1960.

Gordon, John B. *Reminiscences of the Civil War.* New York: Charles Scribner's Sons, 1903. Reprint, Time Life Books, 1981.

Gould, Joseph. *The Story of the Forty-eighth, a Record of the Campaigns of the Forty-eighth Regiment Pennsylvania Veteran Volunteer Infantry During the Four Eventful Years of Its Service in the War For the Preservation of the Union.* Philadelphia: Alfred M. Slocum Co., printer, 1908.

Green, Robert M. *History of the One Hundred and Twenty-fourth Pennsylvania Volunteers.* Philadelphia: Ware Bros. Co., 1907.

Gregg, J. Chandler. *Life in the Army, in the Departments of Virginia, and the Gulf.* Philadelphia: Perkinpine & Higgins, 1866.

Hardin, George D. "The Military Experience of James A. Peifer." *North Carolina Historical Review,* 32 (1955): 385-409.

Hardin, Martin D. *History of the Twelfth Regiment Pennsylvania Reserve Volunteer Corps.* New York: Martin D. Hardin, 1890.

Hays, Gilbert Adams. *Under the Red Patch, Story of the Sixty-third Regiment Pennsylvania Volunteers, 1861-1864.* Pittsburgh: Sixty-third Pennsylvania Volunteers Regimental Association, 1908.

Hays, John. *The 130 Regiment, Pennsylvania Volunteers in the Maryland Campaign and the Battle of Antietam.* Carlisle, Pa.: Herald Printing Co., 1894.

History of the 127th Regiment Pennsylvania Volunteers. Lebanon, Pa.: The Report Publishing Co., 1902.

Hitchcock, Frederick L. *War From the Inside.* Philadelphia: J. B. Lippincott Co., 1904.

Hodge, Robert W., ed. *The Civil War Letters of Perry Mayo*. East Lansing, Mich.: Publications of the Museum, Michigan State University Cultural Series, 1, No. 3, 1967.

Holmes, Oliver Wendell. "My Hunt After 'The Captain.' " *The Atlantic*. December, 1862, 738-64.

_____. *The Poetical Works of Oliver Wendell Holmes*. vol. 2. Boston: Houghton Mifflin Company, the Riverside Edition, 1908.

Hoy, Francis H., Sr. "Harrisburg in the Days of the Civil War." *Harrisburg Telegraph*. October 3, 1905.

Hunt, Jerome Leslie. "The History of the 55th Pennsylvania Volunteer Infantry Regiment." M.S. Thesis. Illinois State University 1979.

Judson, Amos M. *History of the Eighty-Third Regiment Pennsylvania Volunteers*. Erie, PA: B. F. H. Lynn, Publisher. Reprint Alexandria, Va. Stonewall House, 1985.

Kerr, John. *Oration Delivered at the First Reunion of the One Hundred and Fifty-fifth Regiment, Pennsylvania Veteran Volunteers*. Pittsburgh: Samuel F. Kerr, printer, 1875.

Kiefer, W. R. *History of the 153rd Regiment Pennsylvania Volunteer Infantry*. Easton, Pa.: The Chemical Publishing Co., 1909.

Kieffer, Harry M. *The Recollections of a Drummer Boy*. Boston: Houghton, Mifflin and Co., 1890.

Latta, James W. *History of the First Regiment, National Guard of Pennsylvania*. Philadelphia: J. B. Lippincott, 1912.

Lloyd, William Penn. *History of the First Regiment Pennsylvania Reserve Cavalry*. Philadelphia: King & Baird, Printers, 1864.

Lochren, William. "Narrative of the First Regiment." in *Minnesota in the Civil and Indian Wars*. vol. 1. St. Paul: The Pioneer Press, 1890-93.

Locke, William Henry. *The Story of the Regiment*. Philadelphia: J. B. Lippincott & Co., 1868.

Lockwood, John. *Our Campaign Around Gettysburg*. Brooklyn: A. H. Rome & Brothers, Stationers & Printers, 1864.

Loving, Jerome M. ed. *Civil War Letters of George Washington Whitman*. Durham, N.C.: Duke University Press, 1975.

Martin, James M., et al. *History of the Fifty-seventh Regiment P.V.V.I.* Meadville, Pa.: McCoy & Calvin.

McClure, A. K. *Abraham Lincoln and the Men of War Times*. Philadelphia: Times Publishing Co., 1892.

_____. *Old Time Notes of Pennsylvania*. 2 vols. Philadelphia: John C. Winston Company, 1905.

Merchant, Thomas E. *Eighty-fourth Regiment, Pennsylvania Volunteers*. Philadelphia: Press of Sherman & Co., 1890.

Mott, Smith B. *The Campaigns of the Fifty Second Regiment Pennsylvania Volunteer Infantry*. Philadelphia: J. B. Lippincott, 1911.

Moyer, H. P. *History of the Seventeenth Regiment Pennsylvania Volunteer Cavalry.* Lebanon, Pa.: Sowers Printing Co.

Muffly, Joseph W. *The Story of Our Regiment, A history of the 148th Pennsylvania Volunteers.* Harrisburg: Meyers print house, 1889.

Nachtigall, Herrman. *Geschichte des 75sten Regiments, Pa. Vols.* Philadelphia: C. B. Kretschman, 1886.

Nesbit, John Woods. *General History of Company D, 149th Pennsylvania Volunteers.* Oakdale, Cal.: Oakdale Printing and Publishing Co., 1908.

Nolan, Alan T. *The Iron Brigade.* New York: The Macmillan Company, 1961. Reprint. Berrien Springs, Mich.: Hardscrabble Books, 1983.

Orwig, Joseph R. *History of the 131st Penn'a Volunteers.* Williamsport, Pa.: Sun Book and Job Printing House, 1902.

Parker, Thomas H. *History of the 51st Regiment of P.V. and V.V.* Philadelphia: King and Baird, Printers, 1869.

Pennsylvania at Gettysburg: Ceremonies at the Dedication of the Monuments Erected by the Commonwealth of Pennsylvania to Major General George G. Meade, Major General Winfield S. Hancock, Major General John F. Reynolds and to Mark the Positions of the Pennsylvania Commands Engaged in the Battle. Harrisburg: Board of Commissioners for the erection of monuments to mark the position of the Pennsylvania commands engaged in the battle of Gettysburg. 2 vols., 1904.

Pennypacker, Samuel W. "Six Weeks in Uniform: Being a Record of a Term in the Military Service of the United States in the Gettysburg Campaign of 1863." In his *Historical and Biographical Sketches.* Philadelphia: Robert A. Tripple, 1883.

Powelson, B. F. *History of Company K of the 140th Regiment Pennsylvania Volunteers.* Steubenville, Ohio: The Carnahan Printing Co., 1906.

Pullen, John J. *The Twentieth Maine, A Volunteer Regiment in the Civil War.* 1957. Reprint. Dayton, Ohio: Morningside Bookshop, 1983.

Reed, John A. *History of the 101st Regiment Pennsylvania Veteran Volunteer Infantry, 1861-1865.* Chicago: L.S. Dickey & Co., 1910.

Richards, H. M. M. *Pennsylvania's Emergency Men at Gettysburg: A Touch of Bushwhacking.* Reading, Pa.: H.M.M. Richards, 1895.

Richards, Louis. *Eleven Days in the Militia During the War of the Rebellion.* Philadelphia: Collins, Printer, 1883.

Rodenbough, Theo. F., et al. *History of the Eighteenth Pennsylvania Cavalry.* New York: Wynkoop, Hallenbeck Crawford Co., 1909.

Rowe, David W. *A Sketch of the 126th Regiment Pennsylvania Volunteers.* Chambersburg, Pa.: Cook & Hays, 1869.

Rowell, John W. *Yankee Cavalrymen.* Knoxville: University of Tennessee Press, 1971.

Schaat, James L. "Company I, First Regiment Pennsylvania Volunteers" A Memoir of Its Service for the Union in 1861." *The Penn Germania.* 13, No. 7 (1912); 538-550.

Simmers, William and Paul Bachschmid. *The Volunteer's Manual or Ten Months with the 153rd Pennsylvania Volunteers.* Easton, Pa.: D. H. Neiman, 1863.

Sipes, William B. *The Seventh Pennsylvania Veteran Volunteer Cavalry: Its Record, Reminiscences and Roster.* Pottsville, Pa.: Miners Journal Print, 1905.

Smith, John. *Transactions of the First Annual Reunion of the 122nd Regiment Pennsylvania Volunteers.* Lancaster, Pa.: New Era Steam Printing House, 1884.

Sprenger, George F. *Camp and Field Life of the 122nd Penn'a Volunteers.* Lancaster, Pa.: New Era Steam Book, 1885.

Stevens, George. *Three Years in the Sixth Corps.* Albany: S. R. Gray, 1866. Reprint. Time Life Books, 1981.

Stewart, Robert Laird. *History of the One Hundred and Fortieth Regiment Pennsylvania Volunteers.* William S. Shallenberger, Chairman of Publication Committee. 1912.

Strangand, George. *Cemetery Tales and Civil War Diary.* Scottdale, Pa.: The Laurel Press Group, 1978.

Sypher, J. R. *History of the Pennsylvania Reserve Corps.* Lancaster, Pa.: Elias Barr & Co., 1865.

Thomson, O. R. Howard and William H. Rauch. *A History of the "Bucktails."* Philadelphia, 1906.

Under the Maltese Cross, Antietam to Appomattox, the Loyal Uprising in Western Pennsylvania, 1862-1865, Campaigns of the 155th Pennsylvania Regiment. Pittsburgh: 155th Regimental Association, 1910.

Wallace, William W., et al. *History of the One Hundred and Twenty-fifth Regiment Pennsylvania Volunteers 1862-1863.* Philadelphia: J. B. Lippincott Co., 1906.

Westbrook, Robert S. *History of the 49th Pennsylvania Volunteers.* Altoona, Pa.: Altoona Times Print, 1898.

White, A. G. *History of Company F of the 140th Pennsylvania Volunteers.* Greenville, Pa.: The Beaver Printery, 1908.

Wingate, George W. *History of the Twenty Second Regiment of the National Guard of the State of New York From Its Organization to 1895.* New York: Edwin W. Dayton, Publisher and Bookseller, 1896.

Woodward, Evan Morrison. *Our Campaigns; or the Marches, Bivouacs, Battles, Incidents of Camp Life and History of Our Regiment During Its Three Years Term of Service, Together with a Sketch of the Army of the Potomac, Under Generals McClellan, Burnside, Hooker, Meade and Grant.* Philadelphia: John E. Potter and Co., 1865.

_____. *History of the Third Pennsylvania Reserve.* Trenton, NJ: MacCrellish & Quigley, Book and Job Printers, 1883.

NEWSPAPERS

The Knapsack. Harrisburg, 1:10 (18 May 1887).
The National Tribune. Washington, D.C. 28 April 1928.
The Harrisburg Patriot and Union.
The Harrisburg Evening Telegraph.
The Pennsylvania Daily Telegraph.
The Pennsylvania Evening Telegraph.

Index